Student Research Workshop 2021

Associated with the 13th International Conference on Recent Advances in Natural Language Processing (RANLP 2021)

Online
1 – 3 September 2021

ISBN: 978-1-7138-4096-1

Printed from e-media with permission by:

Curran Associates, Inc.
57 Morehouse Lane
Red Hook, NY 12571

Some format issues inherent in the e-media version may also appear in this print version.

Printed with permission by Curran Associates, Inc. (2022)

For permission requests, please contact the Association for Computational Linguistics at the address below.

Association for Computational Linguistics
209 N. Eighth Street
Stroudsburg, Pennsylvania 18360

Phone: 1-570-476-8006
Fax: 1-570-476-0860

acl@aclweb.org

Additional copies of this publication are available from:

Curran Associates, Inc.
57 Morehouse Lane
Red Hook, NY 12571 USA
Phone: 845-758-0400
Fax: 845-758-2633
Email: curran@proceedings.com
Web: www.proceedings.com

RANLPStud 2021

Proceedings of the Student Research Workshop

associated with

The 13th International Conference on Recent Advances in Natural Language Processing RANLP'2021

1–3 September, 2021
(held online)

STUDENT RESEARCH WORKSHOP
ASSOCIATED WITH THE INTERNATIONAL CONFERENCE
RECENT ADVANCES IN
NATURAL LANGUAGE PROCESSING'2021

PROCEEDINGS

1–3 September 2021

Series Online ISSN 2603-2821

Designed by INCOMA Ltd.
Shoumen, BULGARIA

Preface

The RANLP 2021 Student Research Workshop (RANLPStud 2021) is a special track of the established international conference Recent Advances in Natural Language Processing (RANLP 2021), now in its thirteenth edition as an online event due to the unusual circumstances related to the global pandemic.

The RANLP Student Research Workshop is being organised for the seventh time and this year is running in parallel with the other tracks of the main RANLP 2021 conference. The target of RANLPStud 2021 is to be a discussion forum and provide an outstanding opportunity for students at all levels (Bachelor, Masters, and Ph.D.) to present their work in progress or completed projects to an international research audience and receive feedback from senior researchers.

The RANLP 2021 Student Research Workshop received a large number of submissions, this year thirty-three (33) papers were submitted to the event covering nearly all the continents: Asia, The Americas (North and South), Europe and Oceania, a fact which was reflecting the record number of events, sponsors, submissions, and participants at the main RANLP 2021 conference.

We have accepted four (4) excellent student papers as long presentations, one of them has received the Best Paper Award in the opening session also attended by mentors from academia and 29 submissions are presented in a shorter form.

We did our best to make the reviewing process in the interest of our authors, by asking our reviewers to give as exhaustive comments and suggestions as possible as well as to maintain an encouraging attitude. Each student submission was reviewed by at least 2 Programme Committee members, which are specialists in their field and were carefully selected to match the submission's topic.

This year, as usual, we invited both strictly Natural Language Processing (NLP) papers, and submissions at the borderline between two sciences (but bearing contributions to NLP. The topics of the accepted submissions include: Computational treatment of humour, sarcasm and irony;Computer-aided language learning;Computational cognitive modelling ; Corpus annotation; Crowdsourcing;Deep learning for NLP; Discourse text summarisation;Fact checking;Information extraction;Language resources and corpora;Lexicography;Lexicon; Machine translation, including statistical machine translation and neural machine translation;NLP for biomedical texts;NLP for social media;Natural language generation;Natural language processing for educational applications;Opinion mining and sentiment analysis;Pragmatics;Phonetics and phonology;Semantics; Similarity;Syntax ;Text and web mining; Translation technology including translation memory systems; Word embeddings; Word-sense disambiguation.

We are thankful to the members of the Programme Committee for having provided such exhaustive reviews and even accepting additional reviews, and to the conference mentors, who provided additional comments to participants.

We would like especially to thank all members of the Organising Committee (listed in alphabetical order) for their long and devoted work : Souhila Djabri, Dinara Gimadi,Tsvetomila Mihaylova and Ivelina Nikolova-Koleva. THANK YOU for making this event possible within a very short time limit.

The RANLPStud 2021 Organisers

Souhila Djabri, University of Alicante, Spain
Dinara Gimadi, University of Wolverhampton, United Kingdom
Tsvetomila Mihaylova, Institute of Telecommunications, Lisbon, Portugal
Ivelina Nikolova-Koleva, Bulgarian Academy of Sciences and Sirma AI, Bulgaria

Organizers:

Souhila Djabri (University of Alicante, Spain)
Dinara Gimadi (University of Wolverhampton, United Kingdom)
Tsvetomila Mihaylova (Institute of Telecommunications, Lisbon, Portugal)
Ivelina Nikolova-Koleva (Bulgarian Academy of Sciences and Sirma AI, Bulgaria)

Programme Committee:

Aida Kostikova (New Bulgarian University, Bulgaria)
Ali Hatami (University of Wolverhampton, United Kingdom)
Alistair Plum (University of Wolverhampton, United Kingdom)
Andrey Tagarev (Sirma AI, Bulgaria)
Burcu Can Buglalilar (University of Wolverhampton, United Kingdom)
Cengiz Acartürk (Middle East Technical University, Turkey)
Constantin Orăsan (University of Surrey, United Kingdom)
Darya Filippova (University of Wolverhampton, United Kingdom)
Dean Hunter (University of Wolverhampton, United Kingdom)
Dinara Gimadi (New Bulgarian University, Bulgaria)
Elena Murgolo (Aglatech14, Italy)
Emma Franklin (University of Wolverhampton, United Kingdom)
Frédéric Blain (University of Wolverhampton, United Kingdom)
Georgi Karadzhov (University of Cambridge, United Kingdom)
Georgi Georgiev (Releva.ai, Bulgaria)
Ivan Koychev (Sofia University, Bulgaria)
Ivelina Nikolova-Koleva (Bulgarian Academy of Sciences and Sirma AI, Bulgaria)
Jessica López Espejel (Université Sorbonne Paris Nord, France)
Le An Ha (University of Wolverhampton, United Kingdom)
Maria Kunilovskaya (Research Group in Computational Linguistics, United Kingdom)
Maria Carmela Cariello (University of Pisa, Italy)
Marie Escribe (University of Wolverhampton, United Kingdom)
Momchil Hardalov (Sofia Univeristy, Bulgaria)
Necva Bölücü (Hacettepe University, Turkey)
Nikola Spasovski (University of Wolverhampton, United Kingdom)
Preslav Nakov (Qatar Computing Research Institute, HBKU, Qatar)
Raheem Sarwar (University of Wolverhampton, United Kingdom)
Richard Evans (University of Wolverhampton, United Kingdom)
Sandra Kübler (Indiana University, United States)
Sara Može (University of Wolverhampton, United Kingdom)
Shaifali Khulbe (University of Wolverhampton, United kingdom)
Sonia Kropiowska (University of Wolverhampton, United Kingdom)
Souhila Djabri (University of Alicante, Spain)
Svetla Boytcheva (Bulgarian Academy of Sciences and Sirma AI, Bulgaria)
Svetla Koeva (Bulgarian Academy of Sciences, Bulgaria)
Tharindu Ranasinghe (University of Wolverhampton, United Kingdom)
Tsvetomila Mihaylova (Institute of Telecommunications, Lisbon, Portugal)
Yasen Kiprov (Sofia University, Bulgaria)

Table of Contents

Humor Generation and Detection in Code-Mixed Hindi-English
Kaustubh Agarwal and Rhythm Narula 1

Towards Code-Mixed Hinglish Dialogue Generation
Vibhav Agarwal, Pooja Rao and Dinesh Babu Jayagopi 7

Hinglish to English Machine Translation using Multilingual Transformers
Vibhav Agarwal, Pooja Rao and Dinesh Babu Jayagopi 16

SiPOS: A Benchmark Dataset for Sindhi Part-of-Speech Tagging
Wazir Ali, Zenglin Xu and Jay Kumar 22

Sarcasm Detection and Building an English Language Corpus in Real Time
Oliver Cakebread-Andrews 31

Correcting Texts Generated by Transformers using Discourse Features and Web Mining
Alexander Chernyavskiy, Dmitry Ilvovsky and Boris Galitsky 36

Introducing linguistic transformation to improve translation memory retrieval. Results of a professional translators' survey for Spanish, French and Arabic
Souhila Djabri and Rocío Caro Quintana 44

Using Transfer Learning to Automatically Mark L2 Writing Texts
Tim Elks 51

Bilingual Terminology Extraction Using Neural Word Embeddings on Comparable Corpora
Darya Filippova, Burcu Can and Gloria Corpas Pastor 58

Web-sentiment analysis of public comments (public reviews) for languages with limited resources such as the Kazakh language
Dinara Gimadi 65

Disambiguating Grammatical Number and Gender With BERT
Annegret Janzso 69

Towards a Language Model for Temporal Commonsense Reasoning
Mayuko Kimura, Lis Kanashiro Pereira and Ichiro Kobayashi 78

Text Preprocessing and its Implications in a Digital Humanities Project
Maria Kunilovskaya and Alistair Plum 85

Compiling a specialised corpus for translation research in the environmental domain
Anastasiia Laktionova 94

Paragraph Similarity Matches for Generating Multiple-choice Test Items
Halyna Maslak and Ruslan Mitkov 99

Neural Borrowing Detection with Monolingual Lexical Models
John Miller, Emanuel Pariasca and Cesar Beltran Castañon 109

Does local pruning offer task-specific models to learn effectively ?
Abhishek Kumar Mishra and Mohna Chakraborty 118

On Reducing Repetition in Abstractive Summarization
Pranav Nair and Anil Kumar Singh 126

Improving Abstractive Summarization with Commonsense Knowledge
Pranav Nair and Anil Kumar Singh 135

A Dataset for Research on Modelling Depression Severity in Online Forum Data
Isuri Anuradha Nanomi Arachchige, Vihangi Himaya Jayasuriya and Ruvan Weerasinghe 144

Handling synset overgeneration: Sense Merging in BTB-WN
Ivaylo Radev and Zara Kancheva 154

On the Evolution of Word Order
Idan Rejwan and Avi Caciularu 162

EmoPars: A Collection of 30K Emotion-Annotated Persian Social Media Texts
Nazanin Sabri, Reyhane Akhavan and Behnam Bahrak 167

A Review on Document Information Extraction Approaches
Kanishka Silva and Thushari Silva 174

Towards New Generation Translation Memory Systems
Nikola Spasovski and Ruslan Mitkov 180

Question answering in Natural Language: the Special Case of Temporal Expressions
Armand Stricker 184

Building A Corporate Corpus For Threads Constitution
Lionel Tadonfouet Tadjou, Fabrice Bourge, Tiphaine Marie, Laurent Romary and Éric de la Clergerie 193

Generating Answer Candidates for Quizzes and Answer-Aware Question Generators
Kristiyan Vachev, Momchil Hardalov, Georgi Karadzhov, Georgi Georgiev, Ivan Koychev and Preslav Nakov 203

Toward Discourse-Aware Models for Multilingual Fake News Detection
Francielle Vargas, Fabrício Benevenuto and Thiago Pardo 210

Automatic Transformation of Clinical Narratives into Structured Format
Sylvia Vassileva, Gergana Todorova, Kristina Ivanova, Boris Velichkov, Ivan Koychev, Galia Angelova and Svetla Boytcheva 219

Humor Generation and Detection in Code-Mixed Hindi-English

Kaustubh Agarwal, Rhythm Narula
Department of Computer Science and Engineering
Netaji Subhas University of Technology
New Delhi, India
{kaustubh, rhythm.narula}.co19@nsut.ac.in

Abstract

Computational humor generation is one of the hardest tasks in natural language generation, especially in code-mixed languages. Existing research has shown that humor generation in English is a promising avenue. However, studies have shown that bilingual speakers often appreciate humor more in code-mixed languages with unexpected transitions and clever word play. In this study, we propose several methods for generating and detecting humor in code-mixed Hindi-English. Of the experimented approaches, an Attention Based Bi-Directional LSTM with converting parts of text on a word2vec embedding gives the best results by generating 74.8% good jokes and IndicBERT used for detecting humor in code-mixed Hindi-English outperforms other humor detection methods with an accuracy of 96.98%.

1 Introduction

Humor is one of the most powerful tools of communication capable of transforming negative sentiments and emotions to positive ones (Savage et al., 2017, Castro et al., 2016). From the early 1990's, computer science researchers and linguistic scholars have attempted to generate humor using computers giving rise to the field of computational humor generation. However, the task of humor generation has proven to be one of the most difficult tasks in natural language generation due to the lack of fundamental knowledge of how brains perceive and generate humor and its intimate link with the inner workings of the brain (Binsted et al., 2006).

While the field of computational humor generation is nowhere near saturation, deep learning techniques have shown promising results (Ren and Yang, 2017). Meanwhile, studies have shown that appreciating humor in jokes involves resolution and incongruity-detection, both of which require a strong command over the medium of communication of the joke (Ayçiçeği-Dinn et al., 2018). The added element of surprise and clever wordplay by rhyming a logically apt word from another language in a joke adds to its humor (Schröter, 2005). These studies and observations show that code-mixed joke generation can prove effective in creating humor. Code-mixing refers to the insertion of words, phrases, and morphemes of one language into a statement or an expression of another language (Alex, 2008).

India has around 350 million people that speak code-mixed Hindi-English (popularly known as Hinglish) (GTS, 2019), and according to David Crystal, a British linguist at the University of Wales, the world's Hinglish speakers may soon outnumber native English speakers. This makes Hinglish one of the most widely spoken code-mixed languages worldwide.

In this paper, we aim to generate and detect humor in code-mixed Hindi-English. Although a lot of work has been carried out on humor generation and detection in English (Zhang et al., 2020, Petrović and Matthews, 2013, Winters et al., 2019, Dybala et al., 2010, Winters et al., 2018), and humor detection in code-mixed Hindi-English (Khandelwal et al., 2018), humor generation in code-mixed languages is relatively unexplored. To the best of our knowledge, we are the first to attempt humor generation in code-mixed languages.

The contributions of our work include

1. Exploration of novel methodologies to generate humor in code-mixed Hindi-English.
2. Using transformers and other deep learning models to create classifiers to detect humor in code-mixed Hindi-English.

2 Related Works

Early papers date back to 1994 when Graeme Ritchie and Kim Binsted designed a computer

Proceedings of the Student Research Workshop associated with RANLP-2021, pages 1–6,
held online, Sep 1–3, 2021.
https://doi.org/10.26615/issn.2603-2821.2021_001

program called JAPE (Joke Analysis and Production Engine) which was used to generate question-answer type of puns. It was in 2005 when Graeme Ritchie introduced various pun generation mechanisms. They divided puns into two major categories of self-contained puns which are portions of text that can be used as humorous objects in a wide variety of situations. Their best preconditions to be used are preferred know-how (of the surrounding lifestyle, and so on) and contextually integrated puns which are used with a broader discourse and some more text (Ritchie, 2005).

Past endeavors using template-based approaches depend on formats and several constraints which intensely compel the quality and variety of generated sentences. Most past research is focused towards using layouts which are helpful for generating template based jokes, but they are often rigid. None of the frameworks intended to be innovative as the skeletons of the sentences are fixed. Owing to this, over time the quest of joke generation has shifted from template-based approaches to neural networks.

Various work has been done for pun generation using the LSTM approach. The initial model was proposed by Ren and Yang (2017)'s current affair jokes generator which was trained on a joke corpus along with news data for current affairs using LSTM RNN as architecture and GloVe as vector representation for training data (Amin and Burghardt, 2020). The results however, were not satisfactory. Another such attempt was made by using a conditioned neural language model that was trained using general text corpus which was then passed through a decoding algorithm (Yu et al., 2018). Though these neural network techniques gave creative outputs, they lacked humor in comparison to template-based approaches which showed fairly good humor despite lacking creativity. In this paper we take a deeper dive into humor generation using neural networks and attempt to generate humor using deep learning models in code-mixed Hindi-English.

3 Proposed Methodology

The proposed methodology consists of two sections, each covering a major contribution of this paper.

3.1 Humor Detection

For the purpose of humor detection, deep learning models and transformers have been used. To create embeddings, we have scraped a dataset of 412k Hinglish tweets from Twitter and pre-processed them by removing rare words, hashtags, mentions and Uniform Resource Locators (URLs) to create word embeddings. For better comparison of results, we have used the dataset of 3453 jokes in code-mixed Hindi-English created by Khandelwal et al. (2018).

mBERT BERT is a bi-directionally trained language model which helps it to obtain a deeper sense of the language flow compared to single direction trained models (Devlin et al., 2019). mBERT takes a multilingual dataset to train the model. It uses a multi-layer bidirectional transformer encoder which is capable of learning deep bidirectional representations and can easily be fine-tuned for several tasks including humor detection. All the more explicitly, given a sentence, our approach first obtains its token representation which is fed to the output layer which acts as a binary classifier by using class labels. The final output layer generates scores which are used to further train the model by calculating the mean squared error between the predicted score and label (Mao and Liu, 2019).

IndicBERT Just like mBERT, IndicBERT is also used to solve a variety of NLP tasks in the multilingual context. IndicBERT is a multilingual ALBERT model pre-trained solely on 12 significant Indian dialects consisting of about 9 billion tokens and evaluated using a variety of tasks. It has much fewer parameters as compared to other multilingual models like mBERT (Kakwani et al., 2020) and performs better than mBERT on most tasks involving Indic languages. The major advantage of this model is that it performs well even with small training datasets and excels in doing cross-lingual learning which is beneficial while using Indian languages which lack these resources.

3.2 Humor Generation

We have explored humor generation in code-mixed Hindi-English using two methods.

3.2.1 Training deep learning models on Hindi-English jokes

The most direct method of generating humor in code-mixed Hindi-English is by using deep learning models to generate text on a dataset of code-mixed Hindi-English jokes. However, training deep learning models on Hindi-English jokes by using English word embeddings leads to unintelligible words and jokes due to lack of understanding of Hindi words. To resolve this problem, we have used the embeddings from the 412K Hinglish tweets mentioned earlier. We have used Word2Vec (Mikolov et al. (2013a), Mikolov et al. (2013b)) and FastText (Bojanowski et al., 2017, Joulin et al., 2017) for generating word embeddings.

3.2.2 Converting English jokes to code-mixed Hindi-English

For this method, we have used deep learning models trained on a dataset of 200K English jokes created by Pungas (2017). The embeddings are created using Word2Vec and FastText but only for English text instead of Hindi-English text. The generated jokes are purely in English. We have experimented with two methods to convert this English text (jokes) to code-mixed Hindi-English:

1. Converting parts of text: Using a part-of-speech tagger, singular and plural nouns have been converted from each English joke to Hindi. While converting multiple other parts-of-speech have been tested, it often leads to unintelligible results in the context of the entire sentence.

2. Using Pre-trained Encoder and Transfer Learning: A Semi-supervised Approach to Generate Code-Mixed Text using Pre-trained Encoder and Transfer Learning as proposed by Gupta et al. (2020) is used to convert jokes generated in English to code-mixed Hindi-English jokes.

The jokes generated by these techniques contain code-mixed elements of Hindi and English.

The following architectures have been used to create models for each of the aforementioned methods

1. LSTM: Hochreiter and Schmidhuber (1997)

2. Bi-directional LSTM: Schuster and Paliwal (1997)

3. Attention Based Bi-directional LSTM: Zhou et al. (2016)

For generating jokes using these models, the first word or sentence could be provided as an input or could be chosen randomly by the model. While choosing a word would be ideal for generating jokes on a particular topic, randomly choosing words would give room for creativity. Ideally, the model should then pick the word with highest probability of occurring in a given context since that would lead to a better joke based on its learning from the training data. However, this could lead to boring and conservative predictions (Ren and Yang, 2017). This can be countered by using weighted-pick strategies that encourages the model to take greater risks at the cost of getting poor jokes more often. The model thus picks random words from the vocabulary according to the weights, which are the probabilities coming from the last softmax layer.

4 Experimental Results

4.1 Humor Detection

The dataset of jokes in code-mixed Hindi-English created by Khandelwal et al. (2018) is used for training transformers and deep learning models for detecting humor. Each transformer is trained for a total of 5 epochs, and each deep learning model has been trained for 20 epochs with a 15 percent validation split for each.

The hyper-parameters used for all RNNs are: dropout for recurrent state = 0.2, dropout for input state = 0.2, number of LSTM units = 150

Each transformer and deep learning model performs the task of binary classification to detect whether a particular text is humorous or not. Deep learning models have been given the word embeddings of Hindi-English text as described earlier. As evident from Table-1, IndicBERT gives the best classification results among the tested architectures, and transformers significantly outperformed other deep learning models.

Model	Accuracy
LSTM	74.48%
Bi-Directional LSTM	74.80%
Attention Bi-Directional LSTM	79.31%
mBERT	95.37%
IndicBERT	96.98%

Table 1: Humor Detection Accuracies on the dataset of jokes in code-mixed Hindi-English created by Khandelwal et al. (2018)

Model	Percentage of Good Jokes	
	Word2Vec	**FastText**
LSTM	68.8%	67.2%
Bi-Directional LSTM	69%	68.9%
Attention Based Bi-Directional LSTM	72.4%	71.3%

Table 2: Percentage of good jokes generated by training deep learning models on Hindi-English jokes

Thus, with a validation accuracy of 96.98%, IndicBERT outperforms mBERT that has a validation accuracy of 95.37%.

4.2 Humor Generation

We have experimented with two different types of humor generation techniques. In both techniques, the hyper-parameters for the RNNs are: dropout for recurrent state = 0.2, dropout for input state = 0.2, number of LSTM units = 300.

4.2.1 Training deep learning models on Hindi-English jokes

For creating jokes using a dataset of Hindi-English jokes, we experimented with Word2Vec and FastText embeddings created using a dataset of 412k Hinglish tweets from Twitter. We generated 1000 jokes using each deep learning model and ran it on the IndicBERT classifier created for humor detection to find the percentage of good jokes generated by the deep learning model. Table-2 shows the percentage of good jokes created using this joke generation method for each deep learning model.

Among the tested architectures, Attention Based Bi-Directional LSTM gives the best result with 72.4% good jokes with Word2Vec embeddings. It is also observed that Word2Vec gives slightly better results than the corresponding FastText embeddings. Possible reasons for this observation may include the fact that code-mixed data does not allow n-grams to be the primary criterion for classification.

4.2.2 Converting English jokes to code-mixed Hindi-English

For creating jokes in English and converting them to code-mixed Hindi-English we again experimented with Word2Vec and FastText embeddings but only for English. From each deep learning model, 1000 jokes are generated. These 1000 jokes in English are converted to code-mixed Hindi-English by two methods- converting parts of text, and using Pre-trained Encoder and Transfer Learning. The obtained code-mixed Hindi-English jokes are passed through the previously created IndicBERT classifier. The percentage of good jokes generated are shown in Table-3.

It can be observed from Table 3 that Attention Based Bi-directional LSTM created from English jokes converted to code-mixed Hindi-English by converting parts of text gives the best results by creating 74.8% good jokes. It can be deduced that usage of unexpected and unusual words adds to the element of surprise in between an English joke and adds to the element of humor more than converting the entire sentence to a logical code-mixed joke.

Table-4 gives samples of good and bad jokes generated from each of the methods. All Hindi words are written in the Devanagari script to differentiate between English and Hindi words used in a joke. It is noteworthy that a substantial amount of humor is lost in translation of the joke to English

Model	Percentage of Good Jokes			
	Converting Parts Of Text		**Using Pre-trained Encoder and Transfer Learning**	
	Word2Vec	**FastText**	**Word2Vec**	**FastText**
LSTM	69.4%	69.1%	69.2%	68.8%
Bi-directional LSTM	71.5%	70.9%	70.7%	70.2%
Attention Based Bi-directional LSTM	74.8%	73.2%	74.2%	73.6%

Table 3: Percentage of good jokes generated by converting English jokes to code-mixed Hindi-English

Method	Good Joke	Translation	Bad Joke	Translation
Training deep learning models on Hindi-English jokes	Aunty जो सोचती हैं उसकी परवाह क्यों करें... troll किया तो डरने क्या	Why should we care what aunty thinks? Why worry if we trolled?	कितने भी phone बनाते हैं वे एक जैसे दिखेंगे	How many ever phones they make all will look the same.
Converting English jokes to code-mixed Hindi-English by converting parts of text	I call my गणित संकट	I call my mathematics trouble	What's a राक्षस 's favorite खाना? डाक का कबूतर	What's a monster's favorite food? The messenger pigeon
Converting English jokes to code-mixed Hindi-English using pre-trained encoder and transfer learning	क्या आप bear ki हत्या करना चाहते हैं? Personally, I would पर I can bear-ly see it.	Do you want to murder a bear? Personally, I would but I can bear-ly see it.	आप बस attention चाहते हैं. Teenage girl है क्या	You just want attention. Are you a teenage girl?

Table 4: Samples of good and bad jokes generated by each method in native scripts

as presented in the table.

5 Conclusion and Future Work

In this paper, we propose novel approaches for humor generation in code-mixed Hindi-English and explored the idea of using deep learning models for generating and detecting humor in it. One of the proposed approaches uses LSTM, Bi-Directional LSTM and Attention Based LSTM for generating jokes in code-mixed Hindi-English using Hinglish word embeddings and the other uses the same deep learning approaches to generate jokes in English which are further transformed into code-mixed Hindi-English by converting selective parts of text or using a pre-trained encoder and transfer learning method. The produced jokes were evaluated using IndicBERT which performed better than other humor detection models with an accuracy of 96.98%. The proposed conversion of parts of a joke generated in English gave the best results in humor generation by producing 74.8% good jokes on word2vec embedding. Compared to the state of the art humor detection models, our proposed approach performed better at detecting humor on code-mixed Hindi-English data. Since humor generation in code-mixed Hindi-English is unexplored, this paper proposes a baseline for future work.

Future work may include extension of humor generation to other code-mixed languages, usage of contextualized embeddings, and better deep learning techniques that understand humor more deeply. Furthermore, better models can be built using iterative data augmentation in such low-resource scenarios. Appropriate usage of phonetic models to generate similar sounding words with contrasting meanings in the parent code-mixed languages under consideration could be another potential avenue for future research.

References

Beatrice Alex. 2008. *Automatic Detection of English Inclusions in Mixed-lingual Data with an Application to Parsing*. Ph.D. thesis.

Miriam Amin and Manuel Burghardt. 2020. A survey on approaches to computational humor generation. In *Proceedings of the The 4th Joint SIGHUM Workshop on Computational Linguistics for Cultural Heritage, Social Sciences, Humanities and Literature*, pages 29–41, Online. International Committee on Computational Linguistics.

Ayşe Ayçiçeği-Dinn, Simge Şişman-Bal, and Catherine L Caldwell-Harris. 2018. Are jokes funnier in one's native language? *HUMOR*, 31(1):5–37.

K. Binsted, B. Bergen, S. Coulson, A. Nijholt, O. Stock, C. Strapparava, G. Ritchie, R. Manurung, H. Pain, A. Waller, and D. O'Mara. 2006. Computational humor. *IEEE Intelligent Systems*, 21(2):59–69.

Piotr Bojanowski, Edouard Grave, Armand Joulin, and Tomas Mikolov. 2017. Enriching word vectors with subword information. *Transactions of the Association for Computational Linguistics*, 5:135–146.

Santiago Castro, Matías Cubero, Diego Garat, and Guillermo Moncecchi. 2016. Is this a joke? detecting humor in spanish tweets. In *Lecture Notes in Computer Science*, pages 139–150. Springer International Publishing.

Jacob Devlin, Ming-Wei Chang, Kenton Lee, and Kristina Toutanova. 2019. BERT: Pre-training of deep bidirectional transformers for language understanding. In *Proceedings of the 2019 Conference of the North American Chapter of the Association for Computational Linguistics: Human Language Technologies, Volume 1 (Long and Short Papers)*, pages 4171–4186, Minneapolis, Minnesota. Association for Computational Linguistics.

Pawel Dybala, Michal Ptaszynski, Jacek Maciejewski, Mizuki Takahashi, Rafal Rzepka, and Kenji Araki. 2010. Multiagent system for joke generation: Humor and emotions combined in human-agent conversation. *Journal of Ambient Intelligence and Smart Environments*, 2:31.

GTS. 2019. Hinglish - the Biggest Language you've Never Heard of with 350 Million Speakers.

Deepak Gupta, Asif Ekbal, and Pushpak Bhattacharyya. 2020. A semi-supervised approach to generate the code-mixed text using pre-trained encoder and transfer learning. In *Findings of the Association for Computational Linguistics: EMNLP 2020*. Association for Computational Linguistics.

Sepp Hochreiter and Jürgen Schmidhuber. 1997. Long short-term memory. *Neural Computation*, 9(8):1735–1780.

Armand Joulin, Edouard Grave, Piotr Bojanowski, and Tomas Mikolov. 2017. Bag of tricks for efficient text classification. In *Proceedings of the 15th Conference of the European Chapter of the Association for Computational Linguistics: Volume 2, Short Papers*, pages 427–431, Valencia, Spain. Association for Computational Linguistics.

Divyanshu Kakwani, Anoop Kunchukuttan, Satish Golla, Gokul N.C., Avik Bhattacharyya, Mitesh M. Khapra, and Pratyush Kumar. 2020. IndicNLPSuite: Monolingual corpora, evaluation benchmarks and pre-trained multilingual language models for Indian languages. In *Findings of the Association for Computational Linguistics: EMNLP 2020*, pages 4948–4961, Online. Association for Computational Linguistics.

A. Khandelwal, Sahil Swami, S. Akhtar, and Manish Shrivastava. 2018. Humor detection in english-hindi code-mixed social media content : Corpus and baseline system. *ArXiv*, abs/1806.05513.

Jihang Mao and W. Liu. 2019. A bert-based approach for automatic humor detection and scoring. In *IberLEF@SEPLN*.

Tomas Mikolov, Kai Chen, Greg S. Corrado, and Jeffrey Dean. 2013a. Efficient estimation of word representations in vector space.

Tomas Mikolov, Ilya Sutskever, Kai Chen, Greg Corrado, and Jeffrey Dean. 2013b. Distributed representations of words and phrases and their compositionality. In *Proceedings of the 26th International Conference on Neural Information Processing Systems - Volume 2*, NIPS'13, page 3111–3119, Red Hook, NY, USA. Curran Associates Inc.

Saša Petrović and David Matthews. 2013. Unsupervised joke generation from big data. In *Proceedings of the 51st Annual Meeting of the Association for Computational Linguistics (Volume 2: Short Papers)*, pages 228–232, Sofia, Bulgaria. Association for Computational Linguistics.

Taivo Pungas. 2017. A dataset of english plaintext jokes.

H. Ren and Quan Yang. 2017. Neural joke generation.

Graeme Ritchie. 2005. Computational mechanisms for pun generation. In *Proceedings of the Tenth European Workshop on Natural Language Generation (ENLG-05)*.

Brandon M. Savage, Heidi L. Lujan, Raghavendar R. Thipparthi, and Stephen E. DiCarlo. 2017. Humor, laughter, learning, and health! a brief review. *Advances in Physiology Education*, 41(3):341–347.

Thorsten Schröter. 2005. Shun the pun, rescue the rhyme? : The dubbing and subtitling of language play in film.

M. Schuster and K.K. Paliwal. 1997. Bidirectional recurrent neural networks. *IEEE Transactions on Signal Processing*, 45(11):2673–2681.

Thomas Winters, Vincent Nys, and Daniel Schreye. 2018. *Automatic Joke Generation: Learning Humor from Examples*, pages 360–377.

Thomas Winters, Vincent Nys, and Danny De Schreye. 2019. Towards a general framework for humor generation from rated examples. In *Proceedings of the Tenth International Conference on Computational Creativity, ICCC 2019, Charlotte, North Carolina, USA, June 17-21, 2019*, pages 274–281. Association for Computational Creativity (ACC).

Zhiwei Yu, Jiwei Tan, and Xiaojun Wan. 2018. A neural approach to pun generation. In *Proceedings of the 56th Annual Meeting of the Association for Computational Linguistics (Volume 1: Long Papers)*, pages 1650–1660, Melbourne, Australia. Association for Computational Linguistics.

Hang Zhang, Dayiheng Liu, Jiancheng Lv, and Cheng Luo. 2020. Let's be humorous: Knowledge enhanced humor generation. *ArXiv*, abs/2004.13317.

Peng Zhou, Wei Shi, Jun Tian, Zhenyu Qi, Bingchen Li, Hongwei Hao, and Bo Xu. 2016. Attention-based bidirectional long short-term memory networks for relation classification. In *Proceedings of the 54th Annual Meeting of the Association for Computational Linguistics (Volume 2: Short Papers)*, pages 207–212, Berlin, Germany. Association for Computational Linguistics.

Towards Code-Mixed Hinglish Dialogue Generation

Vibhav Agarwal, Pooja Rao S B*, Dinesh Babu Jayagopi
International Institute of Information Technology Bangalore, India
* University of Lausanne, Switzerland
{vibhav.agarwal,jdinesh}@iiitb.ac.in, pooja.rao@unil.ch

Abstract

Code-mixed language plays a crucial role in communication in multilingual societies. Though the recent growth of web users has greatly boosted the use of such mixed languages, the current generation of dialog systems is primarily monolingual. This increase in usage of code-mixed language has prompted dialog systems in a similar language. We present our work in Code-Mixed Dialog Generation, an unexplored task in code-mixed languages, generating utterances in code-mixed language rather than a single language that is more often just English. We present a new synthetic corpus in code-mix for dialogs, CM-DailyDialog, by converting an existing English-only dialog corpus to a mixed Hindi-English corpus. We then propose a baseline approach where we show the effectiveness of using mBART like multilingual sequence-to-sequence transformers for code-mixed dialog generation. Our best performing dialog models can conduct coherent conversations in Hindi-English mixed language as evaluated by human and automatic metrics setting new benchmarks for the Code-Mixed Dialog Generation task.

1 Introduction

Due to the popularity of different social media and messaging platforms over the last decade, there has been a significant increase in internet users, mainly from multilingual societies. Multilingual speakers regularly combine languages in what is commonly called code-mixing or code-switching while communicating with other multilingual speakers. This has resulted in a substantial influx of mixed language data in the form of comments, conversations, and other forms of communication. Traditional natural language processing tasks like tokenization and tagging, semantic processing, machine translation, and text generation face new and interesting challenges due to this language mixing.

Dialog Systems have been of great interest amongst the natural language processing community for widespread applications. These systems are broadly categorized into three categories: task-oriented dialog system (Wen et al., 2017; Williams and Zweig, 2016), open-ended conversational systems (Shang et al., 2015; Xing et al., 2017), and interactive question answering system. Traditional Dialog Systems have mostly relied on a rule or template-based approach (Williams et al., 2013).

The success of deep neural networks with a considerable amount of training data has led towards end-to-end trained sequence-to-sequence (seq2seq) (Sutskever et al., 2014) models that enhance the generality and diversity of the text generated. Recent advances in attention-based mechanisms (Bahdanau et al., 2015) and Transformers (Vaswani et al., 2017) have shown significant performance improvement and shifted the communities' approach and interest in training larger models. However, all of these prior works use monolingual data and specifically English.

The increasing use of code-mixed languages and ubiquitous nature of multilingual speakers call for catering to the needs of such users in a multilingual fashion with a dialog system, the need for a Code-Mixed Dialog Generational System. A recent study by Bawa et al. (2020) shows that in a real-life setting, people prefer chatbots that engage in code-mixed language.

Code-mixing in informal contexts like newsgroups, tweets, comments and blogs has made it difficult to define a uniform structure to the language. However, linguists have formulated various hypotheses (Belazi et al., 1994; Pfaff, 1979; Poplack, 1981) and constraints (Sankoff and Poplack, 1981; Sciullo et al., 1986; Joshi, 1982) that can define a general rule for code-mixing.

With the rise of large pretrained language mod-

Proceedings of the Student Research Workshop associated with RANLP-2021, pages 7–15,
held online, Sep 1–3, 2021.
https://doi.org/10.26615/issn.2603-2821.2021_002

els like (Devlin et al., 2019; Radford et al., 2019; Conneau et al., 2020), there's been a lot of improvement in machine translation and multilingual models. Prior works (Khanuja et al., 2020b; Gupta et al., 2020) show the effectiveness of large multilingual pretrained language models like mBERT (Devlin et al., 2019) and XLM (Conneau and Lample, 2019) on code-mixed data.

Our work attempts to utilize these large seq2seq pre-trained multilingual transformer-based models for the code-mixed dialog generation task. Specifically, our contributions are as follows.

- We propose a synthetic code-mixed dialog dataset, CM-DailyDialog. This is the first benchmark dataset in Hindi-English mixed language for dialog generation generated from translating DailyDialog (Li et al., 2017) to code-mix.

- We set new benchmarks for the code-mixed dialog generation task on the CM-DailyDialog. We finetune the mBART model for the dialog generation in two ways to generate coherent dialog, as seen from both automatic and human evaluation metrics.

- To create CM-DailyDialog, we train a machine translation model. We use monolingual English data as our input instead of a parallel English and Hindi corpus. This differs from earlier work on code-mixed Machine Translation (Gupta et al., 2020; Garg et al., 2018) where they process a parallel corpus for training, making our approach less resource-intensive.

2 Related Work

Code-mixing refers to the interleaving of words belonging to different languages. Code-mixing is most common in multilingual cultures, and it is becoming more common as the number of people using social media and messaging services on the internet grows (Ansaldo et al., 2008). This has lead to a rising research interest in recent years, and several tasks have been conducted as part of code-switching workshops (Diab et al., 2014, 2016). There has been a lot of advancements in solving different code-mixed tasks like language identification (Solorio et al., 2014; Molina et al., 2016), named-entity recognition (Rao and Devi, 2016; Aguilar et al., 2018), question answering (Chandu et al., 2018), part-of-speech tagging (Jamatia et al., 2018), and information retrieval (banerjee et al., 2016). Very recently, a code-mixed version of the GLUE benchmark was proposed by Khanuja et al. (2020b) which introduced a common benchmark for all the tasks.

2.1 Code-Mixed Machine Translation

Machine Translation on Code-Mixed language is a relatively less explored area. There are only a few studies on English to Hinglish Code-Mixed language despite a large population of Code-Mixed speakers in South Asian countries. Dhar et al. (2018) collects a dataset of 6,096 Hinglish-English bitexts and proposes a pipeline where they identify the languages involved in the code-mixed sentence, compute the matrix language and then translate the resulting sentence into a target language. Srivastava and Singh (2020) collects a diversified large parallel corpus called PHINC, consisting of 13,738 Hinglish-English bitexts. Gupta et al. (2020) propose a code-mixed text generator built upon the encoder-decoder framework. They propose using features from a pre-trained cross-lingual transformer based model XLM (Conneau and Lample, 2019) along with Pointer-Generator (See et al., 2017) model as its decoder for the code-mixed text generation.

2.2 Conversational Dialog Systems

This work focuses on open-ended conversational dialog systems, which are interchangeably also called dialog systems here. Conversational systems engage in more open-ended conversations with no specific objective or task to solve in contrast to a task-oriented dialog system. In the open domain, conversational dialog systems fall again into two categories: retrieval-based and generative dialog systems. We take the generative model approach for a code-mixed dialog model rather than retrieve them from a fixed set as it is more dynamic and interactive.

Traditional dialog systems have mostly relied on hand-crafted rules or templates (Williams et al., 2013). Recently, a more data-driven approach is used to enhance the generality and diversity of the text generated in other domains. Researches used RNN (Rumelhart et al., 1986) and LSTM (Hochreiter and Schmidhuber, 1997) based encoder-decoder architectures for the dialog systems. Since the popularity of attention-based mechanisms (Bahdanau et al., 2015), these also have been widely adapted to boost performance. Recent works like DialoGPT (Zhang et al., 2020), BlenderBot (Smith et al., 2020) and Meena (Adiwardana et al., 2020) are just a few examples of the open domain conversational agents.

Although much work has been done in dialog systems, mostly all of it is for English conversations. This is because, in most of the work, the dataset used is monolingual. The only recent work involving a multilingual conversational system is by Chen et al. (2019) which performs dialog generation on English and Chinese data. It uses a shared memory mechanism with a seq2seq encoder-decoder like architecture and is trained using multi-task learning (Caruana, 1997).

3 System Overview

This section describes the benchmark dataset for code-mixed dialog generation: CM-DailyDialog, the English to Hinglish translation model used to generate this dataset, and our mBART based dialog generation model.

3.1 CM-DailyDialog dataset

There is no standardized dataset available for multilingual dialog generation; therefore, we choose to generate a synthetic dataset to train our model for code-mixed dialog. We use a standardized and popular English dialog dataset called DailyDialog (Li et al., 2017) and translate the utterances and conversations from English to Code-Mixed using our mBART model (**mBART-en_cm**) defined in Section 3.1.1. This results in the CM-DailyDialog dataset consisting of 11,118 conversations in the training set and 1,000 conversations in both test and validation sets.

We also use the Code-Mixed NLI conversation dataset from the GLUECoS benchmark (Khanuja et al., 2020a). This dataset contains roughly 1,800 training and roughly 500 test conversations extracted from movies.

We first process the multi-turn conversations from the CM-DailyDialog dataset into triplets of utterances using a sliding window approach. The first two utterances in that triplet are served as contextual inputs to the model, while the third utterance is served as the ground truth on which the loss is calculated. This processing of conversations into triplets of utterances increased the size of our dialog dataset from 13,118 to 76,745 data points. Similarly, we process the Code-Mixed NLI dataset into similar triplets, expanding our working dataset from 1,800 to 2,128 unique dialog triplets in the train set and by roughly 500 triplets in the test set. We choose to process these multi-turn conversations into splits of 3 and not say 5 or any other number because of increased computational costs for the mBART model to process such long conversations.

We describe our English to Hinglish translation model mBART-en_cm and the dataset used for its training in the following section.

3.1.1 Machine Translation model

We use an mBART model finetuned on English to Code-Mixed data described in Section 3.1.2 as our machine translation model to convert the English DailyDialog dataset to Code-Mixed form. We denote this model as **mBART-en_cm**. mBART is a multilingual seq2seq denoising bidirectional auto-encoder pre-trained using the same objective as BART (Lewis et al., 2020) but on large-scale monolingual corpora of 25 languages. It is based on the transformer (Vaswani et al., 2017) architecture and consists of 12 encoder and decoder layers, each with 16 attention heads and model dimensions being 1024 resulting in roughly 680 million parameters.

3.1.2 Dataset for Translation

We use the following datasets to finetune and test our *mBART-en_cm* model for English to Hinglish translation task:

- **CMU Hinglish** is an extended Code-Mixed form of the Document Grounded Conversation dataset by Zhou et al. (2018). It consists of roughly 10,000 English and Hinglish Code-Mixed sentences.
- **Reverse PHINC** is the reverse version of the PHINC (Srivastava and Singh, 2020) dataset but we switch the source and target pairs for our task. It contains roughly 13,000 Hinglish and parallel English translations.
- **LinCE** (Aguilar et al., 2020) Benchmark provides an English to Hinglish Code-Mixed dataset as part of their Code-Mixing benchmark for Machine Translation and GLUE. The dataset consists of roughly 10,000 English and Code-Mixed pairs.

We use these datasets individually and in conjunction to see any improvement with increased

Dataset	BLEU	Perplexity	CMI_{test}
mBART-dialog			
CM-DailyDialog	4.11	17.4	27.5
CM-DailyDialog + Code-Mixed NLI	1.54	13.6	22.6
mBART-dialog^{+}			
CM-DailyDialog	**8.11**	20.54	**28.9**
CM-DailyDialog + Code-Mixed NLI	5.74	12.93	26.8

Table 1: mBART performance on Dialog Generation

data.

3.2 Code-Mixed Dialog Model

We use the end-to-end multilingual training of the mBART. In literature, there is minimal work utilizing the BART architecture for dialog generation. De Bruyn et al. (2020) is one such work. It utilizes BART for knowledge grounding and knowledge retrieval in dialogs. Our approach attempts to leverage multilingualism by using the pre-trained BART for multilingual dialog generation and presents a few baselines for future work. We compare two strategies for finetuning mBART model for dialog generation:

- **mBART-dialog:** We finetune the mBART model on a Code-Mixed dialog dataset. In our case, we use triplet utterances to train our model.
- **mBART-dialog^{+}:** We finetune the mBART model in a dual curriculum learning method where we first finetune the mBART on an English to Code-Mixed translation task and then on a Code-Mixed dialog dataset.

4 Experimental Setup

In this section, we describe our experimental setup for both our mBART-en_cm model and the dialog model described in Section 3.1.1 & 3.2 respectively.

Our proposed approach is written in Pytorch (Paszke et al., 2019), and the mBART model weights and architecture used are from the HuggingFace's Transformer (Wolf et al., 2020) package. We use only the *mbart-cc-25* weights in all our modeling. All the mBART based models were trained using the AdamW optimizer with weight decay. We used all the default hyperparameters except the number of training epochs. We finetuned all our mBART models for five epochs only. As discussed in Section 2, there is extremely limited prior work and literature on multilingual dialogs. Therefore, there is no baseline for us to compare our model to and we report our numbers as it is.

Datasets	BLEU	CMI_{test}
LinCE Benchmark	11	28.3
CMU Hinglish	**11.53**	**32.5**
CMU Hinglish + LinCE Benchmark + Reverse PHINC	11.25	31.9

Table 2: BLEU score on test set for English to Hinglish Translation using mBART-en_cm model

As discussed in Section 3.1, we process our datasets from English to Code-Mixed and then into triplets. We split our processed CM-DailyDialog dataset into 8:1:1 splits for training, validation, and test set and use the additional Code-Mixed NLI dataset in conjunction with the CM-DailyDialog dataset to see any performance improvement with the increased data. We evaluate both our mBART-dialog and mBART-dialog^{+} models on BLEU and perplexity metric and report our scores in the Table 1. To gauge the language mixing performance of our models, we also use the Code-Mixing Index (CMI) (Gambäck and Das, 2016). We report sacrebleu as our BLEU metric using the HuggingFace's Dataset package.

We also show the performance of our *mBART-en_cm* model on different datasets for the monolingual English to Hinglish translation task using metrics like sacrebleu(reported as BLEU) and Code-Mixing Index in Table 2.

5 Results

Table 1 shows that the model trained using the dual curriculum learning method (mBART-dialog^{+}) per-

	Train set	Dev set	Test set
# of English tokens	295,565	54,150	32,676
# of Hindi tokens	546,535	86,231	67,505
# of Other tokens	77,519	13,493	10,721
Code-Mixing Index (CMI)	35	38.5	32.6

Table 3: Statistics of the generated CM-DailyDialog dataset

Error Category	Freq.
Mistranslated/Partially Translated	13
Morphology/Syntax Issues	12
NER mistranslation	1
No error	24

Table 4: Error Analysis on 50 randomly sampled test translated sentences from our best performing mBART-en_cm model on CMU Hinglish Dataset

forms better both on the BLEU as well as the CMI metric. This boost in performance might be due to the model understanding code-mixed language after the first finetune and, as a result, adapting better over the code-mixed dialogs in the second finetune. We also observe that simply increasing the data does not necessarily increase the model performance and leads to a significant drop in this case. This drop might be due to the inconsistent Hindi vocabulary in the romanized form in different datasets. The same Devanagari token can be represented in various Roman scripts in different datasets. This can cause the model not to have a fixed code-mixed vocabulary, causing this confusion and, hence, a drop in model performance.

Table 2 shows our mBART-en_cm model performance on different datasets. As observed previously, increasing the data leads to a drop in performance, which may be due to different datasets' vocabulary discrepancies. We use the best performing model, i.e. trained on the CMU Hinglish dataset and use that to generate our CM-DailyDialog dataset as described in Section 3.1.

Table 3 shows some of the statistics of the CM-DailyDialog dataset. The CMI scores for all the splits for our generated dataset are close to that of the real world code-mixed datasets like Dhar et al. (2018). This strengthens our intent to utilize this synthetic code-mixed dialog dataset for our dialog generation model.

5.1 Error Analysis of mBART-en_cm Translations

Considering BLEU and CMI ratings do not give insight into translation errors, we use error analysis to further assess the quality of our CM-DailyDialog dataset. We assess the quality of our mBART-en_cm model's translations on the test set by grouping the different errors generated by the model into three error categories and a no error category. We randomly sample 50 sentences from our test set and bucket them into categories. We follow the error analysis categories from Gautam et al. (2021). We employ three human raters that classify the sampled translations into the error buckets. Graduate students (non-native English speakers) familiar with the usage of code-mixed language, specifically Hinglish, in everyday life are the human annotators involved in this research. We report our numbers as a mode of three rater evaluations to account for the subjectivity among the raters. Mistranslated/Partially translation category indicates if the translation has low or no semantic resemblance with the source sentence. Morphological/Syntactical errors indicate if the translation has the same semantic meaning as the source sentence but has minor grammatical or syntax errors. NER mistranslations refer to the situation where the model translates the named entities in the generated output.

Table 4 shows the results of the error analysis over the described errors categories for the 50 test translations. We observe that the model makes 12 syntactical errors and 13 partial/mistranslations out of the 50 samples. After a more nuanced analysis of these numbers, we find that most of the syntax errors were 1-2 token errors or misalignment of those tokens. We also found that out of the 13 partial/mistranslations, only 15% of the translations were complete mistranslations. Most of the sentences in this error category were partial translations where the model failed to translate and

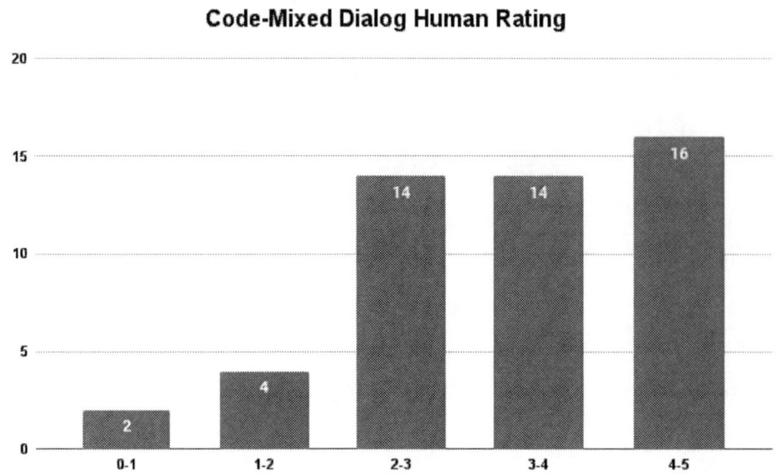

Figure 1: Bucketed average rating of 3 raters over the Code-Mixed dialogs quality from the range of 1-5

code-mix simultaneously.

5.2 Human Evaluation of Code-Mixed Dialog

To further strengthen the assessment of the generated code-mixed dialog, we perform a human evaluation of our best performing dialog model (mBART-dialog$^+$ trained on CM-DailyDialog). We employ three human raters who rate the generated follow-up dialog given prior contextual dialogs. These contextual dialogs refer to the first two utterances in the triplets that we processed in Section 3.1. As previously stated, the raters here are Graduate students familiar with the usage of Hinglish. The raters were instructed to rate the quality of the dialog on a scale of 1-5, with 1 being the lowest. The quality was assessed in terms of both the coherence in the dialog and the code-mixing. We do this analysis on 50 randomly sampled dialog generations from the test set. The results of the human ratings can be seen in Figure 1 as the mean of all three raters.

As it can be seen from Figure 1, 60% of the dialog utterances achieve a score greater than 3. 88% of the dialog utterance are scored above 2. These numbers indicate that our machine-generated code-mixed dialog followups are of good quality both in terms of coherence as well as code-mixing.

6 Conclusion

We introduce a new benchmark dataset for code-mixed dialog generation, CM-DailyDialog, a code-mixed version of the DailyDialog. Our work proposes using multilingual Transformers (mBART) and demonstrates how they help in code-mixed dialog generation. We also introduce a new monolingual English to Code-Mixed machine translation model using mBART. With our comprehensive experiments, we show the effectiveness of our approach in terms of machine translation and dialog generation and set new benchmarks in the Code-Mixed dialog generation task. The manual error analysis illustrates the quality of the new dataset, although it is synthetically generated. In terms of both automatic and human evaluation metrics, we show that the dialog generated from our model is of high quality.

As part of the future work, we would like to improve our machine translation model to improve our CM-DailyDialog data that further boosts our dialog generation. Another huge scope of improvement is in the vocabulary discrepancy in different datasets, and we wish to resolve this to further boost our modeling and performance.

References

Daniel Adiwardana, Minh-Thang Luong, David R. So, Jamie Hall, Noah Fiedel, Romal Thoppilan, Zi Yang, Apoorv Kulshreshtha, Gaurav Nemade, Yifeng Lu, and Quoc V. Le. 2020. Towards a Human-like Open-Domain Chatbot. *arXiv:2001.09977 [cs, stat]*. ArXiv: 2001.09977.

Gustavo Aguilar, Fahad AlGhamdi, Victor Soto, Thamar Solorio, Mona Diab, and Julia Hirschberg, editors. 2018. *Proceedings of the Third Workshop on Computational Approaches to Linguistic Code-Switching*. Association for Computational Linguistics, Melbourne, Australia.

Gustavo Aguilar, Sudipta Kar, and Thamar Solorio. 2020. LinCE: A centralized benchmark for linguistic code-switching evaluation. In *Proceedings of the 12th Language Resources and Evaluation Conference*, pages 1803–1813, Marseille, France. European Language Resources Association.

Ana Inés Ansaldo, Karine Marcotte, Lilian Scherer, and Gaelle Raboyeau. 2008. Language therapy and bilingual aphasia: Clinical implications of psycholinguistic and neuroimaging research. *Journal of Neurolinguistics*, 21(6):539–557.

Dzmitry Bahdanau, Kyunghyun Cho, and Yoshua Bengio. 2015. Neural machine translation by jointly learning to align and translate. In *3rd International Conference on Learning Representations, ICLR 2015, San Diego, CA, USA, May 7-9, 2015, Conference Track Proceedings*.

Somnath banerjee, Kunal Chakma, Sudip Kumar Naskar, Amitava Das, Paolo Rosso, Sivaji Bandyopadhyay, and Monojit Choudhury. 2016. Overview of the Mixed Script Information Retrieval (MSIR). In *Proceedings of FIRE 2016*. FIRE.

Anshul Bawa, Pranav Khadpe, Pratik Joshi, Kalika Bali, and Monojit Choudhury. 2020. Do multilingual users prefer chat-bots that code-mix? let's nudge and find out! *Proc. ACM Hum.-Comput. Interact.*, 4(CSCW1).

Hedi M. Belazi, Edward J. Rubin, and Almeida Jacqueline Toribio. 1994. Code switching and x-bar theory: The functional head constraint. *Linguistic Inquiry*, 25(2):221–237.

Rich Caruana. 1997. Multitask Learning. *Machine Learning*, 28(1):41–75.

Khyathi Chandu, Ekaterina Loginova, Vishal Gupta, Josef van Genabith, Günter Neumann, Manoj Chinnakotla, Eric Nyberg, and Alan W. Black. 2018. Code-mixed question answering challenge: Crowd-sourcing data and techniques. In *Proceedings of the Third Workshop on Computational Approaches to Linguistic Code-Switching*, pages 29–38, Melbourne, Australia. Association for Computational Linguistics.

Chen Chen, Lisong Qiu, Zhenxin Fu, Dongyan Zhao, Junfei Liu, and Rui Yan. 2019. Multilingual Dialogue Generation with Shared-Private Memory. *arXiv:1910.02365 [cs]*. ArXiv: 1910.02365.

Alexis Conneau, Kartikay Khandelwal, Naman Goyal, Vishrav Chaudhary, Guillaume Wenzek, Francisco Guzmán, Edouard Grave, Myle Ott, Luke Zettlemoyer, and Veselin Stoyanov. 2020. Unsupervised cross-lingual representation learning at scale. In *Proceedings of the 58th Annual Meeting of the Association for Computational Linguistics*, pages 8440–8451, Online. Association for Computational Linguistics.

Alexis Conneau and Guillaume Lample. 2019. Cross-lingual language model pretraining. In *Advances in Neural Information Processing Systems 32: Annual Conference on Neural Information Processing Systems 2019, NeurIPS 2019, December 8-14, 2019, Vancouver, BC, Canada*, pages 7057–7067.

Maxime De Bruyn, Ehsan Lotfi, Jeska Buhmann, and Walter Daelemans. 2020. Bart for knowledge grounded conversations. In *Converse@ KDD*.

Jacob Devlin, Ming-Wei Chang, Kenton Lee, and Kristina Toutanova. 2019. BERT: Pre-training of deep bidirectional transformers for language understanding. In *Proceedings of the 2019 Conference of the North American Chapter of the Association for Computational Linguistics: Human Language Technologies, Volume 1 (Long and Short Papers)*, pages 4171–4186, Minneapolis, Minnesota. Association for Computational Linguistics.

Mrinal Dhar, Vaibhav Kumar, and Manish Shrivastava. 2018. Enabling code-mixed translation: Parallel corpus creation and MT augmentation approach. In *Proceedings of the First Workshop on Linguistic Resources for Natural Language Processing*, pages 131–140, Santa Fe, New Mexico, USA. Association for Computational Linguistics.

Mona Diab, Pascale Fung, Mahmoud Ghoneim, Julia Hirschberg, and Thamar Solorio, editors. 2016. *Proceedings of the Second Workshop on Computational Approaches to Code Switching*. Association for Computational Linguistics, Austin, Texas.

Mona Diab, Julia Hirschberg, Pascale Fung, and Thamar Solorio, editors. 2014. *Proceedings of the First Workshop on Computational Approaches to Code Switching*. Association for Computational Linguistics, Doha, Qatar.

Björn Gambäck and Amitava Das. 2016. Comparing the level of code-switching in corpora. In *Proceedings of the Tenth International Conference on Language Resources and Evaluation (LREC'16)*, pages 1850–1855, Portorož, Slovenia. European Language Resources Association (ELRA).

Saurabh Garg, Tanmay Parekh, and Preethi Jyothi. 2018. Code-switched language models using dual RNNs and same-source pretraining. In *Proceedings of the 2018 Conference on Empirical Methods in Natural Language Processing*, pages 3078–3083, Brussels, Belgium. Association for Computational Linguistics.

Devansh Gautam, Prashant Kodali, Kshitij Gupta, Anmol Goel, Manish Shrivastava, and Ponnurangam Kumaraguru. 2021. CoMeT: Towards code-mixed translation using parallel monolingual sentences.

In *Proceedings of the Fifth Workshop on Computational Approaches to Linguistic Code-Switching*, pages 47–55, Online. Association for Computational Linguistics.

Deepak Gupta, Asif Ekbal, and Pushpak Bhattacharyya. 2020. A semi-supervised approach to generate the code-mixed text using pre-trained encoder and transfer learning. In *Findings of the Association for Computational Linguistics: EMNLP 2020*, pages 2267–2280, Online. Association for Computational Linguistics.

Sepp Hochreiter and Jürgen Schmidhuber. 1997. Long short-term memory. *Neural Comput.*, 9(8):1735–1780.

Anupam Jamatia, Björn Gambäck, and Amitava Das. 2018. Collecting and Annotating Indian Social Media Code-Mixed Corpora. In *Computational Linguistics and Intelligent Text Processing*, pages 406–417, Cham. Springer International Publishing.

Aravind K. Joshi. 1982. Processing of sentences with intra-sentential code-switching. In *Coling 1982: Proceedings of the Ninth International Conference on Computational Linguistics*.

Simran Khanuja, Sandipan Dandapat, Sunayana Sitaram, and Monojit Choudhury. 2020a. A new dataset for natural language inference from code-mixed conversations. In *Proceedings of the The 4th Workshop on Computational Approaches to Code Switching*, pages 9–16, Marseille, France. European Language Resources Association.

Simran Khanuja, Sandipan Dandapat, Anirudh Srinivasan, Sunayana Sitaram, and Monojit Choudhury. 2020b. GLUECoS: An evaluation benchmark for code-switched NLP. In *Proceedings of the 58th Annual Meeting of the Association for Computational Linguistics*, pages 3575–3585, Online. Association for Computational Linguistics.

Mike Lewis, Yinhan Liu, Naman Goyal, Marjan Ghazvininejad, Abdelrahman Mohamed, Omer Levy, Veselin Stoyanov, and Luke Zettlemoyer. 2020. BART: Denoising sequence-to-sequence pre-training for natural language generation, translation, and comprehension. In *Proceedings of the 58th Annual Meeting of the Association for Computational Linguistics*, pages 7871–7880, Online. Association for Computational Linguistics.

Yanran Li, Hui Su, Xiaoyu Shen, Wenjie Li, Ziqiang Cao, and Shuzi Niu. 2017. DailyDialog: A manually labelled multi-turn dialogue dataset. In *Proceedings of the Eighth International Joint Conference on Natural Language Processing (Volume 1: Long Papers)*, pages 986–995, Taipei, Taiwan. Asian Federation of Natural Language Processing.

Giovanni Molina, Fahad AlGhamdi, Mahmoud Ghoneim, Abdelati Hawwari, Nicolas Rey-Villamizar, Mona Diab, and Thamar Solorio. 2016. Overview for the second shared task on language identification in code-switched data. In *Proceedings of the Second Workshop on Computational Approaches to Code Switching*, pages 40–49, Austin, Texas. Association for Computational Linguistics.

Adam Paszke, Sam Gross, Francisco Massa, Adam Lerer, James Bradbury, Gregory Chanan, Trevor Killeen, Zeming Lin, Natalia Gimelshein, Luca Antiga, Alban Desmaison, Andreas Köpf, Edward Yang, Zachary DeVito, Martin Raison, Alykhan Tejani, Sasank Chilamkurthy, Benoit Steiner, Lu Fang, Junjie Bai, and Soumith Chintala. 2019. Pytorch: An imperative style, high-performance deep learning library. In *Advances in Neural Information Processing Systems 32: Annual Conference on Neural Information Processing Systems 2019, NeurIPS 2019, December 8-14, 2019, Vancouver, BC, Canada*, pages 8024–8035.

Carol W. Pfaff. 1979. Constraints on language mixing: Intrasentential code-switching and borrowing in spanish/english. *Language*, 55(2):291–318.

Shana Poplack. 1981. *Syntactic structure and social function of code-switching*, pages 169–184.

Alec Radford, Jeff Wu, Rewon Child, David Luan, Dario Amodei, and Ilya Sutskever. 2019. Language models are unsupervised multitask learners.

Pattabhi R. K. Rao and S. Devi. 2016. Cmee-il: Code mix entity extraction in indian languages from social media text @ fire 2016 - an overview. In *FIRE*.

David E. Rumelhart, Geoffrey E. Hinton, and Ronald J. Williams. 1986. Learning representations by back-propagating errors. *Nature*, 323(6088):533–536.

David Sankoff and Shana Poplack. 1981. A formal grammar for code-switching. *Papers in Linguistics - International Journal of Human Communication*, 14:3–46.

Anne-Marie Di Sciullo, Pieter Muysken, and Rajendra Singh. 1986. Government and code-mixing. *Journal of Linguistics*, 22(1):1–24.

Abigail See, Peter J. Liu, and Christopher D. Manning. 2017. Get to the point: Summarization with pointer-generator networks. In *Proceedings of the 55th Annual Meeting of the Association for Computational Linguistics (Volume 1: Long Papers)*, pages 1073–1083, Vancouver, Canada. Association for Computational Linguistics.

Lifeng Shang, Zhengdong Lu, and Hang Li. 2015. Neural responding machine for short-text conversation. In *Proceedings of the 53rd Annual Meeting of the Association for Computational Linguistics and the 7th International Joint Conference on Natural Language Processing (Volume 1: Long Papers)*, pages 1577–1586, Beijing, China. Association for Computational Linguistics.

Eric Michael Smith, Mary Williamson, Kurt Shuster, Jason Weston, and Y-Lan Boureau. 2020. Can you put it all together: Evaluating conversational agents' ability to blend skills. In *Proceedings of the 58th Annual Meeting of the Association for Computational Linguistics*, pages 2021–2030, Online. Association for Computational Linguistics.

Thamar Solorio, Elizabeth Blair, Suraj Maharjan, Steven Bethard, Mona Diab, Mahmoud Ghoneim, Abdelati Hawwari, Fahad AlGhamdi, Julia Hirschberg, Alison Chang, and Pascale Fung. 2014. Overview for the first shared task on language identification in code-switched data. In *Proceedings of the First Workshop on Computational Approaches to Code Switching*, pages 62–72, Doha, Qatar. Association for Computational Linguistics.

Vivek Srivastava and Mayank Singh. 2020. PHINC: A parallel Hinglish social media code-mixed corpus for machine translation. In *Proceedings of the Sixth Workshop on Noisy User-generated Text (W-NUT 2020)*, pages 41–49, Online. Association for Computational Linguistics.

Ilya Sutskever, Oriol Vinyals, and Quoc V. Le. 2014. Sequence to sequence learning with neural networks. In *Advances in Neural Information Processing Systems 27: Annual Conference on Neural Information Processing Systems 2014, December 8-13 2014, Montreal, Quebec, Canada*, pages 3104–3112.

Ashish Vaswani, Noam Shazeer, Niki Parmar, Jakob Uszkoreit, Llion Jones, Aidan N. Gomez, Lukasz Kaiser, and Illia Polosukhin. 2017. Attention is all you need. In *Advances in Neural Information Processing Systems 30: Annual Conference on Neural Information Processing Systems 2017, December 4-9, 2017, Long Beach, CA, USA*, pages 5998–6008.

Tsung-Hsien Wen, David Vandyke, Nikola Mrkšić, Milica Gašić, Lina M. Rojas-Barahona, Pei-Hao Su, Stefan Ultes, and Steve Young. 2017. A network-based end-to-end trainable task-oriented dialogue system. In *Proceedings of the 15th Conference of the European Chapter of the Association for Computational Linguistics: Volume 1, Long Papers*, pages 438–449, Valencia, Spain. Association for Computational Linguistics.

Jason Williams, Antoine Raux, Deepak Ramachandran, and Alan Black. 2013. The dialog state tracking challenge. In *Proceedings of the SIGDIAL 2013 Conference*, pages 404–413, Metz, France. Association for Computational Linguistics.

Jason D. Williams and Geoffrey Zweig. 2016. End-to-end LSTM-based dialog control optimized with supervised and reinforcement learning. *arXiv:1606.01269 [cs]*. ArXiv: 1606.01269.

Thomas Wolf, Lysandre Debut, Victor Sanh, Julien Chaumond, Clement Delangue, Anthony Moi, Pierric Cistac, Tim Rault, Remi Louf, Morgan Funtowicz, Joe Davison, Sam Shleifer, Patrick von Platen, Clara Ma, Yacine Jernite, Julien Plu, Canwen Xu, Teven Le Scao, Sylvain Gugger, Mariama Drame, Quentin Lhoest, and Alexander Rush. 2020. Transformers: State-of-the-art natural language processing. In *Proceedings of the 2020 Conference on Empirical Methods in Natural Language Processing: System Demonstrations*, pages 38–45, Online. Association for Computational Linguistics.

Chen Xing, Wei Wu, Yu Wu, Jie Liu, Yalou Huang, Ming Zhou, and Wei-Ying Ma. 2017. Topic aware neural response generation. In *Proceedings of the Thirty-First AAAI Conference on Artificial Intelligence, February 4-9, 2017, San Francisco, California, USA*, pages 3351–3357. AAAI Press.

Yizhe Zhang, Siqi Sun, Michel Galley, Yen-Chun Chen, Chris Brockett, Xiang Gao, Jianfeng Gao, Jingjing Liu, and Bill Dolan. 2020. DIALOGPT : Large-scale generative pre-training for conversational response generation. In *Proceedings of the 58th Annual Meeting of the Association for Computational Linguistics: System Demonstrations*, pages 270–278, Online. Association for Computational Linguistics.

Kangyan Zhou, Shrimai Prabhumoye, and Alan W Black. 2018. A dataset for document grounded conversations. In *Proceedings of the 2018 Conference on Empirical Methods in Natural Language Processing*, pages 708–713, Brussels, Belgium. Association for Computational Linguistics.

Hinglish to English Machine Translation using Multilingual Transformers

Vibhav Agarwal, Pooja Rao S B*, Dinesh Babu Jayagopi
International Institute of Information Technology Bangalore, India
* University of Lausanne, Switzerland
{vibhav.agarwal,jdinesh}@iiitb.ac.in, pooja.rao@unil.ch

Abstract

Code-Mixed language plays a very important role in communication in multilingual societies and with the recent increase in internet users especially in multilingual societies, the usage of such mixed language has also increased. However, the cross translation between the Hinglish Code-Mixed and English and vice-versa has not been explored very extensively. With the recent success of large pretrained language models, we explore the possibility of using multilingual pretrained transformers like mBART and mT5 for exploring one such task of code-mixed Hinglish to English machine translation. Further, we compare our approach with the only baseline over the PHINC dataset and report a significant jump from 15.3 to 29.5 in BLEU scores, a 92.8% improvement over the same dataset.

1 Introduction

Code-Mixing is the interleaving of tokens from different languages but in the same conversation. Code-Mixing is a common phenomenon in multilingual societies like India, China, Mexico, and in the last decade itself, there has been a massive surge of internet users and specifically from multilingual societies due to the popularity of various social media and messaging platforms. This has lead to a massive surge in mixed language data in the form of comments, conversations, etc. Unfortunately due to the informal nature of the code-mixed, it is hard to set a uniformly defined structure. However, linguists have formulated various hypotheses (Belazi et al., 1994; Pfaff, 1979; Poplack, 1981) and constraints (Sankoff and Poplack, 1981; Sciullo et al., 1986; Joshi, 1982) that can define a general rule for code-mixing.

Recent advances in attention-based mechanisms (Bahdanau et al., 2015) and transformers (Vaswani et al., 2017) have again shown significant performance improvement and shifted the communities' approach and interest in training larger neural models with deeper architecture. With the rise in large pretrained language models like (Devlin et al., 2019; Radford et al., 2019), there's been a lot of improvement in natural language processing problems. Prior work done in code-mixing like that of (Khanuja et al., 2020; Gupta et al., 2020) show the effectiveness of large multilingual pretrained language models like mBERT (Devlin et al., 2019) and XLM (Conneau and Lample, 2019) on code-mixed data. While GLUECoS attempts to set GLUE benchmark using finetuned mBERT, Gupta et al. (2020) shows the effectiveness of machine translation from a parallel corpus of English and Hindi to code-mixed sentence using XLM and Pointer-Generator model. Srivastava and Singh (2020); Dhar et al. (2018) proposes new task of Hinglish code-mixed to English translation and Srivastava and Singh (2020) collects a new social media code-mixed dataset called PHINC consisting of Hinglish code-mixed and parallel English sentences.

Our work attempts to utilize large seq2seq pretrained multilingual transformer based models like mT5 and mBART for the Hinglish to English machine translation task. We propose a dual curriculum learning method where first the models are trained for an English to code-mixed translation task and then finetuned again for a code-mixed to English task. There has been very little prior work involving this task and most of the work dealt with the English to code-mixed translation task for synthetic data generation. Our translation from code-mixed to English shows a significant improvement over the PHINC dataset and even beats the baseline presented by the PHINC dataset by a margin of 92.8%.

The rest of the paper is as follows - Section 2 talks about the prior work done in code-mixed machine translation and large multilingual pretrained

Proceedings of the Student Research Workshop associated with RANLP-2021, pages 16–21,
held online, Sep 1–3, 2021.
https://doi.org/10.26615/issn.2603-2821.2021_003

transformers. Section 3 discusses our model and the dataset used for the Hinglish to English translation. Section 4 addresses our experiments and our qualitative results for our approach. Finally, Section 5 addresses the conclusive remarks for this paper and presents a direction for future work.

2 Related Work

Code-Mixing refers to the interleaving of words belonging to different languages. This happens predominately in multilingual societies and is increasing rapidly with the increase in internet users on social media and messaging platforms. This has lead to a rapid increase in research interest in recent years and several tasks have been conducted as part of Code-Switching workshops (Diab et al., 2014, 2016). Most of the work in these workshops was single NLP problem-specific which were solved using specifically tailored models like Language Identification (Solorio et al., 2014; Molina et al., 2016), Named Entity Recognition (Rao and Devi, 2016; Aguilar et al., 2018), Question Answering (Chandu et al., 2018), Parts-of-Speech tagging (Jamatia et al., 2018), and Information Retrieval (banerjee et al., 2016). This was changed by Khanuja et al. (2020) which introduced a common benchmark for all the tasks using a single finetuned mBERT (Devlin et al., 2019) model downstreamed for all the benchmark tasks.

2.1 Code-Mixed Machine Translation

Machine Translation on code-mixed language is a relatively less explored area. There are only a few studies on English-Hinglish code-mixed language including the work of Dhar et al. (2018); Gupta et al. (2020); Srivastava and Singh (2020) despite a large populous of code-mixed speakers in South Asian countries. Dhar et al. (2018) collects a dataset of 6,096 Hinglish-English bitexts and propose a pipeline where they identify the languages involved in the code-mixed sentence, compute the matrix language and then translate the resulting sentence into the target language. Srivastava and Singh (2020) collects a large parallel corpus called PHINC, consisting of 13,738 Hinglish-English bitexts that they claimed was better than those of Dhar et al. (2018) in terms of diversity, quality, and generality. They propose a pipeline where they selectively identify token languages and then translate Hindi phrases to English using a monolingual translation system while keeping the rest of the phrases intact. This is the only work that addresses a Hinglish to English machine translation task. Gupta et al. (2020) propose a code-mixed text generator built upon the encoder-decoder framework, where the linguistic features obtained from a transformer based language model are encoded using the encoder. They proposed using features from a pretrained cross-lingual transformer based model XLM (Conneau and Lample, 2019) along with Pointer-Generator (See et al., 2017) model as its decoder for the code-mixed text generation.

2.2 Multilingual Pretrained Models

Transformer-based neural models have increasingly become a go-to solution for any NLP problem using models trained with a self-supervised objective like BERT (Devlin et al., 2019), BART (Lewis et al., 2020), and T5 (Raffel et al., 2020). In cross-lingual or multilingual domains, there has been a rapid increase in the number of models built upon BERT, BART, or T5 architecture or they use a similar architecture. Works like mBERT, mBART (Liu et al., 2020), mT5 (Xue et al., 2021), XLM (Conneau and Lample, 2019) and XLM-R (Conneau et al., 2020) are a few examples of such models. While mBERT and XLM-R are encoder only architectures that could be used for downstream classification tasks, XLM is a seq2seq encoder-decoder task-specific model, built mostly for translation tasks. Models like mBART and mT5 are seq2seq encoder-decoder architecture that can solve multiple downstream tasks like summarization, translation, or any other language generational task without any additional modeling head. These models are trained on multiple languages at once with a self-supervised objective like span corruption, permutation, etc. While mBART is pretrained on 25 languages on the same BART objective, mT5 is pretrained on 101 languages on the T5 model's objective. None of these multilingual models are trained on any code-mixed language or at least are not aware of their pretraining data consisting of code-mixed data. Therefore, it becomes an important question to verify and validate these model performances on code-mixed languages.

3 System Overview

In this Section, we propose our mBART and mT5 based machine translation model and the dataset used for finetuning the same.

Hinglish Code-Mixed to English Translation		
Mujhe lagta hai wo captured humanoid amphibian creature play karta hai	→	I think he plays a captured humanoid amphibian creature.
main character ek orphan hai jo ek river mein paya gaya	→	The main character is an orphan who is found in a river.
kya aapko lagtha hein ki ache movie ko high-profile actors hi chahiye?	→	Do you think a good movie should have high-profile actors?
Main suprised hu ye itna low hai	→	I'm suprised how low it is.

Table 1: Samples from the Hinglish to English translation task. Red tokens refer to the Hindi tokens in the Roman script.

3.1 Machine Translation model

We use mBART and mT5 models finetuned on Hinglish code-mixed to English data as described in Section 3.2. mBART is a multilingual seq2seq denoising bidirectional auto-encoder pretrained using the same BART (Lewis et al., 2020) objective but on large-scale monolingual corpora of 25 languages. It is based on the same transformer (Vaswani et al., 2017) architecture and consists of 12 encoder and decoder layers each with 16 attention heads and model dimensions being 1024 resulting in roughly 680 million parameters. mT5 is the multilingual variant of the T5 model pretrained on 101 languages. It has a similar transformer architecture with 2 encoder and decoder layers each, model dimensions being 1024 and 12 attention heads resulting in approximately 770 million parameters.

3.2 Dataset

We use the following datasets to finetune and test our models for Hinglish code-mixed to English translation task:

- **CMU Hinglish** is an extended code-mixed form of the Document Grounded Conversation (Zhou et al., 2018) dataset. It consists of roughly 10,000 English and Hinglish code-mixed sentences.
- **PHINC** (Srivastava and Singh, 2020) consists of Hinglish code-mixed to English translation pairs. It contains roughly 13,000 parallel pairs.

For both of the datasets, we transliterate the Hindi Devanagari script into its Roman script form using CSNLI (Bhat et al., 2017, 2018) and Microsoft Translator.

4 Experiments & Results

In this section, we describe our experimental setup and our finetuning results for our models described in Section 3.

4.1 Experimental Setup

Our proposed approach is written in Pytorch (Paszke et al., 2019) and all the transformer based models and their associated weights are from the HuggingFace's Transformer (Wolf et al., 2020) package. We use *mbart-cc-25* model weights for mBART and *mt5-base* model weight for mT5 in all our modeling. Both the mBART and mT5 models were trained using the AdamW optimizer with weight decay. We used all the default hyperparameters except the number of training epochs, mBART was trained for 5 epochs while the mT5 took larger epochs (50) to converge the training.

We train both of our models in a dual curriculum learning method where we first finetune it on a English to code-mixed data so that model identifies what code-mixed language looks like and then we finetune it again on the Hinglish code-mixed gold dataset for our final task. We show some of the example translations of our best performing model in Table 1. We show the performance of both mT5 and mBART models on the datasets described in Section 3.2 in Table 2. For the BLEU evaluation, we use the *sacrebleu* metric from HuggingFace's Dataset package.

Baseline: Our only comparative baseline is defined by Srivastava and Singh (2020) where they collect a code-mixed dataset from social media and conversations called PHINC and propose a machine translation pipeline built on top of Google Translate with a BLEU score of 15.3.

Datasets	BLEU score
Original Baseline	
PHINC	15.3
mBART model (ours)	
CMU Hinglish → Reverse CMU Hinglish	24.0
CMU Hinglish → PHINC	25.3
mT5 model (ours)	
CMU Hinglish → Reverse CMU Hinglish	28.6
CMU Hinglish → PHINC	**29.5**

Table 2: BLEU score for code-mixed Hinglish to English Translation

4.2 Results

As shown in Table 2, we first finetune our mBART and mT5 models on the CMU Hinglish dataset. These finetuned models have a BLEU score of 11.53 and 11.23 respectively. These are then further finetuned for our final task of Hinglish to English translation. We perform and analyse the second finetune on both the flipped CMU Hinglish dataset and the PHINC dataset.

All four variations of our dual finetuned mBART and mT5 models outperform the original baseline. While the best performing mBART model improves over the baseline by 65.3%, mT5 model beats the PHINC baseline by a margin of 92.8%. This shows the prowess of the large pretrained multilingual transformers in code-mixed translation tasks.

5 Conclusion

Our work proposes using large multilingual transformers (mBART and mT5) and demonstrates how finetuning them in a dual curriculum learning method improves the performance of code-mixed Hinglish to English machine translation tasks. We show a very significant improvement over the PHINC baseline by a margin of 92.8% over the BLEU scores.

As part of the future work, we would like to further improve our machine translation model by using a large amount of synthetic code-mixed data to improve our English to code-mixed translation model, which would further improve our performance on the code-mixed to English translation task. We would also like to extend this work to other low resource and code-mixed languages.

References

Gustavo Aguilar, Fahad AlGhamdi, Victor Soto, Thamar Solorio, Mona Diab, and Julia Hirschberg, editors. 2018. *Proceedings of the Third Workshop on Computational Approaches to Linguistic Code-Switching*. Association for Computational Linguistics, Melbourne, Australia.

Dzmitry Bahdanau, Kyunghyun Cho, and Yoshua Bengio. 2015. Neural machine translation by jointly learning to align and translate. In *3rd International Conference on Learning Representations, ICLR 2015, San Diego, CA, USA, May 7-9, 2015, Conference Track Proceedings*.

Somnath banerjee, Kunal Chakma, Sudip Kumar Naskar, Amitava Das, Paolo Rosso, Sivaji Bandyopadhyay, and Monojit Choudhury. 2016. Overview of the Mixed Script Information Retrieval (MSIR). In *Proceedings of FIRE 2016*. FIRE.

Hedi M. Belazi, Edward J. Rubin, and Almeida Jacqueline Toribio. 1994. Code switching and x-bar theory: The functional head constraint. *Linguistic Inquiry*, 25(2):221–237.

Irshad Bhat, Riyaz A. Bhat, Manish Shrivastava, and Dipti Sharma. 2017. Joining hands: Exploiting monolingual treebanks for parsing of code-mixing data. In *Proceedings of the 15th Conference of the European Chapter of the Association for Computational Linguistics: Volume 2, Short Papers*, pages 324–330, Valencia, Spain. Association for Computational Linguistics.

Irshad Bhat, Riyaz A. Bhat, Manish Shrivastava, and Dipti Sharma. 2018. Universal Dependency parsing for Hindi-English code-switching. In *Proceedings of the 2018 Conference of the North American Chapter of the Association for Computational Linguistics:*

Human Language Technologies, Volume 1 (Long Papers), pages 987–998, New Orleans, Louisiana. Association for Computational Linguistics.

Khyathi Chandu, Ekaterina Loginova, Vishal Gupta, Josef van Genabith, Günter Neumann, Manoj Chinnakotla, Eric Nyberg, and Alan W. Black. 2018. Code-mixed question answering challenge: Crowdsourcing data and techniques. In *Proceedings of the Third Workshop on Computational Approaches to Linguistic Code-Switching*, pages 29–38, Melbourne, Australia. Association for Computational Linguistics.

Alexis Conneau, Kartikay Khandelwal, Naman Goyal, Vishrav Chaudhary, Guillaume Wenzek, Francisco Guzmán, Edouard Grave, Myle Ott, Luke Zettlemoyer, and Veselin Stoyanov. 2020. Unsupervised cross-lingual representation learning at scale. In *Proceedings of the 58th Annual Meeting of the Association for Computational Linguistics*, pages 8440–8451, Online. Association for Computational Linguistics.

Alexis Conneau and Guillaume Lample. 2019. Cross-lingual language model pretraining. In *Advances in Neural Information Processing Systems 32: Annual Conference on Neural Information Processing Systems 2019, NeurIPS 2019, December 8-14, 2019, Vancouver, BC, Canada*, pages 7057–7067.

Jacob Devlin, Ming-Wei Chang, Kenton Lee, and Kristina Toutanova. 2019. BERT: Pre-training of deep bidirectional transformers for language understanding. In *Proceedings of the 2019 Conference of the North American Chapter of the Association for Computational Linguistics: Human Language Technologies, Volume 1 (Long and Short Papers)*, pages 4171–4186, Minneapolis, Minnesota. Association for Computational Linguistics.

Mrinal Dhar, Vaibhav Kumar, and Manish Shrivastava. 2018. Enabling code-mixed translation: Parallel corpus creation and MT augmentation approach. In *Proceedings of the First Workshop on Linguistic Resources for Natural Language Processing*, pages 131–140, Santa Fe, New Mexico, USA. Association for Computational Linguistics.

Mona Diab, Pascale Fung, Mahmoud Ghoneim, Julia Hirschberg, and Thamar Solorio, editors. 2016. *Proceedings of the Second Workshop on Computational Approaches to Code Switching*. Association for Computational Linguistics, Austin, Texas.

Mona Diab, Julia Hirschberg, Pascale Fung, and Thamar Solorio, editors. 2014. *Proceedings of the First Workshop on Computational Approaches to Code Switching*. Association for Computational Linguistics, Doha, Qatar.

Deepak Gupta, Asif Ekbal, and Pushpak Bhattacharyya. 2020. A semi-supervised approach to generate the code-mixed text using pre-trained encoder and transfer learning. In *Findings of the Association for Computational Linguistics: EMNLP 2020*, pages 2267–2280, Online. Association for Computational Linguistics.

Anupam Jamatia, Björn Gambäck, and Amitava Das. 2018. Collecting and Annotating Indian Social Media Code-Mixed Corpora. In *Computational Linguistics and Intelligent Text Processing*, pages 406–417, Cham. Springer International Publishing.

Aravind K. Joshi. 1982. Processing of sentences with intra-sentential code-switching. In *Coling 1982: Proceedings of the Ninth International Conference on Computational Linguistics*.

Simran Khanuja, Sandipan Dandapat, Anirudh Srinivasan, Sunayana Sitaram, and Monojit Choudhury. 2020. GLUECoS: An evaluation benchmark for code-switched NLP. In *Proceedings of the 58th Annual Meeting of the Association for Computational Linguistics*, pages 3575–3585, Online. Association for Computational Linguistics.

Mike Lewis, Yinhan Liu, Naman Goyal, Marjan Ghazvininejad, Abdelrahman Mohamed, Omer Levy, Veselin Stoyanov, and Luke Zettlemoyer. 2020. BART: Denoising sequence-to-sequence pre-training for natural language generation, translation, and comprehension. In *Proceedings of the 58th Annual Meeting of the Association for Computational Linguistics*, pages 7871–7880, Online. Association for Computational Linguistics.

Yinhan Liu, Jiatao Gu, Naman Goyal, Xian Li, Sergey Edunov, Marjan Ghazvininejad, Mike Lewis, and Luke Zettlemoyer. 2020. Multilingual denoising pre-training for neural machine translation. *Transactions of the Association for Computational Linguistics*, 8:726–742.

Giovanni Molina, Fahad AlGhamdi, Mahmoud Ghoneim, Abdelati Hawwari, Nicolas Rey-Villamizar, Mona Diab, and Thamar Solorio. 2016. Overview for the second shared task on language identification in code-switched data. In *Proceedings of the Second Workshop on Computational Approaches to Code Switching*, pages 40–49, Austin, Texas. Association for Computational Linguistics.

Adam Paszke, Sam Gross, Francisco Massa, Adam Lerer, James Bradbury, Gregory Chanan, Trevor Killeen, Zeming Lin, Natalia Gimelshein, Luca Antiga, Alban Desmaison, Andreas Köpf, Edward Yang, Zachary DeVito, Martin Raison, Alykhan Tejani, Sasank Chilamkurthy, Benoit Steiner, Lu Fang, Junjie Bai, and Soumith Chintala. 2019. Pytorch: An imperative style, high-performance deep learning library. In *Advances in Neural Information Processing Systems 32: Annual Conference on Neural Information Processing Systems 2019, NeurIPS 2019, December 8-14, 2019, Vancouver, BC, Canada*, pages 8024–8035.

Carol W. Pfaff. 1979. Constraints on language mixing: Intrasentential code-switching and borrowing in spanish/english. *Language*, 55(2):291–318.

Shana Poplack. 1981. *Syntactic structure and social function of code-switching*, pages 169–184.

Alec Radford, Jeff Wu, Rewon Child, David Luan, Dario Amodei, and Ilya Sutskever. 2019. Language models are unsupervised multitask learners.

Colin Raffel, Noam Shazeer, Adam Roberts, Katherine Lee, Sharan Narang, Michael Matena, Yanqi Zhou, Wei Li, and Peter J. Liu. 2020. Exploring the limits of transfer learning with a unified text-to-text transformer.

Pattabhi R. K. Rao and S. Devi. 2016. Cmee-il: Code mix entity extraction in indian languages from social media text @ fire 2016 - an overview. In *FIRE*.

David Sankoff and Shana Poplack. 1981. A formal grammar for code-switching. *Papers in Linguistics - International Journal of Human Communication*, 14:3–46.

Anne-Marie Di Sciullo, Pieter Muysken, and Rajendra Singh. 1986. Government and code-mixing. *Journal of Linguistics*, 22(1):1–24.

Abigail See, Peter J. Liu, and Christopher D. Manning. 2017. Get to the point: Summarization with pointer-generator networks. In *Proceedings of the 55th Annual Meeting of the Association for Computational Linguistics (Volume 1: Long Papers)*, pages 1073–1083, Vancouver, Canada. Association for Computational Linguistics.

Thamar Solorio, Elizabeth Blair, Suraj Maharjan, Steven Bethard, Mona Diab, Mahmoud Ghoneim, Abdelati Hawwari, Fahad AlGhamdi, Julia Hirschberg, Alison Chang, and Pascale Fung. 2014. Overview for the first shared task on language identification in code-switched data. In *Proceedings of the First Workshop on Computational Approaches to Code Switching*, pages 62–72, Doha, Qatar. Association for Computational Linguistics.

Vivek Srivastava and Mayank Singh. 2020. PHINC: A parallel Hinglish social media code-mixed corpus for machine translation. In *Proceedings of the Sixth Workshop on Noisy User-generated Text (W-NUT 2020)*, pages 41–49, Online. Association for Computational Linguistics.

Ashish Vaswani, Noam Shazeer, Niki Parmar, Jakob Uszkoreit, Llion Jones, Aidan N. Gomez, Lukasz Kaiser, and Illia Polosukhin. 2017. Attention is all you need. In *Advances in Neural Information Processing Systems 30: Annual Conference on Neural Information Processing Systems 2017, December 4-9, 2017, Long Beach, CA, USA*, pages 5998–6008.

Thomas Wolf, Lysandre Debut, Victor Sanh, Julien Chaumond, Clement Delangue, Anthony Moi, Pierric Cistac, Tim Rault, Remi Louf, Morgan Funtowicz, Joe Davison, Sam Shleifer, Patrick von Platen, Clara Ma, Yacine Jernite, Julien Plu, Canwen Xu, Teven Le Scao, Sylvain Gugger, Mariama Drame, Quentin Lhoest, and Alexander Rush. 2020. Transformers: State-of-the-art natural language processing. In *Proceedings of the 2020 Conference on Empirical Methods in Natural Language Processing: System Demonstrations*, pages 38–45, Online. Association for Computational Linguistics.

Linting Xue, Noah Constant, Adam Roberts, Mihir Kale, Rami Al-Rfou, Aditya Siddhant, Aditya Barua, and Colin Raffel. 2021. mT5: A massively multilingual pre-trained text-to-text transformer. In *Proceedings of the 2021 Conference of the North American Chapter of the Association for Computational Linguistics: Human Language Technologies*, pages 483–498, Online. Association for Computational Linguistics.

Kangyan Zhou, Shrimai Prabhumoye, and Alan W Black. 2018. A dataset for document grounded conversations. In *Proceedings of the 2018 Conference on Empirical Methods in Natural Language Processing*, pages 708–713, Brussels, Belgium. Association for Computational Linguistics.

SiPOS: A Benchmark Dataset for Sindhi Part-of-Speech Tagging

Wazir Ali and **Zenglin Xu**
SMILE Lab, School of Computer Science and Engineering
University of Electronic Science and Technology of China, Chengdu 611731, China
{aliwazirjam,zenglin}@gmail.com

Jay Kumar
Data Mining Lab,School of Computer Science and Engineering
University of Electronic Science and Technology of China, Chengdu 611731, China

Abstract

In this paper, we introduce the SiPOS dataset for part-of-speech tagging in the low-resource Sindhi language with quality baselines. The dataset consists of more than 293K tokens annotated with sixteen universal part-of-speech categories. Two experienced native annotators annotated the SiPOS using the Doccano text annotation tool with an inter-annotation agreement of 0.872. We exploit the conditional random field, the popular bidirectional long-short-term memory neural model, and self-attention mechanism with various settings to evaluate the proposed dataset. Besides pre-trained GloVe and fastText representation, the character-level representations are incorporated to extract character-level information using the bidirectional long-short-term memory encoder. The high accuracy of 96.25% is achieved with the task-specific joint word-level and character-level representations. The SiPOS dataset is likely to be a significant resource for the low-resource Sindhi language.

1 Introduction

Annotated corpus is an essential resource for developing automatic natural language processing (NLP) systems (Ali et al., 2020). Such language resources (LRs) play a significant role in the digital survival of human languages (Jamro, 2017). The part-of-speech (POS) tagging is a fundamental preprocessing task in various NLP applications (Mahar and Memon, 2010), used to assign appropriate in-context POS tags to each word. One of the main challenges (Britvić, 2018) in POS tagging is ambiguity since one word can take several possible POS labels. Another problem is the unspoken or complex POS or words. Both of these problems are not rare in natural languages. Moreover, there is a lack of benchmark labeled datasets for Sindhi POS tagging. To tackle these challenges, we propose a novel benchmark SiPOS tagset.

Sindhi is a rich and complex morphological language (Rahman, 2010). It is a low-resource language (Ali et al., 2019) which lacks primary LRs for mature computational processing. Sindhi is being written in two famous writing systems of Persian-Arabic, Devanagari, and more recently Roman (Sodhar et al., 2019) is also getting popularity. However, Persian-Arabic is standard script as well as frequently used in literary work, online communication, and journalism. Sindhi POS tagging has been previously investigated in various scripts including Persian-Arabic,Devanagari (Jamro, 2017), and Roman (Sodhar et al., 2019). However, the low-resource Sindhi language lacks a POS labeled dataset for its supervised text classification.

In this paper, we introduce a novel benchmark SiPOS dataset for the low-resource Sindhi language. Due to the scarcity of open-source POS labeled data, two native experienced annotators performed the POS annotation of Sindhi text using the Doccano (Nakayama et al., 2018) text annotation tool. To the best of our knowledge, this is the first attempt to address the Sindhi POS tagging at a large scale by proposing a new gold-standard SiPOS dataset[1] and exploiting conditional random field (CRF), bidirectional long-short-term memory (BiLSTM) network, and self-attention for its evaluation. Our novel contributions are as follows:

- We reveal a novel open-source gold-standard SiPOS dataset for the low-resource Sindhi language. We manually tagged more than 293k tokens of the Sindhi news corpus using the Doccano text annotation tool.

- We compute the inter-annotator agreement and exploit machine learning models of CRF and BiLSTM, self-attention to evaluate the proposed dataset with different settings.

[1]The SiPOS dataset is publicly available @ https://github.com/AliWazir/SiPOS-Dataset

Proceedings of the Student Research Workshop associated with RANLP-2021, pages 22–30,
held online, Sep 1–3, 2021.
https://doi.org/10.26615/issn.2603-2821.2021_004

- Besides pre-trained GloVe, fastText word-level representation, the task-specific character-level word representations are incorporated to extract character-level information using BiLSTM encoder.

2 Related Work

The labeling of natural language text with POS tags can be a complicated task, requiring much effort, even for trained annotators (Rane et al., 2020). A large number of LRs are publicly available for high-resource languages such as English (Marcus and Marcinkiewicz), Chinese, Indian languages (Baskaran Sankaran and Subbarao, 2008; Khan et al., 2019) and others (Petrov et al., 2012). Unlike rich-resourced languages such as English and Chinese with abundant publicly accessible LRs, Sindhi is relatively low-resource (Ali et al., 2019), which lacks the POS tagged dataset that can be utilized to train a supervised or statistical algorithm.

Previously, Mahar and Memon (2010) proposed a Sindhi POS labeled dataset consists of 33k tokens. Later, Dootio and Wagan (2019) published a new dataset containing 6.8K lexicon, which is insufficient to train a robust supervised classification algorithm. More recently, (Rahman et al., 2020) annotated 100K words by employing a multi-layer annotation model, which comprises different annotation layers like POS, morphological features, dependency structure, and phrase structure. But their dataset is not publicly available. Except for Sindhi Persian-Arabic, the POS tagged datasets in Devanagari (Motlani et al., 2015), and Roman (Sodhar et al., 2019) scripts have also been introduced. The POS tagged corpus of Sindhi-Devanagari consists of 44K tokens, while Sindhi-Roman (Sodhar et al., 2019) only contains 100 sentences. The review of existing work shows that the low-resource Sindhi language lacks a benchmark POS labeled dataset for its supervised text classification.

3 Corpus Acquisition and Annotation

In this section, we illustrate the opted annotation methodology. We utilized the news corpus (Ali et al., 2019) of popular and most circulated Sindhi newspapers of Kawish and Awami-Awaz (see Table 1. Two native graduate students of linguistics were engaged for the annotation purpose using the Doccano (Nakayama et al., 2018) text annotation tool to assign a POS label to each token. The detailed annotation process is illustrated as under:

Table 1: The statistics of news articles utilized for the annotation of SiPOS tagset.

Resource	Articles	Sentences	tokens
Kawish	563	3 769	1 58 145
Awami-Awaz	458	3 015	1 35 539
Total	1 021	6 784	2 93 684

3.1 Preprocessing

Sindhi news corpus contains a certain amount of unwanted data (Ali et al., 2019). Thus, filtering out such data and normalizing it is essential to obtain a more authentic vocabulary for the annotation project. The preprocessing steps consist of the following steps:

- Removal of unwanted multiple punctuation marks from the start and end of the sentences.
- Filtration of noisy data such as non-Sindhi words, special characters, HTML tags, emails, URLs, etc.
- Tokenization to normalize the text, removal of duplicates, and multiple white spaces.

Moreover, it requires human efforts and careful assessment for the consistency in the labeled dataset. Sindhi Persian-Arabic is being written in the right to left direction (Jamro, 2017). An example of a Sindhi sentence is given in Table 2 with language-specific and corresponding universal part-of-speech (UPOS) tags. A Sindhi word comprises one or more clitics or segments (Narejo and Mahar, 2016), typically a stem to which prefix and suffix may be attached. Therefore, the tagging can be done for each clitic in sequence or a word simultaneously. For the annotation, we used Doccano (Nakayama et al., 2018) to assign a POS label to each token. The Doccano is an open-source annotation platform for sequence labeling and machine translation tasks. We engaged two native graduate students of linguistics for the annotation purpose. The annotators also used an online Sindhi Thesaurus portal[2] in case of ambiguity or confusion while deciding a POS label for a token. Moreover, the project supervisor also worked with annotators to monitor annotation quality by following the annotation guidelines (Dipper et al., 2004; Petrov et al., 2012).

[2] http://dic.sindhila.edu.pk/

Table 2: An example of a Sindhi sentence with its corresponding language specific and universal part-of-speech tags. The Roman transliteration of each token is given for the ease of reading.

.	آهي	ويندو	ڪرايو	عمل	سان	سختي	تي	ميڊيا	اليڪٽرانڪ	۽	پرنٽ	**Sentence**
SYM	**AUX**	**VERB**	**VERB**	**NOUN**	**ADP**	**NOUN**	**ADP**	**NOUN**	**NOUN**	**CONJ**	**NOUN**	**UPOS**
PUNCT	**AUX**	**VB**	**VB**	**NN**	**ADP**	**NN**	**ADP**	**NN**	**NN**	**CONJ**	**NN**	**Tag**
بيهڪ جي نشاني	فعل معاون	فعل	فعل	اسم	حرفِ جر	اسم	حرفِ جر	اسم	اسم	حرف جملو	اسم	**Sindhi POS**

3.2 Consistency Evaluation

To ensure annotation consistency, we measure the inter-annotator agreement to investigate the consistency in which annotators agreed to the tags. To measure inter-annotator agreement, we chose to use Cohen's Kappa (Cohen, 1960). Cohen's Kappa measures the inter-annotator agreement between two annotators. Since we have two annotators, we compute this measure for POS tag pairs that show agreement between two annotators, which leads to two results. The inter-annotator agreement comes out to be 0.872 with a confidence percentile of 95%. Cohen's Kappa value shows that the dataset is of acceptable quality.

3.3 SiPOS Dataset

The SiPOS has been annotated using the news corpus (Ali et al., 2019) of Kawish and Awami-Awaz Sindhi newspapers. Sindhi grammar (Oad, 2012) give Sindhi POS of nouns, verbs, adjectives, adverbs, pronouns, prepositions, conjunctions, numerals, articles, and interjections. The dataset consists of more than 293k tokens annotated with sixteen Sindhi POS and UPOS categories, respectively. The complete statistics of the utilized news corpus in the annotation is given in Table 1. The detailed label distribution in the SiPOS is given in Table 3.

4 Evaluation Methods

We evaluate the SiPOS for the consistency in the dataset by computing the inter-annotator agreement using Cohen's Kappa (Cohen, 1960) coefficient. We evaluate the proposed SiPOS dataset by exploiting CRF, BiLSTM and integrating CRF and self-attention in the BiLSTM network for strong baselines. Moreover, pre-trained GloVe, fastText word representations, and task-specific character-level, and joint $Word_{Character}$ level representations are incorporated to extract word-level and character-level information using the BiLSTM encoder.

4.1 Conditional Random Field

We initially evaluate the SiPOS dataset using a CRF (Lafferty et al., 2001), widely used in sequence classification (Sutton et al., 2012) tasks. The CRF is useful to consider the relationship between labels and jointly decode the most suitable chain of labels for a given input sentence (Huang et al., 2015).

4.2 Representation Learning

Representation learning aims to capture the useful semantic, syntactic, and morphological information (Santos and Zadrozny, 2014) in NLP tasks (Bojanowski et al., 2017). We use pre-trained GloVe (Pennington et al., 2014), fastText (Bojanowski et al., 2017) word-level representations, character-level representations as well as joint character-level and word-level $Word_{Character}$ representations (Shao et al., 2017; Matteson et al., 2018) to extract the word-level features. Pre-trained word representations enable neural models to exploit the raw textual data larger than annotated data. Then, we jointly learn the task-specific character-level word representations (Liu et al., 2018) using the BiLSTM network. The task-specific contextual representations include the POS-based knowledge.

4.2.1 GloVe

The GloVe (Pennington et al., 2014) is a word representation model that relies on two methods of global word-to-word co-occurrence statistics and local context window. We obtain the pre-trained GloVe representation by training on the large corpus of more than 61 million words (Ali et al., 2019). We train GloVe with AdaGrad by choosing the context window of 5 and the 300-dimensional word representations. We filter out Sindhi stop words (Ali et al., 2019) in the preprocessing step.

4.2.2 fastText

The fastText (Bojanowski et al., 2017) is similar to Word2vec (Mikolov et al., 2013). It uses subword

Table 3: Complete statistics of SiPOS dataset with the number of POS in each label. The highest proportion in the POS labels is noun, followed by preposition and verb.

Count	SPOS	UPOS	Tag	POS type
65,611	اسم	NOUN	NN	Noun
54,810	حرفِ جر	ADP	ADP	Preposition
41,882	فعل	VERB	VB	Verb
21,849	صفت	ADJ	ADJ	Adjective
20,627	ضمير اشارو	DET	DET	Determiner
20,281	نشاني	SYM	PUNCT	Punctuation, symbol
19,823	ظرف	ADV	ADV	Adverb
11,546	اسم خاص	PROPN	NNP	Proper noun
11,015	حرف جملو	CONJ	CONJ	Conjunction
10,553	فعل معاون	AUX	AUX	Auxiliary verb
7,878	ضمير	PRON	PRON	Pronoun
4,888	صفت عددي	NUM	NUM	Numerical adjective
1,424	أذارولفظ	-	FOW	Borrowed words
1,091	نامعلوم	X	UNK	Unknown
282	حرف جملو شرطيه	SCON	SCON	Subordinating conjunction
124	حرف ندا	INTJ	INTJ	Interjection

information in the prediction model to obtain word representations. We train fastText on recently proposed unlabelled Sindhi corpus (Ali et al., 2019) of more than 61 million words. In training, we use the recommended sub-sampling (Bojanowski et al., 2017), negative sampling, the minimum and maximum length of character ngrams (Grave et al., 2018), minimum word count, learning rate, 300-dimensional representations, and default context window size.

4.2.3 Character-level Word Representations

The character-level representations have an advantage in handling the out-Of-the-vocabulary problem because they can learn almost all character representations from even small or moderate corpus (Jia and Ma, 2019). In other words, these representations are good at inferring unseen words and sharing information about morpheme-level regularities. The BiLSTM network learns the character-level representations of words and associates them with usual word representations to perform POS tagging. We employ task-oriented strategy (Liu et al., 2018) for character-level and joint $Word_{Character}$ level representations learned through BiLSTM network (Shao et al., 2017; Matteson et al., 2018) which are different from pretrained word representations. The BiLSTM is good at capturing prefixes and suffixes from the given input text (Zhang et al., 2018). It consists of interconnected bidirectional forward $\overrightarrow{LSTM}$ and backward $\overleftarrow{LSTM}$ hidden layers, which efficiently encode the contextual information.

4.3 Neural POS Taggers

4.3.1 BiLSTM

The BiLSTM network (Schuster and Paliwal, 1997) has been broadly used in a variety of sequence labelling tasks (Huang et al., 2015; Ma and Hovy, 2016; Peters et al., 2017) including POS tagging (Kann et al., 2018). In this work, we evaluate the SiPOS dataset using the BiLSTM network. The model consists of representations layer, BiLSTM encoder, and softmax for each position in the final layer. The bidirectional layers extract character-level, word-level features and then adopt a random initialization method to transform words into representations. The BiLSTM word-level (pre-train) model is the same as BiLSTM (word-level) but adopts GloVe and fastText for representations. Similar to pre-trained GloVe, fastText, the dimension of word representations was set to 300 to initialize the representation layer, and a context window size of 5 was selected. The dimension of character-level representation was set to 50 in character-level models.

4.3.2 Extensions of Neural Model

The CRF and BiLSTM network form strong baselines. Then, we add more variants such as CRF decoder, self-attention, and character-level feature representations. The CRF is employed on the top of the neural models (Huang et al., 2015; Ma and Hovy, 2016; Shen et al., 2018) as a decoder. Moreover, the self-attention (Vaswani et al., 2017) is used above the encoder layers (Shen et al., 2018) to boost the model performance by focusing on tokens with more meaning that contribute to label prediction. Thus, we integrate self-attention for performance analysis into the BiLSTM and BiLSTM-CRF models to deeply capture semantic information and lexical features. In the word-level models, a sequence of words is given as an input where each word is represented in the word representation. However, the character-level models (Shao et al., 2017) consider each sentence as a sequence of characters (Matteson et al., 2018), and outputs a label distribution for each character, then concatenated to word representations. The character-level representations use the one-dimensional neural network or any other model to find the numeric representations of words by looking at their character-level compositions. Our final BiLSTM-Attention-CRF model relies upon joint task-specific character-level and word-level representations, BiLSTM encoder, self-attention, and CRF as depicted in Figure 1.

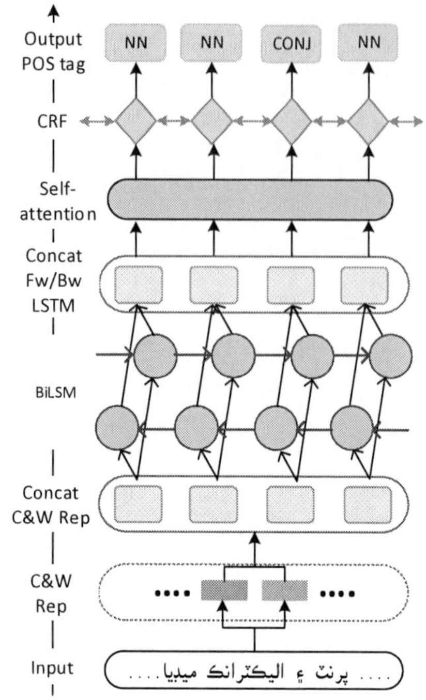

Figure 1: The overall architecture of the BiLSTM-Attention-CRF model. Task-specific joint character-level and word-level representations are regarded as input to the BiLSTM encoder. Then encoder captures the contextual features. The output of the BiLSTM encoder layer is fed into the self-attention layer before decoding through a hidden layer. Finally, we employ CRF to yield the output tag sequence. Concat denotes the concatenation operation; Rep is the representation learning, C&W is the character-level and word-level representations, while Fw&Bw represents the forward, backward LSTM layers.

4.4 Experimental Setting

Since our baseline models and extended neural baselines only rely on labeled training data, no external resources are used. The SiPOS dataset is split into train, validation, and test sets. We report the token level POS tagging accuracy on the large classes in a test collection. All the experiments were conducted on GTX $1080Ti$ Nvidia GPUs using TensorFlow (Abadi et al., 2016).

4.5 Training

We evaluated several hyperparameter configurations (Reimers and Gurevych, 2017) and picked optimal parameters that work well on the SiPOS dataset. The optimization is performed using Adam (Kingma and Ba, 2015) with a learning rate of 0.01 and decay of 0.8, respectively. The BiLSTM hidden layer has 200 units for each direction. A dense layer follows each hidden unit. We project input features by utilizing the dense layer. The batch size was set to 32 for all experiments, except for the CRF, set to 16. A dropout (Srivastava et al., 2014) of 0.25% was applied at the unit representation layer for all the reported neural models with the best performance. Epoch count was set to 50 with early-stopping (Caruana et al., 2001) after five epochs with no improvement in the validation set. We use identical hyperparameters for all neural models.

4.6 Results and Analysis

In this section, we present the results of CRF, BiLSTM baselines, and extended BiLSTM-CRF, BiLSTM-Attention, BiLSTM-Attention-CRF neural POS taggers by employing four representation learning approaches. We conducted several experiments to validate the SiPOS dataset to determine the quality and whether the neural models rely upon the pre-trained word-level, character-level, joint representations, or otherwise due to setting up more model parameters. All the neural models are used to predict the labels in the SiPOS dataset. We initialize pre-trained GloVe, fastText word representations, task-specific character-level, and joint representations learned through BiLSTM encode for the neural models. The results of the CRF and four neural POS taggers are presented in Table 4 with POS tagging accuracy using GloVe word representations. Table 5 shows the results of fastText, the performance of the neural models is depicted in Table 6 using character-level representations learning, and Table 7 presents the results of joint representation learning. In contrast to GloVe, the character-level representations yield better performance. However, the neural POS taggers surpass GloVe and character-level representations with fastText. It is because of the representation learning at the character level with the subword model. The presented results also demonstrate that the CRF is dominant over softmax in neural models. Moreover, it is also important to note that self-attention has enhanced the accuracy across all the experiments. Furthermore, joint word-level and character-level representations are dominant over pre-trained word representations and task-specific character-level representations. However, the performance of the character-level neural models is close to the fastText. It is imperative to mention that joint character-level word representations surpass both pre-trained and character-level representation learning. Our final BiLSTM-Attention-CRF model yields the best accuracy using all types of representation learning compared to BiLSTM, BiLSTM-attention, and BiLSTM-CRF. It surpasses all the models by yielding an accuracy of 96.25% with task-specific joint character-level and word-level representations. The empirical results demonstrate the slight performance difference between pre-trained word-level, task-specific character-level, and joint representations. Thus, it can be determined in the performance comparison that representation learning greatly impacts the performance of the neural network models. Conclusively, it can be observed that the BiLSTM-Attention-CRF with joint representation learning gave us the most significant improvement in the overall accuracy over pre-trained GloVe, fastText, and task-specific character-level representations.

Table 4: POS tagging accuracy (%) using CRF initial baseline and neural models on pre-trained GloVe word representations. Bold font denotes the best results on the GloVe.

Model	Accuracy
CRF	90.34
BiLSTM	92.73
BiLSTM-CRF	93.26
BiLSTM-Attention	93.58
BiLSTM-Attention-CRF	**93.89**

Table 5: POS tagging accuracy (%) on the pre-trained fastText word representations. Bold font denotes the best results on the fastText.

Model	Accuracy
BiLSTM	94.21
BiLSTM-CRF	94.74
BiLSTM-Attention	94.89
BiLSTM-Attention-CRF	**95.32**

Table 6: POS tagging accuracy (%) on the task-specific character-level representations. Bold font highlights the best results.

Model	Accuracy
BiLSTM	93.86
BiLSTM-CRF	94.25
BiLSTM-Attention	94.43
BiLSTM-Attention-CRF	**95.19**

Table 7: POS tagging accuracy (%) on neural models using task-specific joint character-level and word-level representations. Bold font shows the best results across all the experiments.

Model	Accuracy
BiLSTM	94.37
BiLSTM-CRF	94.78
BiLSTM-Attention	**95.49**
BiLSTM-Attention-CRF	**96.25**

5 Conclusion and Future Work

In this paper, we propose a novel benchmark SiPOS dataset for the low-resource Sindhi language. The dataset consists of more than 293K tokens, annotated using the Doccano text annotation tool. We exploit CRF as the initial baseline and BiLSTM model by incorporating CRF as a decoder and self-attention mechanism for the performance gain. The BiLSTM-Attention-CRF model yields a high accuracy of 96.25% with the joint task-specific character-level and word-level representations. The proposed open-source SiPOS dataset will be a sophisticated addition to the resources for the Sindhi language. In the future, we intend to pre-train bidirectional encoder representations from transformers (BERT) and generative pre-trained transformer (GPT) language models for Sindhi text classification.

Acknowledgements

We thank to the anonymous reviewers for concrete suggestions. This work was funded by the National Key R&D Program of China (No. 2018YFB1005100 & No. 2018YFB1005104).

References

Martín Abadi, Paul Barham, Jianmin Chen, Zhifeng Chen, Andy Davis, Jeffrey Dean, Matthieu Devin, Sanjay Ghemawat, Geoffrey Irving, Michael Isard, et al. 2016. Tensorflow: A system for large-scale machine learning. In *12th USENIX Symposium on Operating Systems Design and Implementation (OSDI) 16)*, pages 265–283.

Wazir Ali, Jay Kumar, Junyu Lu, and Zenglin Xu. 2019. Word embedding based new corpus for low-resourced language: Sindhi. *arXiv preprint arXiv:1911.12579*.

Wazir Ali, Junyu Lu, and Zenglin Xu. 2020. SiNER: A large dataset for Sindhi named entity recognition. In *Proceedings of The 12th Language Resources and Evaluation Conference*, pages 2946–2954. European Language Resources Association.

Monojit Choudhury Tanmoy Bhattacharya Pushpak Bhattacharyya Girish Nath Jha S. Rajendran K. Saravanan L. Sobha Baskaran Sankaran, Kalika Bali and K.V. Subbarao. 2008. A common parts-of-speech tagset framework for Indian languages. In *Proceedings of the Sixth International Conference on Language Resources and Evaluation (LREC'08)*, Marrakech, Morocco.

Piotr Bojanowski, Edouard Grave, Armand Joulin, and Tomas Mikolov. 2017. Enriching word vectors with subword information. *Transactions of the Association for Computational Linguistics*, 5:135–146.

Tihana Britvić. 2018. *Semi-supervised neural part-of-speech tagging*. Ph.D. thesis, University of Zagreb. Faculty of Science. Department of Mathematics.

Rich Caruana, Steve Lawrence, and C Lee Giles. 2001. Overfitting in neural nets: Backpropagation, conjugate gradient, and early stopping. In *Advances in neural information processing systems*, pages 402–408.

Jacob Cohen. 1960. A coefficient of agreement for nominal scales. *Educational and psychological measurement*, 20(1):37–46.

Stefanie Dipper, Michael Götze, and Stavros Skopeteas. 2004. Towards user-adaptive annotation guidelines. In *Proceedings of the 5th International Workshop on Linguistically Interpreted Corpora*, pages 23–30.

Mazhar Ali Dootio and Asim Imdad Wagan. 2019. Syntactic parsing and supervised analysis of Sindhi text. *Journal of King Saud University-Computer and Information Sciences*, 31(1):105–112.

Edouard Grave, Piotr Bojanowski, Prakhar Gupta, Armand Joulin, and Tomas Mikolov. 2018. Learning word vectors for 157 languages. In *Language Resources and Evaluation Conference*, CONF.

Zhiheng Huang, Wei Xu, and Kai Yu. 2015. Bidirectional LSTM-CRF models for sequence tagging. *arXiv preprint arXiv:1508.01991*.

Wazir Ali Jamro. 2017. Sindhi language processing: A survey. In *2017 International Conference on Innovations in Electrical Engineering and Computational Technologies (ICIEECT)*, pages 1–8. IEEE.

Yaozong Jia and Xiaopan Ma. 2019. Attention in character-based BiLSTM-CRF for Chinese named entity recognition. In *In Proceedings of the 4th International Conference on Mathematics and Artificial Intelligence*, pages 1–4.

Katharina Kann, Johannes Bjerva, Isabelle Augenstein, Barbara Plank, and Anders Søgaard. 2018. Character-level supervision for low-resource pos tagging. In *Proceedings of the Workshop on Deep Learning Approaches for Low-Resource NLP*, pages 1–11.

Wahab Khan, Ali Daud, Khairullah Khan, Jamal Abdul Nasir, Mohammed Basheri, Naif Aljohani, and Fahd Saleh Alotaibi. 2019. Part of speech tagging in Urdu: Comparison of machine and deep learning approaches. *IEEE Access*, 7:38918–38936.

D Kingma and J Ba. 2015. Adam: A method for stochastic optimization. *San Diego*.

John Lafferty, Andrew McCallum, and Fernando CN Pereira. 2001. Conditional random fields: Probabilistic models for segmenting and labeling sequence data.

Qian Liu, He-Yan Huang, Yang Gao, Xiaochi Wei, Yuxin Tian, and Luyang Liu. 2018. Task-oriented word embedding for text classification. In *Proceedings of the 27th International Conference on Computational Linguistics*, pages 2023–2032.

Xuezhe Ma and Eduard Hovy. 2016. End-to-end sequence labeling via bi-directional LSTM-CNNs-CRF. In *Proceedings of the 54th Annual Meeting of the Association for Computational Linguistics (Volume 1: Long Papers)*, pages 1064–1074.

Javed Ahmed Mahar and Ghulam Qadir Memon. 2010. Sindhi part of speech tagging system using wordnet. *International Journal of Computer Theory and Engineering*, 2(4):538.

Mitchell P Marcus and Mary Ann Marcinkiewicz. Building a large annotated corpus of English: The penn treebank. *Computational Linguistics*, 19(2).

Andrew Matteson, Chanhee Lee, Youngbum Kim, and Heui-Seok Lim. 2018. Rich character-level information for korean morphological analysis and part-of-speech tagging. In *Proceedings of the 27th International Conference on Computational Linguistics*, pages 2482–2492.

Tomas Mikolov, Ilya Sutskever, Kai Chen, Greg S Corrado, and Jeff Dean. 2013. Distributed representations of words and phrases and their compositionality. In *Advances in Neural Information Processing Systems*, pages 3111–3119.

Raveesh Motlani, Harsh Lalwani, Manish Shrivastava, and Dipti Misra Sharma. 2015. Developing part-of-speech tagger for a resource poor language: Sindhi. In *Proceedings of 7th Conference on Language and Technology, Poznan, Poland.*

Hiroki Nakayama, Takahiro Kubo, Junya Kamura, Yasufumi Taniguchi, and Xu Liang. 2018. doccano: Text annotation tool for human.

Waqar Ali Narejo and Javed Ahmed Mahar. 2016. Morphology: Sindhi morphological analysis for natural language processing applications. In *2016 International Conference on Computing, Electronic and Electrical Engineering (ICE Cube)*, pages 27–31. IEEE.

JD Oad. 2012. *Implementing GF resource grammar for Sindhi language. Doctor dissertation.* Ph.D. thesis, M. Sc. thesis, Chalmers University of Technology, Gothenburg, Sweden.

Jeffrey Pennington, Richard Socher, and Christopher Manning. 2014. Glove: Global vectors for word representation. In *Proceedings of the Conference on Empirical Methods in Natural Language Processing*, pages 1532–1543.

Matthew Peters, Waleed Ammar, Chandra Bhagavatula, and Russell Power. 2017. Semi-supervised sequence tagging with bidirectional language models. In *Proceedings of the 55th Annual Meeting of the Association for Computational Linguistics*, pages 1756–1765.

Slav Petrov, Dipanjan Das, and Ryan McDonald. 2012. A universal part-of-speech tagset. In *Proceedings of the Eighth International Conference on Language Resources and Evaluation (LREC'12)*, pages 2089–2096.

Mutee U Rahman. 2010. Towards Sindhi corpus construction. In *Proceedings of the Conference on Language and Technology.*

Mutee U Rahman, Tafseer Ahmed, and Muhammad Shaheer Memon. 2020. Development of annotated corpus resources of Sindhi. *LANGUAGE & TECHNOLOGY*, page 49.

Gajanan Rane, Nilesh Joshi, Geetanjali Rane, Hanumant Redkar, Malhar Kulkarni, and Pushpak Bhattacharyya. 2020. Part-of-speech annotation challenges in marathi. In *Proceedings of the WILDRE5–5th Workshop on Indian Language Data: Resources and Evaluation*, pages 1–6.

Nils Reimers and Iryna Gurevych. 2017. Optimal hyperparameters for deep lstm-networks for sequence labeling tasks. *arXiv preprint arXiv:1707.06799.*

Cicero D Santos and Bianca Zadrozny. 2014. Learning character-level representations for part-of-speech tagging. In *Proceedings of the 31st international conference on machine learning (ICML-14)*, pages 1818–1826.

Mike Schuster and Kuldip K Paliwal. 1997. Bidirectional recurrent neural networks. *IEEE transactions on Signal Processing*, 45(11):2673–2681.

Yan Shao, Christian Hardmeier, Jörg Tiedemann, and Joakim Nivre. 2017. Character-based joint segmentation and POS tagging for Chinese using bidirectional RNN-CRF. In *Proceedings of the Eighth International Joint Conference on Natural Language Processing*, pages 173–183.

T Shen, T Zhou, G Long, J Jiang, and C Zhang. 2018. Bi-directional block self-attention for fast and memory-efficient sequence modeling. In *Proceedings of the International Conference on Representation Learning.*

Irum Naz Sodhar, Akhtar Hussain Jalbani, Muhammad Ibrahim Channa, and Dil Nawaz Hakro. 2019. Parts of speech tagging of Romanized Sindhi text by applying rule based model. *IJCSNS*, 19(11):91.

Nitish Srivastava, Geoffrey Hinton, Alex Krizhevsky, Ilya Sutskever, and Ruslan Salakhutdinov. 2014. Dropout: a simple way to prevent neural networks from overfitting. *The journal of machine learning research*, 15(1):1929–1958.

Charles Sutton, Andrew McCallum, et al. 2012. An introduction to conditional random fields. *Foundations and Trends® in Machine Learning*, 4(4):267–373.

Ashish Vaswani, Noam Shazeer, Niki Parmar, Jakob Uszkoreit, Llion Jones, Aidan N Gomez, Łukasz Kaiser, and Illia Polosukhin. 2017. Attention is all you need. In *Advances in Neural Information Processing Systems*, pages 5998–6008.

Meishan Zhang, Nan Yu, and Guohong Fu. 2018. A simple and effective neural model for joint word segmentation and pos tagging. *IEEE/ACM Transactions on Audio, Speech, and Language Processing*, 26(9):1528–1538.

Sarcasm Detection and Building an English Language Corpus in Real Time

Oliver Cakebread-Andrews
University of Wolverhampton
o.p.cakebread-andrews@wlv.ac.uk

Abstract

This is a research proposal for doctoral research into sarcasm detection, and the real-time compilation of an English language corpus of sarcastic utterances. It details the previous research into similar topics, the potential research directions and the research aims.

1 Introduction

Within the discipline of computational linguistics, and specifically in the field of sentiment analysis, Sarcasm Detection is a fast-growing area of research. In the past twelve months alone there have been multiple papers written on the subject of sarcasm and irony detection (Aboobaker & Illavarasan, 2020; Avvaru et al., 2020; Buzea et al., 2020; Eke et al., 2021). Sarcasm Detection uses Natural Language Processing models along with sentiment analysis based on linguistic cues such as hyperbole or polarity shifts, as well as context to decode whether or not an utterance is sarcastic. Pelser & Murrell (2019) give the example of *"Great! I love waking up sick!"*, which is easy for a human to detect as sarcastic due to "strong polarity shifts", but would remain a challenge for a machine. Suggested applications for research into sarcasm detection include improving the understanding of users' or customers' emotions and opinions about policies, products or services for businesses and governments or policy-makers (Eke et al., 2021; Vyas & Uma, 2019).

2 Background and Literature Review

2.1 Data Collection

In order to obtain data of sarcastic utterances for corpora used in algorithmic training, many studies used social media (Baruah et al., 2020; Bharti, 2019) such as Reddit (Ghosh et al., 2020; Mishra, Kaushik, & Dey, 2020) and Twitter (Avvaru et al., 2020; Ghosh et al., 2020). This provides a wealth of naturally generated, authentic data that is often already tagged as sarcastic (hashtags in the case of Twitter and /s in the case of Reddit), making it easy to collect and categorise. This study would similarly utilise Reddit to develop a novel corpus of sarcastic utterances for the purpose of training an algorithm to detect sarcasm. It appears that in the vast majority of cases, researchers use either an existing corpus of sarcastic utterances (Ghosh et al., 2018; Ghosh et al., 2020) such as the one compiled by Khodak et al. (2018), or more commonly according to Eke et al. (2019), they gather their own unique data to use just in their study (Avvaru et al., 2020; Ghosh et al., 2020; Ren et al., 2018). These corpora generally tend to be considerably smaller (e.g. 4000 Tweets (Ghosh et al., 2020), 5000 Tweets (Jaiswal, 2020), 39000 Tweets (Ghosh & Veale, 2016), 900 Tweets (González-Ibánez et al., 2011)) though this could be due in part to Twitter's restrictions on how many Tweets can be freely downloaded through their API. Although there are exceptions such as Kunneman et al. (2015) who created a corpus of 406 thousand Dutch Tweets. Indeed, it has been noted as recently as 2021 (Eke et al., 2021) that there is a lack of training data for classifiers. It seems that there have not been any major attempts to create a dynamic corpus that continues to automatically detect sarcastic utterances and update the data by adding to the corpus, and consequently learning from the additions. Therefore, the first aim of this study would be to compile a corpus of sarcastic data from Reddit, as well as potentially other sources, that can be used to train an algorithm to detect additional sarcastic utterances in real-time and continuously update, and learn from, the corpus.

2.2 Methodology

Various methodologies and learning models have been employed in to detect sarcasm and irony including, but not limited to, the more

Proceedings of the Student Research Workshop associated with RANLP-2021, pages 31–35,
held online, Sep 1–3, 2021.
https://doi.org/10.26615/issn.2603-2821.2021_005

traditional models such as Support Vector Machines (SVM) (Castro, et al., 2019; González-Ibánez et al., 2011) and more modern neural network models like Long Short Term Memory (LSTM) and Bi-Directional LSTM (Avvaru et al., 2020; Ghosh et al., 2018; Ghosh et al., 2020), Convolutional Neural Networks (CNN), (Castro, et al., 2019; Jaiswal, 2020), Deep Neural Networks (DNN) (Ghosh & Veale, 2016) and Hierarchical Fusion Model (Pelser & Murrell, 2019). CNN and LSTM have been by far the most popular methods for approaching sarcasm detection in the past decade. However, many of the more recent studies have tended to use Bidirectional Encoder Representations from Transformers (BERT) (Avvaru et al., 2020; Baruah et al., 2020) or suggested using BERT in future work (Eke et al., 2021). Therefore, this study is likely to use LSTM, Bi-LSTM, CNN or BERT models for analysis, or a combination of multiple models as has been seen in other papers (Kumar & Garg, 2019; Zhang et al., 2019)

Current accuracy rates of sarcasm detection models can vary quite widely depending on a multitude of factors such as models used, training data and what is being tested. Focussing on the more recent studies, which can be assumed to take advantage of the most modern methods for increased accuracy, there are studies using Bi-LSTM with F-scores from the high 70s (Kumar & Garg, 2019; Mishra et al., 2020) for Reddit, to the low 90s (Mishra et al., 2020) for Twitter, low to high 70s for studies using BERT models (Avvaru et al., 2020; Jaiswal, 2020) and mid 80s for multimodal studies using LSTM (Cai et al., 2019) and slightly lower for BERT (Xu et al., 2020). In the 2020 Sarcasm Detection Shared Task (2020), Ghosh, Vajpayee and Muresan reported findings ranging from 59 to 83 on Reddit and 68 to 93 on Twitter. Studies on Twitter seem to consistently outperform Reddit. Whether this is because comments on Reddit can be much longer, there has been more research conducted on Twitter (as evidenced in the second paragraph) or whether there is some other reason is unclear. Due to the greater opportunity for improvement, the initial focus of this study will be on Reddit, but there is certainly a possibility of expanding to Twitter as well.

Whilst all the studies are researching sarcasm or irony detection, the main focus of analysis varies according to the study, such as semantics (Xu et al., 2020), hyperbole (Kunneman et al., 2015) emojis (Wiguna et al., 2021), and taking the utterance with (Jaiswal, 2020; Baruah et al., 2020) or without context. There have also been several studies done into multimodal sarcasm detection (Castro, et al., 2019; Pelser & Murrell, 2019; Cai et al., 2019). Limitations with current multimodal studies seem to be small corpora (Castro, et al., 2019), or the same corpora (Xu et al., 2020), lack of consideration of multiple participants (Wang et al., 2020) and lack of audio (Cai et al., 2019; Castro, et al., 2019; Pelser & Murrell, 2019). Due to social media posts often taking advantage of multiple formats, extending the scope of this future study to include multimodal analysis will be considered at a later stage in the research.

2.3 Languages

The overwhelming majority of studies continue to be based on English, but other languages are emerging as subjects of sarcasm detection, such as Dutch (Kunneman et al., 2015), Spanish (Frenda & Patti, 2019; Ortega-Bueno et al., 2019), Romanian (Buzea et al., 2020), Arabic (Ranasinghe et al., 2019), Hindi (Jain et al., 2020). Despite this, there are still many languages with negligible or no studies of sarcasm detection done in that medium, leaving the opportunity to transfer the findings from the English study onto these other languages. Japanese for example seems to have very few studies published related to sarcasm detection (Hiai & Shimada, 2018). While there are plenty of examples of studies into cross-linguistics transfer learning, there appears to be very few that focus on, or even mention, sarcasm (Chronopoulou et al., 2019; Tavan et al., 2020). Moving further away from Germanic and Romance languages and cultures may mean limited results, however it is a further aim of this study to discover what patterns and similarities can be found when transferring results to a second language.

3 Aims of the Study

To summarise the aims and focus of this research, there are two current aims which will be the main focus of the research. They are as follows:

1. To compile a large corpus of English sarcastic utterances that will be updated in real-time using social media
2. To use a combination of natural language processing techniques and deep neural networks to identify sarcasm with high accuracy

The first aim is to try and tackle the issue of a lack of large and up-to-date corpora to provide training data for detection algorithms and models. The second is to attempt to improve the current detection rates, particularly on natural data that is unrelated to the training set.

There are also two potential further research directions that may be undertaken depending on the eventual feasibility of introducing other areas of research. These aims are the following:

1. To expand the scope of the study to multimodal analyses to take into consideration images and potentially audio
2. To use transfer learning to transfer findings to a non-European language such as Japanese

These additional directions would be to attempt to expand into areas of sarcasm detection that currently have had little to no research conducted into them.

References

Aboobaker, J., & Illavarasan, E. (2020). A Survey on Sarcasm Detection and Challenges. *2020 6th International Conference on Advanced Computing and Communication Systtems (ICACCS).* https://doi.org/10.1109/ICACCS48705.2020.9074163

Avvaru, A., Vobilisetty, S., & Mamidi, R. (2020). Detection Sarcasm in Conversation Context Using Transformer-Based Models. *Proceedings of the Second Workshop on Figurative Language Processing.* http://dx.doi.org/10.18653/v1/2020.figlang-1.15

Baruah, A., Das, K., Barbhuiya, F., & Dey, K. (2020). Context-Aware Sarcasm Detection Using BERT. *Proceedings of the Second Workshop on Figurative Language Processing.* http://dx.doi.org/10.18653/v1/2020.figlang-1.12

Bharti, S. K. (2019). *Sarcasm Detection in Textual Data: A Supervised Approach.* Doctoral Dissertation. https://doi.org/10.4018/978-1-5225-7186-5.CH010

Buzea, M., Trăuşan-Matu, S., & Rebedea, T. (2020). Automatic Irony Detection for Romanian Online News. *24th International Conference on System Theory, Control and Computing.* https://doi.org/10.1109/ICSTCC50638.2020.9259715

Cai, Y., Cai, H., & Wan, X. (2019). Multi-Modal Sarcasm Detection in Twitter with Hierarchical Fusion Model. *Proceedings of the 57th Annual Meeting of the Association for Computational Linguistics.* http://dx.doi.org/10.18653/v1/P19-1239

Castro, S., Hazarika, D., Pérez-Rosas, V., Zimmermann, R., Mihalcea, R., & Poria, S. (2019). Towards Multimodal Sarcasm Detection (An _Obviously_ Perfect Paper). *Proceedings of the 57th Annual Meeting of the Association for Computational Linguistics.* http://dx.doi.org/10.18653/v1/P19-1455

Chronopoulou, A., Baziotis, C., & Potamianos, A. (2019). An Embarrassingly Simple Approach for Transfer Learning from Pretrained Language Models. *Proceedings of the 2019 Conference of the North.* http://dx.doi.org/10.18653/v1/N19-1213

Eke, C. I., Norman, A. A., & Shuib, L. (2021). Multi-feature fusion framework for sarcasm identification on twitter data: A machine learning based approach. *PLOS ONE, 16*(6). https://doi.org/10.1371/journal.pone.0252918

Eke, C. I., Norman, A. A., Shuib, L., & Nweke, H. F. (2019). Sarcasm identification in textual data: systematic review, research challenges and open directions. *Artificial Intelligence Review, 53*(6), 4215-4258. https://doi.org/10.1007/s10462-019-09791-8

Frenda, S., & Patti, V. (2019). Computational models for irony detection in three spanish variants. *Proceedings of the Iberian Languages Evaluation Forum (IberLEF 2019), co-located with 34th Conference of the Spanish Society for Natural Language Processing (SEPLN 2019).* CEUR. http://hdl.handle.net/2318/1795396

Ghosh, A., & Veale, D. T. (2016). Fracking Sarcasm using Neural Network. *Proceedings of the 7th Workshop on Computational Approaches to Subjectivity, Sentiment and Social Media*

Analysis. http://dx.doi.org/10.18653/v1/W16-0425

Ghosh, D., Fabbri, A. R., & Muresan, S. (2018). Sarcasm Analysis Using Conversation Context. *Computational Linguistics, 44*(4), 755-792. https://doi.org/10.1162/coli_a_00336

Ghosh, D., Vajpayee, A., & Muresan, S. (2020). A Report on the 2020 Sarcasm Detection Shared Task. *Proceedings of the Second Workshop on Figurative Language Processing.* http://dx.doi.org/10.18653/v1/2020.figlang-1.1

González-Ibánez, R., Muresan, S., & Wacholder, N. (2011). Identifying sarcasm in twitter: a closer look. *roceedings of the 49th Annual Meeting of the Association for Computational Linguistics: Human Language Technologies*, (pp. 581-596). https://aclanthology.org/P11-2102

Hiai, S., & Shimada, K. (2018). Sarcasm Detection Using Features Based on Indicator and Roles. *Advances in Intelligent Systems and Computing*, 418-428. https://doi.org/10.1007/978-3-319-72550-5_40

Jain, D., Kumar, A., & Garg, G. (2020). Sarcasm detection in mash-up language using soft-attention based bi-directional LSTM and feature-rich CNN. *Applied Soft Computing*, 91. https://doi.org/10.1016/j.asoc.2020.106198

Jaiswal, N. (2020). Neural Sarcasm Detection using Conversation Context. *Proceedings of the Second Workshop on Figurative Language Processing.* http://dx.doi.org/10.18653/v1/2020.figlang-1.11

Khodak, M., Saunshi, N., & Vodrahalli, K. (2018). A Large Self-Annotated Corpus for Sarcasm. *ArXiv.* https://aclanthology.org/L18-1102

Kumar, A., & Garg, G. (2019). Sarcasm Detection Using Feature-Variant Learning Models. *Proceedings of ICETIT 2019*, (pp. 683-693). https://doi.org/10.1007/978-3-030-30577-2_61

Kunneman, F., Liebrecht, C., Mulken, M. V., & Bosch, A. V. (2015). Signalling sarcasm: From hyperbole to hashtag. *Information Processing & Management, 51*(4), 500-509. https://doi.org/10.1016/j.ipm.2014.07.006

Mishra, P., Kaushik, S., & Dey, K. (2020). Bi-ISCA: Bidirectional Inter-Sentence Contextual Attention Mechanism for Detecting Sarcasm in User Generated Noisy Short Text. *arXiv.* https://arxiv.org/abs/2011.11465

Ortega-Bueno, R., Rangel, F., Hernández Farıas, D., Rosso, P., Montes-y-Gómez, M., & Medina Pagola, J. E. (2019). Overview of the task on irony detection in Spanish variants. *Proceedings of the Iberian languages evaluation forum (IberLEF 2019), co-located with 34th conference of the Spanish Society for natural language processing (SEPLN 2019).* CEUR.

Pelser, D., & Murrell, H. (2019). Deep and Dense Sarcasm Detection. *ArXiv.* https://arxiv.org/abs/1911.07474

Ranasinghe, T., Saadany, H., Plum, A., Mandhari, S., Mohamed, E. O., & Mitkov, R. (2019). RGCL at IDAT: Deep Learning models for Irony Detection in Arabic Language. *Proceedings of the IDAT@FIRE2019.* CEUR Workshop Proceedings. http://hdl.handle.net/2436/622828

Ren, Y., Ji, D., & Ren, H. (2018). Context-augmented convolutional neural networks for twitter sarcasm detection. *Neurocomputing, 308*, 1-7. https://doi.org/10.1016/j.neucom.2018.03.047

Tavan, E., Rahmati, A., & Ali Keyvanrad, M. (2020). Persian Emoji Prediction Using Deep Learning and Emoji Embedding. *2020 10th International Conference on Computer and Knowledge Engineering (ICCKE).* https://doi.org/10.1109/ICCKE50421.2020.9303639

Vyas, V., & Uma, V. (2019). Approaches to Sentiment Analysis on Product Reviews. *Advances in Business Information Systems and Analytics*, 15-30. https://doi.org/10.4018/978-1-5225-4999-4.CH002

Wang, X., Sun, X., Yang, T., & Wang, H. (2020). Building a Bridge: A Method for Image-Text Sarcasm Detection Without Pretraining on Image-Text Data. *Proceedings of the First International Workshop on Natural*

Language Processing Beyond Text. http://dx.doi.org/10.18653/v1/2020.nlpbt-1.3

Wiguna, B. S., Hudiyanti, C. V., Alqis Rausanfita, A., & Arifin, A. Z. (2021). Sarcasm Detection Engine for Twitter Sentiment Analysis using Textual and Emoji Feature. *Jurnal Ilmu Komputer Dan Informasi, 41*(1), 1-8. https://doi.org/10.21609/jiki.v14i1.812

Xu, N., Zeng, Z., & Mao, W. (2020). Reasoning with Multimodal Sarcastic Tweets via Modeling Cross-Modality Contrast and Semantic Association. *Proceedings of the 58th Annual Meeting of the Association for Computational Linguistics.* http://dx.doi.org/10.18653/v1/2020.acl-main.349

Zhang, S., Zhang, X., Chan, J., & Rosso, P. (2019). Irony detection via sentiment-based transfer learning. *Information Processing & Management, 56*(5), 1633-1644. https://doi.org/10.1016/j.ipm.2019.04.006

Correcting Texts Generated by Transformers using Discourse Features and Web Mining

Alexander Chernyavskiy, Dmitry Ilvovsky
HSE University
Moscow, Russia
alschernyavskiy@gmail.com
dilvovsky@hse.ru

Boris Galitsky
Oracle Inc.
Redwood Shores CA USA
bgalitsky@hotmail.com

Abstract

Recent transformer-based approaches to NLG like GPT-2 can generate syntactically coherent original texts. However, these generated texts have serious flaws: global discourse incoherence and meaninglessness of sentences in terms of entity values. We address both of these flaws: they are independent but can be combined to generate original texts that will be both consistent and truthful. This paper presents an approach to estimate the quality of discourse structure. Empirical results confirm that the discourse structure of currently generated texts is inaccurate. We propose the research directions to correct it using discourse features during the fine-tuning procedure. The suggested approach is universal and can be applied to different languages. Apart from that, we suggest a method to correct wrong entity values based on Web Mining and text alignment.

1 Introduction

Natural Language Generation (NLG) task is one of the most challenging and important tasks in NLP. There are various types of NLG tasks: text summarization, machine translation, knowledge aggregation and multimedia information construction such as music generation. We consider tasks where the main goal is to construct a text that cannot be distinguished from a human-written text, by a human or a recognition system.

The most successful and universal models for solving NLP tasks are models based on the idea of transformers. Hence GPT (Radford et al., 2018) and its larger modifications GPT-2 (Radford et al., 2019) and GPT-3 (Brown et al., 2020) successfully perform text generation tasks. However, they still have drawbacks. First of all, fragments in some generated texts do not cohere well with each other, despite the correct syntactic structure. Ko and Li (2020) demonstrated that even the words that indicate discourse relations (such as "but", "after" and "because") can be generated improperly, and proposed an auxiliary model to correct them. More problems arise at a higher level, associated with the consistency between sentences. The model sometimes generates a completely incorrect discourse structure triggered by an inability to plan it. Even the order of the discourse relations should be corrected.

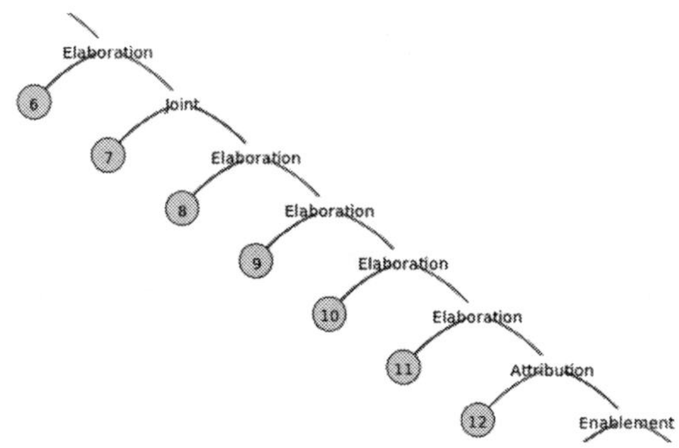

Figure 1: A part of the discourse tree for the generated text: "... *[named john]*[6] *[who survives a major accident]*[7] *[and is saved by a state of the art experimental operation]*[8] *[that turns him into a robotic machine-like agent]*[9] *[who has tools and contraptions of all sorts]*[10] *[built into his body at his use]*[11] *[when he says]*[12]...".

We conducted experiments for GPT-2 and distinguished two types of its mistakes. Firstly, it does not generate well an overall discourse structure (RST is described in Sect. 3). Accordingly, in some cases, contradictions can be found in it. We fine-tuned GPT-2 on lower-cased movie reviews. Here are examples of typical mistakes in the generated texts.

Let us consider the example demonstrated in Figure 1. The sentence has too many "Elaboration" and "Joint" rhetorical relations, which are default

Proceedings of the Student Research Workshop associated with RANLP-2021, pages 36–43,
held online, Sep 1–3, 2021.
https://doi.org/10.26615/issn.2603-2821.2021_006

ones. Moreover, thought structure is not reflected in this discourse tree as it looks like a chain. Generally, genuine discourse trees are more balanced.

Another illustrative example of generated text:

> *with enough fine performances from all of them , this is one of the best cult films ever made. ⟨. . .⟩ it does have some nice gore and some pretty well chosen actors but it is definitely not one of the best cult films of all time .*

In this case, the core text idea is contained in the last sentence. The first part is used to elaborate it. However, there is a contradiction, and a contrast relation does not contribute to coherence.

Apart from that, the "final" summary is in the middle of the text in some cases. It is not followed by the "end of sequence" token and continues by Elaboration. As a result, the text is duplicated.

In addition, for specific areas like medical texts, GPT-2 uses incorrect values of entities since it does not utilize any knowledge base.

Our example is from the 19th century literature domain. The seed to GPT content generation is in bold.

> ***Pushkin wrote the originial chapters of Yevgenii Onegin,*** *then Alexander Pushkin sent letters to Nikolay Gogol, Mikhil Lermontov, and others. While in Saint Petersburgh, Pushkin was approached by Rodion Romanovich Krafft. Krafft wanted Pushkin to be an English translator of a German edition of his poem*

Here, 'then' part of the first sentence seems plausible. Then the reader proceeds to the invented person Krafft, and a random, implausible text starts. To continue impress the reader with a smooth flow of text, we need to find a real person like Krafft related to Pushkin via translation.

The bottom sentences need to be replaced with following:

> *In the 1960's, Vladimir Nabokov, the only writer to simultaneously hold the position as a giant of both Russian and English literature, published an English translation of Pushkin's masterpiece.*

Hence most entities from GPT text generation need to be replaced.

This paper presents empirical proof that GPT-2 generates wrong discourse structure in some cases and proposes ideas for the development of text generation in two directions:

1. Correction of the general consistency of the text, namely its discourse structure. We plan to investigate methods that allow the model to generate Elementary Discourse Units connected by discourse relations in the correct order and use the correct words to express it. Besides, we propose a method to estimate the overall quality of the discourse structure.

2. Correction of generated entity values using external knowledge bases, Web Mining and alignment.

These directions complement each other and can be used sequentially. So, firstly, we correct the discourse structure of the text using additional fine-tuning. Then, we utilize external knowledge to correct the exact specific entity values and get meaningful text.

Our paper is organized as follows. Firstly, we summarize related work and introduce base concepts. Then, we discuss our ideas, preliminary results, and propose directions for further research.

2 Related Work

2.1 General View

In this paper, we consider approaches that can generate unique coherent texts. One of the major problems in open-domain content generated by a deep learning based system is its meaninglessness. Although overall syntactic and logical structure, obtained via averaging of texts from the training dataset, looks plausible in most cases, and some individual phrases might make sense, almost each sentence is meaningless. The main advantage of such raw content is that it is **original.**

Recent approaches to NLG based on external knowledge bases provide good results (Liu et al., 2017; Freitag and Roy, 2018). At the same time, most research considers the only superficial description of a simple piece of structured data such as attribute-value pairs of fixed or very limited schema, like E2E (Novikova et al., 2017) and WikiBio (Lebret et al., 2016). For real-world complex databases, it is often more desirable to provide descriptions involving abstraction and a logical inference of higher generality about database tables and records. For instance, readers should get a kind of a summary over a structured, relational or no-SQL database.

2.2 Knowledge-based Planning

Most data-to-text datasets do not naturally contain content plans. These plans can be derived following an information extraction approach, by mapping the text in the summaries onto entities in the structured data, their values, relations and types.

Ciampaglia et al. (2015) showed that we can leverage any collection of factual human knowledge, such as Wikipedia, for automatic fact checking. The authors follow the paradigm of epistemic closure, computationally building a support for statements by mining the connectivity patterns on a knowledge graph. The initial task is to compute the support of simple statements of fact using a large-scale knowledge graph obtained from Wikipedia. Generally speaking, fact checking can be seen as a special case of link prediction in knowledge graphs (Nickel et al., 2016).

2.3 Style and Discourse Correction

Another way is integration of plans into the training process of the generation system without any knowledge bases. This suffices to solve the second aforementioned problem associated with planning the global structure. Some researchers suggest ways to generate consistent long texts.

Peng et al. (2018) proposed a method to generate text endings based on a pre-planned intent (e.g. "happyEnding", "sadEnding", or "cannotTell") which is predicted due to an additional neural model.

Biran and McKeown (2015) proposed neural text generation based on the selected discourse relations which can be chosen using n-grams. Ji et al. (2016) suggested a similar approach but predicted discourse relations using RNN. Harrison et al. (2019) investigated an approach that allows generating text depending on the need of the "Contrast" relation. One of the main goals was that the model itself should be able to determine which items are suitable for contradistinction and which values are acceptable for them. The idea of using the intent is very important and can be used for discourse planning too, and we propose ways to integrate it in GPT fine-tuning.

Bosselut et al. (2018) suggested an RL-based approach with rewards associated with the correctness of the discourse structure. However, due to the complexity of assessing the correctness of the discourse, the authors trained the model only to generate the correct order of sentences. The sentence coherence was considered as an approximation of the discourse structure.

Post-processing can also be used to correct discourse by analogy with correcting entity values. Ko and Li (2020) considered the word-level discourse correction for GPT-2. The proposed approach predicts the masked discourse connective given the rest of the sentence. Thus, it improves consistency within sentences. The quality was verified due to the human-annotated relations. It should be highlighted that this approach does not consider long relations. Moreover, human annotations may be costly. Our ideas allow to partially solve it.

At the same time, the consistency of generated texts still remains not at a high level, and there are quite a few articles devoted to its investigation. In addition, there are even fewer papers devoted to the correction of the discourse itself.

3 Rhetorical Structure Theory

Rhetorical Structure Theory (RST) proposed by Mann and Thompson (1987) allows to represent any text as a binary tree. Its nodes correspond to text spans and edges conform to discourse relations between them.

The tree is constructed step by step. At the first step, the leaves of the tree are Elementary Discourse Units (shortly EDUs). They contain introductory words, single thoughts, or clauses. Further, some of these nodes are connected via corresponding discourse relations like "Elaboration", "Joint" and "Summary", and form new nodes associated with bigger text spans. Then, the updated set of nodes is connected due to the corresponding discourse relations and so forth. In the end, the text span associated with the root node is the full entire text.

RST distinguishes two types of nodes: Nucleus and Satellite. Nodes of the first type contain key information necessary to understand meaning of the text. Nodes of the second type comprise supplementary information.

Figure 2 demonstrates an example of a discourse tree constructed by the open-source ALT document-level discourse parser (Joty et al., 2012) fot the following text:

"[Media accounts have portrayed past moves as cuts, as well.]^1 [Whats more,]^2 [when Walker intro-

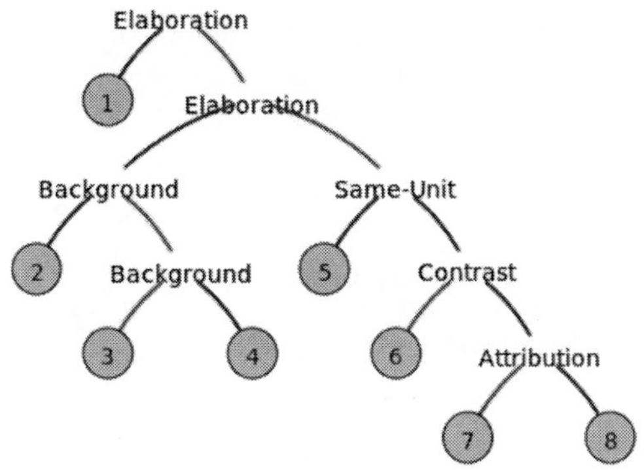

Figure 2: Discourse tree constructed by the ALT parser. Dark blue edges are drawn to Nucleus nodes and light red arrows are drawn to Satellite nodes.

duced his budget,][3] [he also described the changes as cuts.][4] [So,][5] [Walker made a generally accurate statement about the increase,][6] [but by dismissing the talk of cuts][7] [he left out a lot of context and important details on his budget move.][8]"

Here, EDUs are limited by brackets.

4 Discourse Correction

4.1 Methods

Our first idea is to utilize external discourse markers during GPT-2 fine-tuning. The model can be trained to generate them. In a sense, the generated marker will assist to plan next words during generation. In this case, it is necessary to ensure that the model learns planning, not labeling. In details, our suggestions can be described as follows.

Let the GPT-2 model be fine-tuned on a large dataset from the selected subject area. It can be fine-tuned once again using an additional smaller set $\{X_{\text{real\_ft}}\}$ of texts from the same area. So, the set of generated texts $\{X_{\text{fake}}\}$ will be constructed. These are texts that the base model generates with the unmodified training process.

At the same time, we can modify real texts using their discourse structure to add more useful information to the training process. For example, special tokens related to discourse relations can be added. One of the most obvious options is to utilize $\langle \text{R} \rangle$ tokens (e.g. $\langle \text{Contrast} \rangle$) before the corresponding connectives. The updated texts denoted as $\{X_{\text{real\_ft\_disco}}\}$ are used to fine-tune the model instead of $\{X_{\text{real\_ft}}\}$. Thus, another set of fake texts will be generated. The aforementioned special tokens should be removed from them to get raw texts $\{X_{\text{fake\_disco}}\}$. Also, the model tokenizer must treat any $\langle \text{R} \rangle$ token as one subtoken.

We construct fake texts using another correct set $\{X_{\text{real}}\}$. To make the texts more similar in terms of semantic embeddings, for each text from $\{X_{\text{real}}\}$ we generate the text in $\{X_{\text{fake}}\}$ and the text in $\{X_{\text{fake\_disco}}\}$ that have the same words in the beginning.

We propose a criterion to check the improvement of the discourse structure using a recursive neural network (Chernyavskiy and Ilvovsky, 2020) denoted as RSTRecNN. This model was suggested for discourse-based text classification.

Let two discriminative RSTRecNN models $\mathcal{M}$ and $\mathcal{M}_{\text{disco}}$ are trained to solve binary classification tasks $\{X_{\text{real}}\}$ vs $\{X_{\text{fake}}\}$ and $\{X_{\text{real}}\}$ vs $\{X_{\text{fake\_disco}}\}$ respectively. The classifier will pay more attention to the order of EDUs and to the discourse relations between them than to the words meanings since the semantic embeddings are close. Therefore, if the quality of $\mathcal{M}_{\text{disco}}$ is lower than that of $\mathcal{M}$, then it has become more difficult for the classifier to distinguish fake texts using its discourse structure. Thus, in this case the goal of discourse correction will be achieved.

In addition, $\mathcal{M}$ itself suffices to test the hypothesis that the discourse needs to be corrected for the base GPT-2 model. In this aspect, if the accuracy for $\mathcal{M}$ is close to 0.5, then the generated discourse structure is already good (since the dataset is balanced).

4.2 Experimental Details

We conducted experiments for IMDB movie reviews. We added 50,000 examples from a Kaggle competition [1] to the base dataset with 2000 texts from (Pang and Lee, 2004). As the preprocessing, we lowercased all texts.

The base GPT-2 model was fine-tuned on 32,400 texts, and we utilized 3,600 texts as the validation set. GPT-2 was fine-tuned for 3 epochs with a learning rate 5e-5. The final validation perplexity is 28.17. We used 10,000 texts as $\{X_{\text{real\_ft}}\}$ for the second fine-tuning. The ALT parser was applied for discourse labeling.

We did not utilize "Elaboration", "Joint" and "Same-Unit" relations since they are the most popular and do not make much sense. The discourse parser distinguished 19 unique discourse relations, and the relative frequencies of "Elaboration","Joint'

[1] https://www.kaggle.com/lakshmi25npathi/imdb-dataset-of-50k-movie-reviews

Model	Max Acc.	Mean ± Std Acc.
$\mathcal{M}$	0.822	0.807 ± 0.009
$\mathcal{M}_{\text{disco}}$	0.819	0.810 ± 0.006

Table 1: Model performance for two variants of the datasets.

and "Same-Unit" are 0.44, 0.12 and 0.11 correspondingly. Also, we did not use rare relations such as "Manner-Means", "TextualOrganization" and "Topic-Change" (the relative frequency is lower than 0.001). Broadly speaking, we considered only meaningful popular non-trivial relations.

We generated texts with length exceeding 300 since the discourse mistakes for long texts are more obvious. $\{X_{\text{real}}\}$ included 1250 texts. Nucleus sampling technique (Holtzman et al., 2019) was used because its results were superior to that of top-*k* sampling (Fan et al., 2018).

4.3 Results

Table 1 demonstrates the results for the models $\mathcal{M}$ and $\mathcal{M}_{\text{disco}}$. One can see that the accuracy for $\mathcal{M}$ is much higher than 0.5 Thus, the discourse structure for real and fake texts differs considerably.

The table shows that the maximal accuracy (over 6 runs) for $\mathcal{M}$ is higher than that for $\mathcal{M}_{\text{disco}}$. However, there is no significant difference between the models.

It is important to note that there are much fewer special tokens in raw $\{X_{\text{fake\_disco}}\}$ than in the labeled $\{X_{\text{real}}\}$. Moreover, the biggest part of the generated special tokens are quite obvious and in most cases stand in front of their indicators.

4.4 Future Work

There are several directions for further research:

- Customization of the loss function. For instance, we can modify loss weights for the classes associated with the special tokens.
- Modification of special tokens. It may be important to generate tokens associated with the beginning or end of EDUs. In this way, we will also experiment with $\langle R_{\text{start}} \rangle$ and $\langle R_{\text{end}} \rangle$ tokens instead of $\langle R \rangle$.
- Modification of the sampling process. We can check the global discourse coherence using RSTRecNN after generating new EDU at the stage of generation. In the case of bad structure, we will generate it again.
- Customization of the attention module in GPT-2. We plan to add discourse information in the attention module. Accordingly, new words will be generated using the current discourse structure during the training process.

5 Correction of Entity Values

5.1 Methods

Our second major contribution is to correct entity values using web or external knowledge bases. The entities that need to be corrected comprise titles, names and so forth.

Our intent is to take the meaningless raw generated content and cross-breed it with the one taken piece-by-piece from various sources, so that each sentence is not original but truthful. We borrow the structure and content flow from the generated text, and factoids are taken from true texts mined from the web to correspond to the generated sentences.

To obtain true sentences, we form a query from the generated sentence by retaining noun phrases and other significant phrases, and forming OR query. We then search against the whole web, a given web source such as Wikipedia, an intranet or a specific index containing authoritative documents. Iterating through search results, the true sentences which are the closest to the generated sentences are identified. Aligning the raw generated sentence and the identified true sentence, we observe which entities and values in the generated sentences are incorrect and substitute them.

Firstly, we determine what kind of linguistic data should be taken from the generated text, and which – from the true text. Sources such as syntax and discourse we attempt to use from the raw text (the text generated by base GPT or by discourse-based fine-tuned GPT), and once we determine that it is not possible, we obtain from the true text. Once we perform a substitution of a phrase from true to generated, we know which linguistic sources can be retained in the raw generated text. Table 2 demonstrates the partition of data sources.

We use a non-symmetric operation of alignment between generated and true text (Galitsky, 2020). This alignment occurs at the level of the whole text, paragraphs, sentences and phrases. To assess a similarity between texts, paragraphs, sentences and phrases, we apply a symmetric operation of generalization (Galitsky et al., 2012). However, to obtain a proper text aligning generated and true texts, the operation is not symmetric since we use distinct

Data	Generated sentences	True sentences
Source of the text	text generated by DL	real text obtained from sources like web
Syntactic flow	if possible	if required
Discourse flow	if possible	if required
Coreference structure	if possible	if required
Logical flow	if possible	if required
Idea	original "idea"	existing idea, if the original idea is too distant from the topic
Entities	except entities are most likely wrong and need to be substituted	correct entities
Other	actions can be retained, if confirmed by	phrases

Table 2: Merging linguistic data types from generated and true texts.

sources depending on the source type. An entity from a true sentence kills an entity from a generated sentence, but rest of the phrase is taken from generated sentence to retain the logical structure, discourse and coreference. Exploring the ways to identify a piece of true content to repair a flawed raw content, we observe that it is a complex multi-step process requiring conventional linguistic analysis at multiple layers and also a special substitution technique operating at various levels of abstraction.

5.2 Future Work

Other research directions include neural methods inspired by the fact-checking task. To check a given statement, some methods (Thorne et al., 2018; Nie et al., 2019) extract a corresponding justification or refutation from a big data corpus (e.g. Wikipedia texts). This extracted text contains the correct entity value and we can substitute the hidden value with it. This approach does not use the Web but requires a more complex search phase. For instance, we can use deep neural models like BERT (Devlin et al., 2018) to find relevant articles and paragraphs.

6 Conclusion

In this paper, we investigated the current transformer-based approaches to natural language generation. We proposed two challenging research directions: an improvement of overall discourse structure and a correction of entity values to construct meaningful texts.

These directions are independent but complement each other well. By learning how to solve both problems, we expect to be able to generate coherent long texts with meaningful, plausible thoughts. Our idea is to first generate discursively and syntactically coherent text using the custom fine-tuned GPT-2 model. Further, utilizing the non-learning technique based on web mining and text alignment, we replace values of wrong factoid entities with truthful ones.

We proposed a method to evaluate the quality of overall discourse structure and experimentally confirm that GPT-2 generates texts with a mistaken and inconsistent structure in some cases. We suggested some ideas to integrate additional knowledge about discourse into the GPT-2 fine-tuning and generation processes.

Apart from that, we suggested a way to correct wrong entity values in generated texts using web mining. We propose the partition of information types from two sources (generated texts and texts from external knowledge base) to apply a syntactic and semantic alignment.

We suggested some ways to develop a universal approach that will not be just English language-specific and can be applied to other languages. At the moment, there are open-source discourse parsers for Russian, German, Spanish, and we can utilize them without modifying the approach.

Acknowledgments

The article was prepared within the framework of the HSE University Basic Research Program and funded by the Russian Academic Excellence Project '5-100'.

References

Or Biran and Kathleen McKeown. 2015. Discourse planning with an n-gram model of relations. In *Proceedings of the 2015 Conference on Empirical Methods in Natural Language Processing*, pages 1973–1977, Lisbon, Portugal. Association for Computational Linguistics.

Antoine Bosselut, Asli Celikyilmaz, Xiaodong He, Jianfeng Gao, Po-Sen Huang, and Yejin Choi. 2018. Discourse-aware neural rewards for coherent text generation. *CoRR*, abs/1805.03766.

Tom B. Brown, Benjamin Mann, Nick Ryder, Melanie Subbiah, Jared Kaplan, Prafulla Dhariwal, Arvind Neelakantan, Pranav Shyam, Girish Sastry, Amanda Askell, Sandhini Agarwal, Ariel Herbert-Voss, Gretchen Krueger, Tom Henighan, Rewon Child, Aditya Ramesh, Daniel M. Ziegler, Jeffrey Wu, Clemens Winter, Christopher Hesse, Mark Chen, Eric Sigler, Mateusz Litwin, Scott Gray, Benjamin Chess, Jack Clark, Christopher Berner, Sam McCandlish, Alec Radford, Ilya Sutskever, and Dario Amodei. 2020. Language models are few-shot learners.

Alexander Chernyavskiy and Dmitry Ilvovsky. 2020. *Recursive Neural Text Classification Using Discourse Tree Structure for Argumentation Mining and Sentiment Analysis Tasks*, pages 90–101.

Giovanni Luca Ciampaglia, Prashant Shiralkar, Luis Mateus Rocha, Johan Bollen, Filippo Menczer, and Alessandro Flammini. 2015. Computational fact checking from knowledge networks. *PLoS ONE*, 10.

Jacob Devlin, Ming-Wei Chang, Kenton Lee, and Kristina Toutanova. 2018. BERT: pre-training of deep bidirectional transformers for language understanding. *CoRR*, abs/1810.04805.

Angela Fan, Mike Lewis, and Yann N. Dauphin. 2018. Hierarchical neural story generation. *CoRR*, abs/1805.04833.

Markus Freitag and Scott Roy. 2018. Unsupervised natural language generation with denoising autoencoders. In *EMNLP*.

Boris Galitsky. 2020. *Employing Abstract Meaning Representation to Lay the Last-Mile Toward Reading Comprehension*, pages 57–86.

Boris A. Galitsky, Josep Lluis de la Rosa, and Gábor Dobrocsi. 2012. Inferring the semantic properties of sentences by mining syntactic parse trees. *Data & Knowledge Engineering*, 81-82:21–45.

Vrindavan Harrison, Lena Reed, Shereen Oraby, and Marilyn A. Walker. 2019. Maximizing stylistic control and semantic accuracy in NLG: personality variation and discourse contrast. *CoRR*, abs/1907.09527.

Ari Holtzman, Jan Buys, Maxwell Forbes, and Yejin Choi. 2019. The curious case of neural text degeneration. *CoRR*, abs/1904.09751.

Yangfeng Ji, Gholamreza Haffari, and Jacob Eisenstein. 2016. A latent variable recurrent neural network for discourse relation language models. *CoRR*, abs/1603.01913.

Shafiq Joty, Giuseppe Carenini, and Raymond T Ng. 2012. A novel discriminative framework for sentence-level discourse analysis. In *Proceedings of the 2012 Joint Conference on Empirical Methods in Natural Language Processing and Computational Natural Language Learning*, pages 904–915. Association for Computational Linguistics.

Wei-Jen Ko and Junyi Jessy Li. 2020. Assessing discourse relations in language generation from GPT-2. In *Proceedings of the 13th International Conference on Natural Language Generation*, pages 52–59, Dublin, Ireland. Association for Computational Linguistics.

Rémi Lebret, David Grangier, and M. Auli. 2016. Neural text generation from structured data with application to the biography domain. In *EMNLP*.

Tianyu Liu, Kexiang Wang, Lei Sha, Baobao Chang, and Zhifang Sui. 2017. Table-to-text generation by structure-aware seq2seq learning. *CoRR*, abs/1711.09724.

William Mann and Sandra Thompson. 1987. Rhetorical structure theory: A theory of text organization.

Maximilian Nickel, Kevin Murphy, Volker Tresp, and Evgeniy Gabrilovich. 2016. A review of relational machine learning for knowledge graphs. *Proceedings of the IEEE*, 104(1):11–33.

Yixin Nie, Haonan Chen, and Mohit Bansal. 2019. Combining fact extraction and verification with neural semantic matching networks. In *AAAI*.

Jekaterina Novikova, Ondřej Dušek, and Verena Rieser. 2017. The e2e dataset: New challenges for end-to-end generation. pages 201–206.

Bo Pang and Lillian Lee. 2004. A sentimental education: Sentiment analysis using subjectivity summarization based on minimum cuts. *CoRR*, cs.CL/0409058.

Nanyun Peng, Marjan Ghazvininejad, Jonathan May, and Kevin Knight. 2018. Towards controllable story generation. In *Proceedings of the First Workshop on Storytelling*, pages 43–49, New Orleans, Louisiana. Association for Computational Linguistics.

A. Radford, Jeffrey Wu, R. Child, David Luan, Dario Amodei, and Ilya Sutskever. 2019. Language models are unsupervised multitask learners.

Alec Radford, Karthik Narasimhan, Tim Salimans, and Ilya Sutskever. 2018. Improving language understanding by generative pre-training.

James Thorne, Andreas Vlachos, Oana Cocarascu, Christos Christodoulopoulos, and Arpit Mittal. 2018. The fact extraction and VERification (FEVER) shared task. In *Proceedings of the First Workshop on Fact Extraction and VERification (FEVER)*, pages 1–9, Brussels, Belgium. Association for Computational Linguistics.

Introducing linguistic transformation to improve translation memory retrieval Results of a professional translators' survey for Spanish, French and Arabic

Souhila Djabri
University of Alicante
sd89@alu.ua.es

Rocío Caro Quintana
University of Wolverhampton, UK
R.Caro@wlv.ac.uk

Abstract

Translation memory systems (TMS) are the main component of computer-assisted translation (CAT) tools. They store translations allowing to save time by presenting translations on the database through matching of several types such as fuzzy matches, which are calculated by algorithms like the edit distance. However, studies have demonstrated the linguistic deficiencies of these systems and the difficulties in data retrieval or obtaining a high percentage of matching, especially after the application of syntactic and semantic transformations as the active/passive voice change, change of word order, substitution by a synonym or a personal pronoun, for instance. This paper presents the results of a pilot study where we analyze the qualitative and quantitative data of questionnaires conducted with professional translators of Spanish, French and Arabic in order to improve the effectiveness of TMS and explore all possibilities to integrate further linguistic processing from ten transformation types. The results are encouraging, and they allowed us to find out about the translation process itself; from which we propose a pre-editing processing tool to improve the matching and retrieving processes.

1 Introduction

Computer-assisted translation tools are expanding by offering translators increasingly useful solutions; they are composed of several tools such as terminology databases, the integration of machine translation engines and translation memories (TM). Translation memories are the most relevant; their function is to store previous translations so that when translating a new segment, the user can automatically retrieve from a database its equivalent in the target language, avoiding having to translate a segment already recorded in the database (Simard, 2020). Previously, the system automatically splits the source text into segments or units and searches for a similar translation by matching of several levels. The segments are usually sentences beginning with a capital letter and ending with a full stop through the segmentation by punctuation (Oliver, 2016). Among these matching, the fuzzy matches retrieve segments from the TM that are almost similar to their equivalents in the target language and allow a translation with less post-editing. The percentage of these matches is usually calculated using an algorithm based on edit distance or Levenshtein distance (Levenshtein, 1966). In addition Tezcan, Bulté, & Vanroy (2021) reported that fuzzy matching techniques use different approaches to estimate the degree of similarity between two sentences by calculating: the percentage of tokens (or characters) that appear in both segments potentially allowing for synonyms and paraphrase, the length of the longest matching sequence of tokens, or n-gram matching, the edit distance between segments, the most commonly used metric in CAT tools, automated MT evaluation metrics such as translation edit rate (TER), the amount of overlap in syntactic parse trees, or a more recently proposed method, the distance between continuous sentence representations.

However, different authors consider different percentages for the fuzzy matches: 70% and 95% (Ranashingue, Orasan, & Mitkov, 2020) or between 1% and 99% (Bowker & Corpas Pastor, 2015). Fuzzy matches do not have an exact definition since they depend on personal settings of each user and TMS. The most important aspect is to have a high percentage of matching. To this end, several studies are being carried out in order to increase the matching percentage and improve the data retrieval.

Proceedings of the Student Research Workshop associated with RANLP-2021, pages 44–50,
held online, Sep 1–3, 2021.
https://doi.org/10.26615/issn.2603-2821.2021_007

The rest of the article is structured as follows: Section 2 presents previous related work, Section 3 describes the methodology of this research, the survey design and data collection, Section 4 presents, analyses and discusses the qualitative and quantitative data divided in three subsections: participants profile (4.1), use of TMS (4.2), and human evaluations of semantic and syntactic transformations (4.3). Finally, the findings, the conclusions and future work will be presented in Section 5.

2 Related work

Recent research conducted by Ranasinghe et al., (2021), Ranasinghe, Orasan & Mitkov (2020) propose a new approach of new generation translation memories using deep learning techniques. The study conducted by members of the Research Group in Computational Linguistics at the University Wolverhampton showed how to improve the performance of these systems. The authors introduced sentence encoders to improve TMS matching and retrieving processes as an alternative to conventional algorithms. Other related work by Djabri (2020) presents a comparative study for Spanish, French and Arabic applying ten semantic and syntactic transformations to calculate and analyze 1500 original and transformed segments in three pair languages: Spanish-French (ES-FR), French-Spanish (FR-ES), and Arabic-Spanish (AR-ES) with two TMS: SDL Trados and MemoQ in order to identify the TMS deficiencies and propose solutions to improve the systems. The analysis of empirical data indicates that the matching scores decrease between language pairs of the same language family such as ES-FR/FR-ES because of the transformations, but it also shows that Arabic as a source language faces other difficulties when it comes to translating into Spanish, where several segments have no matching. Arabic also registered lower matching percentage with MemoQ, which seems to have more difficulties with the word order transformation than SDL Trados despite that Modern Standard Arabic has a rich and flexible morphology in terms of word order (Bassam & al, 2017) and there are several possibilities of syntactic typology: Verb, Subject, Object (VSO), Subject, Verb, Object (SVO) and Verb, Object, Subject (VOS). For Spanish, the first results show that MemoQ has considerable difficulties when it comes to transform the active/passive voice and the substitution of a word by a synonym. SDL Trados faces difficulties with the substitution of two words by their synonyms and the change of the word order, sentence and/or clause order. As for French, these systems record lower matching when transforming the active/passive voice and replacing a word by a personal pronoun despite the nature of the French language with a frequent use of the passive voice unlike the Spanish language where the use of the passive voice is limited (Weber, 2014). These results indicate that TMS need to integrate more linguistic processing to improve the data retrieval.

Similarly, others researches (Silvestre Baquero & Mitkov, 2017) demonstrated the importance of integrating more language processing in TMS after the calculation and analysis of fuzzy matches. The authors suggested lexical, semantical and syntactical transformations for English-Spanish/Spanish-English and it was observed that Spanish as a target language has more lexical and syntactical difficulties due to the syntactic complexity of Spanish. Consequently, the research demonstrated the shortcomings and the linguistics limitations of TMS.

However, improving TMS retrieving processes still needs human assessment by professional translators, not only from a linguistic and computational point of view. This paper, which presents the second phase of our research on different possibilities to improve the TMS matching process, discuss the results of questionnaires conducted with native speakers and professional translators of Spanish, French and Arabic. The objective is to continue to evaluate the empirical data obtained on the first phase and analyze all the qualitative and quantitative data in order to draw conclusions about different aspects, in particular on how to apply these linguistic transformations to improve the TMS efficiency.

3 Survey Design and Data Collection

The objective of this research is to explore the possibilities to improve the TMS matching process through the evaluation of ten linguistic transformations for Spanish, French and Arabic: 1) Change active to passive voice, 2) Change passive to active voice, 3) Change the word, sentence or clause order, 4) Replace one word with its synonym, 5) Replace two words with their synonyms, 6) Replace two words with their synonyms and change the word, phrase or clause order, 7) Replace one word into a personal pronoun, 8) Replace one word into a personal pronoun and change the word, sentence or clause order, 9) Change active to passive voice and replace one word with its synonym, and 10) Change active to passive voice and replace one word into a personal pronoun. For the survey[1], we selected ten original segments with their corresponding transformation as mentioned previously for each language pair: ES-FR, FR-ES, and AR-ES. We collected and built multilingual corpora from the United Nations General Assembly, Internal Regulation and share it with the participants in Excel files.[2]

The questionnaire was designed with Google Forms in three languages (Spanish, French and Arabic) according to the participants' profile. The choice of these three languages is based on two main reasons i) addressing the participants with their native language and/or working language allows us to have clear assessments and avoid communication ambiguities and ii) the three languages are the language pairs analyzed in the first phase of our research. Thus, it is a logical continuation.

Regarding the data collection, the participants were contacted in early January 2021 and the questionnaires were shared online by emailing the participants and explaining the stages of the research with a guideline[3] in three languages so every participant had to choose their language. Once accepted, the participants completed the questionnaires between 17 and 27 January 2021.

Furthermore, all participants are graduated, post graduated or professional translators in different fields, including two participants who are PhD students in translation. The participants come from i) Algeria and Egypt for the Arabic language, ii) Spain for the Spanish language, and finally iii) from France for French language (see 4.1).

4 Analysis, discussion of quantitative and qualitative data

In this section, we present and analyze the results of the questionnaires. First, we present the collected data with tables, graphs and/or descriptive statistics depending on the nature of the questions: open and closed ones (Saldanha & O'Brien, 2014); then, we analyze the participants answers, question by question according to the questionnaire order. We will present and discuss the human assessment covering three subsections i) participants profile, ii) use of TMS, and finally iii) human evaluation of the linguistic transformation.

4.1 Participants' profile

With regard to the participants' profile (15, 5 for each language), the first question related to their experience in translation obtained fifteen affirmative responses, i.e. 100% of participants are professional translators for Spanish, French or Arabic which is a significant advantage since all the participants are part of the studied discipline and work in the field.

The second question is presented to define the years of professional experience each participant (P) has. For Spanish participants (ES), the number of years of experience are between three and ten years. With regard to French participants (FR), the translators have experience from three to eight years. Finally, Arabic participants (AR) have a professional experience between three and ten years (see Figure 1).

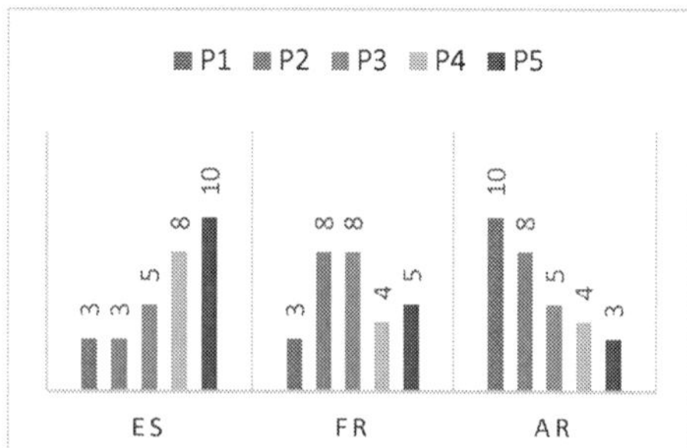

Figure 1: Years of professional experience of the participants.

The third question defines the field or specialty of participants. This question supports the results that indicates that most translators are specialized in technical translation and TMS are generally intended to translate technical and repetitive texts

[1] The full survey is available in the following links for Spanish, French, Arabic with an English translation.

[2] The original and transformed segments for each language pair are available at the following link.

[3] The questionnaires guidelines are available at the following link.

(Timonera & Mitkov, 2015) or texts with specific typology, even if the TMS are used for all types of texts: general, administrative, technical and specialized (Leblanc, 2016). Therefore, determining the specialty is of importance. The results indicate that four Spanish translators are specialized in legal and administrative translation. Other specialties are related to economy, construction, transport, and translation of medical texts. For French, it was found that three of the five translators are specialized in legal and administrative translation; the fourth participant indicated other specialties: translation in the field of Information Technology, Human Rights and Marketing; the fifth participant is specialized in translation related to the field of transport. As for the Arabic translators, three participants are specialized in legal translation; the other two responses indicate medical and economical translation respectively.

4.2 Use of TMS

As for the TMS use (question 4), 60% of Spanish, French and Arabic translators report using TMS. In other words, nine out of fifteen translators use TMS.

On the other hand (question 5), when participants are asked about which TMS they usually use (MemoQ, SDL or another TMS), 20% of Spanish translators use MemoQ and 80% use another TMS. However, no translators from French use MemoQ or SDL, the French translators reported using another TMS apart from these two. Finally, only one translator for Arabic language (20%) uses SDL and 80% use a different TMS.

4.3 Human Evaluation and Linguistic Transformation

The third subsection of the questionnaire corresponds to the analysis of the human evaluation of the ten transformations applied in order to analyze the possibilities of improving the matching process for the three pair languages and to study how to integrate them by analyzing different related aspects from a translation point of view. Five questions are dedicated to this group. To do this, participants were invited to read the ten examples corresponding to their language presented in Excel spreadsheets (see footnote 2). Each Excel spreadsheet consists of two columns: the first called "original segments" which includes the segments without any transformation and the second column called "transformed segments" where each segment is transformed by applying the ten semantic or syntactic modifications.

The spreadsheet is prepared for each language to obtain an unambiguous assessment where each participant chooses one of the three Excel files according to their language.

In the next step, transformations are evaluated by comparing them with the original segments The participants were asked to give their assessment on an increasing linear scale (from 1 to 5 or from ambiguous to clear transformations). Spanish translators give evaluations that are between three and five (see Figure 2): 40% have an average evaluation (moderately clear transformations), 20% indicate that the transformations are almost clear, and 40% indicate that the transformations are clear by granting a five.

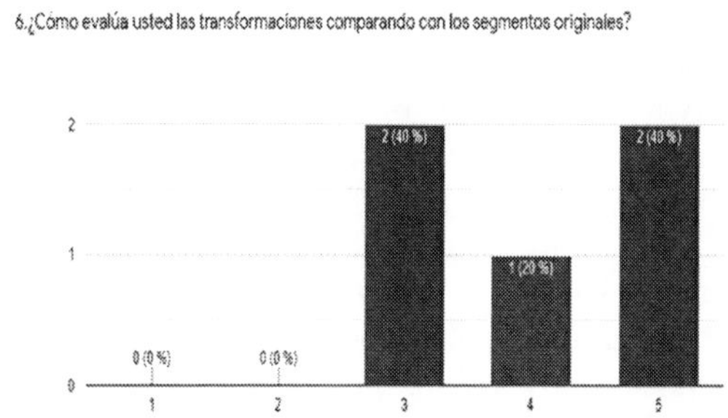

Figure 2: Linear scale for Spanish transformations.

As for the French language, the evaluations are between two and five (see Figure 3): 2 participants gave a 5 (40%), however, the other participants selected 2, 3 and 4 each one (20% for each category) for the semantical and syntactical transformations; they considered them almost ambiguous, moderately clear and almost clear.

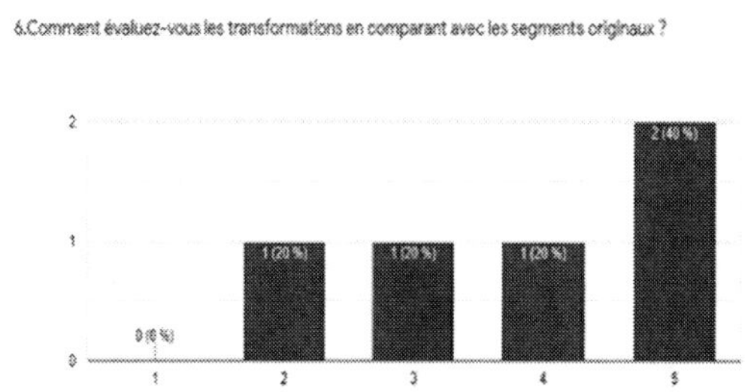

Figure 3: Linear scale for French transformations.

For Arabic (see Figure 4), the assessments range from two to five: 20% say the transformations are almost ambiguous, 40% think they are almost clear, and 40% think they are clear.

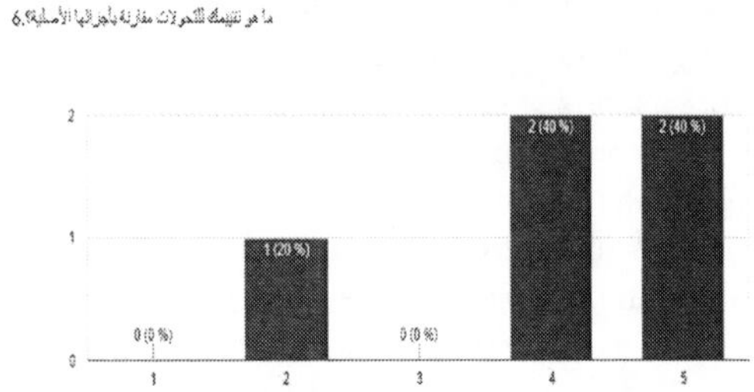

Figure 4: Linear scale for Arabic transformations.

After analyzing the three linear scales, it is observed that all the participants do not consider any of the transformations ambiguous since they have rated the transformations from 2 to 5.

Following that, the seventh question aims at whether translators will integrate these ten transformations into their future translations, the results indicate that all the answers for Spanish and Arabic are affirmative, that is, 100% of the participants will integrate these transformations. As for French, 80% of the participants said they wanted to integrate these transformations into their future translations and 20% did not want to do so. These evaluations confirm the possibilities of integrating more language processing into the TMS given that not only translators have given evaluations that are mostly favorable but also wish to add them to their work for Spanish, French and Arabic.

The participants then indicate what type of transformation they could apply in their translation in order to define the linguistic changes to be proposed to improve the matching process. We present below the transformation with the highest score for each language (see Table 1). For Spanish, most are related to transformation four, seven and nine, i.e. 80% to i) replace a word with it synonym, ii) replace a word with a personal pronoun, iii) change active to passive voice and replace a word with its synonym.

With regard to French, transformations four and five are the ones that obtain the highest percentage with 80%; participants indicate that they are able to replace a word or two words with their respective synonyms without changing the word order. In addition, participants could apply transformations one, two, three and seven, i.e. change active to passive voice, change passive to active voice, change the word, sentences and/or clauses order as well as replace a word with a personal pronoun. For Arabic, transformation four gets a total of 100%, Arabic translators prefer the substitution of a word by its synonym.

Spanish	French	Arabic
Replace a word with its synonym.	Replace a word with its synonym.	Replace a word with its synonym.
Replace a word with a personal pronoun.	Replace two words with their respective synonyms.	
Change active to passive voice and replace a word with its synonym.	Change active to passive voice.	
	Change passive to active voice	
	Change the words, sentences and/or clauses order	
	Replace a word with a personal pronoun.	

Table 1: Linguistic transformations translators would apply.

The second to last question aims to add other language transformations where translators are asked which transformations they wish to add in addition to our ten transformations (see Table 2). There are two proposals for Spanish: omission and addition. For French, it was found that the reformulation, the addition of relative pronouns and the change of masculine/feminine form. Finally, Arabic translators also add the reformulation of the original segments to the ten transformations already proposed.

Spanish	French	Arabic
Omission	Reformulation	Reformulation
Addition	Change of masculine/feminine form	
	Relative pronouns	

Table 2: Translators' suggestions.

Finally, we asked about the translation process itself. For this purpose, we have defined three categories of this process: pre-editing process (Pre-E), editing during the assisted translation (AT) and post-editing process (Post-E). The Pre-E process is the preparation prior to the computer-assisted translation where translators modify the source text by correcting possible errors, changing the word order, remove the use of passive voice or set an appropriate terminology (Arenas, 2019). For us, this process is elaborated before uploading the file to the TMS while the second process (AT) is performed during the translation after uploading the source text into the TMS since we consider that in this phase the translators could set the segmentation of the imported document (for instance, split or combine segments or adjust the alignment of the parallel documents). As for the third process (Post-E), it refers to the revision and correction of the translation provided by the TMS.

Therefore, the surveyed translators would include these transformations during the translation with 60% of the answers for Spanish, French and Arabic (see Figure 5), that is to say that the participants indicate to integrate these transformations after uploading the document in the system while 20% include these same transformations before the AT process or during the Pre-E. On the other hand, 20% include transformations at the end of the AT process (Post-E process). These results clearly demonstrate that translators not only employ linguistic transformations such as synonym substitution, change active-passive voice etc., but also that the pre and post-editing process is not as significant compared to the process of adding transformations during translation and after uploading the document into the system.

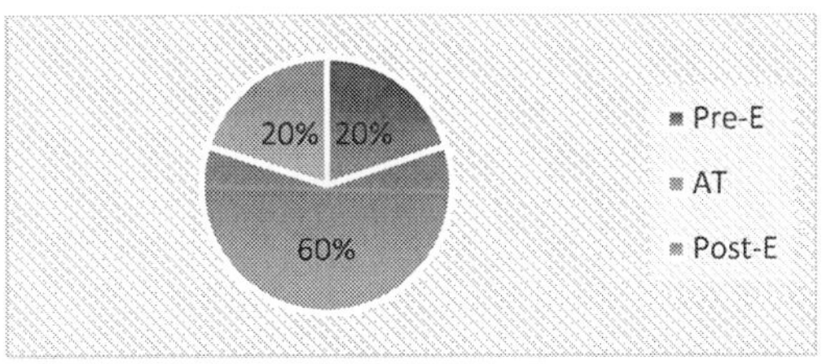

Figure 5: The translation process.

5 Conclusions and Future Research

In this paper, we have presented the results of a questionnaire survey conducted among professional translators specializing in different fields for the Spanish, French and Arabic languages. The objective of this survey, which is the second phase of our research, is to find out how to improve the matching and data retrieval process by applying semantical and syntactical transformations as well as to study the different ways of integrating these transformations and other related proposals. The findings related to the participants profile as well as the use of TMS indicate that 60% of participants use TMS to translate mainly legal and/or administrative texts with 67% of the calculated specialties.

The analysis of the quantitative and qualitative data related to the third part of the questionnaire, i.e. the semantical and syntactical transformations, showed that translators from Spanish apply transformations by synonymy, by personal pronoun, change active/passive voice and prefer transformations with one or two modifications without having to change the words order, sentences and/or clauses order. As for the translators of French, they also apply transformation by synonymy, change active/passive, passive/active voice and substitution by a personal pronoun. All translators from Arabic indicate that they prefer substitution with a synonym without changing the word order; they only make one change in the original segment.

Similarly, our ten initial transformations receive a favorable evaluation from professional translators, which supports our approach to the possibility of integrating them through linguistic processing adapted to each language. All these transformations and other proposals can be integrated during the translation process with 60% of the answers for Spanish, French and Arabic. Thus, it is important to reflect that in the translation process itself the participants prefer editing at the same time of translating, instead of the process of pre-editing the source text before it is uploaded into the system and post-editing which only represent 20% of the participants.

In addition, the participants propose to integrate other types of transformations that we consider to be techniques or strategies used by translators to improve their work, such as reformulation, addition, omission, as well as the change of grammatical gender, or relative pronoun. These proposals will be studied exhaustively in order to consider how we can integrate translation strategies or techniques to improve the efficiency of the TMS providing ideally an editing tool or an automatic paraphrasing process integrated in the TMS.

Finally, these results will be further developed and improved as we plan to continue this research and propose new approaches, especially regarding the translation process itself and how to use translation techniques and strategies in that process.

Acknowledgements

We would like to thank Professor Doctor Ruslan Mitkov (University of Wolverhampton, United Kingdom) and Professor Doctor Gloria Corpas Pastor (University of Malaga, Spain) for their valuable feedback.
Also, we are grateful for the support of the participants and the time they devoted to help our research.

References

Arenas, A. G. (2019). Pre-editing and post-editing. In *The Bloomsbury Companion to Language Industry Studies*. https://doi.org/10.5040/9781350024960.0019

Bassam, H., Asm, M., Nadim, O., & Abeer, T. (2017). *Formal Description of Arabic Syntactic Structure in the Framework of the Government and Binding Theory*. *18*(3), 611–625. https://doi.org/10.13053/C

Bowker, L., & Corpas Pastor, G. (2015). Translation Technology. *Oxford Handbooks Online*, (November), 1–26. https://doi.org/10.1093/oxfordhb/9780199573691.013.007

Djabri, S. (2020). Análisis contrastivo de las coincidencias parciales en español, francés y árabe mediante transformaciones lingüísticas. *Skopos*, *11*, 103–120.

Leblanc, M. (2016). *La traduction spécialisée à l ' ère des nouvelles technologies : quel effet sur le texte de spécialité ? The impact of new translation technologies on specialized texts*. *1*, 77–92. https://doi.org/10.14746/strop.2016.425.006

Levenshtein, V. I. (1966). Binary Codes Capable of Correcting Deletions, Insertions, and Reversals. *Soviet Physics Doklady*, *10*(8), 707–710.

Oliver, A. (2016). *La traducción asistida por ordenador*. Barcelona: Oberta UOC Publishing, SL.

Saldanha, G., & O'Brien, S. (2014). Research Methodologies in Translation Studies. In *Research Methodologies in Translation Studies*. https://doi.org/10.4324/9781315760100

Silvestre Baquero, A., & Mitkov, R. (2017). *Translation Memory Systems Have a Long Way to Go*. 44–51. https://doi.org/10.26615/978-954-452-042-7_006

Simard, M. (2020). Building and using parallel text for translation. In M. O'hagan (Ed.), *The Routledge Handbook of Translation and Technology* (2020th ed., pp. 78–90). https://doi.org/10.4324/9781315311258

Tezcan, A., Bulté, B., & Vanroy, B. (2021). Towards a better integration of fuzzy matches in neural machine translation through data augmentation. *Informatics*, *8*(1), 2–27. https://doi.org/10.3390/informatics8010007

Ranasinghe, T., Orasan, C., & Mitkov, R. (2020). Intelligent Translation Memory Matching and Retrieval with Sentence Encoders. arXiv preprint arXiv:2004.12894.

Ranashinge, T., Mitkov, R., Orasan, C., and Caro Quintana, R., (2021) "Semantic Textual Similarity based on Deep Learning: Can it improve matching and retrieval for Translation Memory tools?" Parallel Corpora: Creation and Applications. John Benjamins.

Timonera, K., & Mitkov, R. (2015). Improving Translation Memory Matching through Clause Splitting. *Proceedings of the Workshop on Natural Language Processing for Translation Memories (NLP4TM)*, 17–23.

Weber, E. (2014). La traducción de la voz pasiva francesa al español: ¿cuestión de lengua o cuestión de traducción? *Mutatis Mutandis*, *7*(2), 368–385.

Using Transfer Learning to Automatically Mark L2 Writing Texts

Tim Elks
Research Institute of Information and Language Processing, University of Wolverhampton
Oxford University Press
t.j.elks@wlv.ac.uk, tim.elks@oup.com

Abstract

The use of transfer learning in Natural Language Processing (NLP) has grown over the last few years. Large, pre-trained neural networks based on the Transformer architecture are one example of this, achieving state-of-the-art performance on several commonly used performance benchmarks, often when fine-tuned on a downstream task. Another form of transfer learning, Multitask Learning, has also been shown to improve performance in Natural Language Processing tasks and increase model robustness.

This paper outlines preliminary findings of investigations into the impact of using pre-trained language models alongside multitask fine-tuning to create an automated marking system of second language learners' written English. Using multiple transformer models and multiple datasets, this study compares different combinations of models and tasks and evaluates their impact on the performance of an automated marking system.

1 Introduction and related work

Human marking of learner productive skills is a costly part of the test development process both in terms of direct financial outlay to external markers and internal resource. Assessors are paid for marking candidates' written test responses and attending training while managing the marking process requires recruiting, training, and monitoring assessors, along with ensuring they are paid for the correct number of responses marked. This cost also increases linearly, meaning that as more candidates enrol to take the test, the number of assessors increases, as does the resource required to manage this increased pool of assessors. It therefore does not scale effectively. Further to this, there are also issues regarding reliability of assessors. Despite efforts by test developers to ensure their assessors mark consistently to the given criteria, human markers often demonstrate inconsistencies as shown by research conducted into inter-rater and intra-rater reliability (Coniam and Falvey, 1999).

One way of attempting to address this issue is to implement an automated marking system. This would make a significant difference to test developers who would be able to save significant resource while improving the reliability of their written assessments. Many test developers already use automated marking in their assessment products, such as Linguaskill (Cheung et al., 2017) from Cambridge Assessment, e-rater (Chen et al., 2017) from ETS, and PTE Academic (ins, 2019) from Pearson. It is also an area which has attracted much research (Chen et al., 2010; Briscoe et al., 2010; Phandi et al., 2015; Nguyen and Dery, 2016; Dong and Zhang, 2016; Farag, 2016; Cummins et al., 2016; Cummins and Rei, 2018; Farag and Yannakoudakis, 2019). This has meant different approaches have been used for automated essay marking and have employed a range of different algorithms.

1.1 Traditional methods

Rudner and Liang (2002) conceptualised automated marking as a classification problem, employing Naive Bayes; Chen et al. (2010) adopted an unsupervised clustering approach; and Briscoe et al. (2010) used a linear batch perceptron classifier. This approach could be well suited to classifying test takers on the CEFR (North, 2006), given the discreet categories, although they are ordinal in nature.

Conversely, regression has been used in several studies. Phandi et al. (2015) employed linear regression, as did Yannakoudakis et al. (2018), who did so with as a ranking regression task, though the authors also suggest using other regression algorithms, and Chen et al. (2016) used support vector machines and decision tree regression models.

Proceedings of the Student Research Workshop associated with RANLP-2021, pages 51–57,
held online, Sep 1–3, 2021.
https://doi.org/10.26615/issn.2603-2821.2021_008

1.2 Neural network methods and pre-trained language models

More recently, Neural Network methods have been widely applied to the problem. Nguyen and Dery (2016) and Boulanger and Kumar (2018) both applied deep learning to essay grading and found initial results to be highly competitive with state-of-the-art results using manually extracted features. Both studies used LSTMs (Hochreiter and Schmidhuber, 1997) to achieve this performance, whereas Farag (2016) and Dong and Zhang (2016) adopted CNNs (LeCun et al., 1989) to achieve high performance.

The advent of the Transformer architecture (Vaswani et al., 2017) and pre-trained language models, such as BERT (Devlin et al., 2018), RoBERTa (Liu et al., 2019) and ELECTRA (Clark et al., 2020), has opened up a new avenue of research in Automated Essay Scoring (AES). Results, however, have been mixed and the field has not seen the large performance increases that appeared in other areas of NLP. Rodriguez et al. (2019) investigated the use of pre-trained models in AES and found that they outperformed traditional machine learning techniques. They also narrowly performed better than an LSTM model, when not as an ensemble of LSTMs – but as a single model. However, the LSTM performed better when combined with others to form an ensemble. Ormerod et al. (2021) found BERT base to outperform LSTMs on an AES task, though not as well as a combined LSTM and CNN model with attention. The author, however, found that the optimum combination was when BERT was combined with manually extracted features. Mayfield and Black (2020), in contrast, found that pre-trained models did not provide any increased performance to n-gram based models but were much more computationally expensive.

1.3 Multitask Learning

Another form of transfer learning, Multitask Learning (MTL), has also been used to tackle the problem of AES, though has received less focus as a research area than pre-trained language models. MTL attempts to improve performance on a given objective by simultaneously training the model to complete a related auxiliary task – the idea being that the model will learn useful information while training on the auxiliary task which will then transfer to the principal task, improving the model's performance (Ruder, 2019). Cummins et al. (2016) took a constrained MTL approach in order to mitigate the need for large volumes of task specific training data. The authors showed that a high performance model was obtainable with very little or no task-specific training data. Further to this, Cummins and Rei (2018) found that by training an automated marker alongside an error detection objective, the automated marker's performance was improved significantly. Farag and Yannakoudakis (2019) applied an MTL approach to coherence modelling and found that by training the model to predict coherence scores for a document while training the same model to predict token level grammatical roles, the model achieved a new state-of-the-art.

One aspect of the MTL literature worth noting is that in researching this paper, only Craighead et al. (2020) used a multitask learning approach which utilized more than a single sub-task. This study took spoken word transcriptions of a speaking test to predict a learners score.

2 Research Questions

The questions that this paper sets out to investigate are:

- Does the use of pre-trained language models improve the performance of an automated marking system of L2 written English?
- Does the use of MTL with pre-trained language models improve the performance of an automated marking system of L2 written English?

3 Task definition

To address the first research question, several models were created in order to achieve suitable comparison. The first model provided a baseline against which the more sophisticated and computationally expensive techniques could be compared. This model was created from manually extracted features, and aimed to be a simplification of the model features described by Yannakoudakis et al. (2011) by using 1-3 grams of tokens, POS and dependency tags, and distances to other grammatical relations. These features were extracted using SpaCy (Honnibal et al., 2020). The task was defined as a standard regression task unlike Yannakoudakis et al. (2011) which used a rank preference approach. These features were then used to train a Random Forest (Breiman, 2001). The second model used the BERT base architecture (Devlin et al., 2018), but with all the model's weights randomly initialized. The third and fourth used BERT base (Devlin et al., 2018) and RoBERTa base (Liu et al., 2019) pretrained models. It was decided not to include an untrained version of RoBERTa because of its architectural similarity to BERT. The Transformers library implementations of the models were used (Wolf et al., 2020). All BERT models used its *uncased* variant.

Each model was trained on a dataset of human-marked written responses to test questions. See below for further information on the dataset used.

3.1 Automated marking task

The primary task in this study is predicting a mark for a written text provided by a learner of English. The data used for this task were taken from the response database of the Oxford Test of English – an English proficiency test developed by the Oxford University Press for learners of English. A subset of responses was sampled so as to achieve an even number of responses as possible across the marking scale, first language groups, gender, and assessor providing the mark. This resulted in a final dataset of 7,596 responses. From this, training, development and test sets were produced. The results reported here were those obtained from predictions on the test set.

The dependent variable, or ground truth, was a score on a scale from 0-21. This is the sum of three marking criteria used on the Oxford Test of English, *Organization*, *Grammar* and *Lexis*. The test uses four criteria in total but *Task Fulfilment*, which rates the extent to which the learner has answered the prompt, was not used because only responses were used for model training.

3.2 Auxiliary tasks

In order to address the second research question, several other tasks were required as subtasks. For this paper, three subtasks were defined:

- an error detection task which required the model to determine whether a sentence was deemed to be acceptable English or not. This was a binary classification task, similar to Cummins and Rei (2018), but at the sentence level as opposed to the token level. This task used the COLA corpus (Warstadt et al., 2018) which consists of 10,000 sentences each tagged 1, 0 depending on their linguistic acceptability.
- an error detection task which required the model to classify tokens by type of error (correct, lexical, grammatical, lexico-grammatical, form, style or missing). This task used a corpus of responses from the Oxford Test of English which had been expertly tagged for their linguistic appropriateness according to a simplified version of the Louvain tagset (Dagneaux et al., 1996).
- a lexis prediction task which required the model to predict the CEFR level of each token. This was chosen in order to train the network to become sensitive to the differences between less and more advanced lexis with regards to learners' linguistic development. This task used the responses from the automated marker task and tagged each token by its CEFR level according to the Oxford 3,000 and Oxford 5,000 word lists. The task was to predict the CEFR level of each token in the response.

Due to the lack of research in training multiple auxiliary tasks as part of an automated marking system, all combinations of the above tasks were trained and the results presented here.

4 Results

4.1 Training and evaluation approach

For each neural model, the same training scheme and training configurations were applied. Each was trained for 5 epochs and was evaluated against the test set at the end of each epoch (the development set was used for preliminary testing and whose results are not reported here). The model which obtained the best RMSE was chosen as the best performing model and whose results are presented here. The metrics presented are the Mean Absolute Error (MAE), Root Mean Square Error (RMSE), and Spearman's rank correlation. Default model training hyper-parameters were used because no search had been conducted at this stage of the study due to time and processing constraints. The hyper-parameters used are shown in table 1.

4.2 Task results

Table 2 shows the results of the models trained only on the automated marking task to compare the effectiveness of using pre-trained language models for automated marking.

Table 3 shows the results of the models trained with the multitask approach. The RoBERTa pre-

Hyperparameter	value
Learning rate	1e-5
Epochs	5
Batch size	16
Gradient accum. steps	1
Weight decay	0
Learning sheduler	linear
Warmup steps	0

Table 1: Comparison of model performance

Model	MAE	RMSE	Sp. r
Manual features	2.79	3.70	.788
BERT not pre	2.82	3.64	.827
BERT pre	2.41	3.35	.892
RoBERTa pre	**2.39**	**3.28**	**.893**

Table 2: Comparison of model performance

trained model was fine-tuned on the primary automarking task alongside the sub-tasks mentioned above. All combinations of tasks were tested in order to verify the impact of each task on the automated marker's performance. *Sent. err* refers to the first auxiliary task which predicts errors at sentence level, *Token. err* refers to the task which predicts error type at the token level, and *CEFR* refers to the task which predicts the associated CEFR level of a particular token.

Tasks	MAE	RMSE	Sp. r
Sent. err.	2.32	3.18	.892
Token err.	2.31	3.12	.892
CEFR	**2.29**	**3.03**	**.893**
Sent. err. + CEFR	2.31	3.09	.889
Token err. + CEFR	2.56	3.49	**.893**
Sent. err. + token err.	2.31	3.09	.889
All tasks	2.38	3.16	.887

Table 3: Comparison of task performance

5 Discussion

The Transformer-based language models performed better than that which used manually extracted features across all the reported metrics. Also, the two models which used pre-trained weights reported superior metrics to those which had not. These results sit in contrast to those found by Mayfield and Black (2020) who reported no performance improvement when using pretrained transformer models. One explanation for this might be the difference in domains. Mayfield and Black (2020) was fine-tuned and tested on five datasets from the ASAP competition (Shermis, 2014) which, though similar in approach, did not mark language learners for their competence in English. This point highlights a critical difference in standard AES and marking the quality of a learners' English. Marking discursive essays requires the assessor to focus on much higher-level textual features compared to that of marking an essay written as part of and ESOL exam. For example, the scoring rubric for ASAP question 1 asks the assessor to focus on whether the *main idea(s) ... stand out*, the text *makes connections and shares insights*, or whether it is *clear, focused or interesting*. This can be contrasted with the Oxford Test of English scoring rubric (OUP, 2019) which focuses on lower-level aspects of the text, requiring responses to demonstrate *a high degree of grammatical accuracy* and *a wide range of cohesive devices.* Understanding such high-level and potentially subjective aspects are likely to be more problematic for language models than issues of grammatical accuracy.

One reason for the increased performance of RoBERTa compared to that of BERT is likely to be the most most obvious differences between the two pre-training approaches. RoBERTa (Liu et al., 2019) is a similar model to BERT but with several key differences: the authors used more training data, they removed the next sentence prediction task, the token sequence length was increased, and the masking pattern applied was dynamically changed during training. This meant that the authors reported improved performance on BERT across the same tasks, mirroring these preliminary results.

Regarding the performance of the MTL models, the vast majority of those which used MTL preformed better than those trained only on the score prediction task. However, the models trained on a single auxiliary task produced higher correlations more consistently than those trained on more than one task, though this trend was not true for the MAE and RMSE metrics, which, showed no obvious trend.

Figures 1 and 2 show scatter plots of the human mark against the automated marker. Although the model shown in figure 1 performed better across the selected evaluation metrics, the model trained on all tasks produced predictions that were much

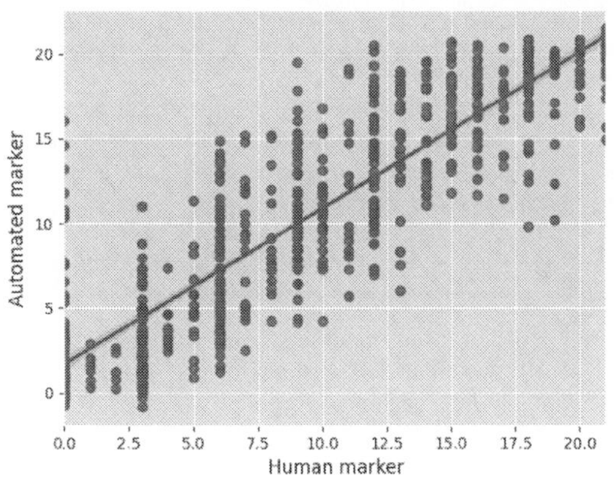

Figure 1: Predictions of MTL model trained with CEFR token level task

more centralized and less erratic. This effect can also be seen in the average standard deviation of predictions for each true score (2.48 for all tasks and 2.56 for the CEFR task alone).

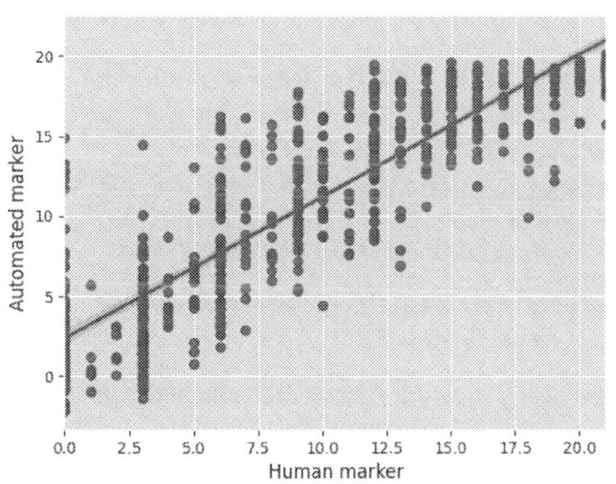

Figure 2: Predictions of MTL model trained with all tasks

Furthermore, when looking at the RMSE for the predictions split by each human mark, the model trained on all tasks was more accurate for all true scores 10-19 but the model trained with only the CEFR auxiliary task was more accurate for all true scores 0-9 and 20-21. This effect can also be seen in figures 1 and 2 where the CEFR trained model made several predictions at the top end of the scale but the model trained on all tasks never predicted the highest possible score.

One potential explanation for this effect is that the model trained on all tasks is not able to differentiate effectively between the higher scores and so clusters many predictions just below the top end of the grade scale in order to be close the true score most frequently. Another explanation might be that as the number of tasks increases, more responsibility is being placed on the model to find a single representation that can be used to predict multiple outputs with only a single transformation in the task specific layer. By increasing the depth of the task specific heads with more transformer layers, this issue might improve, though would not remove the model's dependence on a single representation.

6 Conclusion

Preliminary findings in this research project have shown that pre-trained language models can perform better at automatically grading a learner's English than both traditional methods and the same models without pre-training. The picture regarding the MTL approach is less clear, with the impact of multiple tasks included in training producing opaque results when looking beyond the reported metrics. However, The study has shown that an MTL approach can benefit model performance, but that the impact of using multiple tasks can be unpredictable.

There are several limitations with the study in its current form. Firstly, no model hyperparameter search was conducted to produce the results presented here. This means that some models might perform much better if trained with other hyperparameter values. Another limitation is that it has not explored other prediction methods. For example, as part of the multitask approach, a separate head could be trained to predict each of the three marking criteria as opposed to a total mark. Another limitation and perhaps the most important, is that because the dataset is not available to the wider community, comparison of this approach over others is not possible. One solution to this would be to apply this approach to a freely available dataset such as the Cambridge FCE dataset (Yannakoudakis et al., 2011).

7 Further research

Several issues to be investigated come directly out of the presented findings. Firstly, a more detailed analysis of the predictions made by models trained on multiple tasks compared to those trained on a single task is needed. This could be approached by looking more closely at the distributions of predictions made by the models to see if they do concentrate a much higher rate of predictions just below the top end of the scoring scale in order minimise error without being able to effectively distinguish between texts at those levels. Another way to better understand the performance of the models would be to use another metric, such as a weighted quadratic kappa, which is a more commonly used metric for AES than those presented here and would improve the comparability of results.

Another area of further research would be to introduce manually extracted features and use these alongside MTL training. This approach was demonstrated by Ormerod et al. (2021) to be greatly beneficial for AES systems and would be interesting to introduce with an MTL approach.

Although improvements to automated scoring were seen when trained alongside related tasks, there are other potential benefits from taking such an approach not mentioned in this paper. One such area is providing automated feedback to the learner. Rather than discarding the classification heads for the auxiliary tasks after training, the output predictions of these heads could be used to provide learners with information that could help them improve. For example, the output of the classification head used for the sentence-level error correction task could be used to indicate to the learner which sentences were more likely to contain an error, which they could then address and focus on to improve their writing. Although it would not necessarily be prudent to offer this kind of feedback in a high-stakes proficiency test, this could be very useful as part of a placement test or progress test.

Another benefit of this approach with regards providing learners feedback is that it would simplify the complexity of such a system as it would not require re-training a separate system specifically to perform the feedback task. It would be more simple to replace the final layer of the automarker with a classification head trained on a feedback relevant task. One problem, however, might be that because including more tasks appears to degrade the performance of the model, the more varied forms of feedback the model might give, the greater the reduction in performance of the scoring might be.

References

2019. Pearson Test of English Academic: Automated Scoring. Technical report, Pearson Education Ltd.

David Boulanger and Vivekanandan Kumar. 2018. Deep learning in automated essay scoring. In *International Conference on Intelligent Tutoring Systems*, pages 294–299. Springer.

Leo Breiman. 2001. Random forests. *Machine learning*, 45(1):5–32.

Ted Briscoe, Ben Medlock, and Øistein Andersen. 2010. Automated assessment of ESOL free text examinations. Technical Report UCAM-CL-TR-790, University of Cambridge, Computer Laboratory.

Jing Chen, James Fife, Isaac Bejar, and André Rupp. 2016. Building e-rater® scoring models using machine learning methods. *ETS Research Report Series*.

Jing Chen, Mo Zhang, and Isaac I Bejar. 2017. An investigation of the e-rater® automated scoring engine's grammar, usage, mechanics, and style microfeatures and their aggregation model. *ETS Research Report Series*, 2017(1):1–14.

Yen-Yu Chen, Chuanjun Liu, Chia-Hoang Lee, and Tao-Hsing Chang. 2010. An unsupervised automated essay scoring system. *IEEE Intelligent Systems*, 25:61–67.

Kevin Cheung, Jing Xu, and Gad Lim. 2017. Linguaskill writing trial report.

Kevin Clark, Minh-Thang Luong, Quoc V Le, and Christopher D Manning. 2020. Electra: Pre-training text encoders as discriminators rather than generators. *arXiv preprint arXiv:2003.10555*.

D. Coniam and P. Falvey. 1999. *Melbourne Papers in Language Testing*, 8(2):1–19.

Hannah Craighead, Andrew Caines, Paula Buttery, and Helen Yannakoudakis. 2020. Investigating the effect of auxiliary objectives for the automated grading of learner english speech transcriptions. In *Proceedings of the 58th Annual Meeting of the Association for Computational Linguistics*, pages 2258–2269.

Ronan Cummins and Marek Rei. 2018. Neural multi-task learning in automated assessment. *arXiv preprint arXiv:1801.06830*.

Ronan Cummins, Meng Zhang, and Edward Briscoe. 2016. Constrained multi-task learning for automated essay scoring. Association for Computational Linguistics.

Estelle. Dagneaux, S. Denness, Sylvain. Granger, and Fanny Meunier. 1996. Error tagging manual.

Jacob Devlin, Ming-Wei Chang, Kenton Lee, and Kristina Toutanova. 2018. Bert: Pre-training of deep bidirectional transformers for language understanding. *arXiv preprint arXiv:1810.04805*.

Fei Dong and Yue Zhang. 2016. Automatic features for essay scoring–an empirical study. In *Proceedings of the 2016 conference on empirical methods in natural language processing*, pages 1072–1077.

Youmna Farag. 2016. *Convolutional Neural Networks for Automated Essay Assessment*. Ph.D. thesis, Master's thesis, University of Cambridge, Computer Laboratory. https://www ....

Youmna Farag and Helen Yannakoudakis. 2019. Multi-task learning for coherence modeling. *arXiv preprint arXiv:1907.02427*.

Sepp Hochreiter and Jürgen Schmidhuber. 1997. Lstm can solve hard long time lag problems. *Advances in neural information processing systems*, pages 473–479.

Matthew Honnibal, Ines Montani, Sofie Van Landeghem, and Adriane Boyd. 2020. spaCy: Industrial-strength Natural Language Processing in Python.

Y. LeCun, B. Boser, J. S. Denker, D. Henderson, R. E. Howard, W. Hubbard, and L. D. Jackel. 1989. Backpropagation applied to handwritten zip code recognition. *Neural computation*, 1(4):541–551.

Yinhan Liu, Myle Ott, Naman Goyal, Jingfei Du, Mandar Joshi, Danqi Chen, Omer Levy, Mike Lewis, Luke Zettlemoyer, and Veselin Stoyanov. 2019. Roberta: A robustly optimized bert pretraining approach. *arXiv preprint arXiv:1907.11692*.

Elijah Mayfield and Alan W Black. 2020. Should you fine-tune bert for automated essay scoring? In *Proceedings of the Fifteenth Workshop on Innovative Use of NLP for Building Educational Applications*, pages 151–162.

Huyen Nguyen and Lucio Dery. 2016. Neural networks for automated essay grading. *CS224d Stanford Reports*, pages 1–11.

Brian North. 2006. The common european framework of reference: Development, theoretical and practical issues.

Christopher M Ormerod, Akanksha Malhotra, and Amir Jafari. 2021. Automated essay scoring using efficient transformer-based language models. *arXiv preprint arXiv:2102.13136*.

OUP. 2019. Oxford test of english test specifications.

Peter Phandi, Kian Ming Adam Chai, and Hwee Tou Ng. 2015. Flexible domain adaptation for automated essay scoring using correlated linear regression. In *EMNLP*.

Pedro Uria Rodriguez, Amir Jafari, and Christopher M Ormerod. 2019. Language models and automated essay scoring. *arXiv preprint arXiv:1909.09482*.

Sebastian Ruder. 2019. *Neural transfer learning for natural language processing*. Ph.D. thesis, NUI Galway.

Lawrence M Rudner and Tahung Liang. 2002. Automated essay scoring using bayes' theorem. *The Journal of Technology, Learning and Assessment*, 1(2).

Mark D Shermis. 2014. State-of-the-art automated essay scoring: Competition, results, and future directions from a united states demonstration. *Assessing Writing*, 20:53–76.

Ashish Vaswani, Noam Shazeer, Niki Parmar, Jakob Uszkoreit, Llion Jones, Aidan N. Gomez, Lukasz Kaiser, and Illia Polosukhin. 2017. Attention is all you need.

Alex Warstadt, Amanpreet Singh, and Samuel R Bowman. 2018. Neural network acceptability judgments. *arXiv preprint arXiv:1805.12471*.

Thomas Wolf, Julien Chaumond, Lysandre Debut, Victor Sanh, Clement Delangue, Anthony Moi, Pierric Cistac, Morgan Funtowicz, Joe Davison, Sam Shleifer, et al. 2020. Transformers: State-of-the-art natural language processing. In *Proceedings of the 2020 Conference on Empirical Methods in Natural Language Processing: System Demonstrations*, pages 38–45.

Helen Yannakoudakis, Ted Briscoe, and Ben Medlock. 2011. A new dataset and method for automatically grading esol texts. In *Proceedings of the 49th annual meeting of the association for computational linguistics: human language technologies*, pages 180–189.

Helen Yannakoudakis, Øistein E Andersen, Ardeshir Geranpayeh, Ted Briscoe, and Diane Nicholls. 2018. Developing an automated writing placement system for esl learners. *Applied Measurement in Education*, 31(3):251–267.

Bilingual Terminology Extraction Using Neural Word Embeddings on Comparable Corpora

Darya Filippova, Burcu Can, Gloria Corpas Pastor

Research Group in Computational Linguistics
University of Wolverhampton
University of Malaga

{d.filippova, b.can}@wlv.ac.uk gcorpas@uma.es

Abstract

Term and glossary management are vital steps of preparation of every language specialist, and they play a very important role at the stage of education of translation professionals. The growing trend of efficient time management and constant time constraints we may observe in every job sector increases the necessity of the automatic glossary compilation. Many well-performing bilingual AET systems are based on processing parallel data, however, such parallel corpora are not always available for a specific domain or a language pair. Domain-specific, bilingual access to information and its retrieval based on comparable corpora is a very promising area of research that requires a detailed analysis of both available data sources and the possible extraction techniques. This work focuses on domain-specific automatic terminology extraction from comparable corpora for the English – Russian language pair by utilizing neural word embeddings.

1 Introduction

Terminology studies represent a strictly hierarchical discipline that forms a basement for global scientific knowledge. One of the main challenges of the term extraction task is mostly associated with the "Deficiency of unique norms and rules among linguists and lexicographers to identify a massive amount of modern terminology vocabulary, systematize and place it on international databases because the appearance of new scientific and technological notions occurs faster than it can be defined" (Bidnenko, 2018). Despite the controversy about the notion on "termhood", the main obstacle in the term extraction process consists in the restricted access to cross-lingual parallel content being a major bottleneck for compiling a high-quality specialised dictionary with minimum effort.

Many well-performing bilingual AET systems are based on processing parallel data, however, such parallel corpora are not always available for a specific domain or a language pair (Uyeama, 2006). Even though the number of parallel corpora available online is gradually increasing, this number is still not sufficient to include a wide range of all possible domains, especially if the domain is relatively new. Comparable corpora, on the contrary, can be an excellent alternative with a lot of potential and greater possibilities for domain- and language adaptability (Pekar et al., 2008). Other advantages of comparable corpora include its relatively cheap construction process and its usefulness in building a domain-specific corpus even for low-resource languages and underrepresented topics. It is important to note that a specialised comparable corpus is traditionally of a smaller size (when compared to a general-language corpus), this is usually related to the scarcity of resources in languages other than English (Hazem and Morin, 2016). Such a corpus may also pose issues associated with the unfavorable duplication of web-crawled texts, noisy data, and a general lack of control over the corpus compilation process. Nevertheless, the use of comparable corpora remains a very promising area of research in both monolingual and bilingual term extraction.

This research is hypothesized on the idea that language specialists are usually provided with the minimum information about an event and little or no additional information about the specific domain they must work with (Gaber et al., 2021). The general pipeline of the terminology extraction process can be divided into three main stages: 1. Building a corpus; 2. Application of term extraction methods; 3. Either automatic or

Proceedings of the Student Research Workshop associated with RANLP-2021, pages 58–64,
held online, Sep 1–3, 2021.
https://doi.org/10.26615/issn.2603-2821.2021_009

manual validation of extracted term candidates. Considering all the advantages of using a bilingual comparable corpus, we would like to exploit its properties in the terminology extraction task and make it domain-independent i.e., adaptable to any other domain where the compilation of corpora is possible; However, this work will be mainly focused on Covid – 19 domain whereas our rationale will be discussed later in the next sections

2 Related Work

2.1 Statistical Term Extraction Methods

The variety of strategies used for the automatic term extraction was developed with one common objective to obtain the most consistent set of terms being the best representation of a domain in question. The commonly agreed approaches used in the task of term extraction can be clustered into three main groups, depending on the methods of scoring the candidate terms (Astrakhantsev, 2018). Thus, these three main categories are also classified as statistical, linguistic, and hybrid, accordingly. Statistical approach was aimed to determine the potential "termhood" [1] of a candidate word by defining the optimum measures of this "termhood" (Pazienza et al., 2006). The history of frequency-based approaches lasts for decades, thus Total TF-IDF algorithm is based on measuring word informativeness, i.e., the importance of a particular word/potential term in a given document (Evans and Lefferts, 1995). C-value is another traditional yet more comprehensive statistical measure, that is commonly used with multiword expressions, this measure does not only consider the frequency of an expression but its length and the frequency of its constituents in a corpus, it is proved to be very efficient when applied to highly technical domains (Frantzi et al., 2000). Mutual Information (MI) is widely used as one of the statistical measures of term frequency where the independent probability of terms is compared to the probability to see these terms together. MI is very useful for identifying high-frequency terms; however, it overestimates multiword terms consisting of rarely seen words (Church et al., 2003). The idea of using frequency information as the feature for identifying terms has not only resulted in specialized scripts but also inspired the development of frequency-based automatic term extractors. One of such tools isan open-source TBXTools[2] developed by A. Oliver and M. V`azquez (2015) with the aim of automating statistical term extraction process and making it realizable for general users with no advanced programming skills. With reference to other language-dependent methods, an attempt to compile a glossary of scientific terms in Russian was made by Bolshakova et al., (2019). Considering the complicated structure of Russian grammar, a set of lexical and syntactic patterns was formed to detect terms based on syntactic and morphological features of the Russian language. Such a collection of rules is very efficient when extracting terms in a particular domain, however a very specific fine-tuning is needed depending on every domain, its size, and language.

2.2 Linguistic and Hybrid Term Extraction

Linguistic methods of term extraction try to identify terms based on their syntactic features. Scholars supporting this approach state that syntactic information is sufficient to determine the termhood of a word (Bourigault, 1992). In their comprehensive review Pazienza et al., (2006) confirm that these two stages can be sufficient for loose term extraction if the initial POS grouping is performed correctly and is based on the deep analysis of the most common syntactic structures of a language in question. Let us consider such a common phrase as "*Health protection*", its equivalent in Russian is "*Охрана здоровья*", however, the chances that we will be able to obtain the same translation equivalent using the frequency-based or linguistic techniques are quite low, as this term could potentially be used in different contexts, thus the declension of the first word may change to genitive case ("*Охраны здоровья*") or dative case ("*Охране здоровья*") and others depending on the context. It is important to note that within a linguistic framework of AET other refinement techniques can be applied for further term filtering, such as the creation of customized lists of unwanted words, general-purpose words, or

[1] Termhood is defined as a potential ability of a word to be a term

[2] https://github.com/aoliverg/TBXTools

functional words followed by the manual validation of subject-matter experts (Pazienza et al., 2006).

The best practice in the traditional approach to AET is to use a combination of both statistical and linguistic techniques to achieve better performance. Such hybrid methods are commonly used in the automated term extraction systems. For example, TermoStat [3] tool was developed with the aim of extracting corpus-specific terminology and performed quite well when extracting simple terms achieving 74% of precision (Drouin, 2003). Another hybrid software used for both term extraction and corpus compilation is SketchEngine [4] . This software supports a range of languages and can even be used for domain-specific bilingual term extraction if a parallel corpus is available (Kilgarriff et al., 2014). Some other tools combine nearly all available traditional approaches (ATR4S software that comprises 15 AET methods, including, but not limited to Average Term Frequency, Residual IDF, Relevance and Weirdness scores, etc.) and deliver good results (Astrakhantsev, 2018). Even though the aforementioned techniques performed quite well in both monolingual and bilingual environment, the growing interest to state-of-the-art machine learning methods led to numerous experiments carried out in a range of NLP tasks including term extraction.

2.3 Experiments With the Word Embedding Techniques

The main impulse in improving the consistency and accuracy of domain-specific terminology sets was to increase the number of features each term can be represented with rather than treating every word as an atomic unit (Amjadian et al., 2016). With the introduction of word embeddings, it became possible to obtain deeper contextual meanings of words being a set of features. Tomas Mikolov (2013) was the first to propose "A method to learn a linear transformation from the source language to the target language" to improve the task of lexicon extraction from bilingual corpora. Thus, Hazem and Morin (2017) attempted to improve bilingual terminology extraction from specialised corpora by exploiting finer granularity of the word embeddings generated by Word2Vec. In their work, it was argued that the traditional approaches are also not suitable for domain-specific term extraction as the word co-occurrence information for a small size comparable corpus is always not reliable as well as pre-trained neural network models are unable to learn the features if the vocabulary is of modest size. This limitation was then addressed by enriching the distributed word representations with the general domain data. The concatenation of distributed word representations trained on a domain-specific corpus and a general corpus helped to improve the quality of extracted terms comparing to previous works where the algorithms were only trained on specialised corpora.

It is important to mention that the introduction of other word embedding architectures influenced further experiments with vector concatenation. So, Amjadian (2016) used the abovementioned CBOW and Skip-gram architectures to produce so-called "global word vectors" trained on a general language corpus and concatenated them with "local context vectors" generated by means of another word embedding architecture called Glove (Pennington et al., 2014). Besides the promising results of the previously described works, there are some other limitations, that were not taken into account, such as the ability to produce bias results due to the unbalanced dimensionality of domain-specific and general word vectors. This limitation was then addressed in a later work of Liu et al., (2018) where they proposed to restrict the size of domain-specific word vectors to 100 comparing to the size of general domain word vectors being set as 300. This fine-tuning allowed to not only preserve the features of both corpora but to also use available pre-trained models with the minimum changes required.

Even though multiple experiments with the various types of word embeddings for inflected and agglutinative languages (Üstün et al., 2018; Romanov and Khusainova, 2019) have shown that morphological subword embeddings perform very well with the Slavic languages, these types of distributed word representations are still limited due to its static nature i.e., inability to change depending on the context. However, more

[3] http://termostat.ling.umontreal.ca/

[4] https://www.sketchengine.eu/

information extraction opportunities occurred with the introduction of the most modern type of deep contextualized word embedding, such as ELMo (Peters et al., 2018), BERT (Devlin et al., 2019). Among other possible applications, the BERT model was also considered in the context of binary classification for associating term candidates with their context (Hazem et al., 2020). Given the wide range of neural network-based term extraction experiments we are convinced that state-of-the-art methods can help to improve the AET task for the English – Russian language pair by either being paired with the traditional methods or by applying modern vector concatenation techniques.

3 Methodology on Automatic Term Extraction and Bilingual Mapping of the Terms

3.1 Comparable Corpora as the Main Source of Data

A good example of data scarcity case can be demonstrated by the availability of parallel datasets for En-Ru language pair on such topics as Coronaviruses and Vaccination. The rapid growth of interest to this topic is disproportional comparing to the amount of available bilingual data. As of July 2021, the only open-source parallel corpus we could find on the web was Corona Crisis Corpora published by TAUS[5] with the aim of ensuring better language coverage. The corpus consists of 192,614 aligned segments and could be very useful for small-scale NLP experiments, however, this data is still not enough to cover all Covid-related domains.

Numerous works in the sphere of term extraction from specialized corpora did not only differ in methods and techniques but also covered many domains and languages. Several factors were considered while choosing a domain for our datasets, which is:

a. Asymmetrical availability of resources – by focusing our experiment mostly on the topic of Covid-19, we believe that we will be able to contribute to the simplification of term extraction process for such domains, where the information in English is prevalent due to their novelty. The topic of the coronavirus remains one of the most popular areas of modern research, however, most up-to-date scientific papers on Covid – 19 are published in English. Consequently, the number of relatively new terms introduced in this language is much greater than it is in any other high-resource languages. This disproportion of terminological equivalents makes the task of glossary compilation even more challenging.

b. Usefulness and timeliness of the topic – despite its novelty, Covid – 19 led to numerous international events where the assistance of language specialists is crucial. We are convinced that this domain will not only remain in high demand for the next several years but will also give rise to the development of other cross-disciplinary domains where the availability of high-quality bilingual terminology sets will be essential.

The comparable corpus of the En-Ru language pair will consist of two monolingual corpora, where the English part of it will be represented by the CORD-19 dataset [6]. This exhaustive, open-source dataset was compiled by the leading research groups of the world as a response to the COVID-19 pandemic and it consists of more than 500 000 scientific articles on SARS-COV-19. The compilation of a corpus in Russian will be performed by the automatic web crawling with the subsequent data cleaning and processing. Several websites will be considered as the main source of data in Russian to ensure that the dataset is represented by scientific papers containing plenty of terms. We would like to follow the methodology of A. Rungsawang (2004) for building the web crawler and to ensure that the information from the web pages is collected in an incremental way to avoid data duplication during the subsequent crawls. Thus, the crawler algorithm will be able to learn from search experience and produce filtered results in case of several crawling attempts. Topic relevancy score will be used together with the boilerplate removal to form the textual data. Besides the possibility to have noisy data that requires special treatment and extra attention, another debatable peculiarity of a comparable corpus remains its "comparability" or similarity of genres of the chosen subcorpora,

[5] https://md.taus.net/corona

[6] The dataset is available at: https://www.kaggle.com/allen-institute-for-ai/CORD-19-research-challenge

therefore the initial selection of data sources will be of paramount importance.

3.2 Word Embeddings as Input to a Neural Network Classifier

Word vectorization is performed by means of pre-trained word embedding models to minimize the effort of parameter engineering and benefit from state-of-the-art algorithms. The final optimal approach will solely depend on the results of the experiments carried out with the concatenation of distributed word representations and changing the dimensionality of word embeddings as well as associating specialized corpora with the external data. There is a range of approaches to using bilingual neural network classifiers to distinguish between the terms and non-terms. Some of such deep learning algorithms are trained on a small set of labelled data and then tested on predicting the class on the big amount of domain-specific unlabelled data (Wang et al., 2016). Hand engineering is a very time-consuming and labor-intensive task that often requires extra supervision and the assistance of subject-matter experts. Following the trend of minimum hand–engineering, another term extraction approach relies on the benefits of using deep contextualized word embeddings as input to Convolutional Neural Networks with minimum supervision (Khosla et al., 2019). We would like to adopt and combine the previous methods proposed by Hazem and Morin (2017), Amjadian et al., (2016), and Liu et al., (2018) and to exploit the idea of the independent training of local and global vectors with minimum fine-tuning of more modern customizable models that are capable of learning the context of words.

3.3 Bilingual Mapping and Results Evaluation

Considering the monolingual training conditions, one of the final stages of our research will be to find the translation equivalents for the set of candidate terms extracted by the classifier. The task of bilingual mapping, as well as various transformation options, were thoroughly studied by Artetxe et al., (2016) where they proposed a framework for learning the optimal vector transformation that outperformed all the previous techniques and helped to solve the task of zero-shot translation[7]. We would like to follow the upgraded version of the suggested multi-step framework proposed by Artetxe et al., (2018) consisting of the orthogonal mapping of the word vectors and reducing their dimensionality. This technique proved to be very efficient when paired with the state-of-the-art word embeddings trained on two corpora of distant language pairs.

As it was mentioned before, considering the uncertainties about the classification and the definition of terms, the task of data validation in this work is quite challenging. It was decided to avoid human evaluation techniques because a.) we are convinced that this task is very subjective for manual evaluation as the entire process of glossary building often depends on personal preferences and the individual level of expertise b.) this process is very labor-intensive and requires the assistance of domain experts that are not always available. Alternately, standard automatic evaluation metrics such as precision, recall, and F score will be used. To ensure proper evaluation of the terminology extraction task the terminology reference list for the En-Ru language pair is required. It is important to mention that the domain of Covid-19 is still a field of active research and new terminology is coined every day, however, we could not find any gold standard datasets that are currently available on the web. Thus, the reference bilingual terminology list will be compiled manually by consolidating several glossaries provided by such organizations as WIPO Pearl [8] and the official terminology database of the European Union [9]. The list of possible reference sources is not exhaustive and will be updated in the course of searching for the most up-to-date open-source termbases published by trustworthy providers.

4 Research Questions

The main motivation of this research relates to the restricted access to cross-lingual content being a major obstacle for compiling a high-quality specialised dictionary with minimum effort.

[7] Zero-shot translation enables the neural network to pick the nearest possible translation equivalent for the words that were not present in the training data set.

[8] COVID 19 multilingual glossary is available at: https://www.wipo.int/pressroom/en/articles/2020/article_0021.html

[9] https://data.europa.eu/data/datasets/covid-19-multilingual-terminology-on-iate?locale=en

Thus, our research questions can be formulated as follows:

- What are the limitations of generating a bilingual dictionary for a specific domain when no additional resources are provided?
- Is it possible to compile bilingual glossaries from bilingual comparable corpora?
- If so, what is the most efficient procedure to perform bilingual term extraction?

It is important to note that we would like to address the realia of working conditions that usually imply a significant amount of information that has to be processed by an interpreter in a short period of time to manually compile a glossary; hence our main goal will be to automate glossary creation process to the maximum possible extent and, at the same time, preserve the accuracy and consistency of specialised terms.

References

Amjadian, E., Inkpen, D., Paribakht, T., & Faez, F. (2016). Local-Global Vectors to Improve Unigram Terminology Extraction. *Proceedings of the 5th International Workshop on Computational Terminology (Computerm2016)*, Osaka, Japan, pages 2-11.

Artetxe, M., Labaka, G., & Agirre, E. (2016). Learning principled bilingual mappings of word embeddings while preserving monolingual invariance. *Proceedings of the 2016 Conference on Empirical Methods in Natural Language Processing*, Austin, Texas, pages 2289–2294. https://doi.org/10.18653/v1/D16-1250

Artetxe, M., Labaka, G., & Agirre, E. (2018). Generalizing and Improving Bilingual Word Embedding Mappings with a Multi-Step Framework of Linear Transformations. *Thirty-Second AAAI Conference on Artificial Intelligence*, pages 5012-5019.

Astrakhantsev, N. (2018). ATR4S: toolkit with state-of-the-art automatic terms recognition methods in Scala. *Language Resources and Evaluation, 5 2*, pages 853-872.

Bidnenko, N. (2018). *Practical and theoretical issues of modern terminology* [Ph.D. Thesis, Alfred Nobel University, Dnipro], pages 3-5.

Bolshakova, E., Efremova, N., & Ivanov, K. (2019). Terminological Information Extraction from Russian Scientific Texts: Methods and Applications. pages 7-11. https://doi.org/10.29007/k93q

Bourigault, A. (1992). Surface Grammatical Analysis for the Extraction of Terminological Noun Phrases. *COLING 1992 Volume 3: The 14th International Conference on Computational Linguistics*, https://www.aclweb.org/anthology/C92-3150

Church, K., Gale, W., Hanks, P., & Hindle, D. (2003). Using Statistics in Lexical Analysis. *Lexical Acquisition: Exploiting On-Line Resources to Build a Lexicon*, pages. 5-9.

Devlin, J., Chang, M., Lee, K., & Toutanova, K. (2019). BERT: Pre-training of Deep Bidirectional Transformers for Language Understanding. *Proceedings of the 2019 Conference of the North American Chapter of the Association for Computational Linguistics: Human Language Technologies, Volume 1 (Long and Short Papers)*, Minneapolis, Minnesota, pages 4171 – 4186.https://doi.org/10.18653/v1/N 19-1423

Drouin, P. (2003). Term extraction using non-technical corpora as a point of leverage. *Terminology*, 9(1), pp.99–115. https://doi.org/10.1075/term.9.1.06dro

Evans A. and R. G. Lefferts. (1995). CLARIT-TREC experiments. In Information Processing and Management: An International Journal, volume 31, pages 385–395.

Frantzi K., Ananiadou S., and Mima H. 2000. Automatic Recognition of Multi-Word Terms: the C-value/NC-value Method. International Journal on Digital Libraries, pages 115–130.

Gaber, M., Corpas Pastor, G., & Omer, A. (2021). Speech-to-Text Technology as a Documentation Tool for Interpreters: a new approach to compiling an adhoc corpus and extracting terminology from video-recorded speeches. *TRANS. Revista de Traductologia*, pages 263-281. https://doi.org/10.24310/TRANS2020.v0i24.7876

Hazem, A., & Morin, E. (2016). Efficient Data Selection for Bilingual Terminology Extraction from Comparable Corpora. *Proceedings of COLING 2016, the 26th International Conference on Computational Linguistics: Technical Papers*, Osaka, Japan, pages 3401–3411.

Hazem, A., & Morin, E. (2017). Bilingual Word Embeddings for Bilingual Terminology Extraction from Specialized Comparable Corpora. *Proceedings of the Eighth International Joint Conference on Natural Language Processing (Volume 1: Long Papers)*, Taipei, Taiwan, pages 485-493.

Hazem, A., Bouhandi, M., Boudin, F., & Daille, B. (2020). TermEval 2020: TALN-LS2N System for Automatic Term Extraction. *Proceedings of the 6th International Workshop on Computational Terminology*, Marseille, France, pages 95-100.

https://www.aclweb.org/anthology/2020.computerm-1.13

Khosla, K., Jones, R., & Bowman, N. (2019). Featureless Deep Learning Methods for Automated Key-Term Extraction. Department of Mathematics. Stanford University. Stanford, pages 2-8.

Kilgarriff, A., Baisa, V., Busta, J., Jakubícek, M., Kovár, V., Michelfeit, J., Rychlý, P., & Suchomel, V.
(2014). The Sketch Engine: ten years on. *Lexicog raphy, pages* 7-36.

Liu, J., Morin, E., & Saldarriaga, P. (2018). Towards a unified framework for bilingual terminology extraction of single-word and multi-word terms. *Proceedings of the 27th International Conference on Computational Linguistics*, Santa Fe, New Mexico, USA, pages 2855–2866.

Mikolov, T., Quoc, V. L. e., & Sutskever, I. (2013). Exploiting Similarities among Languages for Machine Translation. v.1, pages 2-4. https://doi.org/https://arxiv.org/abs/1309.4168

Oliver, A., & Vàzquez, M. (2015). TBXTools: A Free, Fast and Flexible Tool for Automatic Terminology Extraction. *Proceedings of the International Conference Recent Advances in Natural Language Processing*, Hissar, Bulgaria, pages 473–479. https://www.aclweb.org/anthology/R15-1062

Pazienza, M., Pennacchiotti, M., & Zanzotto, F. B. (2006). Terminology extraction: an analysis of linguistic and statistical approaches. *Knowledge Mining pp.255-279*, pages 255-279. https://doi.org/10.1007/3-540-32394-5_20

Pekar, V., Mitkov, R., Blagoev, D., Mulloni, A. (2008). Finding Translations for Low-Frequency Words in Comparable Corpora. *Machine Translation*, 20 (4), pages 247-266

Pennington, J., Socher, R., & Manning, C. (2014). GloVe: Global Vectors for Word Representation. *Proceedings of the 2014 Conference on Empirical Methods in Natural Language Processing (EMNLP)*, Doha, Qatar, pages 1532–1543.

Peters, M., Neumann, M., Iyyer, M., Gardner, M., Clark, C., Lee, K., & Zettlemoyer, L. (2018). Deep Contextualized Word Representations. *Proceedings of the 2018 Conference of the North American Chapter of the Association for Computational Linguistics: Human Language Technologies, Volume 1 (Long Papers)*, New Orleans, Louisiana, pages 2227–2237. https://doi.org/10.18653/v1/N18-1202

Romanov, V., & Khusainova, A. (2019). Evaluation of Morphological Embeddings for English and Russian Languages. *Proceedings of the 3rd Workshop on Evaluating Vector Space Representations for NLP*, Minneapolis, USA, pages 77-81.

Rungsawang, A., & Angkawattanawit, N. (2004). Learnable topic-specific web crawler. *Department of Computer Engineering, Massive Information & Knowledge Engineering*, Bangkok, Thailand, pages 5-12.

Üstün, A., Kurfalı, M., & Can, B. (2018). Characters or Morphemes: How to Represent Words?. *Proceedings of the 3rd Workshop on Representation Learning for NLP*, Melbourne, Australia, pages 144-153.

Uyeama, M. (2006). Building general- and special-purpose corpora by Web crawling. *The 13th NIJL International Symposium, Language Corpora: Their Compilation and Application.*, Tokyo, Japan, pages 2-6.

Wang, R., Liu, W., & McDonald , C. (2016). Featureless Domain-Specific Term Extraction with Minimal Labelled Data. *Proceedings of the Australasian Language Technology Association Workshop 2016*, Melbourne, Australia, pages 103–112. https://www.aclweb.org/anthology/U16-1011.pdf

Web-sentiment Analysis Of Public Comments (Public Reviews) For Languages With Limited Resources Such As The Kazakh Language

Dinara Gimadi, Richard Evans, Kiril Simov
University of Wolverhampton, New Bulgarian University

{gimadi.dinara}@mail.ru

Abstract

In the pandemic period, the stay-at-home trend forced businesses to switch their activities to digital mode, for example, app-based payment methods, social distancing via social media platforms, and other digital means have become an integral part of our lives. Sentiment analysis of textual information in user comments is a topical task in emotion AI because user comments or reviews are not homogeneous, they contain sparse context behind, and are misleading both for human and computer. Barriers arise from the emotional language enriched with slang, peculiar spelling, transliteration, use of emoji and their symbolic counterparts, and code-switching.

1 Introduction

Top free Google Play apps in Kazakhstan are Ashyq, Telegram Messenger, Kaspi, Instagram, e-Gov mobile, OLX, Kolesa, and others. Kazakh-language application reviews are of high interest for companies developing and marketing mobile apps. They are valued by businesses to influence the decision-making of a potential customer and evaluate overall satisfaction or dissatisfaction with products, their new features, and services. The given problem predetermines the following obstacle: in the context of the absence of a standard dataset, comparison of techniques applied, and results obtained is a challenging task. The problem of sentiment classification of Kazakh comments includes code-switching between Kazakh and Russian languages by using Cyrillic script, ambiguous words, and emoji, especially the problem of combining negative emoji with a positive comment or vice versa, which have an impact on the overall tonality of the review. The relevance of the topic is justified by the scarcity of developed models and methods of sentiment analysis of the opinions of social networks users in the Kazakh language. Collection of 3000 labeled reviews data set on web apps and development of a method for achieving more correct results is the main goal, which consists of data compilation, pre-processing part, and classification by testing an aspect-based method.

2 Previous work

Researchers in the area of sentiment analysis and opinion mining have achieved significant progress. According to (Liu et al., 2018), sentiment is a subjective feeling expressed in text. Pang and Lee et al. (2008) stated that analysis of subjective feelings in texts refers to the assemble of techniques from fields such as natural language processing (NLP), information retrieval, and machine learning, to identify and extract subjective information from text reviews

Proceedings of the Student Research Workshop associated with RANLP-2021, pages 65–68,
held online, Sep 1–3, 2021.
https://doi.org/10.26615/issn.2603-2821.2021_010

and classify the documents, sentences or phrases into sentiment categories such as positive, negative and neutral. Sentiment analysis of public comments in Google Play Market has performed automatically with Google Cloud Natural Language API. Google Natural Language processing API is a pre-trained machine learning API for Google sentiment analysis, entity recognition, and syntax analysis. Google Cloud Natural Language sentiment analysis calculates a predicted floating-point value between -1 and 1 to evaluate the entire text string's emotional coloring. There are various directions, in which researchers paved their ways, to gain significant developments. As a rule, sentiment analysis is carried out by applying a linguistic method or a machine learning method, and neural networks. Machine learning techniques include Support Vector Machine (SVM), Logistic Regression, Naive Bayes, Random Forest, Linear Regression, k nearest neighbor (k-NN), and others. Machine learning techniques are supervised if they use pre-existing/ collected opinion datasets, which means 'they have a data set of input observations, each associated with some correct output (a 'supervision signal') according to (Jurafsky and Martin, 2020). Then it automatically learns all types of linguistic attributes and computes a model for each corpus. The trained model is later can be used for the classification of the test dataset. Petter Mæhlum et al. (2019) annotated evaluative reviews at three levels in the Norwegian language concerning being on-topic or not, and expressing the first opinion of the author or not, and a binary classification task about positive and negative sentiments. In this dataset sentences with positive, neutral, and negative categories were hand-labeled by reviewing lexical features and context. Also in Google PlayMarket there are existing labeled sentences. Labeled data includes the following categories: binary – positive and negative sentiment, ternary – positive, neutral and negative sentiment, and quinary – strongly positive, positive, neutral, negative, and strongly negative. Jurafsky and Martin (2020) indicated Naïve Bayes is a generative classifier, which is based on conditional probability, according to which the document belongs to the class, and uses the Bayes formula. The linguistic method by Yergesh et al. (2017) supposed designing sentiment dictionaries of Kazakh words and phrases as well as a set of linguistic rules, in which nouns and noun groups were considered as aspect categories. For example, the app 'Kaspi. Kz bank' has aspects such as technical issues, language, interface, and service to address the opinions of users. Users mention the aspects of the object in a comment with sentiment words. Aspect-based sentiment analysis correlates phrases to the aspects (categories that justify the reason for emotional evaluation). Aspect is a specific topic or feature to which sentiment will be assigned. In user comments from Google Play Market aspects for mobile applications are interface, language, technical performance, design, individual issues, and others. Sitaram et al. (2015), when extracting sentiments from the mixed language of Hindi and English, combined the sentiment of these sentence extracts incrementally, and trained data. Kozhirbayev et al. (2018) approached code-switching in a single two-step framework, consisting of unsupervised normalization and Naïve Bayes classification. Linguistic code-switching (LCS) is a linguistic phenomenon, when two or more languages are used in one sentence shifting traditional grammatical structure of the source language. Moreover, they applied model based on LSTM networks to classify reviews of users. Researchers Zharmagambetov et al. (2016) applied Word2Vec in the sentiment classification task for Kazakh and Russian languages and used these word vectors as an input to deep recurrent neural networks to deal with long term dependency of the textual document.

3 Methodology

This research focuses on the development of a new method for aspect-based sentiment analysis for Kazakh-language reviews of Android apps posted on the Google Play Market. The research questions set during the research planning are:

1) Is the rule-based approach for identifying different aspects of apps mentioned in the reviews, in the context of scarce data, more accurate than the data-driven approach?

2) What techniques of machine learning are relevant to overcome challenges related to the scarcity of language resources and tools?

3) To what extent the output obtained from rule-based and data-driven methods for aspect-based sentiment analysis will correlate with each other?

4) How do emoji contribute to proper sentiment extraction in line with a textual message?

5) Is code-switching in Kazakh-Russian combined sentences can be resolved for sentiment classification by applying machine learning techniques?

The relevance of the research topic is justified by the scarcity of developed models and methods of sentiment analysis of the opinions of social networks users in the Kazakh language. Collection of 3000 labeled reviews data set on web apps and development of a method for achieving more correct results is a contribution and can be used for future research. The object of the research is the user reviews from Android Google Play Market in the Kazakh language. The subject of the research is sentiment analysis methods and algorithms, as a special case of semantic analysis of texts in natural language.

The main steps of sentiment analysis are data compilation and preprocessing, as well as classifying it with the use of machine learning algorithms and neural networks. The first stage contains an accumulation of Kazakh-language reviews of Android apps posted on the Google Play Market. Classification consisted of labeled data such as positive, negative, neutral labels based on my personal standpoint, reviews containing only emoji (without words), emoji and words, reviews with code-switching, Google Play Market ratings (1-5 stars), binary classification by Google Play Market. The compiled data consists of 3000 annotated tokens, which can be used for training and testing.

The second stage includes data preprocessing that implies clearing data from unneeded characters and punctuation marks, converting all words to lower case, extracting stop words that do not possess any semantic load, and removing affixes and endings (stemming), or modifying words into an indefinite form (lemmatization). Up to far tokenization was performed with the use of Python, reduced all tokens to lower case, added notes containing corrected tokens for misspelled tokens, which refers to any type of data created by users, and far from standards of literary language. National Laboratory of Kazakhstan contributed to developing the KazNLP tool for text preprocessing, and NLA-NU laboratories developed Kazakh Dependency Treebank for parsing.

In the third stage, it will be tested whether a rule-based approach for identifying different aspects of apps mentioned in the reviews, in the context of scarce data, is more accurate than a data-driven approach.

4 Current progress

At the current stage, 3000 Kazakh comments are compiled. They were labeled manually according to emotional polarity and compared with pre-defined sentiment classification on Google Play Market, The second stage was followed by defining code-switching, peculiar misspelling, and emoji identification. At the third stage, there is an ongoing process of text pre-processing. User comments were tokenized, lemmatized, and keywords were extracted in Sketch Engine to define a list of aspects. The next step will be processed in order to define the effective way of applying machine learning tasks for sentiment extraction.

Acknowledgements

I would like to express my gratitude to my supervisors Dr Richard Evans (University of Wolverhampton) and Prof Kiril Simov (New Bulgarian University) for their support, recommendations and valuable feedback for my research. I would also like to appreciate Prof Ruslan Mitkov, the EM TTI coordinator, he encouraged me to be brave enough to share my experience with this research.

References

Bing Liu, Lei Zhang and Shuai Wang. 2018. Deep learning for sentiment analysis. *Wiley*

Interdisciplinary Reviews: Data Mining and Knowledge Discovery, 8(4):e1253.

Bo Pang and Lillian Lee. 2008. Opinion mining and sentiment analysis. *Foundations and Trends in Information Retrieval*, 2(1-2):1-135. https://doi.org/10.1561/1500000114

Daniel Jurafsky and James H. Martin. 2020. Naive Bayes and Sentiment Classification. *Speech and Language Processings*. Stanford University Press, USA. https://web.stanford.edu/~jurafsky/slp3/

Petter Mæhlum, Jeremy Barnes, Lilja Øvrelid, and Erik Velldal. 2019. Annotating evaluative sentences for sentiment analysis: a dataset for Norwegian. SANT project (Sentiment Analysis for Norwegian Text. In *the Proceedings of SANT project (Sentiment Analysis for Norwegian Text), Research Council of Norway, 10*

Banu Yergesh, Gulmira Bekmanova, and Altynbek Sharipbay. 2017. Sentiment analysis on the hotel reviews in the Kazakh language. In *Proceedings of the International Conference on Computer Science and Engineering (UBMK).* Pages 790-794. https://doi.org/10.1109/UBMK.2017.8093531

D. Sitaram, Savitha Murthy, Debraj Ray, Devansh Sharma, and Kashyap Dhar. 2015. Sentiment analysis of mixed language employing Hindi-English code switching. In *Proceedings of the International Conference on Machine Learning and Cybernetics (ICMLC).* Pages 271-276.

Zhanibek Kozhirbayev, Zhandos Yessenbayev, and Aibek Makazhanov. 2018. Document and Word-level Language Identification for Noisy User Generated Text. In *Proceedings of IEEE 12th International Conference on Application of Information and Communication Technologies (AICT).* Pages 1-4.

Arman Zharmagambetov and N.S. Sakenovich. 2016. On One Approach of Solving Sentiment Analysis Task for Kazakh and Russian Languages. In *Proceedings of ICCCI 8th International Conference on Computational Collective Intelligence.* Halkidiki, Greece, pages 1-9.
https://doi.org/10.1007/978-3-319-45246-3_51

Disambiguating Grammatical Number and Gender With BERT

Annegret Janzso
Saarland University
Department of Language Science and Technology
66123 Saarbrücken, Germany
s8anjanz@stud.uni-saarland.de

Abstract

Accurately dealing with any type of ambiguity is a major task in Natural Language Processing, with great advances recently reached due to the development of context dependent language models and the use of word or sentence embeddings. In this context, our work aimed at determining how the popular language representation model BERT handles ambiguity of nouns in grammatical number and gender in different languages. This work shows that models trained on one specific language achieve better results for the disambiguation process than multilingual models. Also, ambiguity is generally better dealt with in grammatical number than it is in grammatical gender, reaching greater distance values from one to another in direct comparisons of individual word sense embeddings. The overall results show also that the amount of data needed for training monolingual models as well as application should not be underestimated.

1 Introduction

A challenge in Natural Language Processing (NLP) resides in the accurate automatic sense disambiguation of words and phrases. An often cited example of ambiguity is the one between *bank* ("An institution where one can place and borrow money and take care of financial affairs.") and *bank* ("An edge of river, lake, or other watercourse.") in English.[1] While a person is able to get the right meaning of the word from context, the same skill is now expected from contextual language models.

The goal of our work, however, is to find out if and how well contextual meaning representations can handle sense ambiguities in grammatical gender and number. Further, this paper aims to show differences in disambiguation in between different languages, ambiguity types, and pre-existing models. For these tasks, German and Spanish are used for gender and number ambiguities, and English for number ambiguities only (see section 3). Ambiguity in grammatical number is similar to the example mentioned above, as the plural form of a word might also mean something different from the mere quantity. In this case, the Language Model (LM) needs to disambiguate the meaning of plurals considering only the current context. For grammatical gender ambiguity - that is, words that can occur in more than one gender, with their meaning dependent on that factor - additional cues to the current meaning can be found in words that are connected to the currently observed ambiguous word, such as accordingly gendered determina or adjectives.
This specific skill of disambiguation of LMs is tested on BERT word embeddings (see section 4.2), based on data of three different languages: German (section 3.1) and Spanish (section 3.2), which contain both types of ambiguity, and English (section 3.3), which contains only ambiguity in grammatical number, but has been included due to the large amount of available data for testing (see section 4.1).

2 Related Work

While existing work on ambiguity mostly focuses on a more general definition of the term, grammatical gender and number have mostly been left aside. However, there has been research on gender bias in Language Models. Bartl et al. (2020) found a gender-bias for English in BERT similar to the gender-bias occurring with names of professions. For German, this effect has been found to be less strong, due to morphological gender markings. Seeing how a language without grammatical gender shows a higher gender bias than a language with such, this topic appears to be rather drifting

[1]Definitions taken from Wiktionary: https://en.wiktionary.org/wiki/bank

Proceedings of the Student Research Workshop associated with RANLP-2021, pages 69–77,
held online, Sep 1–3, 2021.
https://doi.org/10.26615/issn.2603-2821.2021_011

in a direction of biological gender and social prejudice connected with gender, which, according to Bartl et al. (2020), can be solved by grammatical gender in form of morphological markings, as this occurs in German. These results show a possibility to search for a gender bias in the disambiguation process of BERT for languages such as German or Spanish.

Concerning ambiguity in grammatical number, Gromann and Declerck (2019) analyses how plural entries included in Princeton WordNet (Princeton University, 2010) are encoded in word embeddings using Word2Vec (Mikolov et al., 2013) and GloVe (Pennington et al., 2014), thereby showing the convergence between distributed representations of plurals bearing a specific sense, as well as their symbolic representation proposed in WordNet. They bring up examples like *people - peoples*: Both words occur in plural form. However, *people* can be treated as a singular term, meaning 'the body of citizens of a state or country' (Definition given by Princeton Wordnet (Princeton University, 2010)). *Peoples* can be used as the plural of people, but can also refer to 'the human beings of a particular nation or community or ethnic group' (Definition given by Princeton Wordnet (Princeton University, 2010)). This shows that:

1. the singular and plural form of a word don't necessarily share all their meanings and

2. a word can function as a plural form for some senses, but as a singular form for other senses

This shows further that there is a lot of possibility for ambiguity in grammatical number, making it just as relevant as grammatical gender in a task of disambiguation.

Considering sense already during training, instead of researching on existing models, has been shown to be a promising approach (see Blevins and Zettlemoyer (2020), Levine et al. (2019)) for English data. These approaches add information on senses or glosses to the training process, thereby considering this additional knowledge in all applicational usage.

Morphological approaches have also shown promising results in English, German (Cotterell and Schütze, 2018) and Hebrew (Avraham and Goldberg, 2017). Future research in that direction will show if these approaches can improve disambiguation of those ambiguities that contain relevant morphological cues (see Corbett (2007)).

Observations of morphological content of sentences, including grammatical number and gender, have shown that BERT achieves better results for morphologically simple languages, in comparison to morphologically more complex languages such as German or Russian (see Edmiston (2020)). This work shows that BERT is able to detect and disambiguate such morphological content based on contextual cues, but does not achieve human-like results.

3 Ambiguity in Grammatical Gender and Number

The present work takes focus on ambiguity occurring in grammatical number and gender.

Ambiguity in grammatical number occurs if a word **w** has a plural **p** that has a standing meaning of its own, that is not only expressing a quantity associated with the word. An example in English is given by the word *glass*; its plural *glasses* can either mean *multiple items of the object named glass*, or *an object that is worn on one's face to increase eyesight*. While both meanings of *glasses* appear to be etymologically related, they do mean different things, and one meaning is independent of the meaning of the singular word *glass*.

Ambiguity in grammatical gender is given when a word **w** is ambiguous, while **w** can be assigned to at two or more different grammatical genders **g** and **g'**, and the standing meaning is dependent on the assigned gender. A German example is displayed in Table 1.

Gender	Word	Meaning
masculine	[der] Kiefer	[the] jaw
feminine	[die] Kiefer	[the] pine tree

Table 1: Differences in gender for the German word *Kiefer* with a change in meaning.

This work deals with grammatical number ambiguity in English, German, and Spanish, and grammatical gender ambiguity in German and Spanish. The following sections handle languages-specific details related to such ambiguities.

3.1 German

The German language contains both grammatical gender and grammatical number ambiguity.

Grammatical number ambiguity often occurs when two words **w** and **p** that look like they are forming a singular-plural pair have different meanings. In fact the two words are not forming such a pair, but are the cases of a singulare tantum and a case of plurale tantum, as can be seen in Table 2

Number	Word	Meaning
Singular	Schuld	guilt
Plural	Schulden	debt

Table 2: Different meanings depending on the grammatical number in German.

Here, **w** equals *Schuld* and **p** equals *Schulden*. The morphological *-en* ending is often added to German nouns to create a plural, making **w** and **p** appear as a singular-plural pair, but they are a pair of singulare tantum and plurale tantum, each with their particular meaning. German has three different grammatical genders: masculine, feminine, and neutral. When the grammatical gender of a word changes, so do its article and adjectives in the sentence, which are a good clue to gender detection, and therefore possibly also for meaning disambiguation. Grammatical gender ambiguity, as described in section 3, occurs when an ambiguous word w can be assigned two or more grammatical genders, and is assigned a different meaning for each. The last part is important, because some words can be used in more than one grammatical gender, without having a different meaning, as shown in Table 3. An example of actual gender ambiguity in German is shown in Table 1.

Gender	Word	Meaning
masculine	[der] Paprika	[the] bell pepper
feminine	[die] Paprika	[the] bell pepper

Table 3: Differences in gender for the German word *Paprika* without a change in meaning.

3.2 Spanish

Just like in German, it is possible to observe both types of ambiguity defined above in section 3 in Spanish. Grammatical number ambiguity usually occurs when the plural **p** of a word **w** is ambiguous, and one meaning has no singular term, or one that is different to **w**. An example can be found in the word *esposa*, as shown in Table 4.

Number	Word	Meaning 1	Meaning 2
Singular	esposa	wife	
Plural	esposas	wives	handcuffs

Table 4: Change in meaning depending on grammatical number in Spanish.

For grammatical gender ambiguity, there are two grammatical genders in Spanish: masculine and feminine. Other than that, it is defined the same way it is for German in section 3.1. An example can be the word *cólera*, as shown in Table 5

Gender	Word	Meaning
masculine	[el] cólera	[the] cholera
feminine	[la] cólera	[the] anger

Table 5: Change in meaning depending on grammatical gender in Spanish.

3.3 English

Since English is (in its majority) genderless, it is enough to state that the present work in English deals only with ambiguity in grammatical number.

Number ambiguity in English usually occurs when the plural p of a word **w** is ambiguous, and one meaning has no singular term, or one that is different to **w**. Other cases - such as a plural p being able to used as a singular term **w**, which can be assigned another plural term **p'** - have been observed in other works (e.g. Gromann and Declerck (2019)) with examples such as *person* for **w**, *people* for **p**, and *peoples* for **p'**. These types of occurrences, however, have not been included in this work.

An example on grammatical number ambiguity in English is described in section 3 with the terms *glass* and *glasses*.

4 Methodology

In the following sections, the methods used to compute and compare embedding vectors are described. Section 4.1 describes the data and its necessary information. Section 4.2 lists the pretrained BERT models that have been used to retrieve results, which then have been evaluated using the methods described in section 4.3. The actual results and evaluation outcomes are later described in section 5.

4.1 Data

Wiktionary (Wikimedia, 2021b) is a free online dictionary, created by the Wikimedia Foundation

(Wikimedia, 2021a), providing a range of XML data dumps. It contains information of over 170 languages, and provides detailed information on every word, including Pronunciation, Etymology, Translations, and of course grammatical number and gender, as well as according meanings and example sentences, when any information of a type is available.

Our work uses three so-called Wiktionary dumps (one per language) from July 2021. Each dump has been parsed by taking individual changes in between dumps into account, and information relevant to the task (title, possible senses, example sentences, possible plurals, grammatical number, grammatical gender) have been filtered out for all noun entries. Some entries of the dump of one language are written for words in another language, e.g. there might be an entry for a Spanish word in the English dump. When this happened for one of the three languages used in this work, these entries have also been parsed and saved in additional files, so they could later be used as additional data for their languages.

Entries without the necessary information (e.g. missing example sentences for context) have been discarded, if there was no other way to retrieve the needed information from another dump.

There are significant differences in the size of each dataset, which have been further adjusted to eliminate entries irrelevant for the tasks at hand - such as word types other than nouns, proper names, and entries without any of the observed ambiguities.

To gather additional example sentences for English entry data, NLTK WordNet (Princeton University, 2010) has been used. For any English noun without an example sentence, the word was looked up in WordNet and all available senses and example sentences have been added to the collected data.[2]

An idea of how much data is available to use per language can be given by an overview of iterations used when computing word embeddings (see Table 12 in the appendix). For each language, only a few examples will be used for representation purposes in this paper. Unfortunately, only a small amount of data is available for Spanish, which means only a small amount of possible comparisons. Overall there was not enough data on Spanish to compute vector embedding distances, which is why this part is not included in the results in section 5.

4.2 BERT

BERT (Devlin et al., 2018) is a bidirectional language model and is by now a commonly used tool for NLP. The goal is to test its ability of disambiguation with regard to grammatical gender and number, as a representative of current methods, by computing word embeddings of ambiguous words in specific contexts and specifics meanings. Also, the many pre-existing models available for BERT eliminate the need to train any models for the purposes of our work.

Four pre-trained models have been used here:

- BERT base uncased (Devlin et al., 2018)
- BERT base multilingual uncased (Devlin et al., 2018)
- BERT base German uncased[3]
- BERT base Spanish wwm uncased (Cañete et al., 2020)

By now, for every language, there is one language-specific pre-trained model; the multilingual model includes all three languages, among others.

4.3 Evaluation Methods

To compare the word embedding vectors created by BERT, three methods for computing distances in vector space have been used: **Cosine**, **Euclidean**, and **Manhattan** distance.

Cosine Distance represents the angle between the origins of two vectors. If cosine distance equals 0, the vectors are identical. The higher the distance value, the more different the vectors are from each other. Under the assumption that words with the same meaning will also have the same or similar embedding vectors, and words with distinguished meanings shouldn't, this means that if BERT can properly disambiguate words in this task, the cosine distance should be rather large for ambiguous words with different meanings. If, however, cosine distance is small and close to 0, this would translate as BERT not properly disambiguating the word in it's multiple meanings.

[2]Some example sentences in WordNet contain a synonym of a word instead of the word that is needed. In these cases, the synonym has been replaced by the word in question. This may lead to grammatical errors within the sentence, which has been ignored.

[3]`https://huggingface.co/dbmdz/bert-base-german-uncased`

Given that computing distance by angle in a multi-dimensional vector space might be imprecise in some cases, additional methods have been used. Euclidean Distance portraits the shortest distance from one point in vector space to another, regardless of dimensionality. Similar to Euclidean Distance, a value of 0 means the embedding vectors appear to be identical, whereas larger values portrait the opposite.

A third method used is Manhattan Distance, which, given a rectangle formed by the two points in vector space, is computed by the sum of the lengths of this rectangle. The resulting values are to be treated similarly to the values of Cosine and Euclidean Distance.

5 Results

Distances are compared between ambiguity-types: Comparing results of number-ambiguity to gender-ambiguity shows which of the two is processed better. Comparison of either to 'classic' ambiguity, without a change in number or gender, shows if there is any improvement due to additional contextual cues. Distances between two different, non-ambiguous words are treated as baseline: When ambiguous words have a similar distance as non-ambiguous words, the disambiguation process was successful. These results are presented in section 5.1.

Differences occurring due to the use of different models (multilingual or language specific) show the relevance of being specific to one language. These comparisons can be found in section 5.2.

Due to a huge lack of data, especially in example sentences that would be required to provide context, no distances could be computed on Spanish data. Computed data on Spanish ambiguity in grammatical gender only contained words where the sense stays the same with either possibility of gender. Computed data on Spanish ambiguity in grammatical number only contained words in singular, but none in plural. Therefore, this language is left out in further comparisons. For all other languages, the words and senses that have been used for comparisons in this paper can be found in Table 13 in the appendix.

Cosine Distances have been left out of the tables for results, as most were computed to be 0.0. Those with different values showed similar tendencies to the results of euclidean and manhattan distance, which can be compared better.

Sg	**Pl**	**Euc**	**Man**
kitchening	kitchenings	$1.54e^{+75}$	$7.68e^{+75}$
wood	woods	0.321458	8.897009
gen	gens	$1.55e^{+75}$	$7.74e^{+75}$
W	**W'**		
kitchening	wood	$1.54e^{+75}$	$7.69e^{+75}$
kitchening	gen	$1.54e^{+75}$	$7.69e^{+75}$
wood	gen	0.0	8.550618

Table 6: Results for ambiguity in grammatical number in English in comparison to words without relation of number (monolingual model)
Sg=Singular, Pl=Plural, Euc=Euclidean Distance, Man=Manhattan Distance, W=Word

Sg	**Pl**	**Euc**	**Man**
kitchening	kitchenings	0.213219	5.906484
wood	woods	0.072258	2.002483
gen	gens	$1.51e^{+75}$	$7.54e^{+75}$
W	**W'**		
kitchening	wood	0.098116	2.719078
kitchening	gen	0.106438	2.949704
wood	gen	0.008322	0.230625

Table 7: Results for ambiguity in grammatical number in English in comparison to words without relation of number (multilingual model)
Sg=Singular, Pl=Plural, Euc=Euclidean Distance, Man=Manhattan Distance, W=Word

W	**G**	**G'**	**Euc**	**Man**
Band	m	n	0.209174	5.799105
Gehalt	n	m	0.086309	2.403371
Leiter	f	m	0.194705	5.395817
W	**W'**	**G**	**Euc**	**Man**
Band	Leiter	m	0.219066	3.717639
Band	Gehalt	n	0.160602	4.445368
Leiter	Gehalt	m	0.144773	4.006747

Table 8: Results for ambiguity in grammatical gender in German in comparison to words without relation of gender (monolingual model)
W=Word, G=Gender, Euc=Euclidean Distance, Man=Manhattan Distance

W	G	G'	Euc	Man
Band	m	n	0.248292	6.871943
Gehalt	n	m	0.198916	5.508927
Leiter	f	m	0.008563	0.237300
W	**W'**	**G**	**Euc**	**Man**
Band	Leiter	m	0.204392	5.665711
Band	Gehalt	n	0.092686	2.568588
Leiter	Gehalt	m	0.062330	1.742512

Table 9: Results for ambiguity in grammatical gender in German in comparison to words without relation of gender (multilingual model)
W=Word, G=Gender, Euc=Euclidean Distance, Man=Manhattan Distance

Sg	Pl	Euc	Man
Schuld	Schulden	0.124265	3.444058
Sasse	Sassen	0.093512	2.590606
Barre	Barren	0.0	1.315709
W	**W'**	**Euc**	**Man**
Schuld	Sasse	0.173317	4.812258
Schuld	Barre	$1.48e^{+75}$	$7.27e^{+75}$
Sasse	Barre	$1.48e^{+75}$	$7.27e^{+75}$

Table 10: Results for ambiguity in grammatical number in German in comparison to words without relation of number (monolingual model)
Sg=Singular, Pl=Plural, Euc=Euclidean Distance, Man=Manhattan Distance

Sg	Pl	Euc	Man
Schuld	Schulden	0.066630	1.846514
Sasse	Sassen	0.167143	4.638568
Barre	Barren	0.017129	0.474700
W	**W'**	**Euc**	**Man**
Schuld	Sasse	0.103715	2.899168
Schuld	Barre	0.034782	0.963905
Sasse	Barre	0.138497	3.853023

Table 11: Results for ambiguity in grammatical number in German in comparison to words without relation of number (multilingual model)
Sg=Singular, Pl=Plural, Euc=Euclidean Distance, Man=Manhattan Distance

5.1 Number and Gender Ambiguity

Cosine distance, euclidean distance, and manhattan distance have been computed for word pairs on grammatical gender for German and grammatical number for English and German. Comparisons of individual words out of those pairs, which do not contain such a relation of grammatical gender or number (respectively), are used as a baseline.

For ambiguity in grammatical number in English, results are found in Tables 6 and 7 for mono- and multilingual models, respectively. Results regarding the differences between the two models can be found in section 5.2. The results show similar results for ambiguous and non-ambiguous word pairs.

For ambiguity in grammatical gender in German, results are found in Tables 8 and 9 for mono- and multilingual models, respectively. The results show similar results for ambiguous and non-ambiguous word pairs, however the ambiguous word pairs achieve slightly larger distances in some cases.

For ambiguity in grammatical number in German, results are found in Tables 10 and 11 for mono- and multilingual models, respectively. Just like for ambiguity in grammatical gender, results for ambiguous and non-ambiguous word pairs are similar, but slightly larger distances have been computed for non-ambiguous word pairs, with exception of the word pair of *Schuld* and *Schulden*, which overall achieved rather high distance values.

5.2 Monolingual and Multilingual Models

For ambiguity in grammatical number in English, results can be found in Table 6 and Table 7 for the mono- and multilingual models, respectively. Overall, the monolingual model was able to disambiguate better than the multilingual model, resulting in greater distances for both methods of distance computations. Distances are greater in the monolingual model for the ambiguous as well as the non-ambiguous case.

For ambiguity in grammatical gender in German, results can be found in Table 8 and Table 9 for the mono- and multilingual models, respectively. Overall, the models achieved very similar results. Both models perform slightly better on ambiguous than on non-ambiguous data.

For ambiguity in grammatical number in German, results can be found in Table 10 and 11 for the mono- and multilingual models, respectively. Overall, the monolingual model was able to disambiguate better than the multilingual model, resulting in greater distances for both methods of distance computations. Distances are slightly greater in the monolingual model for the ambiguous case, but much greater for the non-ambiguous case.

6 Discussion

Given the results found in section 5.1, BERT can disambiguate ambiguity in grammatical number in English similarly well as non-ambiguous word pairs. The same goes for ambiguity in grammatical gender in German. Overall, ambiguity in grammatical number in German could also be disambiguated well, but not as well as for the same type of data in English. A reason for this outcome might be more available data to compute word embeddings from or possible differences in amounts of data per language during training of the individual models.

Ambiguity in grammatical number could be dismbiguated better than for grammatical gender, which is possibly due to additional morphological cues within the word, or in some cases a more notable difference within the provided context.

Given the results found in section 5.2, the monolingual model bert-base-uncased outperformed the multilingual model bert-base-multilingual on English data. Concerning ambiguity in grammatical gender in German, both models performed similarly well on both ambiguous and non-ambiguous data. In the case of ambiguity in grammatical number in German, the monolingual model outperformed the multilingual model, achieving slightly greater results for ambiguous data, and much greater results for non-ambiguous data. Overall did the multilingual model perform better on German data, especially on ambiguity in grammatical gender, while it performs similarly well on ambiguity in grammatical number for both languages. The English monolingual model achieved much larger distances overall in comparison to the German monolingual model.

Using monolingual models is rewarded with better disambiguation, showing that it is well worth the time invested in the creation of such models, as the multilingual counterpart does well, but by far not as good. It is, however, a great way to include minority languages with not enough data to create individual language models. For languages like English and German, however, monolingual models appear to be the way to go, at least for disambiguation tasks.

7 Conclusion

This work shows that basic BERT models for English are better adapt to specific types of ambiguity than those for other languages like German, shown by the greater distances reached in the given evaluation methods. However, the multilingual model did perform better on German data than on English data, showing that a change of focus can improve results on languages with less data, but overall does not perform as well as language specific models.

This work shows a need for well-trained monolingual models, which appear to provide a better possibility of focus on disambiguation tasks. Further, available data such as provided by Wiktionary (Wikimedia, 2021b) needs to increase.

Interesting expansions of this work could come with approaches such as SenseBERT (Levine et al., 2019) - a BERT model that is trained on WordNet (Princeton University, 2010) supersenses - which might be able to achieve better results in disambiguation, and goes along with the findings of Blevins and Zettlemoyer (2020). Switching from word level to a morphological level could also bring up interesting results (Avraham and Goldberg (2017), Cotterell and Schütze (2018)).

Acknowledgements

This work has been partly supported by the Horizon 2020 research and innovation programme with the project Prêt-à-LLOD (grant agreement no. 825182) at DFKI Saarbrücken. I thank Thierry Declerck, Josef van Genabith, and Lucia Donatelli for their helpful advice.

References

Oded Avraham and Yoav Goldberg. 2017. The interplay of semantics and morphology in word embeddings. *CoRR*, abs/1704.01938.

Marion Bartl, Malvina Nissim, and Albert Gatt. 2020. Unmasking contextual stereotypes: Measuring and mitigating bert's gender bias. *CoRR*, abs/2010.14534.

Terra Blevins and Luke Zettlemoyer. 2020. Moving down the long tail of word sense disambiguation with gloss-informed biencoders. *CoRR*, abs/2005.02590.

José Cañete, Gabriel Chaperon, Rodrigo Fuentes, Jou-Hui Ho, Hojin Kang, and Jorge Pérez. 2020. Spanish pre-trained bert model and evaluation data. *PML4DC at ICLR 2020*.

Greville G. Corbett. 2007. Canonical typology, suppletion, and possible words. *Language*, 83(1):8–42.

Ryan Cotterell and Hinrich Schütze. 2018. Joint semantic synthesis and morphological analysis of the derived word. *Trans. Assoc. Comput. Linguistics*, 6:33–48.

Jacob Devlin, Ming-Wei Chang, Kenton Lee, and Kristina Toutanova. 2018. BERT: pre-training of deep bidirectional transformers for language understanding. *CoRR*, abs/1810.04805.

Daniel Edmiston. 2020. A systematic analysis of morphological content in BERT models for multiple languages. *CoRR*, abs/2004.03032.

Dagmar Gromann and Thierry Declerck. 2019. Towards the Detection and Formal Representation of Semantic Shifts in Inflectional Morphology. In *2nd Conference on Language, Data and Knowledge (LDK 2019)*, volume 70 of *OpenAccess Series in Informatics (OASIcs)*, pages 21:1–21:15, Dagstuhl, Germany. Schloss Dagstuhl–Leibniz-Zentrum fuer Informatik.

Yoav Levine, Barak Lenz, Or Dagan, Dan Padnos, Or Sharir, Shai Shalev-Shwartz, Amnon Shashua, and Yoav Shoham. 2019. Sensebert: Driving some sense into BERT. *CoRR*, abs/1908.05646.

Tomás Mikolov, Quoc V. Le, and Ilya Sutskever. 2013. Exploiting similarities among languages for machine translation. *CoRR*, abs/1309.4168.

Jeffrey Pennington, Richard Socher, and Christopher D Manning. 2014. GloVe : Global Vectors for Word Representation. *Proceedings of the 2014 Conference on EMNLP*, pages 1532–1543.

Princeton University. 2010. About wordnet. `https://wordnet.princeton.edu/`.

Wikimedia. 2021a. Wikimedia foundation. `https://wikimediafoundation.org/`.

Wikimedia. 2021b. Wiktionary. `https://www.wiktionary.org/`.

A Appendix

Language	Type	Count
German	Number	1606
	Gender	1672
	Neither	99250
Spanish	Number	22
	Gender	42
	Neither	6233
English	Number	151610
	Neither	203077

Table 12: Amount of iterations per language and ambiguity type used to compute word embeddings.

English		
Word	**Number**	**Sense**
kitchening	Sg	food preparation
kitchenings	Pl	scraps of food waste [...]
wood	Sg	a peckerwood
woods	Pl	A dense collection of trees [...]
gen	Sg	a specific version of something in chronological sequence
gens	Pl	a tribal subgroup [...]
German		
Word	**Gender**	**Sense**
Band	m	singular book that is part of a series [...]
	n	the [...] ribbon that is stretched over a finish line
Gehalt	n	amount of money that is [...] paid to workers
	m	the mental [...] content of a creative work
Leiter	f	stitch in knitted [...] wares [...] that got loose [...]
	m	material that lets energy [...] flow through
Word	**Number**	**Sense**
Schuld	Sg	moral misbehaviour [...]
Schulden	Pl	the entire obligations (passiva) of a person [...]
Sasse	Sg	hunting language: a flat trough, used by rabbits as a spot for rest and hiding
Sassen	Pl	historical landmark in east middle europe [...]
Barre	Sg	area of shallow water
Barren	Pl	metal poured in form

Table 13: Words and senses used for comparisons in this paper; the (translated) senses come from the according entries in Wiktionary

Towards a Language Model for Temporal Commonsense Reasoning

Mayuko Kimura[1] **Lis Kanashiro Pereira**[2] **Ichiro Kobayashi**[3]
Ochanomizu University, Japan
[1,3]{g1720512,koba}@is.ocha.ac.jp
[2]kanashiro.pereira@ocha.ac.jp

Abstract

Temporal commonsense reasoning is a challenging task as it requires temporal knowledge usually not explicitly stated in text. In this work, we propose an ensemble model for temporal commonsense reasoning. Our model relies on pre-trained contextual representations from transformer-based language models (i.e., BERT), and on a variety of training methods for enhancing model generalization: 1) multi-step fine-tuning using carefully selected auxiliary tasks and datasets, and 2) a specifically designed temporal task-adaptive pre-trainig task aimed to capture temporal commonsense knowledge. Our model greatly outperforms the standard fine-tuning approach and strong baselines on the MC-TACO dataset.

1 Introduction

Although recent pre-trained language models such as BERT (Devlin et al., 2019) have achieved great success in a wide range of natural language processing (NLP) tasks, these models may still perform poorly on temporal reasoning scenarios. Ribeiro et al. (2020) has shown that such models often fail to make even simple temporal distinctions, for example, to distinguish the words *before* and *after*, resulting in degraded performance. An especially challenging task is temporal commonsense reasoning. For instance, given two events "going on a vacation" and "going for a walk", while most humans would know that a vacation is typically longer and occurs less often than a walk, computers have difficulty understanding and reasoning about temporal commonsense (Zhou et al., 2019).

In this paper, we focus on developing a model for temporal commonsense reasoning. Following best practices from recent work on enhancing model generalization, we propose a model that enriches pre-trained contextual representations with temporal knowledge and general commonsense knowledge by leveraging carefully selected auxiliary datasets in a multi-step fine-tuning setting. Moreover, we specifically designed a temporal task-adaptive pre-training task aimed to capture temporal commonsense knowledge by masking temporal indicators in text.

We evaluate our model on the challenging Multiple Choice Temporal Common-sense (MC-TACO) dataset (Zhou et al., 2019). In our experiments, our model substantially outperforms the standard fine-tuning approach, as well as other strong baselines.

2 Temporal Commonsense Reasoning Task

This task entirely focuses on a specific reasoning capability: temporal commonsense. Zhou et al. (2019) used crowdsourcing to create the Multiple Choice Temporal Common-sense (MC-TACO) dataset, which collects the temporal knowledge of five temporal properties: (1) duration (how long an event takes), (2) temporal ordering (typical order of events), (3) typical time (when an event occurs), (4) frequency (how often an event occurs), and (5) stationarity (whether a state is maintained for a very long time or indefinitely). It contains 13k tuples, each consisting of a sentence, a question, and a candidate answer, that should be judged as plausible or not. The sentences are taken from different sources such as news, Wikipedia and textbooks. An example from the dataset is below. The correct answer is in **bold**.

> *Paragraph*: Growing up on a farm near St. Paul, L. Mark Bailey didn't dream of becoming a judge.
> *Question*: How many years did it take for Mark to become a judge?
> a) 63 years b) 7 weeks c) **7 years**
> d) 7 seconds e) 7 hours
> *Reasoning Type*: Duration

Proceedings of the Student Research Workshop associated with RANLP-2021, pages 78–84,
held online, Sep 1–3, 2021.
https://doi.org/10.26615/issn.2603-2821.2021_012

We use the MC-TACO dataset for evaluating the performance of our model.

3 Model

Our work uses BERT (Devlin et al., 2019) as the text encoder. It has obtained high performance on several natural language understanding (NLU) benchmarks and it is relatively simple to adapt its architecture to downstream tasks. We focus on exploring different training techniques using BERT (Devlin et al., 2019), given its superior performance on a wide range of NLP tasks. The text encoder and the training methods used in our model are detailed below.

3.1 Text Encoder

BERT (Devlin et al., 2019): We use the $\text{BERT}_{\text{BASE}}$ model and the $\text{BERT}_{\text{LARGE}}$ model released by the authors. The $\text{BERT}_{\text{BASE}}$ model consists of 12 transformer layers, 12 self-attention heads per layer, and a hidden size of 768. The $\text{BERT}_{\text{LARGE}}$ model consists of 24 transformer layers, 16 self-attention heads per layer, and a hidden size of 1024.

3.2 Training Methods

Multi-Step Fine-Tuning: Multi-step fine-tuning works by performing a second stage of pre-training with data-rich related supervised tasks. It has been shown to improve model robustness and performance, especially for data-constrained scenarios (Phang et al., 2018; Camburu et al., 2019). We first fine-tune BERT on carefully selected auxiliary tasks and datasets. This model's parameters are further refined by fine-tuning on the MC-TACO dataset. The auxiliary tasks and datasets we use are detailed below:

Event Duration Prediction Task: This task involves predicting the duration of an event in a span of text. We use TimeML (Saurí et al., 2006; Pan et al., 2006), a dataset with event duration annotated as lower and upper bounds. The task is to decide whether a given event has a duration longer or shorter than a day. An example of a sentence with an event (in bold) that has a duration shorter than a day is shown below:

> In Singapore, stocks **hit** a five year low.

Event Ordering Prediction Task: This task involves predicting the temporal relationship between a pair of input events in a span of text. In our work, we use the MATRES dataset (Ning et al., 2018). It originally contains 13,577 pairs of events annotated with a temporal relation (BEFORE, AFTER, EQUAL, VAGUE). The temporal annotations are performed on 256 English documents (and 20 more for evaluation) from the TimeBank (Pustejovsky et al., 2003), AQUAINT (Graff, 2002) and Platinum (UzZaman et al., 2013) datasets. An example of a sentence with two events (in bold) that hold the BEFORE relation:

> At one point , when it **(e1:became)** clear controllers could not contact the plane, someone **(e2:said)** a prayer.

Commonsense Reasoning Task: We propose to enrich the temporal commonsense reasoning task training by leveraging data from general commonsense knowledge task. Since the commonsense reasoning task commonly also involves reasoning about temporal events, e.g. what event(s) might happen before or after the current event, we hypothesize that temporal reasoning might benefit from it. In our experiments, we use the CosmosQA (Huang et al., 2019) and the SWAG (Zellers et al., 2018) datasets. An example from the CosmosQA dataset is below. The task is to choose the correct answer among four options. The correct answer is in **bold**.

> *Paragraph*: Did some errands today. My prime objectives were to get textbooks, find computer lab, find career services, get some groceries, turn in payment plan application, and find out when KEES money kicks in. I think it acts as a refund at the end of the semester at Murray, but I would be quite happy if it would work now.
>
> *Question*: What happens after I get the refund?
>
> *Option 1*: **I can pay my bills.**
> *Option 2*: I can relax.
> *Option 3*: I can sleep.
> *Option 4*: None of the above choices.

An example from the SWAG dataset is below. The task is to choose the correct ending among four options. The correct answer is in **bold**.

> *Question*: On stage, a woman takes a seat at the piano. She
>
> *Option 1*: sits on a bench as her sister plays with the doll.

Option 2: smiles with someone as the music plays.

Option 3: is in the crowd, watching the dancers.

Option 4: **nervously sets her fingers on the keys.**

We also experimented with task-adaptive pre-training on the MC-TACO dataset followed by fine-tuning on MC-TACO. The task-adaptive pre-training method is explained below.

Task-Adaptive Pre-Training (TAPT): Although BERT achieves good performance on only fine-tuning it on the target task, there might be a distributional mismatch between the pre-trained model and the target dataset. To alleviate this issue, performing continual pre-training using the target dataset can be useful to adapt the pre-trained model to the target task (Gururangan et al., 2020). In this setting, we perform continual pre-training on BERT using the MC-TACO dataset. More specifically, we conduct the masked language modeling and the next sentence prediction tasks on BERT using the MC-TACO dataset. The masked language modeling task randomly replaces a subset of tokens by a special token (e.g., [MASK]), and asks the model to predict them. The next sentence prediction task is a binary classification task that for a given sentence pair determines whether one follows the other in the original text (Liu et al., 2020). In addition, we also experimented with masking only the tokens that have a high TF-IDF score.

Temporal Task-Adaptive Pre-Training (Temporal TAPT): In this setting, instead of randomly mask words in the masked language modeling task, we mask time-related words. Those words include numbers, adverbs, adjectives, prepositions (before/after, every, often, etc.), and units of time (hours, years, etc.).

3.3 Ensemble Model

Ensemble of deep learning models has proven effective in improving test accuracy (Allen-Zhu and Li, 2020). We built different ensemble models by taking a majority vote of the outputs of a few independently trained models. Each single model was trained on standard fine-tuning, multi-step fine-tuning, task-adaptive pre-Training, or temporal task-adaptive pre-Training using BERT.

4 Experiments

4.1 Datasets

In this paper, we use MC-TACO as the training and evaluation dataset. In addition, we use the TimeML, MATRES, CosmosQA, and SWAG datasets as auxiliary datasets in the multi-step fine-tuning setting, as detailed in Section 3.2. The summary of the datasets is shown in Table 1.

	train	val	test
MC-TACO	-	3,783	9,442
TimeML	1,248	-	1,003
MATRES	12,716	-	838
CosmosQA	25,588	3,000	7,000
SWAG	73,546	20,006	20,005

Table 1: Summary of the datasets used in our experiments.

4.2 Implementation Details

For the multi-step fine-tuning experiments, the maximum sequence length, batch size, number of epochs, and the learning rate settings are shown in Table 2. For hyperparameter tuning, the parameters with the best accuracy on performing cross-validation on the MC-TACO evaluation set are chosen. In all experiments, we use $\text{BERT}_{\text{BASE}}$ as the text encoder unless stated otherwise.

	max seq_len	batch_size	# epochs	learning rate
MC-TACO	128	{32,**16**}	{3,4,**5**}	{**1e-5**,2e-5}
TimeML	128	{32,**16**}	{3,**4**,5}	{1e-5,**2e-5**}
MATRES	128	{32,**16**}	{**3**,4,5}	{**1e-5**,2e-5}
TimeML + MATRES	128	{32,**16**}	{**3**,4,5}	{1e-5,**2e-5**}
CosmosQA	256	32	{**1**,3,5}	{1e-5,**2e-5**}
SWAG	256	32	{1,**2**,3}	{1e-5,**2e-5**}

Table 2: Hyperparameter settings for the multi-step fine-tuning experiments. The parameters with best performance are shown in **bold**.

The maximum sequence length, batch size, number of epochs, and the learning rate settings for the TAPT and Temporal TAPT experiments are set to 128, 32, 3, and 3e-5, respectively.

We use the exact match (EM) and F1-score as the evaluation metrics. EM measures how many questions a system correctly labeled all candidate answers, while F1-score measures the average overlap between one's predictions and the ground truth.

4.3 Results

Multi-Step Fine-Tuning: The results of the multi-step fine-tuning experiments are shown in Table 3. We used $\text{BERT}_{\text{BASE}}$ as the text encoder.

fine-tuned on	EM [%]	F1 [%]
MC-TACO	40.9 (42.1)	69.9 (68.2)
TimeML→MC-TACO	41.3 (40.2)	70.3 (67.1)
MATRES→MC-TACO	39.6 (42.0)	69.2 (69.4)
TimeML + MATRES →MC-TACO	40.2 (40.9)	70.2 (67.7)
CosmosQA→MC-TACO	42.2 (41.7)	70.4 (68.9)
SWAG→MC-TACO	**43.0 (42.0)**	**71.7 (67.8)**

Table 3: Test results on multi-step fine-tuning using $\text{BERT}_{\text{BASE}}$. The cross-validation results are shown in parenthesis.

The MC-TACO model denotes the model that uses standard single-stage fine-tuning using MC-TACO, and the TimeML→MC-TACO, TimeML + MATRES, the CosmosQA→MC-TACO, and the SWAG→MC-TACO models denote the models that use multi-step fine-tuning using other datasets as the first stage fine-tuning and MC-TACO as the second-stage fine-tuning. The TimeML + MATRES →MC-TACO model denotes the model that combined the TimeML and MATRES datasets for the first stage of fine-tuning. We can observe that multi-step fine-tuning improved the overall accuracy, although there were some differences depending on the dataset used. The best results were obtained when we fine-tune on SWAG followed by MC-TACO (SWAG→MC-TACO model). This indicates that enriching training with general commonsense knowledge is beneficial.

We also conducted experiments using $\text{BERT}_{\text{LARGE}}$, where we can observe similar tendency in the results compared to $\text{BERT}_{\text{BASE}}$. The results are shown in Table 4.

fine-tuned on	EM [%]	F1 [%]
MC-TACO	42.6 (42.9)	70.9 (71.0)
TimeML→MC-TACO	44.8 (43.7)	72.8 (70.8)
CosmosQA→MC-TACO	**46.3** (43.6)	73.4 (70.7)
SWAG→MC-TACO	46.2 **(44.7)**	**73.6 (72.6)**

Table 4: Test results on multi-step fine-tuning using $\text{BERT}_{\text{LARGE}}$. The cross-validation results are shown in parenthesis.

Task-Adaptive Pre-Training (TAPT): Table 5 shows the Task-Adaptive Pre-Training (TAPT) results where we randomly mask a subset of tokens. In order to check if we could further reduce the mismatch between the pre-trained model and the target task dataset, we also experimented with masking rates higher than BERT's default masking rate of 15%. However, the best accuracy was obtained with the 15% masking probability.

Masking Probability [%]	EM [%]	F1 [%]
15	**44.5 (45.2)**	**71.9 (72.4)**
30	43.5 (44.3)	71.9 (71.3)
60	42.8 (44.6)	71.1 (69.9)

Table 5: Task-Adaptive Pre-Training (TAPT) results when masking words randomly. The cross-validation results are shown in parenthesis.

We also experimented with masking the tokens that have a high TF-IDF score. For each sentence, the candidate words for masking are the top-half words with the highest TF-IDF score. We also remove the stopwords when computing the TF-IDF. We experimented with two stopwords lists: nltk stopwords list [1] and sklearn stopwords list [2]. The results are shown in Table 6. Overall, using the nltk' stopwords achieved the best results.

stopwords = nltk		
Masking Probability [%]	EM [%]	F1 [%]
15	43.3 (43.9)	71.7 (69.4)
30	43.5 (44.3)	71.7 (70.9)
45	**44.4 (42.4)**	**72.3 (69.6)**
60	43.5 (44.3)	71.7 (71.0)
stopwords = sklearn		
Masking Probability [%]	EM [%]	F1 [%]
15	42.0 (43.6)	70.9 (71.4)
30	43.0 (45.3)	71.0 (71.2)
45	**43.0 (46.0)**	**71.4 (72.5)**
60	41.7 (45.8)	70.7 (71.4)

Table 6: Task-Adaptive Pre-Training (TAPT) results when masking words with a high TF-IDF score. The cross-validation results are shown in parenthesis.

Since the accuracy differs between using nltk's stopwords and sklearn's stopwords, we looked at the contents of each stopword and found that the stopwords from sklearn contained words related to time (i.e. numbers, prepositions such as before and after, adverbs, etc.) that ended up being removed, and not being masking candidate words. Therefore, we conducted a similar experiment in which we manually removed the time-related words from the sklearn stopwords. The results of the experiment are shown in Table 7.

As we can observe, the accuracy is higher compared to when using the original sklearn's stop-

[1] https://www.nltk.org/nltk_data/

[2] https://scikit-learn.org/stable/modules/feature_extraction.html#stop-words

Masking Probability [%]	EM [%]	F1 [%]
15	42.6 (42.4)	70.6 (69.9)
30	43.2 (43.5)	71.2 (69.9)
45	**44.1 (43.8)**	**71.8 (71.3)**
60	43.3 (44.3)	71.5 (71.1)

Table 7: Task-Adaptive Pre-Training (TAPT) results when masking words with a high TF-IDF score. The cross-validation results are shown in parenthesis. Here, we use the sklearn's stopwords without the time-related words.

words, indicating that it is not optimal to exclude words related to time from the calculation of TF-IDF. The accuracy of the TF-IDF experiment is about the same as that of randomly selecting words to be masked.

Next, we set a threshold value and try to mask words where TF-IDF exceeds this value. We set different threshold values based on the percentage of the total number of words that will be masked, and we treat them as a hyperparameter. For the stopwords, we use the nltk's stopwords and the sklearn's stopwords excluding the words related to time. The results are shown in Table 8.

TF-IDF Threshold	Masking Probability [%]	EM [%]	F1 [%]
stopwords = nltk			
0.35	19.3	41.8 (42.5)	70.4 (69.2)
0.3	28.5	**42.5 (40.9)**	**71.0 (69.5)**
0.25	45.6	41.8 (42.8)	70.7 (69.0)
stopwords = sklearn - time			
0.35	22.6	42.5 (43.2)	71.2 (68.8)
0.3	31.2	42.0 (40.9)	70.3 (68.1)
0.25	43.2	**42.5 (44.6)**	**71.0 (70.3)**

Table 8: Task-Adaptive Pre-Training (TAPT) results when masking words with a high TF-IDF score. The cross-validation results are shown in parenthesis. Here, we mask all words that exceed a TF-IDF threshold value.

We found that if we masked all the words where TF-IDF exceeded the threshold, the accuracy decreases. Therefore, we randomly select tokens to mask from the words that exceed the threshold value. The results for this setting are shown in Table 9. In some cases, the accuracy was improved over the default case where the tokens are randomly masked. On the other hand, it is difficult to find regularities in the threshold setting and the percentage of masking, thus masking focusing on TF-IDF may not be effective.

Temporal Task-Adaptive Pre-Training (Temporal TAPT): Here, time-related words (numbers, before/after, every, hour, etc.) have a higher masking probability than the other words. The results are shown in Table 10. Different form the TAPT experimentes, here, masking rates higher than BERT's default masking rate of 15% improves the performance, indicating that masking temporal indicators with a higher masking rate further helps the model to acquire temporal knowledge. Moreover, we found that if we masked all the time-related words (100% masking probability), the accuracy would decrease, but if we left a few words unmasked, the accuracy improves.

TF-IDF Threshold	Masking Probability [%]	EM [%]	F1 [%]
stopwords = nltk			
0.35	15	43.0 (44.0)	71.2 (71.0)
	30	43.6 (44.6)	71.2 (70.8)
	45	43.5 (44.1)	71.3 (71.4)
	60	**44.2 (43.1)**	**72.8 (70.3)**
0.3	15	43.1 (44.9)	71.0 (71.1)
	30	43.5 (44.7)	71.6 (71.5)
	45	43.2 (44.1)	71.8 (71.2)
	60	**44.1 (44.3)**	**71.8 (71.6)**
0.25	15	43.6 (43.2)	71.4 (70.6)
	30	**43.8 (44.7)**	71.0 (72.8)
	45	42.8 (44.2)	**72.0 (70.8)**
	60	42.0 (44.7)	71.0 (70.3)
stopwords = sklearn - time			
0.35	15	42.3 (44.3)	71.3 (71.8)
	30	**45.0 (45.8)**	**72.1 (70.9)**
	45	42.9 (44.8)	70.9 (72.1)
	60	45.0 (42.6)	71.9 (68.3)
0.3	15	**44.7 (43.6)**	**72.5 (71.0)**
	30	42.6 (44.8)	71.1 (71.9)
	45	42.8 (42.5)	70.8 (70.1)
	60	43.1 (44.8)	71.3 (70.9)
0.25	15	42.9 (43.6)	71.3 (70.7)
	30	43.4 (43.8)	71.6 (71.0)
	45	42.9 (45.6)	71.3 (70.6)
	60	**43.7 (43.3)**	**71.7 (68.8)**

Table 9: Task-Adaptive Pre-Training (TAPT) results when masking words with a high TF-IDF score. The cross-validation results are shown in parenthesis. Here, we randomly select tokens to mask from the words that exceed the threshold value.

Ensemble Model: We built different ensemble models by taking a majority vote of the outputs of a few independently trained models. Each single model was trained on standard fine-tuning, multi-step fine-tuning, Task-Adaptive Pre-Training, or Temporal Task-Adaptive Pre-Training using BERT. The results are shown in Table 11.

The experimental results show that ensembling improves accuracy. In particular, *pattern 4*, which uses three models: multi-step fine-tuning with CosmosQA, multi-step fine-tuning with SWAG, and

Masking Probability (time-related words) [%]	Masking Probability (others) [%]	EM [%]	F1 [%]
100	0	42.7 (46.6)	71.0 (71.7)
90	10	44.1 (43.3)	71.6 (70.1)
80	20	**45.1 (44.3)**	**72.7 (70.7)**
70	30	42.9 (42.6)	71.9 (69.5)

Table 10: Temporal Task-Adaptive Pre-Training (Temporal TAPT) results. The cross-validation results are shown in parenthesis. Here, time-related words (numbers, before/after, every, hour, etc.) are masked with higher probability than the other words.

model	pattern1	pattern2	pattern3	pattern4
MC-TACO			✓	
TimeML →MC-TACO	✓			
CosmosQA →MC-TACO	✓	✓	✓	✓
SWAG →MC-TACO	✓	✓	✓	✓
TAPT(random)		✓		
Temporal TAPT				✓
EM [%]	45.0	45.6	44.4	**46.5**
F1 [%]	72.9	73.2	72.0	**73.9**

Table 11: Ensemble Model results.

Temporal Task-Adaptive Pre-Training obtained the best performance, with an EM score of 46.5% and an F1-score of 73.9%.

This model also outperformed the model from Zhou et al. (2019): a BERT model with standard fine-tuning, and a time unit normalized BERT model, where the authors further add unit normalization to temporal expressions in candidate answers and fine-tune on the MC-TACO dataset. Table 12 shows the results.

model	EM [%]	F1 [%]
BERT	39.6	66.1
BERT + unit normalization	42.7	69.9
Ours	**46.5**	**73.9**
Human	75.8	87.1

Table 12: Comparison of our best ensemble model with the model from Zhou et al. (2019).

We also compared our best ensemble model with TACOLM, proposed by Zhou et al. (2020). TACOLM is a BERT model pre-trained on explicit and implicit mentions of temporal commonsense, extracted from a large corpus using pattern rules. The results are shown in Table 13. As we can observe, the accuracy of all the five temporal properties was improved by our model.

class	BERT	TACOLM	Ours
Duration	33.4	34.6	**36.9**
Ordering	36.5	35.1	**46.0**
Stationarity	57.6	57.9	**59.3**
Frequency	43.3	45.1	**49.3**
Typical Time	39.5	40.9	**46.2**

Table 13: Comparison of our best ensemble model with TACOLM (Zhou et al., 2020).

4.4 Discussion

In our experiments, we could observe that multi-step fine-tuning outperforms standard single-stage fine-tuning. Also, fine-tuning BERT in the first stage using Temporal TAPT followed by fine-tuning on MC-TACO obtained the best performance among all single models. This indicates that a careful choice of the words to be masked has an impact on the performance. On the other hand, when all the words related to time were masked, the accuracy deteriorated. We hypothesize this is because if all the words were masked, the information about time would disappear from the context, and inferences about temporal common sense would be difficult.

In the TAPT experiments with TF-IDF, we found it difficult to find a regularity regarding the threshold and the ratio of masking, and it is hard to claim that masking based on TF-IDF is effective. In this study, we focus on the temporal commonsense task, and since the data contains more words related to time than other tasks, the value of IDF becomes smaller, and it may be said that TF-IDF might not be optimal.

5 Conclusion

In this paper, we proposed a model for temporal commonsense reasoning. We specifically designed a temporal masked language model task aimed to capture temporal commonsense knowledge by masking temporal indicators in text and used it in a multi-step fine-tuning setting. Moreover, we found out that an ensemble of this model with other models achieves the best results, outperforming other state-of-the-art models. In order to improve our model, we plan to conduct attention and saliency analysis.

Acknowledgements

This study was financially supported by KAKENHI (18H05521). We express our gratitude for the support.

References

Zeyuan Allen-Zhu and Yuanzhi Li. 2020. Towards understanding ensemble, knowledge distillation and self-distillation in deep learning. *arXiv preprint arXiv:2012.09816*.

Oana-Maria Camburu, Vid Kocijan, Thomas Lukasiewicz, and Yordan Yordanov. 2019. A surprisingly robust trick for the winograd schema challenge.

Jacob Devlin, Ming-Wei Chang, Kenton Lee, and Kristina Toutanova. 2019. BERT: Pre-training of deep bidirectional transformers for language understanding. In *Proceedings of the 2019 Conference of the North American Chapter of the Association for Computational Linguistics: Human Language Technologies, Volume 1 (Long and Short Papers)*, pages 4171–4186, Minneapolis, Minnesota. Association for Computational Linguistics.

David Graff. 2002. *The AQUAINT corpus of English news text:[content copyright] Portions© 1998-2000 New York Times, Inc.,© 1998-2000 Associated Press, Inc.,© 1996-2000 Xinhua News Service*. Linguistic Data Consortium.

Suchin Gururangan, Ana Marasović, Swabha Swayamdipta, Kyle Lo, Iz Beltagy, Doug Downey, and Noah A. Smith. 2020. Don't stop pretraining: Adapt language models to domains and tasks. In *Proceedings of the 58th Annual Meeting of the Association for Computational Linguistics*, pages 8342–8360, Online. Association for Computational Linguistics.

Lifu Huang, Ronan Le Bras, Chandra Bhagavatula, and Yejin Choi. 2019. Cosmos QA: Machine reading comprehension with contextual commonsense reasoning. In *Proceedings of the 2019 Conference on Empirical Methods in Natural Language Processing and the 9th International Joint Conference on Natural Language Processing (EMNLP-IJCNLP)*, pages 2391–2401, Hong Kong, China. Association for Computational Linguistics.

Xiaodong Liu, Hao Cheng, Pengcheng He, Weizhu Chen, Yu Wang, Hoifung Poon, and Jianfeng Gao. 2020. Adversarial training for large neural language models. *arXiv preprint arXiv:2004.08994*.

Qiang Ning, Hao Wu, and Dan Roth. 2018. A multi-axis annotation scheme for event temporal relations". In *Proceedings of the 56th Annual Meeting of the Association for Computational Linguistics (Volume 1: Long Papers)*, pages 1318–1328, Melbourne, Australia. Association for Computational Linguistics.

Feng Pan, Rutu Mulkar-Mehta, and Jerry R Hobbs. 2006. Extending timeml with typical durations of events. In *Proceedings of the Workshop on Annotating and Reasoning about Time and Events*, pages 38–45.

Jason Phang, Thibault Févry, and Samuel R Bowman. 2018. Sentence encoders on stilts: Supplementary training on intermediate labeled-data tasks. *arXiv preprint arXiv:1811.01088*.

James Pustejovsky, Patrick Hanks, Roser Sauri, Andrew See, Robert Gaizauskas, Andrea Setzer, Dragomir Radev, Beth Sundheim, David Day, Lisa Ferro, et al. 2003. The timebank corpus. In *Corpus linguistics*, volume 2003, page 40. Lancaster, UK.

Marco Tulio Ribeiro, Tongshuang Wu, Carlos Guestrin, and Sameer Singh. 2020. Beyond accuracy: Behavioral testing of nlp models with checklist. *arXiv preprint arXiv:2005.04118*.

Roser Saurí, Jessica Littman, Bob Knippen, Robert Gaizauskas, Andrea Setzer, and James Pustejovsky. 2006. Timeml annotation guidelines. *Version*, 1(1):31.

Naushad UzZaman, Hector Llorens, Leon Derczynski, James Allen, Marc Verhagen, and James Pustejovsky. 2013. Semeval-2013 task 1: Tempeval-3: Evaluating time expressions, events, and temporal relations. In *Second Joint Conference on Lexical and Computational Semantics (* SEM), Volume 2: Proceedings of the Seventh International Workshop on Semantic Evaluation (SemEval 2013)*, pages 1–9.

Rowan Zellers, Yonatan Bisk, Roy Schwartz, and Yejin Choi. 2018. SWAG: A large-scale adversarial dataset for grounded commonsense inference. In *Proceedings of the 2018 Conference on Empirical Methods in Natural Language Processing*, pages 93–104, Brussels, Belgium. Association for Computational Linguistics.

Ben Zhou, Daniel Khashabi, Qiang Ning, and Dan Roth. 2019. "going on a vacation" takes longer than "going for a walk": A study of temporal commonsense understanding. In *Proceedings of the 2019 Conference on Empirical Methods in Natural Language Processing and the 9th International Joint Conference on Natural Language Processing (EMNLP-IJCNLP)*, pages 3363–3369, Hong Kong, China. Association for Computational Linguistics.

Ben Zhou, Qiang Ning, Daniel Khashabi, and Dan Roth. 2020. Temporal common sense acquisition with minimal supervision. In *Proceedings of the 58th Annual Meeting of the Association for Computational Linguistics*, pages 7579–7589, Online. Association for Computational Linguistics.

Text Preprocessing and its Implications in a Digital Humanities Project

Maria Kunilovskaya
University of Wolverhampton, UK
University of Tyumen, Russia
maria.kunilovskaya@wlv.ac.uk

Alistair Plum
RGCL
University of Wolverhampton, UK
a.j.plum@wlv.ac.uk

Abstract

This paper focuses on data cleaning as part of a preprocessing procedure applied to text data retrieved from the web. Although the importance of this early stage in a project using NLP methods is often highlighted by researchers, the details, general principles and techniques are usually left out due to consideration of space. At best, they are dismissed with a comment "The usual data cleaning and preprocessing procedures were applied". More coverage is usually given to automatic text annotation such as lemmatisation, part-of-speech tagging and parsing, which is often included in preprocessing. In the literature, the term 'preprocessing' is used to refer to a wide range of procedures, from filtering and cleaning to data transformation such as stemming and numeric representation, which might create confusion. We argue that text preprocessing might skew original data distribution with regard to the metadata, such as types, locations and times of registered datapoints. In this paper we describe a systematic approach to cleaning text data mined by a data-providing company for a Digital Humanities (DH) project focused on cultural analytics. We reveal the types and amount of noise in the data coming from various web sources and estimate the changes in the size of the data associated with preprocessing. We also compare the results of a text classification experiment run on the raw and preprocessed data. We hope that our experience and approaches will help the DH community to diagnose the quality of textual data collected from the web and prepare it for further natural language processing.

1 Introduction

In this paper we discuss our experience of preprocessing textual descriptions of cultural events collected from a number of diverse web sources for a DH project. The problems that we faced demonstrate that there is a big difference between the amount of raw data scraped from the web and the amount of data distilled from it through preprocessing for further application of natural language processing (NLP) methods. The web is a unique source of available information that, to an extent, reflects social and cultural trends, and it is increasingly used in sociological and cultural studies. However, it seems that preprocessing and filtering, necessary to ensure reliability of automatic analyses, creates an additional refraction of the original signal registered by the web. This paper offers a description of the data preprocessing stage in a DH project and reports its effects on the quality of text classification on the one hand, and on the size of data available for the analysis as compared to the original web-scraping results on the other hand. We used pre-trained ELMO (Embeddings from Language Model) models for text representation in the classification task. We aim to find a reasonable trade-off between quantity and quality, and try to salvage as many text instances as possible without compromising the performance of NLP methods.

Our specific tasks include:

1. description of a preprocessing pipeline and its application to the data at hand;
2. evaluation of the impact of preprocessing on text classification results;
3. estimation of the impact of preprocessing on the dataset integrity.

The data underlying this project includes texts in at least five languages, with a lot of cases of code-switching. However, for the purposes of the paper we focus on English and Russian subsets of the data.

Proceedings of the Student Research Workshop associated with RANLP-2021, pages 85–93,
held online, Sep 1–3, 2021.
https://doi.org/10.26615/issn.2603-2821.2021_013

2 Related work

The term 'data preprocessing' is used as an umbrella term to refer to a wide range of procedures, including cleaning, filtering, normalising, annotating and transforming raw data. It is not always clear which operations from this list are referred to in a particular description. For example, functions included in a *Keras* preprocessing module convert files in a tree of folders into the *Keras* internal dataset format by creating batches of texts and linking texts to labels, and possibly truncating text to a pre-set maximum length. It assumes that the text files in folders are already suitably prepared for machine learning experiments. In this paper, we focus on the steps that precede this sort of data transformation and have to do with ensuring structural completeness of the data, its cleaning and normalisation.

The link between the quality of the data and the reliability of the research outcomes is well known. It is reflected in the popular 'garbage in, garbage out' wisdom shared by the research communities in data science and NLP. It was famously formulated by John Sinclair, a widely-recognised authority in corpus building and corpus linguistics: "the beginning of any corpus study is the creation of the corpus itself ... The results are only as good as the corpus" (Sinclair, 1991).

Data collection and preprocessing is not only an important stage in a research project, it is also the most tedious and time-consuming step. A popular belief is that it claims up to 80% of the research time. According to a report by *Anaconda* "2020 State of Data Science: Moving From Hype Toward Maturity", based on a survey, which attracted a total of 2,360 responses from researchers from over 100 countries says that "on average 45% of their time is spent getting data ready (loading and cleansing)". [1] Based on the previous research, there is no getting away from this chore, especially if using bag-of-words representations.

Preprocessing is always dependent on the data and task at hand, and it is often so specific to a project that it is not described in detail. Nevertheless, there have been numerous attempts at evaluating the effects of different preprocessing steps for different types of data and NLP tasks. Subramaniam et al. (2009) present a survey of different sources of noise in texts and how these types of noise can be handled. The survey cites techniques such as automatic speech recognition, optical character recognition and machine translation to be the biggest culprits in terms of introducing noise. Kathiravan and Haridoss (2018) go into detail about preprocessing techniques used specifically for information extraction (IE) and information retrieval (IR). While this study utilises all the techniques mentioned previously, it focuses on different stemming approaches, as it is said to be one of the most beneficial preprocessing steps in terms of performance.

In Sergienko et al. (2016) 'text preprocessing' refers to data handling operations such as stop-words filtering with stemming, feature selection, feature transformation and a novel transformation method based on classes of terms. The study proves that using the novel feature transformation method and ensembles of term weighting methods yields good classification results even with very small amounts of features. Similarly, Gonçalves and Quaresma (2005) reports the impact of non-relevant word removal and lemmatisation/stemming in conjunction with data transformation steps in the context of text classification for two languages. Using a Support Vector Machine (SVM) classifier to represent Portuguese data from the law domain as well as English Reuters texts, experiments were carried out on feature reduction and construction, feature subset selection and term weighting. In terms of feature reduction, three configurations were tested including different combinations of non-relevant word removal (including articles, pronouns, adverbs and prepositions), as well as lemmatisation and stemming. Crucially, the authors found that for Portuguese stop-word removal did yield better results, while for English stemming had to also be included to attain better results. Kadhim (2018) propose similar methods for tf-idf based text classification, but also include the removal of HTML tags.

More recently, HaCohen-Kerner et al. (2020) performed an extensive evaluation of common preprocessing steps before text classification. Exploring the impact of all possible combinations of five to six basic preprocessing methods on four benchmark text corpora, the study tested three machine learning methods. The preprocessing methods included spelling correction, conversion to lower case, HTML tag removal, punctuation removal, stop-words removal and reduction of replicated characters. Overall, it is determined that the best

[1] https://www.anaconda.com/state-of-data-science-2020

results could be achieved with a combination of preprocessing methods, while stop word removal to be the most effective preprocessing method that significantly improved text classification. However, the exact combination of methods is said to vary significantly across datasets, leading to the conclusion that every dataset has to be treated accordingly.

The impact of noise on the outcomes of NLP tasks, implemented using BERT-based deep learning methods, such as offensive language identification, informativeness identification and sentiment analysis, is explored in Al Sharou et al. (2021). In line with the above studies, they limit the concept of noise to non-standard appearance of language units (casing, hashtags, code-switching, emoji, URL and punctuation). They found that for some tasks these types of noise are actually useful, and filtering them out results in lower classification results.

Most of the related work is focused on handling text representations such as feature reduction and selection, with some emphases on stop-words removal and lemmatisation/stemming. However, most researchers worked with available datasets that have undergone some sort of preprocessing. In our setting, we dealt the immediate results of crawling and had to extract raw text from it.

3 Data origins and structure

The textual data underlying this study is part of a dataset contracted by a research group for a DH project and collected by a data company following a technical assignment. The dataset includes tables, where each row represents a cultural event announced at one of the seven web services aggregating news about cultural life in various locations across the globe. The project is set within comparative cultural studies and focuses on the types of events advertised in Russia and elsewhere in the world. That is why the sources of data include both international and national publishing platforms, social networks and distributors of information regarding cultural events. A cultural event is understood broadly as any social (public) activity in the spheres of contemporary arts, education, sports, music, theatre, including social activities arranged by restaurants, computer clubs, and private enthusiasts (yoga classes, guided tours, etc). There is an understandable imbalance between the number of cultural events coming from international and Russian sources (see Table 1.

Table 1 has the names and links to these resources as well as the number of raw data points acquired from each website. The content of the web pages was either scraped (e.g. e-flux, Theories and Practice), or accessed through the official API (e.g. Behance, Timepad), or downloaded using open data service (Russian Ministry of Culture).

Data collection did not target any particular time period, but acquired all available announcements. Most of the platform's archives date back to 2003-2004. The data was collected up to mid-2019.

The records of events obtained from these web resources included city and date of the event and its textual description. Besides, each event was characterised by the name of the website section, where it was published, if available (e.g. 'business', 'graphic design', 'lectures'). This raw data was supplemented with additional information about event locations. The diverging thematic groups of events from the websites were manually mapped into seven major categories. The enhanced data tables have 24 columns, which store objective properties of each location: unique event identifier, date, city, synthetic and raw semantic categories, geographic coordinates, country, region, population, social and economic development parameters of the area (GDP, human development index, economic complexity index).

4 Preprocessing Methodology

4.1 Structural Completeness

The first obvious step to take is to ensure the overall structural sanity of the dataset. It makes sense to see whether there are empty values in the columns that are of primary importance for the subsequent analysis. Our project is centered around analysis of descriptions in the 'text' column in conjunction with 'date' and 'city'. Working in *pandas*, one of the most versatile Python libraries for tabled data, we collected the counts of NaN values in each column *i*: (`counts = df[i].isnull().sum()`) into a dictionary keyed on the column names and determined the ratio of NaN per column. It turned out that the text column had 1.67% of empty values (75,918 datapoints). These need to be dropped to avoid further errors in processing.

Similarly, the data stored in text column can be all numbers and contain no alphabetic characters. In this case, this content is hardly of value for subsequent semantic analysis. We found the indices of rows with this issue in 'text' col-

Source	Description	Region	Data points
Behance `api.behance.net/v2/users/X/projects`	Adobe's social media, advertising, architecture, fashion, industrial design	international user profiles	1,184,509
e-flux `www.e-flux.com/announcements`	a publishing platform and archive, artist projects focused on visual arts, inc. education	North America, Europe	10,280
Meetup `www.meetup.com/api/general`	a social media platform for building local communities and discovering what is happening nearby	international, user information	2,635,724
Ministry of Culture `opendata.mkrf.ru/opendata/7705851331-events`	a monitoring archive of cultural events registered by companies and individuals	Russia	84,222
TED `www.ted.com/tedx/events`	announcements of TED-style local events	international	26,001
Timepad `afisha.timepad.ru/`	a online service which helps to manage, promote and attend events	Russia	524,432
Theories and Practice `theoryandpractice.ru/seminars`	announcements for seminars, courses, workshops, master classes	Russia	70,379
Total			4,535,547

Table 1: Sources of cultural data and their coverage

umn with idx=df['text'].str.contains(pat='[a-zA-ZA-Яa-я]', regex=True) and sliced the dataframe on this index to lose additional 18,243 instances (0.4% of the original data size). This also filters out texts entirely in scripts other than Latin or Cyrillic.

Finally, in most cases automatically collected web data is known to carry duplicates, which can unfairly inflate counts of some items. One way to retain only the unique entries is to run `duplicated = df[~df.duplicated(keep='first')]`. A more rigorous approach is to drop rows that have duplicates in the focused column ('text' in our case): `texted.drop_duplicates('text', inplace=True)`.

All preprocessing decisions need to be taken with the view of the main research tasks. For example, it can be important to retain duplicate announcements that appeared on several platforms or on several dates. They indicate re-current events or events with enhanced visibility.

These operations can be computationally demanding, with less powerful computers getting stuck, if all data is fed to one CPU in one processing thread. It makes more sense to partition big datasets and process them in parallel. Our data was naturally split by source, i.e. by the web resource of data origin. Keeping these datasets apart instead of collecting them into one massive file was useful to understand the quality of the data coming from various sources. The overall size of our data was 4.6 GiB uncompressed, with one of the files accounting for 3.8 GiB and throwing out-of-memory error. We split it into 5 files for easier processing. Besides, we found it helpful to perform each preprocessing step as a separate process with its own intermediary output. It gives better control over the preprocessing workflow and allows to fall back to the output of the previous step as a contingency measure in case of errors, instead of running the whole preprocessing pipeline from scratch. For example, we found that some preprocessing libraries require switching to earlier versions of Python than our standard setup. At the time of writing, 'contraction' is available for up to Python3.6 and 'unidecode' up to Python3.7. Additionally, to save disk space we suggest working with single-member archives for each input file. In pandas, it is loaded and saved by adding the keyworded argument (compression='gzip') to the standard commands: `df = pd.read_csv(data1.tsv.gz, compression='gzip')` and `df.to_csv('data1.tsv.gz', compression='gzip')`.

After this initial clean-up step, which is a necessary minimum preprocessing required regardless of the input language, our data shrank by 19% of the original data size.

4.2 Cleaning and Noise Reduction

Language modeling and analysis by NLP techniques require some type of numeric representation of texts. This includes indexing, one-hot representations, frequency-based approaches (e.g. tf-idf), vectorisation based on co-occurrence statistics, which exploits the distributional hypothesis in lexical semantics. We assume that some NLP methods work better when the input text is free of extraneous artefacts, such as HTML tags, encoding errors, literal renditions of Unicode characters such as `\xe2\x80\x93` and `\r\n\t`. They appear in the top of a sorted frequency dictionary built from the raw text and may affect the quality of lemmatisation, which was shown to be useful for automatic semantic analysis in previous work. Although URL and email addresses can be useful for some tasks, we treated them as organisational information, external to the text, and removed them using regular expressions.

The sequence of the operations aimed at removing or reducing noise can be important both for safety and efficiency of the process. For example, if you are prepared to drop texts, shorter than five tokens, it makes sense to run this command for the first time early on in the stack of preprocessing operations to exclude these instances from further processing. Each web resource selected for scraping together with the scraping settings is likely to produce individual types of noise that can be detected by looking at the top of the reverse-ordered frequency dictionaries generated after each procedure or preprocessing step. As a result of several attempts and recursive iterations, we developed a preprocessing pipeline, which includes the following operations:

- insert a space (i) before a capital, following a lowercase character and (ii) after a set of punctuation marks (both are usually a sign of a missing delimiter, such as a newline, e.g. What we'll doGoogle Cloud Study Jams What to bringLaptop);
- drop recurrent commenting phrases typical for some websites (e.g. 'Meeting description' and square-bracketed content (e.g. [masked]);
- drop unnaturally long tokens (over 15 characters), usually a sign of malformed content;
- normalise double and single quotes, dashes, hyphens, tildes, dots, apostrophes;
- remove multiple spaces and all characters, except an allowed set to filter out incorrectly decoded Unicode (e.g. ÄéÊÉÖÂ±ÂÖ) (using a function adapted from the processing pipeline developed by Shavrina and Shapovalova (2017);
- remove tokens that contain no alphanumeric characters, usually noise and orphaned punctuation marks;
- fix literal renditions of HTML entities such as `\&gt, \';`
- fix spaced or mostly spaced strings (e.g. E S H K O L O T F E S T I V A L);
- remove unmotivated repetitions of characters and words;
- weed out items with unmotivated high frequencies unique for each web resource.

It makes sense to finish this stage of language-independent preprocessing with running a language detection module and storing its output in a new attribute (column) to be used at the lemmatisation stage. One major problem with language detection is that some texts in our dataset include mixed code, i.e. they have words written in several languages (e.g. 'Илья Чёрт в The Right Place', 'New Year Mylene Farmer Fan-Club Party в ночном клубе "Jack Jan"). This can be an issue for any automatic language detection. We used an additional heuristic (checking whether any characters are Cyrillic) to correct the prediction of the automatic language detection for mixed code samples, produced by *fasttext* language detection model [2]. Following language identification we dropped all observations in languages other than English and Russian. The number of texts in other languages (Italian, French, Spanish) was disproportional to the bulk of the data, and cumulatively accounted for about 7%.

4.3 Text Normalisation

Machine learning algorithms and lemmatisation pipelines perform better, if the textual data is standardised, e.g. spelling variants are replaced with a one unified convention. Typically, this is done for quotation symbol styles, English contracted forms, and Russian ë. When choosing a specific type of normalisation, it is good to have in mind the requirements to the input at the next stage of data processing, particularly, which linguistic annotation tool (e.g. for lemmatisation) and which numeric representation method is planned for the main study. For example, the Russian model learnt on SynTagRus treebank (Droganova et al., 2018) does not recognise «», one of the double quotes styles, used in Russian texts. We have taken care of quotes at the previous step. In this project, language-specific normalisation concerned expanding English contractions (admittedly an optional task, given the subsequent use of UDpipe, which can process contractions) and normalisation of Russian ë. In cases when lemmatisation does not follow, normalisation measures can include bringing all words to lower case, and stop-words and punctuation removal. Finally, at this stage we filtered out all datapoints with the textual attribute shorter that 5 tokens.

4.4 Automatic Lemmatisation and Filtering

For lemmatisation, we relied on Universal Dependencies (UD) framework using UDPipe module (v1, Straka and Straková, 2017), with the Russian model trained on SynTagRus treebank (v2.5, Droganova et al., 2018). All tokens in our texts were replaced with their lemmas identified by the parsing pipeline. UD-annotations were also used to produce and store lists of lemmas of content words (tagged as NOUN, ADJ or VERB) from each text to be used in solving the main research task, i.e. grouping events by category in an unsupervised machine learning setting. Content lemmas were filtered with stop-words lists [3]. At the time of annotation we discarded instances that had no content words.

5 Results and Discussion

To demonstrate the impact of preprocessing and annotation on the outcomes of the experiments, we compared the results of automatic classification on the texts at different stages of preprocessing (raw tokens, clean tokens, all lemmas, content lemmas). To this end, we selected a subset of 600 event descriptions (in Russian) registered in Tyumen (a big city in Western Siberia, Russia). These datapoints were labelled with the names of the website sections where the respective event was announced (*Timepad* and *Ministry of Culture*). The six categories used as class labels were 'theatre', 'psychology and self-development', 'business', 'sport', 'concerts', 'kids events' and had at least 30 observations in each category. The texts are represented using available ELMO models (Kutuzov and Kuzmenko, 2017), pre-trained on raw and lemmatised corpora matching the types of preprocessing we have in our data. Each text received an averaged vector for all words in it. The ELMO vectors (size 1024) were then transformed into 32-dimensional vectors with *Autoencoder* module from the *Keras* library for Python. These representations were classified with a SVM algorithm with the default *scikit-learn* parameters. The evaluation is performed in 5-fold cross-validation setting. Given the imbalance in our data, we used stratified folds and weighting for underrepresented classes. Table 2 reports accuracy and macro F1-score for each of the preprocessing variants.

	accuracy	**F-score**
raw input	76%	0.72
cleaned tokens	76%	0.72
lemmatised text	80%	0.76
content lemmas	82%	0.78

Table 2: Classification results on versions of input

As can be seen from Table 2, there is no difference between the classifier performance on raw and cleaned tokens, but lemmatisation definitely helps. It is not clear whether preprocessing procedures like those described in Sections 4.2 and 4.3 improve the quality of lemmatisation, but it seems that vectorisation effectively coped with raw text. Frustratingly, all the tedious cleaning procedures did not pay off. One explanation for this counter-

[2] https://fasttext.cc/docs/en/language-identification.html

[3] https://github.com/Alir3z4/python-stop-words

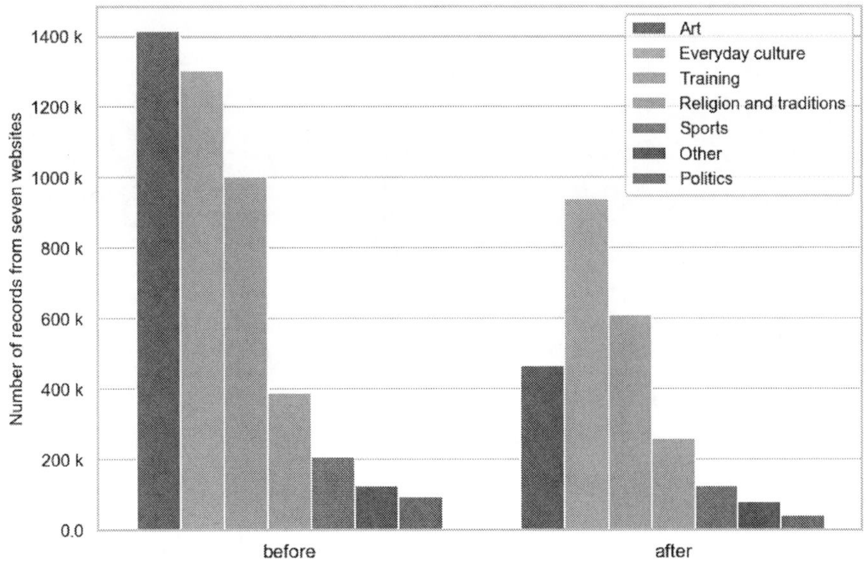

Figure 1: Distributions of events across categories before and after preprocessing

intuitive result is that the Russian data in part was downloaded from an official government-curated archive. The quality of these texts was higher in comparison to the typical user-generated content seen on other web resources.

Another alarming aspect of preprocessing is the portion of the original dataset that gets discarded during preprocessing. Overall, for the dataset at hand, preprocessing claimed 45% of the original size in terms of the number of observations. Importantly, preprocessing affected the ratio of events assigned to various categories. The diverging inventories of categories used for sectioning on the websites were manually mapped into seven thematic groups shown in Figure 1. Figure 1 demonstrates the impact of preprocessing on the distribution of records across the seven thematic categories from all seven web resources. It can be seen that preprocessing resulted in a significant reduction in the 'art' and 'politics' categories (62.7 and 57.4% of registered events lost, respectively). Most of the items lost in the 'arts' category had a link to a media object such as a picture in the 'text' field. It raises a question whether any multi-modal processing can be employed as a contingency measure.

The top three web resources that lost most of the records in preprocessing were *Behance*, *Timepad* and *TED*, which were reduced by 81.9, 54.1 and 55.3% respectively. The highest integrity was characteristic for *e-flux* and *Ministry of Culture*; they had little noise and hardly lost any datapoints. Note that in terms of absolute number of datapoints, *Meetup* remained the biggest source of data, dwarfing *e-flux* into insignificance (with only 10,280 raw records and 10,081 after pre-processing, it is shown as a dot in Figure 2.

For the Tyumen sample, we are left with less than 50% (992 events) of the original number of observations (1864 events), given the preprocessing described above. The number of observations for Manchester (for example) dropped by 35%. Most of the datapoints are discarded due to the lack or insufficiency of text attributes associated with recorded events. Interestingly, in another experiment we set the text lengths threshold to 10 words (as opposed to 5 here) and achieved the classification accuracy of over 90% on just 452 observations, represented as content lemmas, in the same experimental setup. On the one hand, it seems to indicate that a smaller, but higher-quality data returns better results, but on the other hand, can we claim that the results pertain to the original dataset? If half of the datapoints end up in the garbage bin, how can we say that the results reflect the content of the web

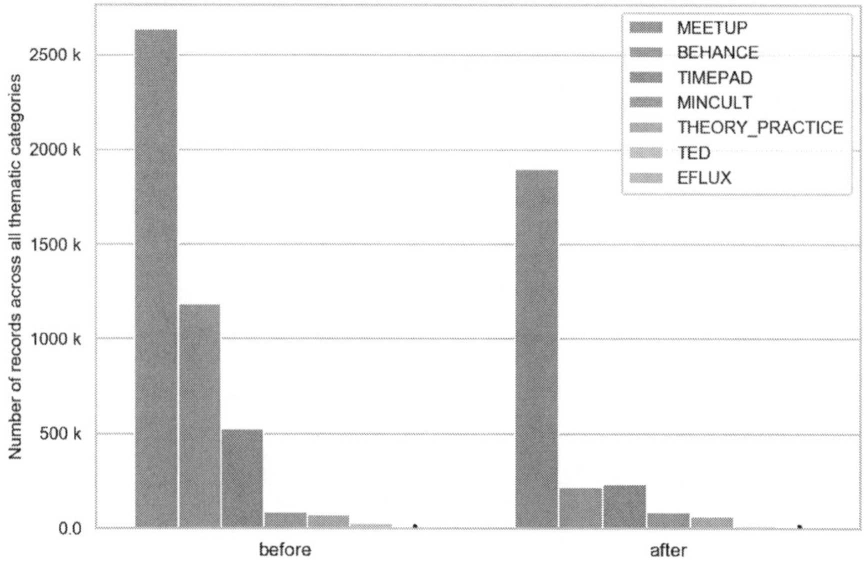

Figure 2: Number of records from seven web resources before and after preprocessing

sources used? Our observations raise issues with the selection of web resources and data collection techniques. We have seen that some websites are more suitable as sources of textual data than others.

6 Conclusion

The paper contains a detailed description of preprocessing steps that were taken to prepare textual data collected from seven web aggregators of cultural information for automatic analysis using NLP methods. We followed the best practices in the field, and expected that cleaner data with 15-40% smaller vocabulary would yield gains in the classifier performance proportional to the efforts invested. However, it seems that these efforts fall with the 80% of work that generates only 20% of profits, following the famous Pareto principle. In the future, we plan to explore the interrelations between types of preprocessing and actual gains seen for different types of language representations, particularly embeddings and classification setups. What is the impact of preprocessing on parsing? Which types of noise can actually be tolerated? One take-away from this project is that selection of web resources is important: some of them return cleaner data than others. It is true that data preprocessing takes most of the research time, too. When reporting the results, in addition to the inaccuracies of analysis, two caveats have to be made with regard to the amount of observations (datapoints) discarded during preprocessing.

Acknowledgements

This work has been partly supported by the Russian Foundation for Basic Research within Project *Cultural Trends in the Tyumen Region in the National and Global Contexts* No. 20-411-720010 p_a_Tyumen region.

References

Khetam Al Sharou, Zhenhao Li, and Lucia Specia. 2021. Towards a Better Understanding of Noise in Natural Language Processing. In *RANLP-2021*, page in print.

Kira Droganova, Olga Lyashevskaya, and Daniel Zeman. 2018. Data conversion and consistency of monolingual corpora: Russian ud treebanks. In *Proceedings of the 17th international workshop on treebanks and linguistic theories (tlt 2018)*, volume 155, pages 53–66.

Teresa Gonçalves and Paulo Quaresma. 2005. Evaluating preprocessing techniques in a text classification problem. *São Leopoldo, RS, Brasil: SBC-Sociedade Brasileira de Computação*.

Yaakov HaCohen-Kerner, Daniel Miller, and Yair Yigal. 2020. The influence of preprocessing on text classification using a bag-of-words representation. *PloS one*, 15(5):e0232525.

Ammar Ismael Kadhim. 2018. An evaluation of preprocessing techniques for text classification. *International Journal of Computer Science and Information Security (IJCSIS)*, 16(6):22–32.

Periasamy Kathiravan and N Haridoss. 2018. Preprocessing for mining the textual data: A review. *vol*, 7:5–8.

Andrey Kutuzov and Elizaveta Kuzmenko. 2017. *WebVectors: A Toolkit for Building Web Interfaces for Vector Semantic Models*, pages 155–161. Springer International Publishing, Cham.

Roman Sergienko, Muhammad Shan, and Wolfgang Minker. 2016. A comparative study of text preprocessing approaches for topic detection of user utterances. In *Proceedings of the Tenth International Conference on Language Resources and Evaluation (LREC'16)*, pages 1826–1831.

Tatiana Shavrina and Olga Shapovalova. 2017. To the methodology of corpus construction for machine learning:«taiga» syntax tree corpus and parser. In *Proceedings of the "Corpora*, pages 78–84.

John Sinclair. 1991. *Corpus, Concordance, Collocation.* Oxford University Press.

Milan Straka and Jana Straková. 2017. Tokenizing, POS Tagging, Lemmatizing and Parsing UD 2.0 with UDPipe. In *Proceedings of the CoNLL 2017 Shared Task: Multilingual Parsing from Raw Text to Universal Dependencies*, pages 88–99.

Venkata Subramaniam, Shourya Roy, Tanveer Faruquie, and Sumit Negi. 2009. A survey of types of text noise and techniques to handle noisy text. In *Proceedings of The Third Workshop on Analytics for Noisy Unstructured Text Data*, pages 115–122.

Compiling a Specialised Corpus for Translation Research in the Environmental Domain

Anastasiia Laktionova
University of Wolverhampton
laktionovaaa@gmail.com

Abstract

The present study is an ongoing research that aims to investigate lexico-grammatical and stylistic features of texts in the environmental domain in English, their implications for translation into Ukrainian as well as the translation of key terminological units based on a specialised parallel and comparable corpora. The research will comprise the process of creation of the English-Ukrainian parallel corpus and a Ukrainian comparable corpus and the exploration of the resource from a translational perspective.

1 Introduction

The research focuses on compiling a parallel English-Ukrainian corpus comprising environmental texts, conducting an analysis to identify genre-specific lexico-grammatical and stylistic features of the texts in the corpus using the corpus management tools, identifying key terminological units in the English corpus and their translations and qualitative analysis of the pairs in order to identify potential inconsistencies and errors, as well as multiple and null translation equivalents associated with specific English terminological units, compiling a comparable Ukrainian corpus of texts based on the key terms of the parallel corpus and conducting quantitative and qualitative lexico-grammatical and stylistic analysis of translated and non-translated (original Ukrainian) texts in the two corpora.

For the corpus, international conventions, protocols and agreements in the environmental domain are collected to serve as a base for analyzing specific lexico-grammatical and stylistic features of from the translation perspective, observing possible differences between translated and native use of language in the domain as well as capturing possible inconsistencies in the translation of terminological units: such as mistranslations, non-translations or multiple translations of terms.

2 Methodology

The methodology that underpins the study is based upon the latest developments in the field of corpus linguistics, which has become an extremely common paradigm for studying various aspects of language, including translation. A corpus can be defined as a collection of authentic texts held in electronic form and assembled according to specific design criteria (Laviosa, 2013, p.228) or a form of linguistic data which represents a collection of written texts (or transcripts of speech) that can be searched by a computer using specialized software (Brezina, 2018, p.1). Corpora can contain texts in several languages, representing either parallel or comparable types. Parallel corpora are corpora that contain native language (L1) source texts and their translations (L2). Comparable corpora contain texts that are collected using the same sampling frame (the same proportions of the texts of the same genres in the same domains etc.) in different languages.

In order to apply a corpus to translation studies it must be compiled in several stages in line with a number of criteria. Scholars outline the following steps in the compilation process: the selection of texts, followed by preprocessing, annotation and alignment, after which the search and retrieval of information will be conducted, and the analysis of

Proceedings of the Student Research Workshop associated with RANLP-2021, pages 94–98,
held online, Sep 1–3, 2021.
https://doi.org/10.26615/issn.2603-2821.2021_014

findings. An important feature of corpus design, applicable for parallel corpora, is text alignment, which means the connection of "the parallel or translational relationship between the source texts and target texts at different levels" (Hu, 2016, p.37). The alignment can be performed at lexical, sentence, paragraph or text level. This process is quite technically challenging, but is crucial for further corpus analysis. Alignment is carried out on segment level and realization of alignment at the sentential level is necessary for the investigation of translation equivalents. At present, some corpus management tools already have in-built alignment functions (for example, SketchEngine (Kilgarriff et al. 2014)), and for this process it is only required to save corpus data in a vertical format. However, in order to make corpus resources even more useful and insightful, it is necessary to perform corpus annotation (manual or automatic) at various levels (phonological, morphological, lexical (POS tagging, lemmatization, semantic annotation), syntactic (parsing, treebanking), and sometimes at discoursal level (adding coreference annotation) depending on the purpose of the research.

For this research, a specialised parallel corpus and a comparable corpus is compiled. The texts in the corpora represent legal environmental documents, such as environmental conventions, protocols, guidelines on legislation approximation and agreements available in English and Ukrainian. The size of the parallel corpus will be around 100,000 tokens and around 50,000 tokens for the comparable corpus in Ukrainian. The size is limited due to the available translations of the English texts: a larger number of documents is adapted, and not translated. It is planned to carry out tokenization of texts in Python, followed by lemmatization. Other most common annotation types include part-of-speech tagging and syntactic parsing, however resources for these types of annotation are not highly developed for Ukrainian and will not necessarily be used for annotation of the corpora. Corpus analysis tools include frequency lists, concordances, keywords and n-grams, as well as statistical methods (frequency, dispersion etc.).

3 Related work

There is a substantial number of monolingual corpus resources for many languages, and a great number of parallel and comparable corpora have been compiled for various languages, for example the Europarl parallel corpus, consisting of the proceedings of the European Parliament, the OPUS (open parallel corpus) which contains texts in 40 languages, the "Oslo Multilingual Corpus", the "ACTRES Parallel Corpus" (P-ACTRES), which contains English source texts and their Spanish target texts, EUR-Lex corpus with documents in the official languages of the EU, English-Norwegian Parallel Corpus and many other. This approach is applied to an increasing number of language pairs and domains.

A specialised corpus contains texts of a particular type, e.g. computer manuals, medical package inserts etc. whereas a general corpus is normally large, balanced, containing as many text types as possible and more representative of a language in general. An example of a specialised corpus in the environmental domain is the EcoLexicon English Corpus (EEC), which contains 23.1 million words and consists of contemporary environmental texts in a wide range of genres (León-Araúz, San Martín and Reimerink, 2018). It was built by the LexiCon research group for the development of EcoLexicon – a terminological knowledge base for the environment. Specialised parallel and comparable corpora have proven to be very useful in domain-specific translation research, terminology extraction and other practical applications.

In case of a general corpus, the size has to be as large as possible, in order for it to represent the variety of a language. However, in a specialized, domain-specific corpus it is easier to achieve representativeness of this particular language type based on a smaller-sized corpus. McEnery, Xiao and Tono (2006), for example, highlight that the representativeness of general and specialised corpora should be measured in different ways: for a general corpus it is related to sampling from a wide range of genres, for a specialised one – it can be measured by the level of 'saturation' or 'closure' at the lexical level. According to the authors, saturation or closure for a linguistic feature (for example, the size of lexicon) of a language type or variety (for example, environmental conventions) means that "the feature appears to be finite or is subject to very limited variation beyond a certain point". It can be concluded, that specialised corpora in a certain subject area have high saturation or concentration of vocabulary that represents this area and it affects the potentially sufficient size of such corpora.

As for the Ukrainian language, there are several large general corpora compiled in the recent years. One of the publicly available corpora is "GRAC" – the General Regionally Annotated Corpus of Ukrainian, which contains more than 400,000,000 tokens and represents most genres of written texts. A specific feature of the corpus is the regional annotation, which means that about half of the texts are attributed with regard to the different regions of Ukraine or countries of the diaspora (Shvedova 2020, p.489). Another available corpus is the Ukrainian Web Corpus of the Leipzig University, which contains a little over 1,5 billion tokens. It contains internet texts from the year 2014 and it is only possible to search word forms to see textual examples or collocations; the corpus also has a feature of graphs, visualizing frequencies of word forms co-occurred in a sentence. As for specialised corpora, there has recently been developed a corpus of texts in the medical domain called UKRMED (Cherednichenko et. al 2020). An example of a specialised comparable corpus is a corpus of political media discourse containing texts in English and Ukrainian (400 texts from 2014-2017) (Romanyshyn, 2020).

Available resources also include some general parallel corpora: Parallel Ukrainian-Russian and Russian-Ukrainian corpora within the Russian National Corpus (6,5 million tokens) and some parallel corpora developed by The Corpus Project of the Laboratory of Ukrainian, that include Polish, French, German, Spanish, Portuguese and a 1,5-million-token English-Ukrainian parallel corpus (bidirectional, mostly containing translation of fiction). There is morphological tagging in parallel corpora, made automatically with the Universal Dependencies system. This parallel corpus is based on the NoSketchEngine Platform and is publicly available online for searching. At present, corpus resources are widely present for English and other common European languages. Despite some active work on development of corpora, they are still not available in sufficient volume for Ukrainian, and especially scarce are bilingual and specialised corpora.

4 Environmental translation

Translation of texts in the environmental domain is challenging due to the relative recency of the environmental science as a specialized field, its multidisciplinary nature, and its fluid terminology, which includes both single-word terms and multiword expressions. Another factor is the urgent social message in many texts, which are fueled by the assumption that time is running out. (Faber and León-Araúz, 2021 p.589). There is research indicating inconsistencies in environmental terminology translation from English. For example, a study by Krimpas and Karadimou (2018) shows evidence for a number of terminological issues in official translations of international environmental conventions translation into Greek. A few studies by Ukrainian researchers also point out potential difficulties in translation of environmental texts focusing on the lexico-semantic aspect (Chervonetsky and Chervonetska, 2015).

In light of the European integration of Ukraine and the respective approximation of Ukrainian legislation to the EU, including the areas of environment and energy, the Ukrainian national government as well as local municipalities constantly adapt various European environmental conventions and use materials translated from English to create according legislation and development plans, implemented in many Ukrainian cities. The materials are actively disseminated to the population and main novel concepts are even introduced to the life in the country and implemented into governments' policies. In view of that, adequate translation of texts in the environmental domain is extremely important, especially for developing countries such as Ukraine. Moreover, it has been pointed out by researchers, that for lesser-used languages, terminology transfer from English can often be observed due to the import of technical advances from European countries where terms are mostly coined in the widely-used English language (Krimpas and Karadimou, 2018, p.22).

5 Research questions

The motivation behind the research is the limited availability of multilingual specialised corpus resources which include the Ukrainian language and the choice of the environmental domain is conditioned by this field being one of the most often communicated and crucial for the developing countries. In the course of the research the following research questions need to be addressed: What are the specific features of international conventions, protocols and agreements in the environmental domain? Is there a difference between translated and native use of language in the domain? How do translations and original texts written in the target language differ in terms of their lexico-grammatical and stylistic features? Are there inconsistencies in the translation of terminological units: are there mistranslations, non-translations or multiple translations of a term? Compilation of a parallel corpus and a comparable corpus will serve as a basis for the investigation.

6 Conclusions

The research focuses on building a parallel and comparable corpus of environmental texts which can be further used for a number of applications, such as terminology or information extraction, research on differences and similarities between the English language and Ukrainian language, or between native and non-native language speakers' output (the translationese or textual fit), language-specific features, universal features, and any typological or cultural differences and potentially for MT. Analysing potential inconsistencies in official translation of terminology in the domain can be applied in terminology resources for translators, specialists developing and enhancing the terminology database or for creating a specialised terminology database.

Acknowledgements

I would like to express my gratitude to my supervisors Dr Maria Stambolieva (New Bulgarian University) and Dr Sara Moze (University of Wolverhampton) for their encouragement, help and valuable feedback for my research. I would also like to thank Prof Ruslan Mitkov, the EM TTI coordinator, for encouraging students to submit their research to the conference.

References

Baker, Mona. 1996. Corpus-based translation studies: the challenges that lie ahead. In H. Somers (ed.) *Terminology, LSP, and Translation: Studies in* 1.
Language Engineering in Honour of Juan C. Sager. 2.
Philadelphia/Amsterdam: John Benjamins, pages 175-186.

Biel, Lucja and Giczela-Pastwa, Justyna. 2016. Metody korpusowe w analizie gatunków specjalistycznych – założenia, perspektywy i ograniczenia. In *Pod pretekstem slow. Ksiega* 3.
jubileuszowa dla Profesora Wojciecha Kubinskiego, Gorszczynska, P. and Karwacka, W. (eds.), Gdansk, Częsci Proste.

Brezina, Vaclav. 2018. Introduction: Statistics Meets Corpus Linguistics, in *Statistics in Corpus Linguistics*, pages 1–37.

Cherednichenko, Olga *et al.* 2020. Collection and processing of a medical corpus in Ukrainian. In *CEUR Workshop Proceedings* (Volume 2604), pages 272–282. Available at: http://ceur-ws.org/Vol-2604/paper21.pdf

Chervonetsky, Volodymyr and Chervonetska, S. 2015. Problems of text translation in the field of ecology from the English language into Ukrainian: lexico-semantic aspect. In Ivashchenko V. (ed.) *Terminolohichnyi visnyk (Collected papers)*, vol.3(2), Kyiv, National Academy of Sciences of Ukraine, pages 94-101.

Cronin, Michael. 2013. Translation and globalization. In Millán C. and Bartrina F. (eds.) *The Routledge Handbook of Translation Studies*. New York: Routledge, pages 491-502.

Faber, Pamela and León-Araúz, Pilar. 2021. Designing Terminology Resources for Environmental Translation. In Ji M. and Laviosa, S. (eds.) *The Oxford Handbook of Translation and Social Practices*. New York: Oxford University Press, pages 587-615.

Hu, Kaibao. 2016. *Introducing Corpus-based Translation Studies*, *Introducing Translation Studies*. Shanghai: Springer.
doi: 10.4324/9781315691862.

Ji, Meng. (ed.). 2019. *Translating and Communicating Environmental Cultures*, New York: Routhledge.

Kilgarriff, Adam *et al.* 2014. The Sketch Engine: ten years on. In *Lexicography*, (1), pages. 7–36. Available at: https://www.sketchengine.eu/wp-content/uploads/The_Sketch_Engine_2014.pdf.

Krimpas, Panagotis G. and Karadimou, Despina. 2018. Terminological issues in official translations of international environmental conventions. In *Parallèles*, 30(1), pages. 21–35.
doi: 10.17462/para.201

Lapshinova-Koltunski, Ekaterina. 2015. Variation in translation: Evidence from corpora. In *New directions in corpus-based translation studies*, *Translation and Multilingual Natural Language Processing*,
Fantinuoli, C. and Zanettin, F. (eds.), Berlin, Language Science Press, pages 93–113.

Laviosa, Sara. 2013. Corpus linguistics in translation studies. In Millán, C. and Bartrina, F. (eds.) *The Routledge Handbook of Translation Studies*. London and New York: Routhledge, pages 228–240.
doi: 10.4324/9780203102893.ch17.

León Araúz, Pilar and García Melania C. 2020. Term and translation variation of multi-word terms. In: Mogorrón Huerta, Pedro (ed.) *Multidisciplinary Analysis of the Phenomenon of Phraseological Variation in Translation and Interpreting*. MonTI Special Issue 6, pages. 210-247.
doi: 10.6035/MonTI.2020.ne6.7

León-Araúz, Pilar, San Martín, A. and Reimerink, A. 2018. The EcoLexicon English Corpus as an Open Corpus in Sketch Engine. In *XVIII EURALEX*

International Congress: Lexicography in Global Contexts, Ljubljana, pages 893–901.
McEnery, Tony and Hardie, Andrew. 2012. *Corpus Linguistics: Method, Theory and Practice*. Cambridge: Cambridge University Press.
McEnery, Tony, Brezina, Vaclav, Gablasova, Dana and Banerjee, Jayanti. 2019. Corpus Linguistics, Learner Corpora, and SLA: Employing Technology to Analyze Language Use. In *Annual Review of Applied Linguistics*, (39): pages.74–92.
Romanyshyn, Natalia. 2020. 'Application of corpus technologies in conceptual studies (based on the concept Ukraine actualization in English and Ukrainian political media discourse). In *CEUR Workshop Proceedings*, 2604, pages 472–488.
Sinclair, John. 2004. Corpus and Text — Basic Principles in *Developing Linguistic Corpora: a Guide to Good Practice*. Edited by M. Wynne. Available at: https://users.ox.ac.uk/~martinw/dlc/chapter1.htm.

Paragraph Similarity Matches for Generating Multiple-choice Test Items

Halyna Maslak and **Ruslan Mitkov**
University of Wolverhampton
Wolverhampton, UK
halyna.maslak@gmail.com
r.mitkov@wlv.ac.uk

Abstract

Multiple-choice questions (MCQs) are widely used in knowledge assessment in educational institutions, during work interviews, in entertainment quizzes and games. Although the research on the automatic or semi-automatic generation of multiple-choice test items has been conducted since the beginning of this millennium, most approaches focus on generating questions from a single sentence. In this research, a state-of-the-art method of creating questions based on multiple sentences is introduced. It was inspired by semantic similarity matches used in the translation memory component of translation management systems. The performance of two deep learning algorithms, doc2vec and SBERT, is compared for the paragraph similarity task. The experiments are performed on the ad-hoc corpus within the EU domain. For the automatic evaluation, a smaller corpus of manually selected matching paragraphs has been compiled. The results prove the good performance of Sentence Embeddings for the given task.

1 Introduction

The Multiple-choice test items (MCQs) are frequently used for knowledge assessment, e.g., ongoing assessment or during an examination. They are also used for career-significant assessment in medical training and certification, e.g., the Medical College Admission Test (MCAT) or the United States Medical Licensing Examination (USMLE) as well as in law schools and as a part of the Multistate Bar Examination (MBE). Some employers also use MCQs to evaluate the knowledge of candidates applying for a job since it is an easy and fast way to do so. Tests of this kind are also extremely popular in game shows like Who Wants to Be a Millionaire? and alike, in myriads of mobile apps or Facebook quizzes. Moreover, the Covid-19 pandemic has already affected significantly the way assessment is conducted in education institutions switching to extensive use of technology. MCQs are recommended to be used for online education, and many virtual learning environments offer in-built tools for the composition of such tests (Burnett and Fuentes, 2020).

For our research, we decided to experiment with the EU law domain. MCQs are used to assess knowledge of job seekers applying for positions in in the European Union institutions. Furthermore, MCQs are frequently used during exams in law schools and universities. Therefore, the primary reason for selecting this domain is our motivation to assist education professionals and offer a helpful tool for knowledge assessment. We conduct the experiments on EU textbooks used in classrooms.

Despite the popularity and extensive use of multiple-choice tests, their manual creation is a laborious and time-consuming task (Mitkov and Ha, 2003; Mitkov et al., 2006). Ambiguously worded questions, too easy or too difficult distractors can lead to the poor performance of test-takers and misleading results.

There have been several attempts to automatically generate multiple-choice questions starting from various NLP techniques, including the use of WordNet, shallow parsing, corpora, ontologies (Mitkov and Ha, 2003; Papasalouros et al., 2008). For the last couple of years, researchers have been experimenting with machine learning (Guo et al., 2016). In recent papers on this topic, deep neural networks are successfully applied for this task (Kumar et al., 2018; Martinez-Gil et al., 2019).

Proceedings of the Student Research Workshop associated with RANLP-2021, pages 99–108,
held online, Sep 1–3, 2021.
https://doi.org/10.26615/issn.2603-2821.2021_015

Furthermore, various strategies have been used for choosing distractors or testing on various types of instructive material (such as linguistics (Mitkov and Ha, 2003) or medical texts (Karamanis et al., 2006), sports domain (Majumder and Saha, 2015), as well as Wikipedia articles (Singh et al., 2013). Most research papers are based on the sentence-based approach, where questions are generated from one sentence that contains a key term (Wang et al., 2018). In recent research, the questions are based on the whole paragraph with the use of deep neural models (Zhao et al., 2018).

We aim to evaluate the performance of two existing deep neural models, doc2vec and SBERT, for the generation of multiple-choice test items based on multiple sentences.

Our contributions are as follows:

- Compiling a corpus of MCQs based on multiple sentences within the EU law domain. As to our knowledge, no such corpus exists or is publicly available.
- Providing a state-of-the-art method for finding semantically similar paragraphs with the use of paragraph embeddings.

The MCQ corpus is needed for the experiments. It should contain the question-answer (QA) pair and the paragraph on which the question is based. In addition, we aim to create the corpus that can be used for knowledge assessment of EU law. Therefore, the QAs should follow the criteria of MCQs used in classroom, i.e. they should not focus on too narrow topics or specific cases. In addition, we want to expand this research in the future by generating distractors automatically. That is why the answer should be concise. The requirements of MCQ corpus design are listed in Section 3.1. More detailed description of the corpus and experiments can be found in the master's dissertation (Maslak, 2021).

2 Related Work

Early research was focused on the use of traditional natural language processing methods for generating questions and distractors automatically. For example, Mitkov and Ha (2003), who were the pioneers in generating MCQs automatically, used such NLP techniques as term extraction, parsing, a corpus, and WordNet. Their system-generated test questions and distractors based on a linguistics textbook. A few years later, Karamanis et al. (2006) generated Multiple-Choice Test Items from medical text using Rapid Item Generation (RIG) and the UMLS thesaurus. A medical textbook served as the source texts, while a much more extensive collection of MEDLINE texts was used as the reference corpus. In another research, Mitkov et al. (2006) employed various NLP techniques such as automatic term extraction, shallow parsing, sentence transformation and computing of semantic distance as well as corpora and ontologies. In contrast to the methodologies that highly depend on the used domain, Papasalouros et al.'s (2008) approach is domain-independent as they employed specific ontology-based strategies and OWL.

Singh Bhatia et al. (2013) proposed selecting sentences using existing test items in the Web as well as presented a technique for creating named entity distractors from Wikipedia. Alsubait et al. (2014) used OWL ontologies to generate multiple-choice test items and proposed a psychologically-based theory to control the question difficulty.

Afzal and Mitkov (2014) suggested an unsupervised dependency-based approach to identify the most important named entities and terms and define semantic relations between them. This approach did not use any prior knowledge about the semantic types of the relations but was based on a dependency tree model. The results were evaluated in respect of their readability, usefulness of semantic relations, relevance, acceptability of questions and distractors and general usability of multiple-choice test items.

A couple of years ago, the focus of the research community shifted towards the use of neural networks for natural language processing tasks. For example, Liang et al. (2018) investigated how machine-learning models, in particular feature-based and neural net (NN) based ranking models, can be used for distractor selection. Gao et al. (2019) proposed a hierarchical encoder-decoder framework to generate question items for reading comprehension questions from real examinations. Susanti et al. (2018) investigated methods for automatically generating distractors for multiple-choice questions on English vocabulary and used semantic similarity and collocation information. Shin et al. (2019) used a topic modeling procedure, machine learning, and natural language processing to generate distractors based on students' misconceptions.

In the aforementioned words, various approaches were used to generate questions or distractors automatically. Mostly, the questions were generated on the basis of a single sentence. In our research, we do not create questions automatically. Instead, we employ the most recent methods of semantic textual similarity matching to find similar paragraphs in the reference corpus. The question-answer pair attached to the incoming paragraph that is fed to the model is transferred to the newly found paragraph and then post-edited to create a new question-answer pair. This approach aims at reducing the teachers' effort to create new test items from scratch.

3 Methodology

This research was inspired by translation memory (TM) matching used in computer-assisted translation (CAT) tools. TM consists of aligned on the sentence level source-and-target pairs (Sikes, 2007). These are the previous translations done by a human translator on the same or similar topic. Basically, after the source text is segmented according to segmentation rules, usually according to sentence-closing punctuation marks, the source sentence is searched in the translation memory. When a similar sentence in the source language is found, its translation is suggested for the target segment. The translation memory matches are retrieved according to a certain threshold chosen by a translator based on how similar the segments are. This score is normally presented in a percentage value. Totally exact segments constitute a 100% match, while exact segments within the same context, i.e., the same sentences or phrases before and after this segment, are called 101% matches or context-matches. The other matches below the 100% score are referred to as fuzzy matches.

In this work, an analogous method is used for finding similar paragraphs. However, there are several differences. Firstly, only one language, English, is used in the experiments. Moreover, the segmentation rules are different. Instead of sentences, paragraphs are used. A paragraph is defined as a sequence of characters ending with closing punctuation marks, i.e., a full stop, exclamation mark, question mark, followed by a new line symbol. Moreover, in the case of lists, such as the text presented in the form of bullet points, additional rules apply. If colons and semicolons are followed by a new line symbol, the new line is removed so that such phrases comprise a part of a larger paragraph. Otherwise, if left unchanged, each new bullet point phrase would make a separate paragraph. The paragraph consisting of a few words is not useful for this research.

To imitate the translation memory matches, two corpora are needed. The Paragraph cell in the above-mentioned MCQ corpus serves as a source text segmented into individual characters. A paragraph is searched for in the huge reference corpus that represents the translation memory. When a similar paragraph is found, it is suggested to a user. The question, anchor, and distractors attached to the source paragraph are used now for the target paragraph. They can be post-edited to reflect the contents of the new paragraph better. Although the reference corpus used in this research does not include any translations, for the simplicity of explaining the mechanism behind the research idea, it is called the translation memory, or TM corpus.

3.1 MCQ Corpus Compilation

For the purposes of this research, a corpus of MCQs is required. It is needed for the experiments to find similar paragraphs in another textbook. Such a corpus is manually compiled and consists of the following elements:

- The paragraph from a chosen book on which the question is based.
- The question referring to the corresponding paragraph.
- The answer.

Such question answering datasets as The Natural Questions corpus (Kwiatkowski et al., 2019), TriviaQA (Joshi et al., 2017), HotpotQA (Yang et al., 2018), QuAC (Choi et al., 2018), QASPER (Dasigi et al., 2021), CaseHOLD (Zheng et al., 2021), OpenBookQA (Mihaylov et al., 2018), SQuAD (Rajpurkar et al., 2016), and MultiRC (Khashabi et al., 2018) were revised to determine whether they can be used in this research. Due to the fact that most of them contain question-answer pairs derived from Wikipedia articles, we did not find them suitable. Instead, we focus on textbooks and other teaching materials for the experiments to imitate real-life in-classroom applications. Moreover, in some cases, it is not possible to create the reference corpus for the above-mentioned QA pairs since it is not clear what materials were used for those datasets. In addition, in some cases, the questions were not based on multiple sentences. Therefore, it would not be reasonable to use such datasets while we aim to work with the European Union law domain and with questions based on a whole paragraph. Consequently, it was decided to develop a new corpus of multiple-choice test items that is based on the selected principles of design.

The criteria for choosing a book for the MCQ corpus were the following:

- The contents of the book cover general information about the European Union, particularly the history of its creation, the founding treaties, the four freedoms, the sources of law, and other basic concepts and legislation. The book should not include any specific details regarding specialised legislation cases. For instance, home affairs law, EU immigration and asylum law, commerce or terrorism are too narrow topics and were not touched upon in the corpus.

- The information presented in the book should mostly be written in full paragraphs rather than in bullet points or stored in tables.

- It should be possible to copy the text easily from the book. Otherwise, retyping the paragraphs would take too much time. Moreover, it is easier to have typos or other errors in this case. Thus, not being able to copy directly from the book constitutes a challenge in terms of both time and human effort.

The chosen book consists of sixteen chapters and covers the following topics from the history and legislation of the European Union: the origins and character of EU law; the development from Community to Union; the political and legal institutions of the European Union; the sources of EU law; the legislative process; enforcement of EU law; Article 267 of the Treaty on the Functioning of the European Union (TFEU); the relationship between EU law and national law – supremacy; the relationship between EU law and national law – direct effect; the Internal Market; citizenship of the Union; the free movement of workers; freedom of establishment and the freedom to provide and receive services under Articles 49 and 56 TFEU; the free movement of goods and Articles 34 and 35 TFEU; Article 28 TFEU and customs tariffs and Article 110 TFEU and discriminatory internal taxation; EU competition law; social policy; discrimination law and Article 157; the wider social influence of the EU. All of these topics are mentioned in the MCQ corpus.

The following criteria for the corpus were selected:

- Paragraphs have to be included for all the questions. Since the research is based on paragraph similarity matching, without the relevant paragraph the question cannot be used for the purposes of this task. In the context of this research, a paragraph refers to either an actual paragraph from the book or a couple of sentences on which the question is based. The Paragraph cell should contain only those sentences that are necessary to answer the question. Therefore, sometimes the actual paragraph from the book has to be cut or shortened to include only the sentences needed to answer the question. It is possible to add sentences from different paragraphs as long as they make sense and the text in the Paragraph cell is 2-5 sentences long. The length of the paragraphs may vary. It is worth underlying that only one sentence cannot constitute a paragraph for this research no matter its size. The number of sentences in the paragraph highly depends on the asked question and the answer. Although it is possible to include longer paragraphs in the MCQ corpus, it is rather challenging to make a question that is based on the information in all the sentences in a large paragraph.

- All the questions in the MCQ corpus should be based on the information in all the sentences in the Paragraph cell. Yes/No or True/False questions are not possible. The questions should be worded as actual questions rather than incomplete statements.

- The answer should consist of one or a few words rather than a long phrase. The answer cannot consist of a whole sentence. It is of paramount importance for the automatic generation of distractors. Although the distractors are not generated for this study, they will be used in future research. In order to retrieve good quality distractors, the anchor should be concise, ideally consist of a couple of words or a number. However, the MCQ corpus is aimed to be easy to use in classrooms. Therefore, the above-mentioned rule about the length of the anchor can be neglected in some cases for the sake of a good multiple-choice test item that can be used unchanged.

In total, the MCQ corpus consists of 200 paragraphs and question-answer pairs. The corpus was checked with a writing tool Grammarly to spot grammar and spelling mistakes, typos, extra spaces and other issues. Furthermore, all the questions were revised by a native speaker of English who is a professional proofreader and qualified linguist. Unfortunately, due to the lack of time and resources, the MCQ corpus was not revised by an expert in EU law. It is an area of further research and developments.

3.2 The reference corpus (TM corpus)

The preparation of the TM corpus started with choosing the relevant book. A procedure similar to choosing the book for the MCQ corpus was used. Overall, the book had to cover the same topics in the EU law and be available in a machine-readable or easy-to-process format. The information should be presented in text in paragraphs rather than in diagrams, charts, tables or images. In contrast to the MCQ corpus, the TM corpus should be of a considerably larger size. While looking for such a book, we encountered several problems. Many books on the EU law are available in hard copies but do not have the copies in the electronic format. In many cases, if it is available in the PDF format, the printed book is scanned. Therefore, even with the use of the optical character recognition (OCR) software, the processed output would be of very low quality and will require a significant amount of time and human resources to be revised manually.

The selected book consists of 1,198 pages and includes similar chapters as the one used for the MCQ corpus. The PDF is processed with a Python program in order to write the text into a text file. The information unrelated to the contents of the relevant paragraphs is omitted. For example, the table of contents, page numbers, headings, headers, footnotes, the list of references as well as any tables or images are not included in the TM corpus file.

Moreover, in the original file, the words at the end of the line are hyphenated. It is a typographical hyphen that has to be removed from the corpus. If it is not done, a substantial amount of information can be lost since for the machine, the same word written with or without a hyphen constitutes different words. Besides, a new line character follows this typographical hyphen, so the word is split into two parts. The hyphens followed by a new line character were deleted, and the parts of the word were glued together. All the hyphenated words with a new line character inside were checked in the Enchant module. It is a spell-checking library for Python. After the new line symbol is deleted, if a hyphenated word is found in the library, it is left untouched. Otherwise, it is glued together.

The other issues with processing the file included the following ones: many chapters include quotes that constitute a large paragraph. They should not be included in the TM corpus since the MCQ corpus can contain the same quotations. For the purposes of this research, we want to retrieve fuzzy matches instead of the exact matches. Therefore, we do not want to have exactly the same paragraphs in both corpora. Since such quotes are written in a different font and size, it was possible for the Python program to omit them.

3.3 Comparison of the MCQ and TM corpora

As mentioned above, the method for finding similar paragraphs resembles the one used for retrieving translation memory matches in a translation management system. Since the MCQ corpus represents a source text, and the reference (TM) corpus embodies the translation memory, it is essential that those corpora have many features in common. Hence, a comprehensive contrastive analysis of both corpora was conducted.

The corpora are compared in terms of the word count, the number of unique words, the average number of words per paragraph, most common words. As previously stated, the MCQ corpus includes 200 multiple-choice test items together with the referencing paragraphs. It estimates to 12,754 words. A word in this context is a sequence of alphanumeric characters split by a space.

Conversely, the reference corpus equals to 399,196 words. It encompasses more than a thousand pages of the processed text. Thus, it is more than 31 times larger than the multiple-choice questions corpus.

The average number of words in a paragraph in the MCQ corpus is 63 words. Likewise, for the TM corpus the number is 57 words.

4 Experiments

Experimenting with semantic textual similarity has been within the scope of recent research in natural language processing. For example, Ranashinghe et al. (2019a) evaluated the implications contextual word embeddings have on unsupervised semantic textual similarity methods. They carried out their experiments with several dataset including the SICK dataset and bio-medical dataset for English as well as the dataset in Spanish. Such methods as cosine similarity using average vectors, Word Mover's Distance and cosine similarity using Smooth Inverse Frequency with contextualised word embeddings were evaluated to calculate semantic similarity between pairs of texts. They came to a conclusion that contextual word embeddings can be employed for various languages and domains for unsupervised machine learning tasks.

Ranasinghe et al. (2019b) experiment with Siamese neural networks (Bromley et al., 1993) for semantic textual similarity. They mention that "Siamese networks contain two or more identical sub-networks. The networks are identical in the sense that they have the same configuration with the same parameters and weights. In addition, parameter updating is mirrored across these sub-networks". The authors state that this type of neural networks performs well for finding similarity or a relationship between two comparable things, e.g., signature verification, face verification, image similarity as well as sentence similarity. In this research, we will use sentence transformers for the paragraph similarity tasks that also use Siamese and triplet network structures.

In Ranasinghe et al. (2020), sentence encoders are used to improve the matching and retrieving process in Translation Memories systems. In our research, we use a similar approach while experimenting with paragraph encoders.

4.1 Doc2vec model

In our experiments, we use a similar technique as in Řehůřek (2014) and Shperber (2017). We use Gensim, a free Python library for topic modelling (Rehurek and Sojka, 2010). It is helpful for training large-scale semantic natural language processing models; representing text as semantic vectors; and finding semantically related documents. It allows to train vector embeddings fast, can be run on any operating system as well as any other platform that supports Python and NumPy. The library is also open-source.

For each paragraph from the MCQ corpus, we retrieve two similar paragraphs from the TM corpus. We also calculate the similarity score for each match.

4.2 Sentence-BERT

Transformer models like BERT are the state-of-the-art nowadays in semantic textual similarity and are salient in natural language processing in general. They are widely used in machine translation and time series prediction; document summarization; document generation; named entity recognition; image processing; video understanding and other tasks. Sentence-BERT (SBERT) is "a modification of the pretrained BERT network that use Siamese and triplet network structures to derive semantically meaningful sentence embeddings that can be compared using cosine-similarity" (Reimers and Gurevych, 2019). It was presented as an advancement of BERT, which requires a lot of computational power and is very slow. For example, BERT needed 65 hours to find the most similar pair in a collection of 10,000 sentences, while SBERT did the same task in five seconds. Although the authors claim that SBERT is very fast and computationally efficient, such speed and performance requires the use of a GPU. For this research, the experiments were conducted on a regular laptop using a CPU only. Therefore, our results are far from such small numbers in terms of speed. The motivation behind the approach of using a CPU only for this research is explained by the fact that the aims of this research is to help education professionals and reduce the teachers' effort in preparing the assessment materials. Therefore, if the used methods require very powerful computers and a lot of computational power with the use of a GPU, it will not be feasible to replicate this method in a real-life classroom setting.

The procedure for finding the similar paragraphs in this research is analogous to the one used with doc2vec. Particularly, for each paragraph from the small ad-hoc corpus of multiple-choice test items, two matching paragraphs are found in the large reference corpus. The similarity scores are also calculated for all the retrieved paragraphs.

In this research, we took the SBERT approach to obtain paragraph vectors. We used the paraphrase-MiniLM-L12-v2 model.

5 Evaluation

In this study, a simple method of automatic evaluation is used. Specifically, the paragraphs from the MCQ corpus are fed to the algorithms. With the help of either doc2vec or SBERT, semantically similar paragraphs are found in the reference corpus. The results are written to a file together with the paragraphs similarity score and the paragraph manually found as a gold standard. Paragraph similarity scores resemble fuzzy matches in translation memory systems. After that, the number of identical matches, i.e., paragraphs produced by the algorithms and the paragraphs from the evaluation corpus, is calculated. The performance of the algorithms is presented in the percentage of correct matches out of 50 paragraphs.

For the purposes of evaluation, a small corpus of fifty paragraphs was made. It consists of a Paragraph column with the paragraphs from the MCQ corpus; a Question column with the questions attached to those paragraphs; and a Match column with the paragraphs similar to the ones in column 1. All the matches are selected manually. In order to do so, the reference corpus is searched for key words manually identified in the paragraph from the MCQ corpus. It is done with the Find option. After that, the found results are checked in terms of their content and size. The paragraph from the MCQ corpus and its match from the reference corpus should talk about the same thing and include the same key words. Moreover, it is important that the question from the MCQ corpus attached to one paragraph can be answered if shown only the paragraph from the reference corpus. In addition, the correct answer (anchor) for this question should also be included in the new match. It was required that the length of both paragraphs was roughly similar where possible.

5.1 Evaluation Results

It was calculated that the performance of doc2vec during the automatic evaluation was 0%, i.e. zero matches out of fifty paragraphs in the evaluation corpus were found. In contrast, in 44% of the cases, SBERT found the correct matches from the evaluation corpus. More rigorous human evaluation is required to check to what extent the automatically obtained paragraphs are similar to the ones in the MCQ corpus. It is assumed that some of the question answer pairs could be post-edited and used in the in-classroom environment. It was also noticed that in some cases, SBERT outperformed human judgement and found the paragraphs with higher similarity scores. In terms of efficiency, SBERT was rather slow when used on a CPU, which is its main drawback.

Table 1 below includes the paragraph similarity scores for both models. It is evident that the difference in performance of the two algorithms is rather significant. The highest score of doc2vec is roughly the same as the lowest score of SBERT. Moreover, the average score of SBERT is higher than any of the results of doc2vec.

doc2vec	SBERT
10 highest scores	
0.58	0.86
0.57	0.86
0.57	0.85
0.57	0.85
0.57	0.85
0.57	0.83
0.57	0.83
0.56	0.83
0.56	0.82
0.56	0.82
Highest score	
0.58	0.86
Lowest score	
0.37	0.57
Average score	
0.51	0.70

Table 1: Similarity scores for doc2vec and SBERT

Furthermore, the efficiency of both algorithms was compared in terms of time needed to perform the task. The time in seconds was recorded for each found match with the help of the Python module

Timeit(). After that, the average time needed to find a single match was calculated. The results for the two algorithms are as follows: doc2vec – 46 seconds; SBERT – 268 seconds (4.4 minutes).

It is worth mentioning that usually the experiments with SBERT are conducted on a GPU. It was done deliberately to check the efficiency of the algorithms under the typical conditions teachers face at schools and non-technical departments in universities. Therefore, although SBERT demonstrated impressive results and even outperformed human judgement, it is very slow without using a GPU.

6 Conclusion and Future Work

In this research, the ways to automatically generate multiple-choice test items from a whole paragraph are investigated. In particular, it was inspired by translation memory matches in modern translation management systems.

The experiments are conducted within the European Union law domain. A small corpus of 200 multiple-choice test items together with the corresponding paragraphs is manually created from scratch. The larger reference corpus (TM corpus) that consists of 1,000+ pages of processed text from a textbook on the same topic was also created.

The performance and efficiency of two deep learning models, doc2vec and SBERT, was tested. Both algorithms provide paragraph vectors used to find semantically similar paragraphs. Although doc2vec was almost six times faster than sentence transformers when run on a regular computer with a CPU, it failed to produce the desired results. In fact, the performance of doc2vec was 0% when evaluated automatically. In contrast, SBERT achieved 44% performance in the same automatic evaluation task. Moreover, in some cases, it outperformed human judgement and found the paragraphs with higher similarity scores than those selected manually. Nevertheless, the fact that SBERT is not computationally efficient when used on a regular laptop remains its main drawback.

In the future, this research can be broadened to include automatic generation of distractors and their evaluation. Moreover, the corpus of multiple-choice test items can be extended. It would also be beneficial to have this corpus revised by an expert on the European Union law. Moreover, in-classroom experiments with the students of law and teachers are needed to fully evaluate the quality of produced multiple-choice test items and to test whether the suggested method truly reduces the teachers' effort in performing knowledge assessment.

References

Naveed Afzal and Ruslan Mitkov. 2014. Automatic generation of multiple choice questions using dependency-based semantic relations. In *Soft Computing* 18.7, pages 1269-1281.

Tahani Alsubait, Bijan Parsia, and Uli Sattler. 2014. Generating Multiple Choice Questions From Ontologies: Lessons Learnt. In *OWLED*, pages 73-84.

Jane Bromley, Isabelle Guyon, Yann LeCun, Eduard Sackinger, and Roopak Shah. 1993. Signature verification using a siamese time delay neural network. In *IJPRAI*, 7, pages 669–688.

Tim Burnett and Stefania Paredes Fuentes. 2020. Assessment in the Time of Pandemic: A Panic-free Guide. In *The Economics Network*.

Eunsol Choi, He He, Mohit Iyyer, Mark Yatskar, Wen-tau Yih, Yejin Choi, Percy Liang, and Luke Zettlemoyer. 2018. *Quac: Question answering in context*, arXiv preprint arXiv:1808.07036. https://doi.org/10.18653/v1/D18-1241

Pradeep Dasigi, Kyle Lo, Iz Beltagy, Arman Cohan, Noah A. Smith, and Matt Gardner. 2021. *A Dataset of Information-Seeking Questions and Answers Anchored in Research Papers*, arXiv preprint arXiv:2105.03011. https://doi.org/10.18653/v1/2021.naacl-main.365

Yifan Gao, Lidong Bing, Piji Li, Irwin King, and Michael R. Lyu. 2019. Generating distractors for reading comprehension questions from real examinations. In *Proceedings of the AAAI Conference on Artificial Intelligence*. Vol. 33. No. 01. 2019, pages 6423-6430.

Qi Guo, Chinmay Kulkarni, Aniket Kittur, Jeffrey P. Bigham, and Emma Brunskill. 2016. Questimator: Generating knowledge assessments for arbitrary topics. In *IJCAI-16: Proceedings of the AAAI Twenty-Fifth International Joint Conference on Artificial Intelligence*.

Mandar Joshi, Eunsol Choi, Daniel S. Weld, and Luke Zettlemoyer. 2017. Triviaqa: A large scale distantly supervised challenge dataset for reading comprehension. In *Proceedings of the 55th Annual Meeting of the Association for Computational Linguistics*, ACL 2017, Vancouver, Canada, July 30 - August 4, Volume 1: Long Papers, pages 1601–1611. https://doi.org/10.18653/v1/P17-1147

Nikiforos Karamanis and Ruslan Mitkov. 2006. Generating multiple-choice test items from medical text: A pilot study. In *Proceedings of the fourth international natural language generation conference,* pages 111-113. https://aclanthology.org/W06-1416

Daniel Khashabi, Snigdha Chaturvedi, Michael Roth, Shyam Upadhyay, and Dan Roth. 2018. Looking Beyond the Surface: A Challenge Set for Reading Comprehension over Multiple Sentences. In *Proceedings of the 2018 Conference of the North American Chapter of the Association for Computational Linguistics: Human Language Technologies*, Volume 1 (Long Papers), pages 252-262. https://doi.org/10.18653/v1/N18-1023

Vishwajeet Kumar, Ganesh Ramakrishnan, and Yuan-Fang Li. 2018. *A framework for automatic question generation from text using deep reinforcement learning*, arXiv preprint arXiv:1808.04961.

Tom Kwiatkowski, Jennimaria Palomaki, Olivia Rhinehart, Michael Collins, Ankur Parikh, Chris Alberti, Danielle Epstein, Illia Polosukhin, Matthew Kelcey, Jacob Devlin, Kenton Lee, Kristina N. Toutanova, Llion Jones, Ming-Wei Chang, Andrew Dai, Jakob Uszkoreit, Quoc Le, and Slav Petrov. 2019. Natural questions: a benchmark for question answering research. In *Transactions of the Association of Computational Linguistics.* https://doi.org/10.1162/tacl_a_00276

Chen Liang, Xiao Yang, Neisarg Dave, Drew Wham, Bart Pursel, and C. Lee Giles. 2018. Distractor generation for multiple choice questions using learning to rank. In *Proceedings of the thirteenth workshop on innovative use of NLP for building educational applications*, pages 284-290. https://doi.org/10.18653/v1/W18-0533

Mukta Majumder and Sujan Kumar Saha. 2015. A system for generating multiple choice questions: With a novel approach for sentence selection. In *Proceedings of the 2nd workshop on natural language processing techniques for educational applications*, pages 64-72. https://doi.org/10.18653/v1/W15-4410

Jorge Martinez-Gil, Bernhard Freudenthaler, and A. Min Tjoa. 2019. Multiple choice question answering in the legal domain using reinforced co-occurrence. In *International Conference on Database and Expert Systems Applications*, pages 138-148.

Todor Mihaylov, Peter Clark, Tushar Khot, and Ashish Sabharwal. 2018. *Can a Suit of Armor Conduct Electricity? A New Dataset for Open Book Question Answering*, arXiv preprint arXiv:1809.02789. https://doi.org/10.18653/v1/D18-1260

Halyna Maslak. 2021. Automatic generation of multiple-choice test items with deep learning (Unpublished master's dissertation). University of Wolverhampton, Wolverhampton, United Kingdom.

Ruslan Mitkov. 2003. Computer-aided generation of multiple-choice tests. In *Proceedings of the HLT-NAACL 03 workshop on Building educational applications using natural language processing*, pages 17-22. https://aclanthology.org/W03-0203

Ruslan Mitkov, Le An Ha, and Nikiforos Karamanis. 2006. A computer-aided environment for generating multiple-choice test items. *In Natural language engineering 12(2)*, pages 177-194.

Andreas Papasalouros, Konstantinos Kanaris, and Konstantinos Kotis. 2008. Automatic Generation Of Multiple Choice Questions From Domain Ontologies. In *e-Learning*, pages 427-434.

Pranav Rajpurkar, Jian Zhang, Konstantin Lopyrev, and Percy Liang. 2016. *SQuAD: 100,000+ Questions for Machine Comprehension of Text*, arXiv preprint arXiv:1606.05250. https://doi.org/10.18653/v1/D16-1264

Tharindu Ranashinghe, Constantin Orasan, and Ruslan Mitkov. 2019a. Enhancing unsupervised sentence similarity methods with deep contextualised word representations. In *RANLP*. https://doi.org/10.26615/978-954-452-056-4_115

Tharindu Ranasinghe, Constantin Orăsan, and Ruslan Mitkov. 2019b. Semantic textual similarity with siamese neural networks. In *Proceedings of the International Conference on Recent Advances in Natural Language Processing (RANLP 2019).* https://doi.org/10.26615/978-954-452-056-4_116

Tharindu Ranasinghe, Constantin Orasan, and Ruslan Mitkov. 2020. *Intelligent Translation Memory Matching and Retrieval with Sentence Encoders*, arXiv preprint arXiv:2004.12894. https://aclanthology.org/2020.eamt-1.19

Radim Rehurek. 2014. Doc2vec tutorial.

Radim Rehurek and Petr Sojka. 2010. Software framework for topic modelling with large corpora. In *Proceedings of the LREC 2010 workshop on new challenges for NLP frameworks*, pages 45-50.

Nils Reimers and Iryna Gurevych. 2019. *Sentence-bert: Sentence embeddings using siamese bert-networks*, arXiv preprint arXiv:1908.10084. https://doi.org/10.18653/v1/D19-1410

Jinnie Shin, Qi Guo, and Mark J. Gierl. 2019. Multiple-choice item distractor development using topic modeling approaches. In *Frontiers in psychology* 10: 825.

Gidi Shperber. 2017. A gentle introduction to Doc2Vec.

Richard Sikes. 2007. Fuzzy Matching in Theory and Practice. In *Multilingual*, 18(6), pages 39–43.

Arjun Singh Bhatia, Manas Kirti, and Sujan Kumar Saha. 2013. Automatic generation of multiple choice questions using wikipedia. In *International conference on pattern recognition and machine intelligence*, pages 733-738.

Yuni Susanti, Takenobu Tokunaga, Hitoshi Nishikawa, and Hiroyuki Obari. 2018. Automatic distractor generation for multiple-choice English vocabulary questions. In *Research and practice in technology enhanced learning 13.1*, pages 1-16.

Yuanlong Wang, Ru Li, Hu Zhang, Hongyan Tan, and Qinghua Chai. 2018. Using Sentence-Level Neural Network Models for Multiple-Choice Reading Comprehension Tasks. In *Wireless Communications and Mobile Computing 2018*.

Zhilin Yang, Peng Qi, Saizheng Zhang, Yoshua Bengio, William W. Cohen, Ruslan Salakhutdinov, and Christopher D. Manning. 2018. *Hotpotqa: A dataset for diverse, explainable multi-hop question answering*, arXiv preprint arXiv:1809.09600. https://doi.org/10.18653/v1/D18-1259

Yao Zhao, Xiaochuan Ni, Yuanyuan Ding, and Qifa Ke. 2018. Paragraph-level neural question generation with maxout pointer and gated self-attention networks. In *Proceedings of the 2018 Conference on Empirical Methods in Natural Language Processing*, pages 3901-3910. https://doi.org/10.18653/v1/D18-1424

Lucia Zheng, Neel Guha, Brandon R. Anderson, Peter Henderson, and Daniel E. Ho. 2021. When Does Pretraining Help? Assessing Self-Supervised Learning for Law and the CaseHOLD Dataset. In *Proceedings of the Eighteenth International Conference on Artificial Intelligence and Law*, pages 159-168.

Neural Borrowing Detection with Monolingual Lexical Models

John E. Miller
jemiller@pucp.edu.pe

Emanuel Pariasca
emanuel.pariasca@pucp.edu.pe

César A. Beltrán Castañón
cbeltran@pucp.edu.pe

Artificial Intelligence/Engineering
Pontificia Universidad Católica del Perú
San Miguel, Lima, Perú

Abstract

Identification of lexical borrowings, transfer of words between languages, is an essential practice of historical linguistics and a vital tool in analysis of language contact and cultural events in general. We seek to improve tools for automatic detection of lexical borrowings, focusing here on detecting borrowed words from monolingual wordlists. Starting with a recurrent neural network lexical model and competing entropies approach, we incorporate a more current Transformer based lexical model. From there we experiment with several different models and approaches including a lexical donor model with augmented wordlist. The Transformer model reduces execution time and minimally improves borrowing detection, and the augmented donor model shows some promise. A substantive change in approach or model seems necessary for significant gains in detection of lexical borrowings.

1 Introduction

When words shows striking similarity between languages, they may be inherited from a common ancestor, borrowed from one contact language into the other, or less frequently, similar by chance or common creative process, e.g., onomatopoeia.

Identification of lexical borrowings, transfer of words between languages, is an integral step in the comparative method of historical linguistics (Campbell, 2013) and a vital tool for investigations of language contact, and cultural influences. Automated or assisted detection of lexical borrowings is one of many important and difficult tasks remaining in historical linguistics (List, 2019a).

We use neural network lexical language models of the phonology and phonotactics of a language to identify lexical borrowings. While language models refer generally to "any system trained only on the task of string prediction" (Bender and Koller, 2020), our lexical language models operate on monolingual wordlists limited to common or essential concepts, with vocabularies limited to language sound segments (phonemes, allophones). A fixed vocabulary of typically less than 100 coded sound segments eliminates the out-of-vocabulary problem, and a limited wordlist size of at most a few thousand lexical entries, reduces the practical model complexity.

We use the recurrent neural network model and competing lexical entropies approach of Miller et al. (2020) as a jumping off point, and incorporate a light-weight forward direction Transformer model from Vaswani et al. (2017) into this approach. We demonstrate our light-weight Transformer model over 41 different languages from the World Loan Database (Haspelmath and Tadmor, 2009) and contrast performance versus the recurrent model of Miller et al. (2020).

We perform several experiments expanding both the technical and application scope of our light-weight Transformer model: 1. develop a direct model approach that discriminates between inherited and borrowed words directly without the need to model inherited and borrowed word entropies separately, 2. enhance competing entropies and direct approaches to account for borrowed words by individual donor language, 3. train multiple borrowed and inherited models, and base decisions on majority vote of model combinations, 4. perform search for best model parameters using experimental sequences of randomly assigned parameter values, 5. explore a limited multi-lingual approach of using an additional donor language table to supplement borrowed words from the recipient language.

Results are evaluated for borrowing detection and, secondarily, execution time. Our light-weight Transformer minimally improves borrowing detection and reduces execution time versus the baseline. Direct detection of borrowed words performs less

Proceedings of the Student Research Workshop associated with RANLP-2021, pages 109–117,
held online, Sep 1–3, 2021.
https://doi.org/10.26615/issn.2603-2821.2021_016

well than the competing entropies approach. Multiple model combinations and parameter search show little improvement over the Transformer model, each with increased execution time. Adding a donor language wordlist minimally improves borrowing detection.

Our contributions are:

- Incorporation of Transformer model and direct approach into the borrowing detection problem,
- Demonstration that the competing entropies approach offers better borrowing detection than the direct approach,
- Demonstration that the multiple models approach and parameter search do not improve borrowing detection,
- Prototyped a way to improve detection performance via added donor wordlists.

2 Related Work

Approaches to Borrowed Word Detection

When words are borrowed into a language, initially, they may retain the phonology, phonotactics, or other features of the donor language. But over time the borrowed words will adapt to the recipient language – making borrowing detection more difficult (Kiparsky, 2014).

Our monolingual wordlist approach gambles that some remnant of the phonology or phonotactics of the donor language will still be perceptible long after the word is borrowed, and that competing entropies lexical models can be used to detect borrowed words. This is the approach taken by Miller et al. (2020) where curated monolingual wordlists of inherited and borrowed words are modeled with Markov chain and recurrent neural network lexical models, and then inherited versus borrowed word decisions are made based on which model estimates the minimum entropy. The approach is modestly successful, yet not sufficient as a tool to determine lexical borrowing. Professional linguists also take into account substantial multilingual and cross-linguistic lexical and contextual information.

An ambitious and complex borrowed word detection approach by Mi et al. (2020, 2018) identifies borrowed words by Uyghur from Turkish, Arabic, Russian and Chinese donors. Word embeddings are calculated using monolingual language models from corpora of Uyghur and donor languages, and then cross-lingual embeddings are constructed between Uyghur and donor languages with the help of bilingual dictionaries. The cross-lingual embeddings are used to identify candidate borrowed words between Uyghur and donor languages. Candidate words are tested as borrowed or inherited based on sound similarity and other language features. This approach is not limited to curated wordlists indexed by concepts. Future research planning will consider (Mi et al., 2020, 2018).

List and Forkel (2021) and List (2019b) repurpose lexical cognate identification methods from multilingual wordlists to the task of identifying borrowed words on a newly developed dataset of South-East Asian languages. Cognate detection, by searching for full or partial cognates based on sound similarity, is applied to identify language family internal cognate sets, and then "cognate sets are compared across language families and clustered into sets of potentially borrowed words" (List and Forkel, 2021, pg 4). We hope to integrate this approach into future research.

Another approach to borrowed word detection is to construct phylogenetic models of language families based on wordlists, including also intruder languages that are not necessarily part of the language family. Observed discrepancies in the model, in particular lexical items that detract from hierarchical family relations and contribute instead to lateral transfers, are likely due to borrowed words (List et al., 2014; Delz, 2014).

Neural Network Language Models

Use of recurrent neural networks to model textual language was popularized by Bengio et al. (2003). The language model is relatively sparse and still useful today with the incorporation of long short-term memory (LSTM) or gated recurrent unit (GRU) cells. Miller et al. (2020) employed a lexical language version of this model.

The attention module by Bahdanau et al. (2015), paired with a recurrent layer, explicitly takes into account the differential contribution of language elements on the position or element being modeled. Vaswani et al. (2017) realized that attention doesn't require a recurrent layer, "all you need is attention", resulting in reduced complexity and cost. They constructed a standard Transformer module of attention, add and normalization, and feed forward layers, and incorporated it into their state of the art translation system. Our lexical language models incorporate a light-weight Transformer module.

Recent advances include Bi-directional Encoder Representations from Transformers (BERT) (Devlin et al., 2018) and many others such as GPT, ElMo, and RoBERT which use millions or billions of parameter language models. This seems overkill since the number of parameters is orders of magnitude greater than a typical wordlist size. However, the method used by BERT of bi-directional training with a masked language model avoids the problem of model dependencies, and similarly the model of Wada et al. (2020) with independent bi-directional models. Both merit further consideration.

3 Materials and Methods

3.1 Materials

Wordlists extracted from all 41 language tables of the World Loan Database (Haspelmath and Tadmor, 2009) are used in our experiments. Tables document concept, value, borrowed status, language donor, etc., and consist of 800 to 2,000 words representing some 1,400 concepts from the Intercontinental Dictionary Series (Key and Comrie, 2015). Tables have recently been updated to add International Phonetic Alphabet (IPA) (Moran and Cysouw, 2018) representations of sound segments for all lexical entries (Tresoldi et al., 2019). A snippet from the Imbabura Quechua language table is shown in Table 1.

Concept	Value	Segments	Borrowed	Donor
World	pacha mama	p a tʃ a + m a m a	False	
Valley	yunga	j u ŋ g a	False	
Foam	putsuju	p u ts u x u	False	
Knife	kuchillo	k u tʃ i ʒ u	True	Spanish

Table 1: Snippet of Imbabura Quechua table.

In the experiment, where an additional Spanish donor wordlist is used in training, the Spanish word table from IDS is used as source, since Spanish is not among the 41 WOLD languages. However, the Spanish language word table from IDS was orthographic, so we transcribed the Spanish to segmented IPA, using the Easy Pronunciation portal (Baytukalov, 2019) to produce a phonetic representation of the Spanish wordlist, and then LingPy (List et al., 2018) with cross-linguistic transcription (List et al., 2021) module and a transcription profile to construct segmented IPA.

3.2 Methods

3.2.1 Neural models and experiments

Recurrent model Miller et al. (2020)'s lexical language model, based on Bengio et al. (2003), was adapted to work with sound segments and estimate lexical entropies using appropriate dropout and regulation (Figure 1). An innovative aspect of their borrowed word detection approach was to train separate models for inherited and borrowed words and have the models compete for which word is inherited or borrowed. Words belong to the model which estimates the lesser entropy for them.

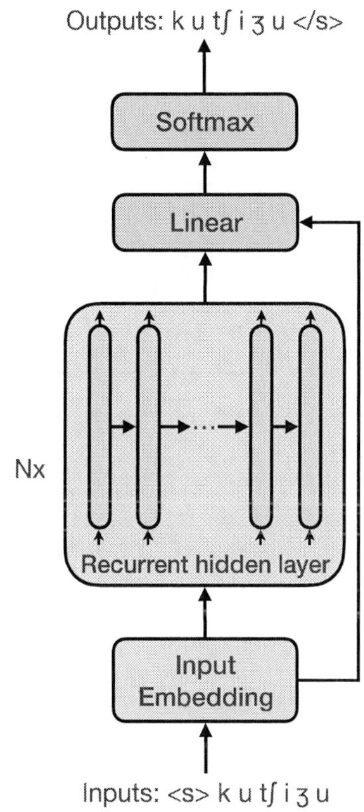

Figure 1: Recurrent Lexical Model

Light-weight Transformer Our technology improvement over the baseline model replaces the recurrent layer with a light-weight Transformer module (Vaswani et al., 2017) which includes Attention (Bahdanau et al., 2015) and Transformer features of adding and normalization layers, and a feed forward layer (Figure 2). The model uses a forward only (left-to-right) causal model — this reduces model complexity and avoids unintended dependencies between inputs and outputs.

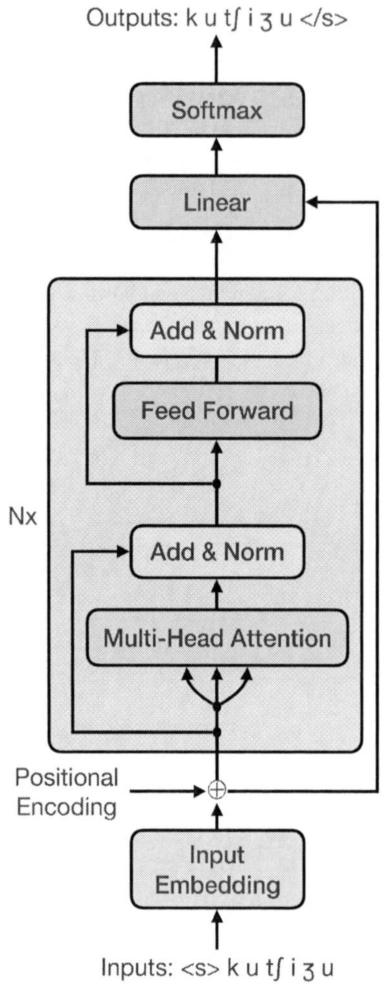

Figure 2: Light-weight Transformer Lexical Model

Direct model - experiment We developed a light-weight Transformer to predict inherited versus borrowed words directly from wordlists without the intermediate calculation of inherited and borrowed word entropies. This model flattens Transformer outputs and optionally merges embeddings (see connector on right of Figure 2) before connecting to the softmax layer.

Word donor - experiment We broadened the problem definition to include donor source of the borrowed words. Inputs include indication of word donor instead of simply inherited versus borrowed, where $d = 0$ designates an inherited word, and $d \in [1, D]$ designates which is the borrowed word donor. A minimum donor wordlist size of 75 words was used to assure enough data to fit donor models; less than 75 word donor sources were combined.

For competing entropy models this results in $D+1$ individual entropy models per language — one for inherited words and one for each donor source. In the decision procedure, all models compete for which has the lowest entropy to select the word. For the direct model, only one model is created and it directly discriminates between donors.

Multiple word models - experiment With competing entropy models, inherited word models are paired with borrowed word models to compete for which estimates the lower entropy for a word and so claims that word. With M inherited and borrowed word models each, there are $M \times M$ model pairs competing to claim words as inherited or borrowed. We developed the multiple models capability, which determines whether a word is inherited or borrowed based on majority vote of the model combinations. Model training and calculation of entropies is much more costly than entropy comparisons, $C \gg c$, so cost of training multiple models and taking majority vote on all entropy comparisons is approximately $(M + M) \times C$.

Parameter search - experiment Each language is unique whether considering the entire language or just phonology and phonotactics in a wordlist. Each lexical model for computing entropy will be different and maybe each configuration of light-weight Transformer parameter settings should be different as well. We developed the capability to run experiments on each training dataset, to determine optimal training parameters based on minimum validation cross-entropy for a lexical model, and then train multiple instances M of each model at the optimal training parameters. Majority vote from combinations of models trained at optimal conditions determine inherited versus borrowed word status.

This experiment is costly. For each training set, there are E experiments; for each experiment, there are I iterations of samples from the training set; for each iteration there are R replicate runs which return validation cross-entropies. Optimal training parameters for inherited and for borrowed words are used to train R model replicates on inherited and borrowed words training data. The resulting $R \times R$ model combinations predict inherited versus borrowed word status based on majority vote, as for multiple word models. So the cost per train-test partition or fold is $2 \times (E \times I \times R + R)$.

Additional donor wordlist - experiment Lack of sufficient borrowed words for training was a detractor so we enhanced our data methods to permit an additional donor wordlist source. This was a limited experiment where we include a Spanish wordlist from IDS (Key and Comrie, 2015), transcribe it to IPA (§3.1), and combine it with Spanish donor borrowed words for target languages where Spanish is the primary donor language: Imbabura Quechua, Mapudungun, Otomi, Q'eqchi', Wichí, Yaqui, and Zinacantán Tzotzil. We applied our enhanced data methods with both competing entropy and direct models for these seven languages.

3.2.2 Decision and Evaluation procedures

Test F1 score for the borrowed word category is the primary evaluation metric, with precision and recall reported as well. Total time duration of execution, combined training and testing, is a secondary measure.

Experiments ran 10-fold cross-validations over all 41 WOLD language tables except for the additional donor wordlist experiment which used just seven language tables. In the 10-fold cross-validation, wordlists are partitioned into 10 different folds of 9/10 training and 1/10 testing data. Models train on training data, predict borrowing on testing data, and summarize detection results from testing as F1 score, precision and recall over all folds. Results are reported here as the average of F1 score, precision, and recall, plus the execution time, over cross-validations and language tables.

Experiments were run under Windows 10 on an Intel portable with 6 cores (12 logical) and 16 GB of memory. TensorFlow 2.4 was configured to use 8 parallel threads; other user tasks were curtailed.

4 Experiments

4.1 Competing Entropies and Direct Models

Parameter settings specific to the recurrent model and constant parameter settings for the light-weight Transformer are shown in Table 2. Typical number of parameters per neural model are also reported. Results of the recurrent neural network competing entropies approach from (Miller et al., 2020) and our replication of that analysis are shown in Table 3. Note that Table 3 also reports Transformer parameter values that vary over experiments.

F1 score measures are similar for original and replicate recurrent neural studies. Execution time for the recurrent model is 1 hr and 57 minutes.

Parameter	Recurrent	Transformer
cell_type	GRU	LSTM
N_layers	1	1
embedding_len	32	32
hidden_internal_len	32	32
merge_embedding	True	True
learning_rate_schedule	Decay	Transformer
decay_factor	0.95	
recurrent_l2	0.001	
recurrent_output_dropout	0.2	
merge_embedding_dropout	0.2	
number of parameters	$\approx 13,000$	$\approx 10,000$

Table 2: Recurrent and Transformer Model Parameters

Light-weight Transformer

Results for the light-weight Transformer with the competing entropies approach on inherited versus borrowed words are shown in Table 3. Trials at 50 and 80 training epochs are reported with learning rate and dropouts held constant. A split settings for inherited and borrowed models is also shown with inherited, 50, and borrowed, 80, epochs. F1 scores are 1 percentage point greater for the greater number of epochs. Performance of the light-weight Transformer is on par or minimally better than the recurrent neural model. Adoption of the light-weight Transformer model reduced execution time.

Inherited versus donor Since borrowed words can vary substantially by word donor, we speculated that fitting an entropy model on borrowed words by donor language could result in better fitting donor models with a commensurate improvement in overall borrowed word prediction. Results for this experiment at 50 and 80 training epochs, and the split 50, 80 epochs settings, are reported for the competing entropies approach in Table 3. Detection performance remains essentially unchanged or slightly reduced for donor models while execution time increased slightly.

Direct neural model

The approach of competing entropy models, may be more complicated than necessary. All the data is available for a direct neural model to use in discriminating between inherited and borrowed words.

Results of our experiment with a light-weight Transformer model to directly discriminate between inherited and borrowed words are reported in Table 3. All trials used 120 training epochs and the same learning rate and dropout parameters. For the competing entropies approach, embeddings are merged with recurrent or light-weight Transformer output before calculating segment probabilities and word entropies. This improved model detection performance. We tested this explicitly with our flattened direct model with merge and no-merge of embeddings.

The direct model scores 5 percentage points lower F1 score than the competing entropies model and takes half again as much time to execute. There is no difference between merge and no-merge of embeddings with the Transformer output.

The direct model for inherited versus donor shows no difference in borrowing detection between inherited versus borrowed and inherited versus donor approaches. Execution times are similar between all experiments on the direct model, and are a litter longer than those for the competing entropies model when training for 80 epochs.

4.2 Multiple Models and Search

An advantage of the competing entropy models approach is that when there are several entropy models, they can be combined with any of their opposite inherited or borrowed word models. In particular, with three models each of inherited and word models, nine competing entropy model pairs can be formed to make borrowed word decisions.

Table 4 reports results for two experiments on competing entropy models where three models each for inherited and borrowed were trained at the same set of conditions and then a majority vote taken over the nine model combinations for borrowed word decisions. The experiment with 80 training epochs, used different learning rates and embedding dropouts for inherited versus borrowed word models, while the experiment at 50 epochs used constant learning rates and dropouts. Detection results are on par with those reported previously for the single competing entropies approach (Table 3). Execution times are increased by a little more than three times that for the single competing entropies approach.

Since the phonology, phonotactics, language culture and contact situation are different for each language, maybe different training parameters are required for each language wordlist. Table 4 reports results of an experiment on competing entropy models where eight experiments on three parameters are performed. Per the experimental method in §3.2.1 one iteration with three replicates each are performed for each randomly chosen experimental condition for each fold of the cross-validation. Parameter settings were randomly sampled from the parameter ranges shown in Table 4. Resulting optimal parameter settings are used to perform three replicate trials on their corresponding inherited or borrowed word model. The nine combinations of inherited and borrowed models take a majority vote on borrowed word decisions.

Parameter search does no better than using multiple inherited and borrowed word models trained at fixed parameter settings, which does no better than a single pair of inherited and borrowed models trained at fixed settings. Execution times have exploded to about a day due to the quantity of model training for search models.

4.3 Added Spanish Donor Table

Several of the Latin American languages in WOLD (Imbabura Quechua, Mapudungun, Otomi, Q'qechi', Wichí, Yaqui, Zinacantán Tzotzil) have Spanish as the primary and only significant language donor. For each of these languages we added the Spanish wordlist in segmented IPA to the existing borrowed words of the training set, and then trained the models and evaluated test performance for these seven languages in a 10-fold cross-validation. This was a crude attempt to take advantage of data quantity with the hope that Spanish phonotactics would translate sufficiently into Spanish borrowed word phonotactics via our light-weight Transformer model.

Table 5 shows detection results using this method. Also shown are the average of detection results over these same seven languages from the light-weight Transformer with competing entropies and direct approaches. We find at best a slight improvement in F1 score by using the Spanish language wordlist. Recall suffers and precision improves as a result of using the Spanish wordlist. Direct model results remain noncompetitive.

5 Discussion

The purpose of this study was to develop and improve tools for automatic or assisted identification of lexical borrowings in monolingual wordlists. We replicated the recurrent lexical model and competing entropies approach of Miller et al. (2020) for detecting borrowed words, producing similar detection results and capturing a baseline execution time.

[1]Precision and Recall, in error in the Original "Baseline - recurrent" model, is corrected here.

Experiment	Epochs	Learning rate	Embed dropout	Attention dropout	Transform dropout	F1 score	Precision	Recall	Time hr:min
Baseline - recurrent									
Original[1]	45	0.01				0.603	0.546	0.697	
Replicated	45	0.01				0.604	0.546	0.699	1:57
Competing entropies - Transformer									
Borrowed	50/80	.0075/.0035	0.4/0.2	0.2	0.1	0.616	0.559	0.713	1:12
Borrowed	50	0.0055	0.3	0.2	0.1	0.606	0.548	0.701	1:08
Borrowed	80	0.0055	0.3	0.2	0.1	0.614	0.557	0.706	1:33
Donor	50/80	.0075/.0035	0.4/0.2	0.2	0.1	0.599	0.527	0.724	1:29
Donor	50	0.0055	0.3	0.2	0.1	0.605	0.536	0.720	1:21
Donor	80	0.0055	0.3	0.2	0.1	0.606	0.533	0.730	1:35
Direct - Transformer - flattened									
Borrowed(nomerge)	120	0.0025	0.3	0.3	0.3	0.559	0.480	0.726	1:49
Borrowed(merge)	120	0.0025	0.3	0.3	0.3	0.557	0.506	0.659	1:53
Donor(nomerge)	120	0.0025	0.3	0.3	0.3	0.544	0.447	0.766	1:47
Donor(merge)	120	0.0025	0.3	0.3	0.3	0.552	0.479	0.694	1:52

Table 3: Competing Entropies and Direct Model Experiments - 10 Fold Cross-validation

Epochs	Learning rate	Embed dropout	Attention dropout	Transform dropout	F1 score	Precision	Recall	Time d:hr:min
Multiple entropy models								
80	.0075/.0035	0.4/0.2	0.2	0.1	0.615	0.559	0.710	4:22
50	0.0055	0.3	0.2	0.1	0.617	0.561	0.708	4:08
Parameter search								
50-100	.0025-.0075	0.1-0.5	0.2	0.1	0.621	0.563	0.715	23:53

Table 4: Parameter Search and Multiple Models Experiments - 10 Fold Cross-validation

We developed a light-weight Transformer model (Bahdanau et al., 2015; Vaswani et al., 2017) and observed that it performed minimally better than par versus the recurrent model in borrowed word detection, and was more responsive with reduced execution times. The light-weight Transformer offers a viable base for exploring different lexical borrowing detection approaches.

5.1 Competing Entropies and Direct Models

Our meta-level design and analysis, contrasts Transformer with recurrent model results, and forms a 2-factor design of: competing entropies versus direct approaches, and inherited and borrowed versus inherited and word donor approaches.

The light-weight Transformer with competing entropies approach performed five percentage points better than the light-weight Transformer with a direct approach. Competing entropies seems a useful approach to test for lexical borrowings, more so than fitting a larger but less meaningful direct neural model.

With inherited versus donor models, we tested whether modeling donors separately would result in better prediction performance, thinking that treating donors individually might give more coherent training and test subsets. Resulting performance was just on par with the corresponding borrowed word approach; no benefit was conveyed by modeling donors separately. This suggests that any benefit due to modeling more coherent language subsets is offset by the reduced sample size for such subsets. This result seems more likely a problem of insufficient data rather than a dismissal of the utility of modeling donors separately.

5.2 Multiple Models and Search

With multiple models and the competing entropies approach, we took the cross product of inherited with borrowed word models and used majority vote to indicate borrowed words. The multiple models approach conferred no advantage. Modeling inherited versus borrowed words seems sufficiently consistent that voting has nothing to add.

Experiment	Epochs	Learning rate	Embed dropout	Attention dropout	Transform dropout	F1 score	Precision	Recall	Time min
Results for Languages with Additional Donor Language Table									
Entropies	100/150	0.0055	0.1	0.1	0.1	0.789	0.841	0.752	52
Direct	120	0.0035	0.3	0.3	0.3	0.735	0.743	0.742	41
Results for Languages without Donor Language Table									
Replicated Baseline - Recurrent						0.777	0.719	0.855	
Competing Entropies Borrowed - Transformer						0.775	0.713	0.855	
Direct Borrowed - Transformer						0.704	0.632	0.830	

Table 5: Additional Spanish Donor Language Table Experiments - 10 Fold Cross-validation - Over Languages: Imbabura Quechua, Mapudungun, Otomi, Q'qechi', Wichí, Yaqui, Zinacantán Tzotzil

Performing parameter search for training of inherited and borrowed word models, was ineffective and costly. Detection results were no better than for multiple models, and execution time over all 41 WOLD languages was about a day. The single competing entropies approach with light-weight Transformer gives almost as good detection results with just 1.5 hours execution time. Again modeling seems sufficiently consistent within the given parameter sampling ranges that no benefit is gained.

5.3 Added Spanish Donor Table

Lack of sufficient data is a major detractor in obtaining good model fits and reproducibility on test cases; this is especially true for highly parameterized models where the parameter counts equal or exceed the data counts. We added training data from a Spanish language wordlist as though they were borrowed words, fake borrowed words, for each of the seven WOLD language tables where Spanish is the primary donor language.

Transformer models learned from actual and fake borrowed words, and produced F1 scores slightly better than par versus the competing entropies approach without data augmentation. Recall decreased and precision increased. This indicates that the Transformer model learned the Spanish wordlist so well that it no longer detected borrowed words that were better adapted to the recipient language. Similarly the better learning prevented inherited words from being confused with Spanish borrowed words. This suggests that with a table of fake borrowed words that conforms more faithfully to word adaption to each language, we could see a meaningful improvement in detection of borrowed words. We observed an improvement for direct detection too, but still with poorer performance versus the competing entropies approach.

6 Conclusion

We constructed an effective and responsive light-weight Transformer model as a lexical language model for use in the competing entropies approach for detection of lexical borrowings. Detection performance was on par to minimally better than that using a recurrent neural network model; execution times were reduced. A direct detection model using a light-weight Transformer showed poorer detection of lexical borrowings than the competing entropy models approach. Entropy seems to capture important evidence about lexical items that our direct model does not.

Incorporation of language donor into detection models performed on par with the the corresponding borrowed word models. Lack of sufficient data detracts more from the model than within language coherence contributes. Majority vote over the cross product of inherited and borrowed word models, and parameter search via random experimental trial design, offer no benefit. This vouches for the relative consistency of model results for current parameter ranges and model architecture.

Addition of a donor language wordlist, as though borrowed words, reduced recall and increased precision. With better simulated borrowed words, rather than simple adoption of the donor wordlist, recall and precision should improve. This offers a promising avenue of investigation.

Acknowledgments

We sincerely thank the reviewers for their helpful and detailed comments. The first author has received funding and encouragement from the Graduate School of the Pontificia Universidad Católica del Perú (PUCP) through the Huiracocha-2019 scholarship program.

References

Dzmitry Bahdanau, Kyunghyun Cho, and Yoshua Bengio. 2015. Neural machine translation by jointly learning to align and translate. *ICLR*.

Timur Baytukalov. Easypronunciation.com [online]. 2019.

Emily Bender and Alexander Koller. 2020. Climbing towards nlu: On meaning, form, and understanding in the age of data. In *Proceedings of the 58th Annual Meeting of the Association for Computational Linguistics*, page 5185–5198, Stroudsberg. Association for Computational Linguistics.

Yoshua Bengio, Réjean Ducharme, Pascal Vincent, and Christian Janvin. 2003. A neural probabilistic language model. *J. Mach. Learn. Res.*, 3:1137–1155.

L. Campbell. 2013. *Historical Linguistics: An Introduction*. Edinburgh University Press.

Marisa Delz. 2014. Mismatches between phylogenetic trees in historical linguistics. Master's thesis, Eberhard-Karls-Universität, Tübingen, Germany.

Jacob Devlin, Ming-Wei Chang, Kenton Lee, and Kristina Toutanova. 2018. BERT: pre-training of deep bidirectional transformers for language understanding. *CoRR*, abs/1810.04805.

Martin Haspelmath and Uri Tadmor, editors. 2009. *World Loanword Database (WOLD)*. Max Planck Institute for Evolutionary Anthropology, Leipzig.

Mary Ritchie Key and Bernard Comrie, editors. 2015. *Intercontinental Dictionary Series (IDS)*. Max Planck Institute for Evolutionary Anthropology, Leipzig.

Paul Kiparsky. 2014. New perspectives in historical linguistics. In Claire Bowern and Bethwyn Evans, editors, *The Routledge Handbook of Historical Linguistics*, pages 64–102. Routledge.

Johan-Mattis List. 2019a. Automatic detection of borrowing (open problems in computational diversity linguistics 2). Web blog at: http://phylonetworks.blogspot.com/2019/03/automatic-detection-of-borrowing-open.html.

Johann-Mattis List. 2019b. Automated methods for the investigation of language contact, with a focus on lexical borrowing. *Language and Linguistics Compass*, 12:1–16.

Johann-Mattis List, Cormac Anderson, Tiago Tresoldi, and Robert Forkel. 2021. Clts. cross-linguistic transcription systems.

Johann-Mattis List and Robert Forkel. 2021. Automated identification of borrowings in multilingual wordlists - version 1; peer review: 2 approved, 1 approved with reservations. *Open Research Europe*, 1:79.

Johann-Mattis List, Simon Greenhill, Tiago Tresoldi, and Robert Forkel. 2018. Lingpy. a python library for historical linguistics. version 2.6.4. Web page. With contributions by Christoph Rzymski, Gereon Kaiping, Steven Moran, Peter Bouda, Johannes Dellert, Taraka Rama, Frank Nagel.

Johann-Mattis List, Shijulal Nelson-Sathi, Hans Geisler, and William Martin. 2014. Networks of lexical borrowing and lateral gene transfer in language and genome evolution. *Bioessays*, 36(2):141–150.

Chenggang Mi, Lei Xie, and Yanning Zhang. 2020. Loanword identification in low-resource languages with minimal supervision. *ACM Trans. Asian Low-Resour. Lang. Inf. Process.*, 19(3).

Chenggang Mi, Yating Yang, Lei Wang, Xi Zhou, and Tonghai Jiang. 2018. A neural network based model for loanword identification in Uyghur. In *Proceedings of the Eleventh International Conference on Language Resources and Evaluation (LREC 2018)*, Miyazaki, Japan. European Language Resources Association (ELRA).

John E. Miller, Tiago Tresoldi, Roberto Zariquiey, César A. Beltrán Castañón, Natalia Morozova, and Johann-Mattis List. 2020. Using lexical language models to detect borrowings in monolingual wordlists. *PLOS ONE*, 15(12):1–23.

Steven Moran and Michael Cysouw. 2018. *The Unicode Cookbook for Linguists: Managing writing systems using orthography profiles*. Zenodo. This is the Language Science Press publication version.

Tiago Tresoldi, Robert Forkel, and Natalia Morozova. 2019. *CLDF dataset derived from Haspelmath and Tadmor's "World Loanword Database" from 2009*. Zenodo, Geneva.

Ashish Vaswani, Noam Shazeer, Niki Parmar, Jakob Uszkoreit, Llion Jones, Aidan N. Gomez, Lukasz Kaiser, and Illia Polosukhin. 2017. Attention is all you need. In *31st Conference on Neural Information Processing Systems (NIPS 2017)*, volume abs/1706.03762.

Takashi Wada, Tomoharu Iwata, Yuji Matsumoto, Timothy Baldwin, and Jey Han Lau. 2020. Learning contextualised cross-lingual word embeddings for extremely low-resource languages using parallel corpora.

Does local pruning offer task-specific models to learn effectively ?

Abhishek Kumar Mishra
Dept. of Electrical & Computer Engineering
Drexel University
Philadelphia, PA, USA
am4862@drexel.edu

Mohna Chakraborty
Dept. of Computer Science
Iowa State University
Ames, IA, USA
mohnac@iastate.edu

Abstract

The need to deploy large-scale pre-trained models on edge devices under limited computational resources has led to substantial research to compress these large models. However, less attention has been given to compress the task-specific models. In this work, we investigate the different methods of unstructured pruning on task-specific models for Aspect-based Sentiment Analysis (ABSA) tasks. Specifically, we analyze differences in the learning dynamics of pruned models by using the standard pruning techniques to achieve high-performing sparse networks. We develop a hypothesis to demonstrate the effectiveness of local pruning over global pruning considering a simple CNN model. Later, we utilize the hypothesis to demonstrate the efficacy of the pruned state-of-the-art model compared to the over-parameterized state-of-the-art model under two settings, the first considering the baselines for the same task used for generating the hypothesis, i.e., aspect extraction and the second considering a different task, i.e., sentiment analysis. We also provide discussion related to the generalization of the pruning hypothesis.

1 Introduction

Significant progress in deep neural networks (DNN) over the last decade (Liu et al., 2017) and access to unlimited online and offline data has revolutionized the research in Natural Language Processing (NLP). Neural-based language models (LMs) (Devlin et al., 2019; Brown et al., 2020) can utilize large volumes of data and discover patterns that can be used to facilitate various downstream tasks (Xu et al., 2019; Sun et al., 2019; Wu and He, 2019; Li et al., 2019; Dai et al., 2020). However, the development and deployment of such LMs require extensive resources that amplify the costs in industry settings and questions the easy deployment of such models onto low resource capable embedded devices such as mobile phones (Wu and He, 2019; Yang et al., 2017). For instance, pre-trained transformer-based LMs such as BERT (Devlin et al., 2019) have demonstrated state-of-the-art results for various applications such as machine reading comprehension, information retrieval, and question answering by extracting contextualized word embedding or fine-tuning BERT for specific functionality (Xu et al., 2019; Li et al., 2019; Dai et al., 2020). However, these models are over-parametrized and thus are memory hungry and time-intensive to deploy on resource-constrained devices. Therefore, it is crucial to develop energy-efficient and cost-effective models for use in production.

Applications in the real world are task-oriented, with a demand for resource-efficient models. So, the models are required to use fewer parameters. Given the need to build smaller task-specific architectures to save memory footprint and computational burden (Henderson et al., 2020; Bender et al., 2021), one popular solution is pruning, a well-vetted topic in computer vision. Pruning (Karnin, 1990) is a compression technique that systematically removes less significant parameters from an existing network to produce a smaller compressed model with similar performance comparing the larger model. The evolution of DNN has lead to the rise of research in pruning, even though the concept of pruning has existed for a long time. Abundant research has been conducted on compressing deep learning-based architectures for computer vision tasks (Li et al., 2016); however, few works have been proposed for compressing the task-specific models in NLP (Liu et al., 2018a).

In this work, we aim to sparsify the models for ABSA tasks. ABSA aims to capture the opinion of the reviewer towards specific aspect in a review. In product-based reviews (reviews for restaurants, websites, etc.), the aspect term describes the attribute of a product, and the opinion term captures the sentiment expressed towards the aspect term.

Proceedings of the Student Research Workshop associated with RANLP-2021, pages 118–125,
held online, Sep 1–3, 2021.
https://doi.org/10.26615/issn.2603-2821.2021_017

An example of the product-based review is depicted in Figure 1. In the review "The food is great however the service is poor." the aspect terms are *food* and *service* and the opinion terms are *great* and *poor*. The sentiment captured by the opinion terms is *positive* and *negative* respectively. Aspect extraction is considered as a sequence labeling task to consider the span of aspect terms. Each term in the span is assigned a label following BIO scheme (Ramshaw and Marcus, 1999) where B and I indicate the beginning and inside of the span, respectively, and O indicates outside of the span.

***Review**: "The **food** is great however the **service** is poor."*

***Target Terms**: Food, Service*
***Sentiment**: Positive, Negative*

Figure 1: Example of a restaurant review

A complex model slows down the speed of inference, and thus a simple model is always preferred over these highly sophisticated architectures (Xu et al., 2018). To this end, we propose pruning a simple Convolutional Neural Network (CNN) (LeCun et al.; Wróbel et al., 2018), trained on general embedding and show that it produces promising results for ABSA tasks. In this paper, we perform an in-depth analysis of local and global pruning to sparsify architectures needed for real-world applications and empirically demonstrate that local pruning offers desirable sparsity with less compromising in performance, inferring that it is more practical in addressing real-world tasks.

Our contributions are as follows:

1. A meta-analysis of pruning a language model used for ABSA tasks.
2. Empirically demonstrates the effectiveness of local pruning over global pruning under the unstructured setting.
3. Empirically illustrates the possibility of generalization of pruning hypothesis and discuss our observations to pave the way for future research in the direction.

The rest of the paper is organized as follows: In Section 2, we provide an overview of related works in the field. In Section 3, we discuss the methodology proposed. Section 4 details the experimental setup, datasets, and results of the experiments. Section 5 concludes the paper and discusses the possible extensions of this work.

2 Related Works

2.1 *Aspect-based Sentiment Analysis*

Analysis of the sentiment expressed by a reviewer for a review has been studied in the past under different settings using supervised (Xu et al., 2019), semi-supervised (Dai and Song, 2019), and unsupervised (He et al., 2017) approaches. To exploit the full potential of supervised approaches, a large amount of labeled data is required, which is expensive to obtain. To alleviate this problem, semi-supervised and unsupervised approaches emphasize understanding features directly from raw corpus. This work focuses on extracting the aspect terms for a given review in a supervised fashion.

2.2 *Pruning*

Due to the over-parameterized nature of the deep neural networks (Mao et al., 2017; Frankle and Carbin, 2019) which lead to several problems like high computational costs, larger memory needs, etc. several compression methods like pruning (Han et al., 2015; Guo et al., 2016), quantization (Courbariaux et al., 2016; Shu and Nakayama, 2017) and knowledge distillation (Hinton et al., 2015) are proposed. Among them, pruning has been an efficient and effective method to reduce the number of parameters without loss of accuracy significantly. Moreover, it helps achieve higher compression rates (Han et al., 2015). Empirically, it has been shown that pruning performs better for sparse models compared to dense models (Lee et al., 2020). Furthermore, there have been many works on pruning for computer vision applications (Han et al., 2015; Li et al., 2017; Molchanov et al., 2017) but very few works exist for natural language processing applications (Joulin et al., 2016; Shu and Nakayama, 2017). Most of the works in NLP applications use quantization for language model compression (Joulin et al., 2016; Shu and Nakayama, 2017; Zadeh et al., 2020; Zafrir et al., 2019) and only a few apply pruning techniques for the purpose (Liu et al., 2018a).

3 Methodology

In this section, we introduce the methodology adopted for this work. We employ magnitude-based unstructured pruning where individual connections are detached based on the magnitude (L_1) of synaptic weights (Li et al., 2016) and then use it to implement both local and global pruning. In unstructured pruning, (Mao et al., 2017), individual connections between neurons or filters of adjacent filters are detached from the network, whereas in structured pruning (Liu et al., 2018b), the entire neurons or filters are detached from the network. In local pruning, (Han et al., 2015), a substantial percentage of connections are detached by contrasting each connection to the other connections in the layer, while in global pruning (Lee et al., 2018), all parameters are put together across all the different layers, and then a global percentage of them are taken to prune.

We have used unstructured pruning over structured pruning considering the in-feasibility of structured pruning due to ample search space for pruning rates per layer (Renda et al., 2020) and for causing large accuracy loss also (Li et al., 2016).

Algorithm 1 Training and pruning

$W \leftarrow randomlyInitialize()$
$M \leftarrow \{1\}^{|W|}$
for $i = 0 : E$ **do**
  $W' \leftarrow weightUpdate(f(X; W))$
  $M' \leftarrow unstructuredPrune(M, L1(W'))$
  $W' \leftarrow Set(f(X; M' \odot W'))$
  $W \leftarrow W'$
  $M \leftarrow M'$
end for

Algorithm 1 shows the proposed pruning algorithm where $f(X; W)$ refers to the neural network model, which is a collection of nested functions parameterized by weight W. W' is the updated weight, M denotes the mask, E represents the number of training epochs, and X is the training dataset. In the algorithm, we prune the language model using gradual pruning (Liu et al., 2018b; Renda et al., 2019). The result after training is the pruned model with desired sparsity. During the training phase, we first perform weight updates to obtain W', later $L1$-norm is applied on the updated weights to remove the least essential weights resulting in an updated binary mask M' that affixes a definite number of parameters to 0. The generated pruned model is $f(X; M' \odot W')$, and $M' \in \{0,1\}^{|W'|}$ and $\odot$ is the element-wise product operator which helps to generate pruned weights. This enables the masked parameters to reactivate during training based on gradient updates. At last, we apply a gradual sparsification schedule with sorting-based weights to achieve desirable sparsification.

To show the effectiveness of the proposed hypothesis, we consider two CNN-based baselines with 4 and 6 convolutional layers respectively working on aspect extraction (AE) task. To study the possibility of pruning hypothesis generalization, we further consider two neural network-based architectures proposed by Xu *et al.* (Xu et al., 2018) and Li *et al.* (Li et al., 2019). The architectures proposed in these works use different language models thus enabling us to perform meta-analysis for our hypothesis. Xu *et al.* (Xu et al., 2018) uses a CNN-based model for aspect term extraction by employing double embeddings (domain + general) whereas Li *et al.* (Li et al., 2019) uses five different versions of BERT-based models to perform AE and sentiment analysis of the extracted aspect terms.

The code is implemented in Pytorch, and the code is available at the url[1].

4 Experiments

The effectiveness of the inferred hypothesis is tested considering two settings. In the first setting, we consider the baselines for the same task of aspect extraction, which is used to generate the hypothesis. In the second setting, we consider the baselines for a different sentiment analysis task to validate the generalization of the hypothesis. We use fastText (Bojanowski et al., 2017) for the general-purpose embedding.

4.1 *Dataset Overview*

Following the baseline papers (Xu et al., 2018; Li et al., 2019), we conduct our experiments on two benchmark datasets from SemEval challenges (Pontiki et al., 2014, 2016). The first dataset is from the laptop domain on subtask 1 of SemEval-2014 Task 4. The second dataset is from the restaurant domain on subtask 1 of SemEval-2016 Task 5. The statistics of the dataset are given in Figure 2.

Experiments	Description	Training + Validation	Testing
Baseline	SemEval-14 Laptop	3045	800
BERT-based Models	SemEval-14 Laptop	3045	800
DE-CNN	SemEval-14 Laptop	3045	800
	SemEval-16 Restaurant	2000	676

Figure 2: Dataset Overview

[1] https://github.com/abhishekkumarm98/Local_Vs_Global-Pruning.git

4.2 *Baselines*

To obtain the proposed hypothesis, we consider two different CNN-based models with 4 and 6 convolutional layers respectively. For both the models, after the convolutional layers, fully connected layer along with a softmax layer is applied. The architecture is shown in Figure 3. Furthermore, we consider general purpose embedding using fastText for both.

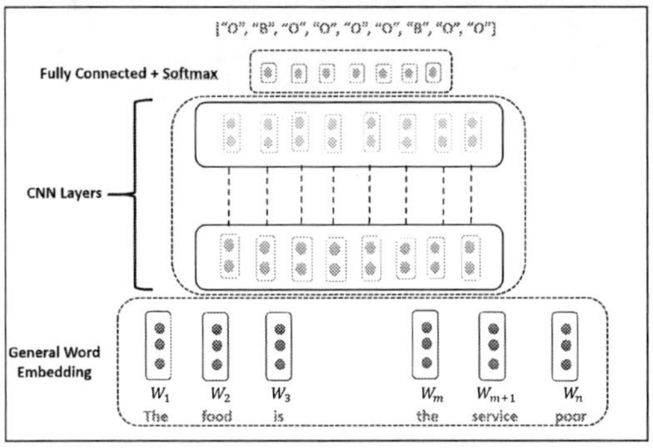

Figure 3: Baseline framework for (Conv-4 and Conv-6) layers where the input to the model is "The food is good however the service is poor".

The embedding layers in the LM provide vector representation at the character, word, or sentence level. Considering the distribution of parameters in the language models, a substantial percentage of parameters come from the embedding layer. During training, we apply different fractions of local and global pruning in an unstructured manner. The average f1-score of the resultant pruned model with respect to the fraction of weights pruned is shown in Figure 4 for SemEval-14 laptop dataset. For the experiments, the hyperparameter settings include epochs (200), batch size (128), learning rate ($1e$-4) with a learning rate scheduler dividing the learning rate by ten after each epoch.

From Figure 4, it can be observed that for both the models, applying local pruning resulted in a considerable average f1-score until 80% of the weights were pruned, whereas applying global pruning resulted in a substantial performance degradation after 40% of the weights were pruned. This observation validates our claim that local pruning is more efficient than global pruning for ABSA tasks.

4.3 *DE-CNN*

In order to validate the generalization of our proposed hypothesis, for the double-embedding CNN-based model, we have trained and pruned on both SemEval-14 laptop and SemEval-16 restaurant

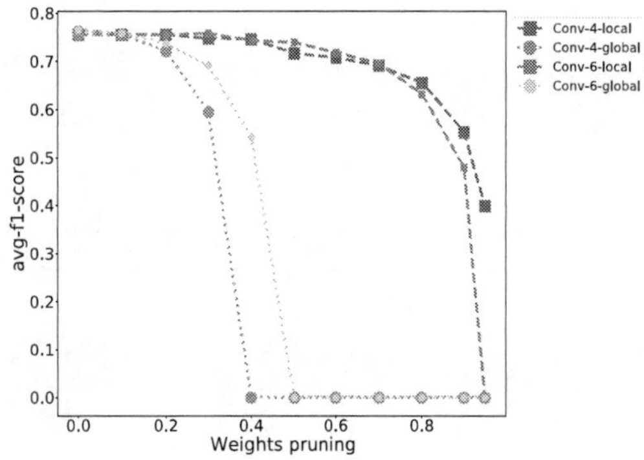

Figure 4: Performance of Conv-4 and Conv-6 models on applying local and global pruning on test set of SemEval-14 laptop.

datasets by applying local and global pruning in an unstructured manner considering the same hyperparameter settings as proposed in the paper. We made a few modifications like changing the number of epochs to 300, introducing a learning rate scheduler, and early stopping to learn effectively and prevent overfitting. Results are shown in Figure 7.

From Figure 7, we can see that for both datasets, SemEval-14 laptop, and SemEval-16 restaurant, we have obtained a considerable f1-score on applying pruning locally until 80% of the weights were pruned, but the model's performance dropped drastically on applying pruning globally immediately after 30% of the weights were pruned.

In the literature, it has been shown that global pruning performs slightly better than local pruning (Blalock et al., 2020) which contradicts our observations. Our in-depth analysis shows that most of the works on pruning are performed for computer vision tasks, and their model architecture is different from the architecture of a LM. Standard model architectures like ResNet-50 (He et al., 2016), VGG-16 (Simonyan and Zisserman, 2014), extensively used in the computer vision domain, have a bunch of convolutional layers, batch normalization layers but lacks embedding layer, a crucial part of any LM. The general embedding layer of a language model contains substantial portions of the total parameters of the model. Figure 8 demonstrates the relative percentage of model parameters in each layer of the DE-CNN model.

We further analyzed the drastic drop in performance when we applied global pruning on the models considered in the baselines and DE-CNN. The results of our analysis are shown in Figure 5.

We have observed that sparsification occurs

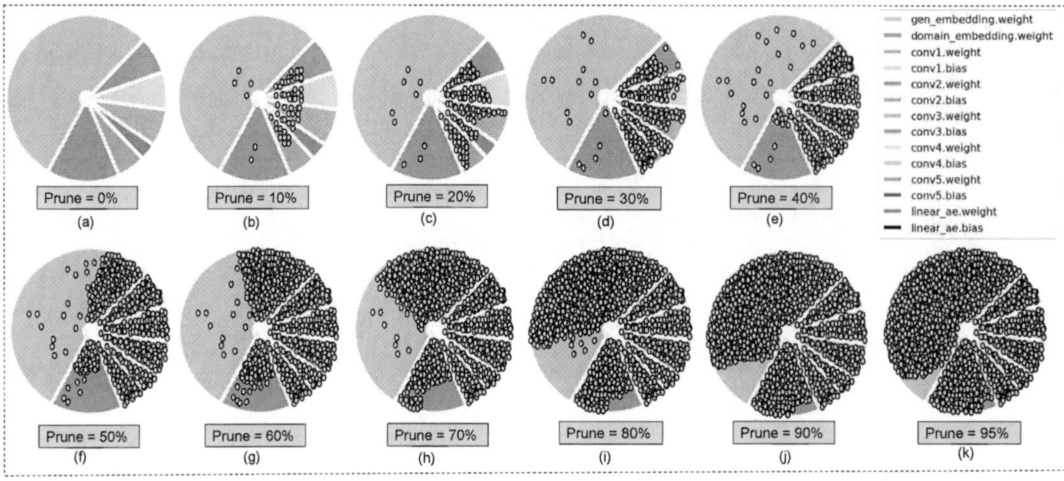

Figure 5: Spread of sparsification across each layer of DE-CNN with respect to different global pruning percentages.

more progressively for all layers except embedding layers as we increase the pruning percentage. From Figure 8, it can be observed that around 70% of the parameters belong to general and domain embedding layers. During global pruning, we pool all the parameters together and then take $L1$-norm to sort the absolute values in the decreasing order. The desired sparsification is applied to the sorted absolute values by setting the parameters to 0. From Figure 5 (b), it can be observed that sparsification has started in all layers, but as we progress, from Figure 5 (e), it can be observed that all layers except the embedding layers are sparsified completely. This leads to concluding that $L1$-norm causes the parameters of all the layers except the embedding layer to be smaller in magnitude resulting in the pruning of convolutional, bias, and fully connected layers ahead of embedding layers. This results in substantial decrement in models performance.

4.4 *BERT-based models*

In order to validate the generalization of our proposed hypothesis, we have trained and pruned the five different versions of BERT based models proposed in (Li et al., 2019) for an end to end ABSA task by applying local and global pruning in an unstructured manner considering the same hyperparameter settings as proposed in the paper. The result is demonstrated in Figure 9.

From Figure 9, it can be observed that applying local pruning resulted in a considerable performance for all the models until 60% of the weight pruning, whereas a substantial performance drop is observed after 30% of the weight pruning when global pruning is applied. The statistics of the crucial embedding layer of the model are shown in Figure 10. The reason for this performance drop is similar to what is observed for DE-CNN, where position type embedding and token type embedding layers are progressively sparsified compared to the word embedding layer as shown in Figure 6.

Furthermore, BERT has 200 layers where embedding, attention, and pooling layers have higher parameters than position and token type embedding layers, resulting in faster sparsification than other layers. Analyzing the phenomenon on the foundation of machine learning makes it analogous to garbage in, garbage out scenarios. Pruning most of the parameters by setting them to 0 results in an improper representation of the input, leading to performance deterioration observed for all the models. As per our analysis, the reason for better performance of local pruning compared to global pruning is because of giving more weightage during pruning to the layers with considerable parameters.

5 Conclusion and Future Works

This paper considers standard pruning techniques for compressing the model for two sub-tasks under ABSA tasks. We propose our hypothesis stating that local pruning is more effective than global pruning for aspect extraction. We empirically then demonstrate the validity of our hypothesis on two benchmark datasets for DE-CNN and show that pruned models can achieve comparable perfor-

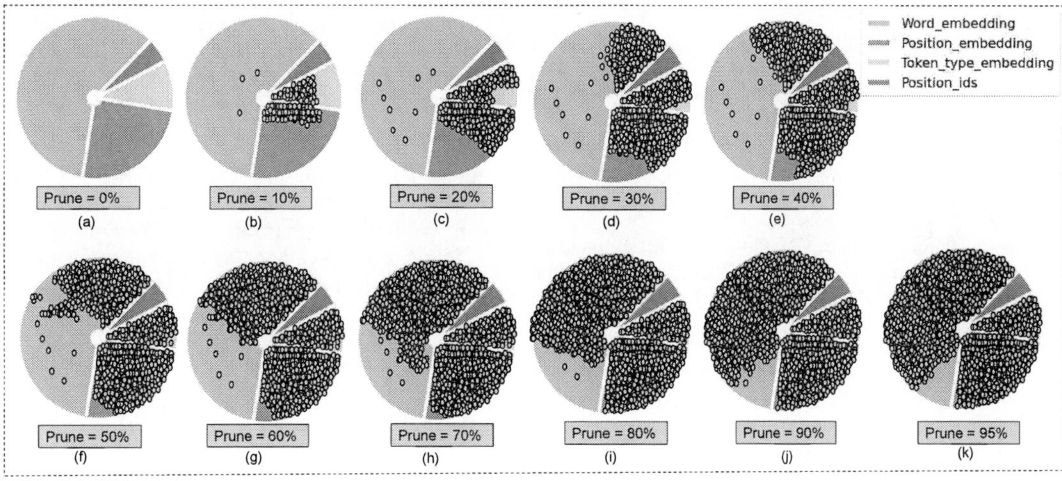

Figure 6: Spread of sparsification across each embedding layer of BERT with respect to different global pruning percentages.

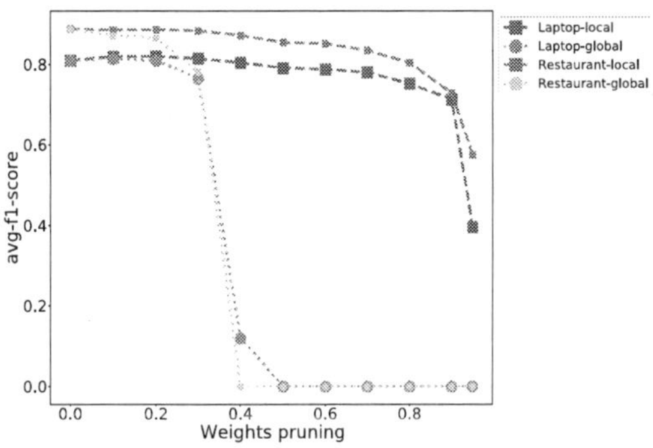

Figure 7: Performance of DE-CNN on test set of SemEval-14 laptop and SemEval-16 restaurant on applying local and global pruning.

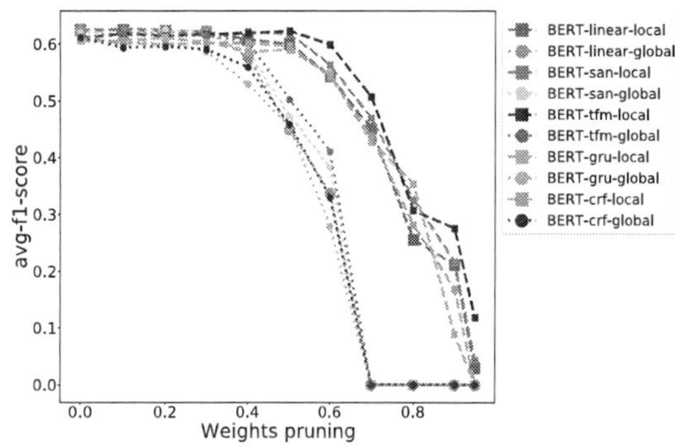

Figure 9: Performance of BERT (linear, crf, tfm, gru, san) on test set of SemEval-14 laptop on applying local and global pruning.

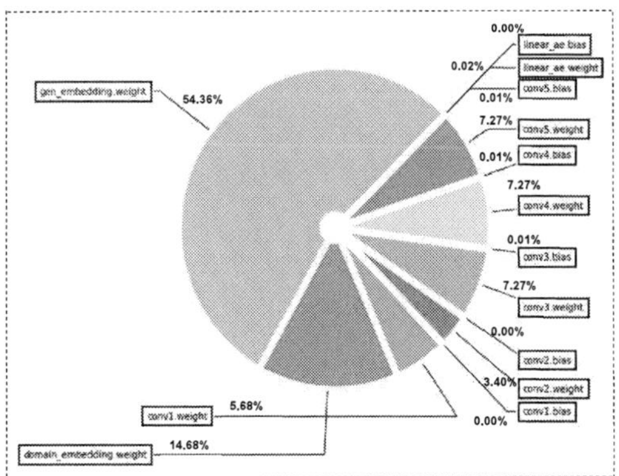

Figure 8: Relative percentage of parameters of each layer of DE-CNN.

Embedding layer's name	Parameters	Percentage
Position_ids	511	0.0005%
Word_embedding	23,440,896	21.4012%
Position_embedding	393,216	0.3591%
Token_type_embedding	1,536	0.0014%

Figure 10: Details of BERT's crucial embedding layers.

mance comparing the original models. We further performed experiments on BERT-based models to verify the effectiveness of generalizing our hypothesis for the sentiment analysis task. In the future, we aim to explore different models on various tasks using other novel pruning-based techniques like global and local gradient magnitude.

Acknowledgement

We thank Adithya Kulkarni for his help and all the reviewers for their constructive comments.

References

Emily M Bender, Timnit Gebru, Angelina McMillan-Major, and Shmargaret Shmitchell. 2021. On the dangers of stochastic parrots: Can language models be too big? In *Proceedings of the 2021 ACM Conference on Fairness, Accountability, and Transparency*, pages 610–623.

Davis Blalock, Jose Javier Gonzalez Ortiz, Jonathan Frankle, and John Guttag. 2020. What is the state of neural network pruning? *arXiv preprint arXiv:2003.03033*.

Piotr Bojanowski, Edouard Grave, Armand Joulin, and Tomas Mikolov. 2017. Enriching word vectors with subword information. *Transactions of the Association for Computational Linguistics*, 5:135–146.

Tom B Brown, Benjamin Mann, Nick Ryder, Melanie Subbiah, Jared Kaplan, Prafulla Dhariwal, Arvind Neelakantan, Pranav Shyam, Girish Sastry, Amanda Askell, et al. 2020. Language models are few-shot learners. *arXiv preprint arXiv:2005.14165*.

Matthieu Courbariaux, Itay Hubara, Daniel Soudry, Ran El-Yaniv, and Yoshua Bengio. 2016. Binarized neural networks: Training deep neural networks with weights and activations constrained to+ 1 or-1. *arXiv preprint arXiv:1602.02830*.

Hongliang Dai and Yangqiu Song. 2019. Neural aspect and opinion term extraction with mined rules as weak supervision. In *Proceedings of the 57th Annual Meeting of the Association for Computational Linguistics*, pages 5268–5277.

Zehui Dai, Cheng Peng, Huajie Chen, and Yadong Ding. 2020. A multi-task incremental learning framework with category name embedding for aspect-category sentiment analysis. In *Proceedings of the 2020 Conference on Empirical Methods in Natural Language Processing (EMNLP)*, pages 6955–6965.

Jacob Devlin, Ming-Wei Chang, Kenton Lee, and Kristina Toutanova. 2019. Bert: Pre-training of deep bidirectional transformers for language understanding. In *Proceedings of the 2019 Conference of the North American Chapter of the Association for Computational Linguistics: Human Language Technologies, Volume 1 (Long and Short Papers)*, pages 4171–4186.

Jonathan Frankle and Michael Carbin. 2019. The lottery ticket hypothesis: Finding sparse, trainable neural networks.

Yiwen Guo, Anbang Yao, and Yurong Chen. 2016. Dynamic network surgery for efficient dnns.

Song Han, Jeff Pool, John Tran, and William J Dally. 2015. Learning both weights and connections for efficient neural networks. *arXiv preprint arXiv:1506.02626*.

Kaiming He, Xiangyu Zhang, Shaoqing Ren, and Jian Sun. 2016. Deep residual learning for image recognition. In *Proceedings of the IEEE conference on computer vision and pattern recognition*, pages 770–778.

Ruidan He, Wee Sun Lee, Hwee Tou Ng, and Daniel Dahlmeier. 2017. An unsupervised neural attention model for aspect extraction. In *Proceedings of the 55th Annual Meeting of the Association for Computational Linguistics (Volume 1: Long Papers)*, pages 388–397.

Peter Henderson, Jieru Hu, Joshua Romoff, Emma Brunskill, Dan Jurafsky, and Joelle Pineau. 2020. Towards the systematic reporting of the energy and carbon footprints of machine learning. *Journal of Machine Learning Research*, 21(248):1–43.

Geoffrey Hinton, Oriol Vinyals, and Jeff Dean. 2015. Distilling the knowledge in a neural network. *arXiv preprint arXiv:1503.02531*.

Armand Joulin, Edouard Grave, Piotr Bojanowski, Matthijs Douze, Hérve Jégou, and Tomas Mikolov. 2016. Fasttext.zip: Compressing text classification models.

Ehud D Karnin. 1990. A simple procedure for pruning back-propagation trained neural networks.

Yann LeCun, Yoshua Bengio, et al. Convolutional networks for images, speech, and time series.

Namhoon Lee, Thalaiyasingam Ajanthan, Stephen Gould, and Philip H. S. Torr. 2020. A signal propagation perspective for pruning neural networks at initialization.

Namhoon Lee, Thalaiyasingam Ajanthan, and Philip HS Torr. 2018. Snip: Single-shot network pruning based on connection sensitivity. *arXiv preprint arXiv:1810.02340*.

Hao Li, Asim Kadav, Igor Durdanovic, Hanan Samet, and Hans Peter Graf. 2016. Pruning filters for efficient convnets. *arXiv preprint arXiv:1608.08710*.

Hao Li, Asim Kadav, Igor Durdanovic, Hanan Samet, and Hans Peter Graf. 2017. Pruning filters for efficient convnets.

Xin Li, Lidong Bing, Wenxuan Zhang, and Wai Lam. 2019. Exploiting bert for end-to-end aspect-based sentiment analysis. In *Proceedings of the 5th Workshop on Noisy User-generated Text (W-NUT 2019)*, pages 34–41.

Liyuan Liu, Xiang Ren, Jingbo Shang, Xiaotao Gu, Jian Peng, and Jiawei Han. 2018a. Efficient contextualized representation: Language model pruning for sequence labeling. In *Proceedings of the 2018 Conference on Empirical Methods in Natural Language Processing*, pages 1215–1225.

Weibo Liu, Zidong Wang, Xiaohui Liu, Nianyin Zeng, Yurong Liu, and Fuad E Alsaadi. 2017. A survey of deep neural network architectures and their applications. *Neurocomputing*, 100(234):11–26.

Zhuang Liu, Mingjie Sun, Tinghui Zhou, Gao Huang, and Trevor Darrell. 2018b. Rethinking the value of network pruning. *arXiv preprint arXiv:1810.05270*.

Huizi Mao, Song Han, Jeff Pool, Wenshuo Li, Xingyu Liu, Yu Wang, and William J Dally. 2017. Exploring the regularity of sparse structure in convolutional neural networks. *arXiv preprint arXiv:1705.08922*.

Pavlo Molchanov, Stephen Tyree, Tero Karras, Timo Aila, and Jan Kautz. 2017. Pruning convolutional neural networks for resource efficient inference.

Maria Pontiki, Dimitrios Galanis, Haris Papageorgiou, Ion Androutsopoulos, Suresh Manandhar, Mohammad Al-Smadi, Mahmoud Al-Ayyoub, Yanyan Zhao, Bing Qin, Orphée De Clercq, et al. 2016. Semeval-2016 task 5: Aspect based sentiment analysis. In *International workshop on semantic evaluation*, pages 19–30.

Maria Pontiki, Dimitris Galanis, John Pavlopoulos, Harris Papageorgiou, Ion Androutsopoulos, and Suresh Manandhar. 2014. "SemEval-2014 task 4: Aspect based sentiment analysis". In *Proceedings of the 8th International Workshop on Semantic Evaluation (SemEval 2014)*, pages 27–35, Dublin, Ireland. Association for Computational Linguistics.

Lance A Ramshaw and Mitchell P Marcus. 1999. Text chunking using transformation-based learning. In *Natural language processing using very large corpora*, pages 157–176. Springer.

Alex Renda, Jonathan Frankle, and Michael Carbin. 2019. Comparing rewinding and fine-tuning in neural network pruning. In *International Conference on Learning Representations*.

Alex Renda, Jonathan Frankle, and Michael Carbin. 2020. Comparing rewinding and fine-tuning in neural network pruning. *arXiv preprint arXiv:2003.02389*.

Raphael Shu and Hideki Nakayama. 2017. Compressing word embeddings via deep compositional code learning.

Karen Simonyan and Andrew Zisserman. 2014. Very deep convolutional networks for large-scale image recognition. *arXiv preprint arXiv:1409.1556*.

Chi Sun, Luyao Huang, and Xipeng Qiu. 2019. Utilizing bert for aspect-based sentiment analysis via constructing auxiliary sentence. In *Proceedings of the 2019 Conference of the North American Chapter of the Association for Computational Linguistics: Human Language Technologies, Volume 1 (Long and Short Papers)*, pages 380–385.

Krzysztof Wróbel, Marcin Pietroń, Maciej Wielgosz, Michał Karwatowski, and Kazimierz Wiatr. 2018. Convolutional neural network compression for natural language processing. *arXiv preprint arXiv:1805.10796*.

Shanchan Wu and Yifan He. 2019. Enriching pre-trained language model with entity information for relation classification. In *Proceedings of the 28th ACM international conference on information and knowledge management*, pages 2361–2364.

Hu Xu, Bing Liu, Lei Shu, and S Yu Philip. 2018. Double embeddings and cnn-based sequence labeling for aspect extraction. In *Proceedings of the 56th Annual Meeting of the Association for Computational Linguistics (Volume 2: Short Papers)*, pages 592–598.

Hu Xu, Bing Liu, Lei Shu, and S Yu Philip. 2019. Bert post-training for review reading comprehension and aspect-based sentiment analysis. In *Proceedings of the 2019 Conference of the North American Chapter of the Association for Computational Linguistics: Human Language Technologies, Volume 1 (Long and Short Papers)*, pages 2324–2335.

Tien-Ju Yang, Yu-Hsin Chen, and Vivienne Sze. 2017. Designing energy-efficient convolutional neural networks using energy-aware pruning. In *2017 IEEE Conference on Computer Vision and Pattern Recognition (CVPR)*, pages 6071–6079. IEEE Computer Society.

Ali Hadi Zadeh, Isak Edo, Omar Mohamed Awad, and Andreas Moshovos. 2020. Gobo: Quantizing attention-based nlp models for low latency and energy efficient inference.

Ofir Zafrir, Guy Boudoukh, Peter Izsak, and Moshe Wasserblat. 2019. Q8bert: Quantized 8bit bert.

On Reducing Repetition in Abstractive Summarization

Pranav Ajit Nair
Indian Institute of Technology (BHU)
Varanasi
pranavajitnair.cse18@itbhu.ac.in

Anil Kumar Singh
Indian Institute of Technology (BHU)
Varanasi
aksingh.cse@iitbhu.ac.in

Abstract

Repetition in natural language generation reduces the informativeness of text and makes it less appealing. Various techniques have been proposed to alleviate it. In this work, we explore and propose techniques to reduce repetition in abstractive summarization. First, we explore the application of unlikelihood training and embedding matrix regularizers from previous work on language modeling to abstractive summarization. Next, we extend the coverage and temporal attention mechanisms to the token level to reduce repetition. In our experiments on the CNN/Daily Mail dataset, we observe that these techniques reduce the amount of repetition and increase the informativeness of the summaries, which we confirm via human evaluation.

1 Introduction

Abstractive summarization (Nallapati et al., 2016; See et al., 2017; Chopra et al., 2016; Rush et al., 2015) aims at capturing the essence of a document in a limited number of words. Despite great performance improvement over the years, many abstractive summarization models still suffer from the repetition problem wherein they tend to repeat the same phrase or ngram over and over again reducing the amount of information conveyed and also reducing the quality of the generated text. For example such a system may generate "He scored five goals. five goals. five goals ...". Such kind of repetition is highly uncommon in human written text.

A true understanding of the problem is still unknown. Some argue that it is because of model architecture (Vig, 2018; Holtzman et al., 2020), other suggest that it is because of the nature of sampling performed by the model which is very different from human natural language (Holtzman et al., 2020). Welleck et al. (2020) suggests that the cause of the problem is maximum likelihood training of language generation models. Holtzman et al. (2020) alleviates this problem to some extend via nucleus sampling and Fan et al. (2018) propose TopK sampling to solve the repetition problem.

To solve this repetition problem for abstractive summarization we adopt two approaches.

1. The unlikelihood training approach proposed by Welleck et al. (2020). Their approach has significantly reduced repetition on several language modeling datasets. We extend their approach to abstractive summarization. In our experiments we observe that the unlikelihood objective significantly reduces repetition and also boosts the model performance in terms of evaluation metric such as ROUGE. All our experiments are based on Transformers (Vaswani et al., 2017). Our model, on the CNN/DailyMail (Chen et al., 2016) dataset outperforms the baseline by a significant margin.

2. See et al. (2017) used the coverage mechanism (Tu et al., 2016) which penalizes the model if the decoder cross attention attends to the same source token multiples times. We propose to extend this idea at the token level where the model is penalized in a similar way if it gives high probability to the same token multiple times while generating the summary. In this way we ensure that model does not assign high probabilities to the same token over and over again. In our experiments we see that this additional regularization not only reduces repetition in the generated summaries but also improves the performance in terms of evaluation metric beating the baseline Transformer.

Our key contributions are:

- We qualitatively and quantitatively analyze repetition in abstractive summarization.

Proceedings of the Student Research Workshop associated with RANLP-2021, pages 126–134,
held online, Sep 1–3, 2021.
https://doi.org/10.26615/issn.2603-2821.2021_018

- We extend the unlikelihood objective for language modeling to abstractive summarization ans show that there is a significant reduction in repetition.
- We propose an extension of the coverage mechanism to the token level to reduce repetition ans show that our approach reduces repetition in abstractive summarization.
- We experiment with the embedding regularizer proposed by Gao et al. (2019) to increase the expressiveness of the token embeddings for transformers, which we suspect would allow the model to utilize rare tokens and help in repetition reduction.
- We also propose an extension of the temporal attention mechanism (Sankaran et al., 2016), which dampens the attention distribution by dividing it with the sum of the previous attention distributions to the token level. We conduct experiments on this approach to verify it's effectiveness on repetition reduction.

2 Related Work

Abstractive summarization aims at capturing the entire essence of a document within a relatively smaller number of words. There has been great progress made in the recent past where better and better architectures have been proposed to solve the problem. See et al. (2017) used pointer generator networks to copy words from the input document. Duan et al. (2019) augmented the Transformer architecture with a contrastive attention mechanism to ignore the irrelevant parts of the document. Zhang et al. (2020a) pretrained a Transformer model for summarization. Paulus et al. (2018) proposed to use rewards from policy gradient reinforcement learning to alleviate exposure bias. Gehrmann et al. (2018) developed a bottom-up copy attention mechanism to over-determine phrases in the document that should be included in the summary. There approach is build upon the pointer generator network (See et al., 2017). Our work unlike previous work tries to reduce the repetition in Transformer models via techniques that have been successfully applied to language modeling.

Several methods have been proposed to reduce repetition in language generation. Holtzman et al. (2020) use different sampling techniques to reduce repetition. Welleck et al. (2020) propose the unlikelihood objective to reduce repetition. Fu et al. (2021) propose to combine pairs of words that often follow each other to reduce repetition. Our work applies such techniques to abstractive summarization where repetition reduces the amount of information conveyed in the summary.

To reduce repetition in abstractive summarization Li et al. (2019) propose a reinforcement learning based approach. They utilize BERTScore (Zhang et al., 2020b) to reward the model for better generations and reduce repetition. Lin et al. (2018) propose a CNN based encoder to perform global encoding of the source side information. Their approach also reduces repetition. Chen and Bansal (2018) propose a reinforcement learning based sentence level neural abstractive summarization model. Unlike these approaches both our approaches explicitly try to reduce repetition without using any heuristic based decoding strategies.

3 Method

In this section we provide the training objectives used by us to reduce repetition. All our models and experiments are based on the standard Transformer encoder-decoder architecture. The input to the encoder is the input document x represented as $x = (x_1, x_2, ..., x_n)$, and the summary to be generated is $y = (y_1, y_2, ..., y_m)$. We can write the loss function obtained via maximum likelihood estimation as:

$$L_{MLE} = -\sum_{i=1}^{m} \log p_\theta(y_i|y_{1,...,i-1}, x) \quad (1)$$

where θ represents the model parameters.

3.1 Unlikelihood Objective

The idea is to decrease the probability of the tokens which have been already generated by the model in the summary to avoid frequent repetition. So for generation of ith word the negative candidates would be $C_i = \{y_1, ..., y_{i-1}\} \setminus \{y_i\}$. The unlikelihood loss for the ith token's generation can be written as:

$$L_{UN} = -\sum_{c \in C_i} \log(1 - p_\theta(c|y_{1,...,i-1}, x)) \quad (2)$$

Thus the total loss for the ith token's generation

is:

$$L^i_{token} = -\log p_\theta(y_i|y_{1,\dots,i-1},x) - \gamma \sum_{c \in C_i} \log(1 - p_\theta(c|y_{1,\dots,i-1},x) \quad (3)$$

We call this objective UOMLE. In all our experiments we use $\gamma = 1$.

3.2 Embedding Regularizer

Gao et al. (2019) propose to minimize the cosine similarity between token embeddings for Transformer models to solve the representation degeneration problem where the word embeddings tend to degenerate over the course of training and form a narrow cone. Since all our experiments are based on the Transformer model we add this regularization term into the model to check for any improvement in the quality of the generated summaries. We suspect that increasing the expressiveness of the embeddings would allow the model to better generate rare words, which in turn would reduce repetition. The regularization loss added is:

$$L_W = \frac{1}{N^2} \sum_{i}^{N} \sum_{i \neq j}^{N} \hat{w_i}^T \hat{w_j} \quad (4)$$

where $\hat{w_i} = \frac{w_i}{\|w_i\|}$ $w_i \in \mathbb{R}^d$, and $W = [w_1, w_2, ..., w_N]^T$ is the embedding matrix. d is the embedding dimension and N is the vocabulary size. We call this objective EmbedReg.

3.3 Coverage Regularizer

Here the model is penalized if it gives high probability to the same token multiple times while generating the summary. The loss function added is an extension of the coverage mechanism used in See et al. (2017). Defining the context vector at time step t as:

$$c_t = \sum_{i=1}^{t-1} p_\theta(\cdot|y_{1,\dots,i-1},x) \quad (5)$$

Let $p_t = p_\theta(\cdot|y_{1,\dots,t-1},x)$. The coverage loss is defined as:

$$L_t = \sum_{j=1}^{N} \min(c_t^j, p_t^j) \quad (6)$$

This coverage loss can be added to the model loss function without any other change to the model making it's implementation fairly straightforward. Thus if the model gives a higher probability to a token which has been previously given a higher probability the loss incurred is higher. We refer to it as CovReg.

3.4 Temporal Mechanism

Sankaran et al. (2016) proposed the temporal attention mechanism. In this approach, each attention distribution is divided by the sum of the previous, which effectively dampens repeated attention. We extend this approach to the token level where the distribution over the vocabulary at every time step is divided by the sum of the vocabulary distributions from the previous time steps. We suspect that this would reduce the probability of generating the same token over and over again since a higher probability of the token in the previous time steps would incur a greater dampening effect. In our experiments we refer to it as TemporalMech.

4 Experiments

We use the CNN/Daily Mail dataset for all our experiments. All our models are Transformer based, we use the Transformer base model with 8 encoder layers, 8 decoder layers, 8 attention heads, 256 is the hidden and embedding dimension and 512 dimensional feed forward layer. We use the linear warm-up followed by square root decay schedule proposed in Vaswani et al. (2017). We train our baseline for 200K iterations with a batch size of 32 and we employ early stopping based on validation loss. We use beam search decoding in all our experiments with a beam size of 4, we also employ a length penalty of 1.0. We use label smoothing with $\alpha = 0.1$. We use Sentencepiece tokenizer in all our experiments. All the experiments are performed using PyTorch on a single NVIDIA Tesla V100 GPU.

4.1 Evaluation metrics

As a token level metric we use fraction of the net token predicted that has previously occurred in a window of l tokens :

$$rep/l = \frac{1}{|S|} \sum_{i=1}^{|S|} \sum_{t=1}^{|y^{(i)}|} \mathbb{I}[\text{argmax} p_\theta(y_t|y_{1,\dots,t-1},x) \in y_{t-l-1:t-1}] \quad (7)$$

Where $\mathbb{I}$ is the indicator function S in the validation/test data and y in the generated summary. For a single token repeat $\mathbb{I}$ is 1.

Model variant	ROUGE-1	ROUGE-2	ROUGE-L	rep/4	seq-rep-4
Baseline	21.55	7.27	23.74	0.3751	0.2336
CovReg	**21.94**	**7.50**	**24.15**	**0.3618**	**0.2204**
TemporalMech	20.50	7.53	22.92	0.3978	0.2413
EmbedReg	20.97	7.31	24.80	0.3757	0.2212
UOMLE	**25.47**	**8.34**	**25.70**	**0.2241**	**0.0966**

Table 1: Results of our final models on the validation set.

Model variant	ROUGE-1	ROUGE-2	ROUGE-L	rep/4	seq-rep-4
Baseline	21.25	7.04	23.55	0.3785	0.2420
CovReg	**21.75**	**7.44**	**24.02**	**0.3634**	**0.2208**
TemporalMech	20.36	7.08	21.34	0.3983	0.2431
EmbedReg	20.81	7.11	23.78	0.3779	0.2214
UOMLE	**25.39**	**8.13**	**25.43**	**0.2255**	**0.0942**

Table 2: Results of our final models on the test set.

A similar sequence level metric to measure repetition will be:

$$\text{seq-rep-n} = 1.0 - \frac{|\text{unique n-grams in y}|}{|\text{n-grams}|} \quad (8)$$

This metric calculates the fraction of unique n-grams in the generated summary. Both the above metrics have been proposed in Welleck et al. (2020).

4.2 Results

The results on the validation set can be found in Table 1 for all the four approaches. From the results we can see that all approaches except the temporal mechanism reduce repetition and increase the the ROUGE scores. An increase in ROUGE scores can be attributed to the fact that reducing repetition allows the model to generate more informative summaries. For the repetition metrics we report rep/4 and seq-rep-4.

The Unlikelihood objective significantly reduces repetition and also increase ROUGE scores, since UOLME explicitly decreases the probability of previously generated words. A reduction in repetition allows the model to generate better summaries which in turn increases the ROUGE scores. The Embedding regularizer method also reduces seq-rep-4. There is no decrease in rep/4 probably because EmbedReg objective does not try to explicitly or implicitly penalize the model for repetition.

From Table 1 one can see that CovReg beats the baseline on the ROUGE metric and reduces repetition as well. Since we penalized the model for giving a high probability to the same token over and over again the model tends to repeat less generating better summaries, which is evident from the ROUGE scores. With TempMech, we see that repetition in the model has increased, also the performance in terms of ROUGE metric drops slightly below that of the baseline. This drop in performance and increase in repetition may be because of the distortion of the probability distribution over the vocabulary as pointed out by See et al. (2017).

We also test a combination of these objectives wherein we combine the EmbedReg method with the UOMLE and CovReg objectives. We find no significant decrease in repetition. Results on the test set for all our models are presented in Table 2.

4.3 Qualitative Analysis

To analyze the generated summaries qualitatively we present summaries generated by UOMLE objective in Table 3. In the first example the baseline model unlike the model trained with UOMLE objective tends to repeat 'second-half' multiple times. In the second example the phrases 'jaw' and '29-year-old' are repeated several times in the baseline, whereas the model trained with UOMLE shows no such repetition, and in the third example the word 'middle' is repeated several times by the baseline. This clearly shows that UOMLE reduces repetition. We also present samples generated with the CovReg objective in Table 4. Here, in the first example the baseline repeats the phrase 'best footballer' several times in the summary, whereas the model trained with CovReg shows no such repetition. Similarly in the second example the baseline repeats 'year' multiple times and in the third ex-

Article: when defenders who have not scored for two years find the net, watford might begin to think this can be the year they return to the premier league. matthew connolly has only been at the club for a month but struck a goal that proved key at a stadium that has humbled all three of their nearest promotion rivals. watford were made to sweat for the three points during a late surge by 10-man nottingham forest, but left having leapfrogged middlesbrough into third, behind norwich in second on goal difference. watford forward odion ighalo celebrates having given the hornets the lead after just four minutes . defender matthew connolly celebrates after putting watford 2-0 up against nottingham forest on wednesday . (Truncated)
UOMLE: matthew connolly' s first-half at the premier league cup of 2014 world cup in his last 16 clash with watford on wednesday . it was a late first-minute ten-minute treatment to be the premier league two-half premier league season after half- macsbury . matthew connolly' s first-half minutes against nottingham forest to make a late on wednesday .
Baseline: matthew connolly' s first-half-rated to four- cent-minute goal . don' first-half minutes of his **second-half from second-half** from a point to four minutes from **second half** half-ry lead for the **second-half** from the **second-half** .

Article: a four-year-old boy has returned home after being mauled by their family' s newly adopted pit bull. gavin tobeck of lacey, washington suffered from a broken cheekbone, jaw and nose bridge, and needed sections of a rib to repair his eye sockets after the attack by their dog smash on april 1. the boy also lost five baby teeth and three permanent tooth buds. in an effort to save her son, 29-year-old alissa evans' friend threw hot coffee on the dog which led to the animal releasing his grip on gavin . (Truncated)
UOMLE: a four-year-old boy has returned to his eye sockets after being mauled by their family' s newly adopted pit bull . the young boy also lost five-year old to repair his eye sockets after being mauled by their dog in a 11th permanent tooth bud .
Baseline: gavin to repair his eye socket, **jaw, jaw, jaw, jaw, jaw, jaw** and nose bridge, **29-year-old** a normal life and nose bridge, **29-year-old** a drug at harborview medical center in a broken cheekbone' s newly adopted pit bull smash on the animal releasing his eye sockets after spending six days at harborview medical center, **29-year-old** a broken cheekbone, **29-year-old** a broken cheekbone, **29-year-old** a normal life .

Article: a pensioner has broke down in tears in court as he was spared jailed after admitting he stabbed his sick wife to death after she begged him to ' bring her suffering to an end' . anthony mann, 78, sat quietly sobbing in the dock as he listened to the details of the mercy killing of his wife janet at their home in nuneaton, warwickshire. he was given a two year suspended sentence after he appeared at leamington justice centre today. anthony mann was spared jail for killing his wife janet after she asked him to end his life . (Truncated)
UOMLE: anthony mann was given a three-month suspended jail term for killing his sick wife . he was given a two-year community community service by the suicide of his life in nunea .
Baseline: anthony mann, 78, sat quietly sobbing in nuneaton, sat quietly sobbing in a kitchen knife, sat quietly sobbing in the **middle of the middle of the middle of the middle of the middle of the middle of the middle of the middle of the middle of the middle of the middle of the middle** of the year .

Table 3: Summaries generated by UOMLE from test set. Repetitions made by the baseline are highlighted.

Article: real madrid striker karim benzema has boldly stated he can win the ballon d' or award during his career. the france international is confident his club success at the bernabeu can force his way into contention for the prestigious award. however benzema' s los blancos team-mate cristiano ronaldo has picked up the last two accolades for the world' s best footballer whereas barcelona talisman lionel messi prevailed between 2009-12. french and real madrid forward karim benzema believes he can win the ballon d' or award in his career . despite the duo' s dominance, benzema is adamant he can compete for the title if he continues to perform for real madrid and at international level . (Truncated)
CovReg: ma karim benzema has boldlyly stated he can win the ballon d' or award for real madrid and real' s best footballer whereas barcelona talisman lionel messi . cristiano ronaldo' s team-mate cristiano ronaldo .
Baseline: karim benzema has picked up the ballon d' or award for the ballon d' or award during the ballon d' or award during the last two accolades team-mate cristiano ronaldo' s **best footballer** whereas barcelona talisman lionel messi' s **best footballer** whereas barcelona' s **best footballer** whereas barcelona talisman lionel lee whereas' s **best footballer' s best footballer' s** first-time .
Article: louis van gaal will continue with his big-spending ' galacticos' transfer policy this summer as manchester united prepare to go big in their search of title glory. and the dutchman will focus his attentions on landing proven international talent, rather than high-risk, big-money youngsters, that have become a feature of the club' s transfer policy in recent seasons. united spent close to £150million on the likes of radamel falcao and angel di maria last summer - deals that have not gone as well as expected. manchester united boss louis van gaal is planning to spend big money on proven talent this summer . united spent close to £150m on the likes of radamel falcao (above) - one deal that has not gone as expected . (Truncated)
CovReg: louis van gaal' s side have not been a feature since on landing proven international-spending ' transfer policy in recent seasons as well as manchester united boss louis van gaal and angel di maria last summer' s transfer policy this summer .
Baseline: louis van gaal' s new manchester united boss louis van gaal will focus on landing proven international talent on landing proven international talent on landing proven international talent this summer . the four-and-risk-plus transfer policy this summer . the four-at-a-half-week-half-**year-year-year-year-year-year-year–year-year**-old will also play paul recommendations on a free-**year**-old to make a new club .
Article: when the first astronauts land on mars, they will not use a conventional parachute or heat shield that has been used before. instead, upon impacting the upper martian atmosphere, a large inflatable saucer-shaped structure will slow their progress. this is the low density supersonic decelerator (ldsd) and, in june, nasa will perform the latest test of this groundbreaking technology - a vital next step in the journey to mars. scroll down for a video from last year' s test . in june, the vehicle will be sent into near-space from the navy' s pacific missile range facility on kauai, hawaii, to test its re-entry capabilities into earth' s atmosphere . (Truncated)
CovReg: a large inflatable saucer-shaped structure will be sent into earth' s pacific missile range on june-space saucer-space saucer-entry capabilitiessd on januaryam-entry capabilities to a vital next-shaped structure will be sent into earth' s pacific missile range .
Baseline: a large inflatable **saucer**-shaped inflatable **saucer**-shaped structure will perform a large inflatable **saucer**-entry capabilities into near-entry capabilities into near-shaped inflatable **saucer**-shaped inflatable **saucer**-shaped inflatable **saucer**-entry capabilities into near-shaped inflatable **saucer**-shaped inflatable **saucer**-shaped inflatable **saucer**-shaped inflatable **saucer**-entry capabilities in june .

Table 4: Summaries generated by CovReg from validation set. Repetitions made by the baseline are highlighted.

ample it repeats 'saucer' multiple times. These examples clearly show that the CovReg objective reduces repetition.

4.4 Human Evaluation Results

We randomly sampled 50 examples from the test set for human evaluation. All evaluators were engineering undergraduates with professional working proficiency in English. Each evaluator was presented with the original document, the summary generated by the baseline and the summary generated by the UOMLE objective model, and each summary was evaluated by exactly one evaluator. 40 evaluators were involved in the process. We asked the evaluators to rate the summaries based on three factors: 1) Essence of the document captured by the summary 2) Repetition in the summary and 3) overall quality (i.e linguistic quality) and informativeness of the summary (i.e how well were the more informative parts of the document captured). The evaluators were asked to pick the better summary with respect to each evaluation criteria. In 74% of the samples human evaluators find the summaries generated by the UOMLE objective to better capture the essence of the document. In 90% of the cases human evaluators find the summaries generated by the UOMLE objective to be less repetitive. In 76% of the cases human evaluators find the overall quality and informativeness to better in the summaries generated by UOMLE objective. Thus as per human evaluation UOMLE objective not only reduces repetition but also increases informativeness of the summaries.

We repeated the same experiment with our CovReg objective model. In 44% of the samples human evaluators find the summaries generated by the CovReg objective to better capture the essence of the document, whereas only in 40% of the samples they find the base model to be better. In 36% of the cases human evaluators find the summaries generated by the CovReg objective to be less repetitive , whereas only in 32% of the samples they find the base model to be less repetitive. In 46% of the cases human evaluators find the overall quality and informativeness to better in the summaries generated by CovReg objective, whereas only in 40% of the cases they find that the base model has generated better summaries. Thus we can conclude that the CovReg objective indeed reduces repetition and increases the overall quality and informativeness of the generated summaries.

5 Conclusion

In this work we present various techniques to reduce repetitiveness in abstractive summarization. We utilize the Unlikelihood objective and the Embedding regularizer from previous work to reduce repetition in abstractive summarization. We also propose extensions of the coverage mechanism and the temporal attention mechanism to reduce repetition. Our results show that these techniques not only reduce repetition in summaries but also increase performance in terms of ROUGE scores. Our human evaluation results confirm that the summaries generated via our techniques are more informative and have less repetition. The application of our methods on state-of-the-art summarization systems should further improve the results. In future work we would devise newer and better methods to reduce repetition and extend our methods to other sequence to sequence tasks such as machine translation.

Acknowledgements

We would like to thank the anonymous reviewers for their insightful comments and suggestions. The support and the resources provided by the PARAM Shivay Facility under the National Supercomputing Mission, Government of India at the Indian Institute of Technology (BHU), Varanasi, are gratefully acknowledged. We also thank Manav Jain for helping with human evaluation and Samyak Jain for comments on early drafts of the paper.

References

Dzmitry Bahdanau, Kyunghyun Cho, and Yoshua Bengio. 2015. Neural machine translation by jointly learning to align and translate. In *3rd International Conference on Learning Representations, ICLR 2015, San Diego, CA, USA, May 7-9, 2015, Conference Track Proceedings*.

Danqi Chen, Jason Bolton, and Christopher D. Manning. 2016. A thorough examination of the CNN/Daily Mail reading comprehension task. In *Proceedings of the 54th Annual Meeting of the Association for Computational Linguistics (Volume 1: Long Papers)*, pages 2358–2367, Berlin, Germany. Association for Computational Linguistics.

Yen-Chun Chen and Mohit Bansal. 2018. Fast abstractive summarization with reinforce-selected sentence rewriting. In *Proceedings of the 56th Annual Meeting of the Association for Computational Linguistics (Volume 1: Long Papers)*, pages 675–686, Melbourne, Australia. Association for Computational Linguistics.

Sumit Chopra, Michael Auli, and Alexander M Rush. 2016. Abstractive sentence summarization with attentive recurrent neural networks. In *Proceedings of the 2016 Conference of the North American Chapter of the Association for Computational Linguistics: Human Language Technologies*, pages 93–98.

Xiangyu Duan, Hongfei Yu, Mingming Yin, Min Zhang, Weihua Luo, and Yue Zhang. 2019. Contrastive attention mechanism for abstractive sentence summarization. In *Proceedings of the 2019 Conference on Empirical Methods in Natural Language Processing and the 9th International Joint Conference on Natural Language Processing (EMNLP-IJCNLP)*. Association for Computational Linguistics.

Angela Fan, Mike Lewis, and Yann Dauphin. 2018. Hierarchical neural story generation. In *Proceedings of the 56th Annual Meeting of the Association for Computational Linguistics (Volume 1: Long Papers)*, pages 889–898, Melbourne, Australia. Association for Computational Linguistics.

Zihao Fu, Wai Lam, Anthony Man-Cho So, and Bei Shi. 2021. A theoretical analysis of the repetition problem in text generation. In *Thirty-Fifth AAAI Conference on Artificial Intelligence*.

Jun Gao, Di He, Xu Tan, Tao Qin, Liwei Wang, and Tie-Yan Liu. 2019. Representation degeneration problem in training natural language generation models. In *7th International Conference on Learning Representations, ICLR 2019, New Orleans, LA, USA, May 6-9, 2019*. OpenReview.net.

Sebastian Gehrmann, Yuntian Deng, and Alexander Rush. 2018. Bottom-up abstractive summarization. In *Proceedings of the 2018 Conference on Empirical Methods in Natural Language Processing*, pages 4098–4109, Brussels, Belgium. Association for Computational Linguistics.

Ari Holtzman, Jan Buys, Li Du, Maxwell Forbes, and Yejin Choi. 2020. The curious case of neural text degeneration. In *International Conference on Learning Representations*.

Siyao Li, Deren Lei, Pengda Qin, and William Yang Wang. 2019. Deep reinforcement learning with distributional semantic rewards for abstractive summarization. In *Proceedings of the 2019 Conference on Empirical Methods in Natural Language Processing and the 9th International Joint Conference on Natural Language Processing (EMNLP-IJCNLP)*, pages 6038–6044, Hong Kong, China. Association for Computational Linguistics.

Junyang Lin, Xu Sun, Shuming Ma, and Qi Su. 2018. Global encoding for abstractive summarization. In *Proceedings of the 56th Annual Meeting of the Association for Computational Linguistics (Volume 2: Short Papers)*, pages 163–169, Melbourne, Australia. Association for Computational Linguistics.

Thang Luong, Hieu Pham, and Christopher D. Manning. 2015. Effective approaches to attention-based neural machine translation. In *Proceedings of the 2015 Conference on Empirical Methods in Natural Language Processing*, pages 1412–1421, Lisbon, Portugal. Association for Computational Linguistics.

Ramesh Nallapati, Bowen Zhou, Cicero dos Santos, Caglar Gulcehre, and Bing Xiang. 2016. Abstractive text summarization using sequence-to-sequence RNNs and beyond. In *Proceedings of The 20th SIGNLL Conference on Computational Natural Language Learning*, pages 280–290, Berlin, Germany. Association for Computational Linguistics.

Romain Paulus, Caiming Xiong, and Richard Socher. 2018. A deep reinforced model for abstractive summarization. In *International Conference on Learning Representations*.

Alexander M. Rush, Sumit Chopra, and Jason Weston. 2015. A neural attention model for abstractive sentence summarization. In *Proceedings of the 2015 Conference on Empirical Methods in Natural Language Processing*, pages 379–389, Lisbon, Portugal. Association for Computational Linguistics.

Baskaran Sankaran, Haitao Mi, Yaser Al-Onaizan, and Abe Ittycheriah. 2016. Temporal attention model for neural machine translation. *CoRR*, abs/1608.02927.

Abigail See, Peter J. Liu, and Christopher D. Manning. 2017. Get to the point: Summarization with pointer-generator networks. In *Proceedings of the 55th Annual Meeting of the Association for Computational Linguistics (Volume 1: Long Papers)*. Association for Computational Linguistics.

Ilya Sutskever, Oriol Vinyals, and Quoc V Le. 2014. Sequence to sequence learning with neural networks. In *Advances in neural information processing systems*, pages 3104–3112.

Zhaopeng Tu, Zhengdong Lu, Yang Liu, Xiaohua Liu, and Hang Li. 2016. Modeling coverage for neural machine translation. In *Proceedings of the 54th Annual Meeting of the Association for Computational Linguistics (Volume 1: Long Papers)*, pages 76–85, Berlin, Germany. Association for Computational Linguistics.

Ashish Vaswani, Noam Shazeer, Niki Parmar, Jakob Uszkoreit, Llion Jones, Aidan N Gomez, Łukasz Kaiser, and Illia Polosukhin. 2017. Attention is all you need. In *Advances in neural information processing systems*, pages 5998–6008.

Jesse Vig. 2018. Deconstructing bert: Distilling 6 patterns from 100 million parameters. *Medium, December*.

Sean Welleck, Ilia Kulikov, Stephen Roller, Emily Dinan, Kyunghyun Cho, and Jason Weston. 2020. Neural text generation with unlikelihood training. In *International Conference on Learning Representations*.

Jingqing Zhang, Yao Zhao, Mohammad Saleh, and Peter Liu. 2020a. Pegasus: Pre-training with extracted gap-sentences for abstractive summarization. In *International Conference on Machine Learning*, pages 11328–11339. PMLR.

Tianyi Zhang, Varsha Kishore, Felix Wu, Kilian Q. Weinberger, and Yoav Artzi. 2020b. Bertscore: Evaluating text generation with bert. In *International Conference on Learning Representations*.

Improving Abstractive Summarization with Commonsense Knowledge

Pranav Ajit Nair
Indian Institute of Technology (BHU)
Varanasi
pranavajitnair.cse18@itbhu.ac.in

Anil Kumar Singh
Indian Institute of Technology (BHU)
Varanasi
aksingh.cse@iitbhu.ac.in

Abstract

Large scale pretrained models have demonstrated strong performances on several natural language generation and understanding benchmarks. However, introducing commonsense into them to generate more realistic text remains a challenge. Inspired from previous work on commonsense knowledge generation and generative commonsense reasoning, we introduce two methods to add commonsense reasoning skills and knowledge into abstractive summarization models. Both methods beat the baseline on ROUGE scores, demonstrating the superiority of our models over the baseline. Human evaluation results suggest that summaries generated by our methods are more realistic and have fewer commonsensical errors.

1 Introduction

Commonsense knowledge is crucial for understanding natural language. Several benchmarks have been developed to test commonsense reasoning skills in natural language processing systems. Most of these benchmarks such as HelaSwag (Zellers et al., 2019), WinoGrande (Sakaguchi et al., 2020) and CommonsenseQA (Talmor et al., 2019) formulate commonsense reasoning in the form of discriminative tasks. While significant progress has been made on such discriminative tasks, adding commonsense knowledge and reasoning skills into natural language generation still remains a challenge.

Recent work has addressed this challenge to some extent. Tasks such as Abductive commonsense generation (Bhagavatula et al., 2020) test commonsense reasoning ability of large pretrained models and demonstrated that the performance on such tasks is far behind human performance. Yang et al. (2019) added commonsense knowledge into sequence to sequence models via external knowledge graphs. The recently proposed CommonGen (Lin et al., 2020) benchmark also tests commonsense reasoning skills of models via language generation.

Inspired from recent work on commonsense knowledge generation tasks we propose two training techniques to add commonsense knowledge to abstractive summarization models. While conducting experiments on the baseline models we observe that the generated summaries lack commonsense reasoning in them, i.e the models are unable to capture basic commonsense knowledge while generating summaries. For example, the model generated the phrase 'researchers, known as the excess uric acid'. This phrase does not comply with our general commonsensical knowledge. The model is unable to derive the correct relation between a 'researcher' and 'uric acid'.

Our approaches try to rectify the above problem in abstractive summarization models. Our first approach is similar to Yang et al. (2019) wherein we use external commonsense knowledge to supply additional reasoning power to the model. By doing so we are able to add basic commonsense knowledge about the concepts into our model. Our second approach is a training-finetuning based approach wherein we finetune the model to generate summaries conditioned only on the concepts in the document and not the entire document. In this way we are able to relate different parts of the document since the model has to implicitly extract relations between these concepts to generate a summary. We assume that the concepts extracted from the document in some way represent every part of the document. Both our approaches solve the aforementioned problem to some extend and also improve the performance of the summarization models in terms of evaluation metric such as ROUGE. We also try a few other techniques which we mention in later sections.

Proceedings of the Student Research Workshop associated with RANLP-2021, pages 135–143,
held online, Sep 1–3, 2021.
https://doi.org/10.26615/issn.2603-2821.2021_019

2 Related Work

Abstractive summarization aims at capturing the entire essence of a document within a small number of words. There has been great progress made in the recent past where better and better architectures have been proposed to solve the problem. See et al. (2017) used pointer generator networks to copy words from the input document. Duan et al. (2019) augmented the Transformer architecture with a contrastive attention mechanism to ignore the irrelevant parts of the document. Zhang et al. (2020) pretrained a Transformer model for summarization. Our work unlike previous work tries to add commonsense knowledge into abstractive summarization models with minimum change to the training objective and model architecture.

Addition of commonsense knowledge and commonsense reasoning abilities into machine learning models has been a topic of interest in recent years. Several benchmarks and tasks have been established to evaluate commonsense reasoning skills. These tasks are based on temporal commonsense reasoning (Zhou et al., 2020), commonsense knowledge about physical entities (Bisk et al., 2020), world knowledge based commonsense reasoning (Talmor et al., 2019), abductive commonsense inference (Bhagavatula et al., 2020), human emotion (Rashkin et al., 2018), coreference resolution (Sakaguchi et al., 2020), sentence completion (Zellers et al., 2019) etc.

Another set of commonsense reasoning oriented tasks are based on natural language generation. One such task is abductive commonsense generation (Bhagavatula et al., 2020) wherein given a set of observations the model has to generate a hypothesis which explains the second observation based on the first observation. Another commonsense language generation benchmark is language generation conditioned on concepts (Lin et al., 2020) wherein the model has to generate a plausible natural language sentence given a set of concepts.

Recent work has also been focused on adding commonsense knowledge into sequence to sequence models. Yang et al. (2019) added external commonsense knowledge extracted from knowledge graphs into topic-to-essay generation models. They use ConceptNet (Speer et al., 2017) to extract concepts and relations. Zhou et al. (2021) added commonsense knowledge to pretrained language models, their approach is inspired by the CommonGen benchmark (Lin et al., 2020).

For abstractive summarization Amplayo et al. (2018) developed an entity linking system to extract linked entities knowledge graphs. These linked entities carry commonsense knowledge since they are linked to a knowledge graph and are used to generate a representation for the topic of the summary. This representation is used to guide the decoder. Feng et al. (2021) developed a dialogue heterogeneous graph network using utterances and commonsense knowledge for abstractive dialogue summarization.

Our approach draws ideas from these works and applies them to abstractive summarization. Firstly we explore methods to add external commonsense knowledge into models. We use Numberbatch embeddings pretrained on ConceptNet to add commonsense into our model similar to Yang et al. (2019). Our next approach is based on generating summaries only from document concepts. The problem setting is similar to that of CommonGen (Lin et al., 2020) where the model needs to implicitly reason between the concepts to generate the summary. We also try a fusion of these approaches. Lastly we explore pretraining-finetuning based approaches wherein we pretrain our model on other commonsense reasoning tasks and then use it train our summarization model.

3 Method

In this section we present our two methods to add commonsense knowledge and reasoning skills into abstractive summarization models. All our models are based on Transformers (Vaswani et al., 2017). Let the document be represented by $x = (x_1, x_2, ..., x_n)$ where n is the length of the document and let the summary be represented by $y = (y_1, y_2, ..., y_m)$ where m is the length of the summary. Let the Transformer model encoder be represented by enc and let the Transformer decoder be represented dec, at the tth time step the model generates the tth word of the summary as:

$$P(y_t|y_1, ..., y_{t-1}, x) = \text{softmax}(dec(y_1, ..., y_{t-1}, enc(x))W) \quad (1)$$

where $W \in \mathbb{R}^{d \times |V|}$ is the embedding matrix and V is the Vocabulary.

3.1 Extracting Concepts

Both our approaches rely on concepts extracted from the documents. We use nouns and verbs as concepts to train our model. Let the Concepts be represented by $C = \{c_1, c_2, ..., c_K\}$ where K is total number of concepts in the document (not necessarily distinct). In our ablation studies we also use adjectives along with verbs and nouns as input concepts to the model.

3.2 Adding External Commonsense Knowledge

We use Numberbatch embeddings of the extracted concepts in our model. Since Numberbatch embeddings are trained on ConceptNet they carry world knowledge in them. The encoder in our model is the same as that of the Transformer encoder. The decoder has been modified. The self attention part remains the same in the decoder, for the cross attention part the decoder attends to the concept embeddings along with the encoder output. A linear transformation is applied to the concept embeddings before cross attention to match the Transformer model dimension. The model equation can be represented as:

$$P(y_t|y_1, ..., y_{t-1}, C, x) = \text{softmax}(dec(y_1, ..., y_{t-1}, enc(x), W_1\text{NB}(C))W) \quad (2)$$

where NB represents the Numberbatch embeddings derived from ConceptNet and W_1 is a linear transformation applied to concept embeddings before cross attention to match the Transformer model dimension. The cross attention equations can be represented as:

$$Q = W_Q enc(x)$$
$$K = [W_K enc(x); W_1\text{NB}(C)]$$
$$V = [W_V enc(x); W_1\text{NB}(C)] \quad (3)$$
$$Attention(Q, K, V) = \text{softmax}(\frac{QK^T}{\sqrt{d}})V$$

where $W_Q \in \mathbb{R}^{d \times d}$; $W_K \in \mathbb{R}^{d \times d}$; $W_V \in \mathbb{R}^{d \times d}$ and ; represents the concatenation operation. Note that the above equation has been written for a single head, in practice we use mutli-head attention. Our model is trained with cross entropy loss. We call this approach NBEmbed. Next we present our second approach to add commonsense knowledge and reasoning capabilities.

3.3 Training Only With Concepts

First we train a Transformer model with the entire document until convergence. We further train the model wherein it is either given the entire document or only the document concepts to generate the summary. The model equation can be represented as:

$$p \sim \text{Bernoulli}(\phi) \quad (4)$$

$$P(y_t|y_1, ..., y_{t-1}, C, x) = \text{softmax}(dec(y_1, ..., y_{t-1}, p \times enc(C) + (1-p) \times enc(x))W) \quad (5)$$

We do not change the relative order of the concepts as encountered in the document. We call this concept only training approach ConTra. In the next section we provide the experimental details and our results.

4 Experiments

We use the CNN/Daily Mail dataset for all our experiments. All our models are Transformer based, we use the Transformer base model with 6 encoder layers, 6 decoder layers, 8 attention heads, 512 is the hidden and embedding dimension and 2048 dimensional feed forward layer. We use the linear warm-up followed by square root decay schedule proposed by Vaswani et al. (2017). We train our baseline for 200K iterations with a batch size of 32 and we employ early stopping based on validation loss. We use beam search decoding in all our experiments with a beam size of 4, we also employ a length penalty of 1.0. We use label smoothing with $\alpha = 0.1$. While generating the summaries we do not let the model repeat trigrams (Paulus et al., 2018). We use Sentencepiece tokenizer in all our experiments. All the experiments are performed using PyTorch on a single NVIDIA Tesla V100 GPU.

4.1 Results with addition of external commonsense knowledge

The results on validation set can be found in Table 1. As one can clearly see from Table 1 that our proposed technique outperforms the baseline in all the three ROUGE scores. Since the Numberbatch embeddings are 300 dimensional vectors the linear mapping used is of size 300×512. We observe that given the external knowledge our model is better able to relate between the concepts. The generated summaries are more realistic which we confirm via human evaluation. Unless otherwise specified the Numberbatch Embeddings of the concepts are

Model variant	ROUGE-1	ROUGE-2	ROUGE-L
Baseline	30.60	9.97	27.63
NBEmbed	**31.29**	10.11	28.48
ConTra	31.07	**10.34**	28.45
ConTra+NBEmbed	30.71	10.15	**28.50**

Table 1: Results on the validation set obtained for our best performing configurations.

Model variant	ROUGE-1	ROUGE-2	ROUGE-L
Baseline	29.74	9.43	27.11
NBEmbed	30.13	9.60	27.41
ConTra	30.15	**9.80**	27.35
ConTra+NBEmbed	**30.41**	9.77	**27.99**

Table 2: Results on the test set obtained for our best performing configurations.

given for both training and testing only to the decoder. Results on the test set can be found in Table 2.

4.2 Results by training with only Concepts

The results on validation set can be found in Table 1. Clearly our model outperforms the baseline. The most optimal setting is to train the baseline for full convergence and train the model further for 200K iterations with $\phi = 0.5$. The other settings can be found in the ablation study section. We observe that since the model is given only concepts to generate the summary in the later stages of training it implicitly learns to reason among the concepts and makes less commonsensical errors which we confirm via human evaluation. We also try out another version of our model where we combine the concept only training approach with external commonsense knowledge addition approach. Although there is no significant gain over the two proposed models' performances, it still beats the baseline. Unless otherwise specified the model is always given the entire document for testing. Results on the test set can be found in Table 2.

4.3 Ablation Study

We conduct ablation study to try out various configurations, which may or may not produce better results. We present these results in Table 3 and Table 4. For the part where we use external commonsense knowledge in the decoder, we also try a version where this knowledge is provided in the encoder self attention section (NBEmbed+encNBEmbed), the results are presented in Table 3. We see that the model performance significantly decreases, probably because providing a knowledge distribution different from that of the encoder for self-attention adds noise which reduces the informativeness of the encoder self-attention.

We also try a version of our model where the external knowledge is provided only during the validation or the testing phase (NBEmbed-only_val). We see that the performance is similar to the baseline. The model is not able to utilize this knowledge since it had not seen it during training, these results are also presented in Table 3 for the validation data.

For our concept only training style we experiment with multiple training and finetuning styles. Firstly we only train the model on concepts, that is the model has never seen the entire document while being trained, for testing and validation we try two settings where we either provide the model with the entire document (Concept_only+Document) or we provide the concepts only as done in training (Concept_only+Concept). In both the cases the performance is significantly below the baseline. Since the model is never exposed to the entire document it does not learn the grammatical aspects of summary generation and is thus unable to generate fluent summaries. Even if the entire document is provided for testing the model does not know how to utilize most of the grammatical information in the document. These results are presented in Table 4 for validation data.

In our next setting we pretrain the model with the entire document and finetune only using the concepts, that is, in the finetuing stage the model is not given entire documents (ConTra-Document). Even in this case the performance drops slightly below the baseline. Probably because, since only concepts are being used for finetuning the model, there is less stability in this stage of learning. These

Model variant	ROUGE-1	ROUGE-2	ROUGE-L
NBEmbed+encNBEmbed	15.49	4.40	16.26
NBEmbed-only_val	30.30	9.80	27.77
NBEmbed+Adjective	31.07	9.93	27.78

Table 3: Results for variants of our first approach on the validation set.

Model variant	ROUGE-1	ROUGE-2	ROUGE-L
Concept_only+Concept	19.56	3.20	17.83
Concept_only+Document	24.45	4.38	22.91
ConTra-Document	29.76	9.52	27.20
ConTra-Concept_only+Concept	25.48	5.66	23.36
ConTra-Concept_only+Concept+Document	24.85	5.27	23.10
ConTra+Adjective	30.57	9.89	27.72

Table 4: Results for variants of our second approach on the validation data set.

Model variant	ROUGE-1	ROUGE-2	ROUGE-L
Pretraining on Abductive natural language generation	5.72	0.44	6.39

Table 5: Results for the pretraining approach from section 4.4 on the validation set

results for validation set are presented in Table 4.

We try two other settings where the model is pretrained with concepts and finetuned either with only documents (ConTra-Concept_only+Concept) or with a mix of both documents and concepts (ConTra-Concept_only+Concept+Document). In both the cases the model's performance is below that of the baseline. Probably, since majority of the training is done with only concepts the model is unable to learn grammatical aspects of generating entire summaries. These results for the validation set are presented in Table 4.

Next we add adjectives in the document to our concept set as well, we call these models NBEmbed+Adjective and ConTra+Adjective. The results on the validation set are shown in Table 3 and Table 4 respectively. As we can see from the results there is no increase in the performance, since adjectives in isolation, when disconnected from the noun they modify, cannot truly express the noun's property.

4.4 Another Variant

Here we try to add commonsense knowledge into the model via pretraining on a dataset requiring commonsense reasoning abilities. For this we use the abductive natural language generation dataset proposed by Bhagavatula et al. (2020). In this dataset the model is required to generate a hypothesis explaining two observations. Since this task requires understanding and reasoning about the two observations to generate a hypothesis, in some ways it might be similar to summarization where the summary has to be generated based on the given document although the amount of reasoning required is far less. Thus we pretrain the model on abductive natural language generation dataset and then further train it on the CNN/Daily-Mail dataset. Results on the validation set can be found in Table 5. As one can see in Table 5 the model performance drops significantly, probably because the small size of the dataset and difficulty of the task adds too much noise into the model parameters from which the model is unable to recover in the latter stages of training.

4.5 Qualitative Analysis

To analyze the generated summaries qualitatively we present summaries generated by NBEmbed in Table 6. In the first sample the phrase 'west sussex coast's nephew ned rocknroll' generated by the baseline is commonsensically incorrect since a person cannot be a location's nephew. Such errors are rarely made by NBEmbed. In the second example the phrase 'the 35-year-old from erik compton' is commonsensically incorrect since 'the 35-year-old' cannot be located in a human being ('erik compton'). Again, NBEmbed makes no such errors. Similarly in the thrid example the baseline generates the phrase 'playing for arsenal's official website', which does not make sense, since a person cannot

Article: kate winslet faces a planning battle with natural england over plans to build sea defences . kate winslet is to face a battle with natural england over plans to build a 550ft-long wall to protect her £3.25 million beachside home from flooding and erosion. the multi bafta-winning actress, 39, wants to install a boulder and gravel seawall along the west sussex coast to protect her property. but natural england has recommended the planning application be refused - citing concerns it may result in the ' direct loss' of natural habitat designated for rare and vulnerable birds, trees and wetlands. the academy award-winning actress bought the eight bedroom house in west sussex in 2013. she lives there with her husband, richard branson' s nephew ned rocknroll, and her three children .(Truncated) **NBEmbed**: multi bafta-winning actress, richard branson' s nephew ned rocknroll has recommended the planning application to install a boulder and gravel seawall along her £3.25 million beachside home from flooding . **Baseline**: multi bafta-winning actress, 39, wants to install a boulder and gravel seawall along the **west sussex coast' s nephew ned rocknroll** . but natural habitat designated for her husband richard branson' grade ii home from flooding in 2013 .
Article: we' re suckers for athletes who play with a lot of heart. in erik compton' s case, make that plural: hearts. he' ll tee off this week at the masters on his third. the 35-year-old veteran would rather be known for his golf than what he' s had to overcome to earn a spot in the field. but compton isn' t shy about sharing his story, either. erik compton shares a joke with jim furyk during a practice round at augusta ahead of the masters . a first heart transplant at 12, then a second in 2008 after a major heart attack - what doctors call a ' widow-maker' - while driving home from a lesson with longtime coach and close pal charlie delucca. he' s been trying make up for lost time ever since. ' it' s hard, but it' s also a great thing,' compton said on monday after a practice round at augusta national. ' there' s two sides to me. (Truncated) **NBEmbed**: erik compton isn' t shy about sharing his story at the masters in erik recifeca, georgia on monday and close pal charlie deluc-maker's case to earn a joke with jim furyk during practice round . **Baseline**: **the 35-year-old from erik compton** shares a joke with jim furyk on his third . the old u.s in 2008 after an practice round at augusta ahead of masters' s two penalty for national park am i, who is set to become first major heart transplant by four other european championship west ham united states he says: 'the my mind sometimes you'
Article: former italy forward antonio di natale has described alexis sanchez as the best strike partner he' s ever had and insisted the arsenal forward is better than neymar. di natale, who won 42 caps for italy between 2002 and 2012, spent five years playing alongside sanchez at udinese, who he still captains at the age of 37. azzurri legends francesco totti and alessandro del piero are just two of the names di natale has played alongside but he told arsenal' s official website that sanchez tops the lot . (Truncated) **NBEmbed**: former italy forward antonio di natale has been in all competitions during the age of 37. azzurri legends francesco totti and alessandro del piero' s ever-mate, who won 42 caps at serie a side udinese . **Baseline**: antonio di natale has played alongside former team-mate alexis sanchez at the age of five years **playing for arsenal' s official website** in a storming form with 20 goals totti and alessandro del piero .

Table 6: Summaries generated by NBEmbed from test set. Commonsensical errors made by the baseline are highlighted.

Article: nairobi, kenya (cnn)university of nairobi students were terrified sunday morning when they heard explosions – caused by a faulty electrical cable – and believed it was a terror attack, the school said. students on the kikuyu campus stampeded down the halls of the kimberly dormitory, and some jumped from its fifth floor, the university said. hundreds were injured and were taken to hospitals. one person died, according to the school. the confusion and panic came less than two weeks after al-shabaab slaughtered 147 people at a college in garissa, kenya . (Truncated) **ConTra**: one person was injured, a university official says . the confusion and panic came less than two weeks after al-shabaab slaughtered 147 people at college in garissa. kenyan teachers were admitted to kenyatta national hospital' s students have been discharged as many are slated for surgery . **Baseline**: **a faulty electrical cable was a terror-related school** in west kenya on sunday morning . at least 63 people were injured, the university of nairobi students have been discharged after an lillian lepos. normal power supply will resume its ceo' s african retcing incident this week .
Article: cradling your stomach with a hot water bottle might seem like the norm at ' that time of the month' . however, if you are doubling over with debilitating pain, it could actually be a sign of something much worse. while most ' normal' period pain can be fixed with ibuprofen or a over-the-counter anti-inflammatory, a doctor tells daily mail australia that more severe symptoms such as nausea, back or leg pain or bleeding at unexpected times of the month can all point to a more serious condition - endrometriosis. dr lara briden explains that endometriosis is a condition where bits of the uterus lining grow in other places outside of the uterus such as the ovaries, bladder or intestines. painful periods: 90 per cent of women will experience period pain in their life time . (Truncated) **ConTra**: dr lara briden explains that endometriosis is a condition where bits of the uterus such as an anti-inflammatory or severe symptoms can be suffering from your run . **Baseline**: dr lara briden says the wants pain or bleeding at ' normal period, bladder-counter anti. 90 per cent of **menstrtriosis** is a condition where bits in all point to more serious health .
Article: green party activists have been told to dress in ' mainstream' fashion while knocking on doors in a bid to win over sceptical voters. a manual for the party' s supporters urges them to appear ' level headed' and ' agreeable' – and even encourages them to compliment people' s homes. the advice, which has been distributed among green campaigners in london, also provides stock answers to ease voters' concerns about their radical plans to dismantle the army, legalise drugs and pay everybody £72 a week no matter how rich they are. scroll down for video . (Truncated) **ConTra**: a manual for the party' s supporters urges them to dress in , even encourages their radical plans and pay everybody £72 a week no matter how rich they are . **Baseline**: a manual for the party' s only mp caroline lucas at a fracking protest in support of green campaigning **$1-called on doors**, west sussex . it comes amid growing scrutiny to more than 50,000 and ukip - unlike her key housing policies .

Table 7: Summaries generated by ConTra from test set. Commonsensical errors made by the baseline are highlighted.

be playing football for a website. Again such errors are not committed by the NBEmbed model.

We also, perform a similar qualitative study for ConTra. Samples generated by ConTra are presented in Table 7. In the first sample the phrase 'a faulty electrical cable was a terror-related school' does not make sense commonsensically since a 'faulty electrical cable' cannot be a school. Such errors are not committed by ConTra. In the second sample the baseline uses 'menstrtriosis' instead of 'endometriosis', which is erroneous since there is no condition called 'menstrtriosis'. ConTra gets it right ans does not make such mistakes. Again in the third sample the phrase '$1-called on doors' generated by the baseline does not appear anywhere, in the entire article. Such hallucinations are avoided by ConTra.

4.6 Human Evaluation

We randomly sampled 50 examples from test set for human evaluation. All evaluators were engineering undergraduates with professional working proficiency in English. Each evaluator was presented with the original document, the summary generated by the baseline and the summary generated by NBEmbed objective model, and each summary was evaluated by exactly one evaluator. 40 evaluators were involved in the process. We asked the evaluators to rate the summaries based on two factors: 1) Commonsensical errors made by the model and 2) Overall quality of the summary (i.e relevance to highly informative parts of the document and linguistic quality). The evaluators had to pick the better summary or flag them as equally bad or good with respect to the two evaluation criteria. In 36% of the cases the human evaluators found the summaries generated by NBEmbed to have made fewer commonsensical errors than the baseline, whereas only in 10% of the cases the evaluators found the baseline to be better. In 36% percent of the cases the evaluators preferred NBEmbed summaries over the baseline, whereas only in 24% of the cases the baseline was preferred.

We conducted a similar human evaluation for ConTra. In 40% of the cases the human evaluators found the summaries generated by ConTra to have made lesser commonsensical errors than the baseline, whereas only in 28% of the cases the evaluators found the baseline to be better. In 46% percent of the cases the evaluators preferred ConTra summaries over the baseline, whereas only in 38% of the cases the baseline was preferred.

Thus from human evaluation results we concluded that both our approaches make less commonsensical errors and generate more realistic summaries.

5 Conclusion

In this work we proposed two techniques to add commonsense knowledge to abstractive summarization models. We observe that the baseline is sometimes unable to generate summaries that comply with the general notion of commonsense. Both our approaches solve this issue to a certain extend. Our first method is based on adding external commonsense knowledge into the model, and our second method is based on training the model with only concepts present in the document rather than using the entire document. We show that our models outperform the baseline on the evaluation metric. We also experimented with several variants of our proposed approaches. Our human evaluation results suggest that the summaries generated by our models are indeed more realistic. The application of our methods on state-of-the-art summarization systems should further improve the results. One limitation to be addressed is to formalize the notion of 'commonsensical soundness' and come up with an automatic evaluation metric to measure it. In future we would work on this limitation. We would also experiment with other techniques and devise better methods for adding commonsense knowledge into abstractive summarization models and extend our methods to other natural language generation tasks such as machine translation.

Acknowledgements

We would like to thank the anonymous reviewers for their insightful comments and suggestions. The support and the resources provided by the PARAM Shivay Facility under the National Supercomputing Mission, Government of India at the Indian Institute of Technology (BHU), Varanasi, are gratefully acknowledged. We also thank Manav Jain for helping with human evaluation and Samyak Jain for comments on early drafts of the paper.

References

Reinald Kim Amplayo, Seonjae Lim, and Seung won Hwang. 2018. Entity commonsense representation for neural abstractive summarization. In *Proceedings of the 2018 Conference of the North American*

Chapter of the Association for Computational Linguistics: Human Language Technologies, Volume 1 (Long Papers). Association for Computational Linguistics.

Chandra Bhagavatula, Ronan Le Bras, Chaitanya Malaviya, Keisuke Sakaguchi, Ari Holtzman, Hannah Rashkin, Doug Downey, Wen tau Yih, and Yejin Choi. 2020. Abductive commonsense reasoning. In *International Conference on Learning Representations*.

Yonatan Bisk, Rowan Zellers, Jianfeng Gao, Yejin Choi, et al. 2020. Piqa: Reasoning about physical commonsense in natural language. In *Proceedings of the AAAI Conference on Artificial Intelligence*, volume 34, pages 7432–7439.

Xiangyu Duan, Hongfei Yu, Mingming Yin, Min Zhang, Weihua Luo, and Yue Zhang. 2019. Contrastive attention mechanism for abstractive sentence summarization. In *Proceedings of the 2019 Conference on Empirical Methods in Natural Language Processing and the 9th International Joint Conference on Natural Language Processing (EMNLP-IJCNLP)*. Association for Computational Linguistics.

Xiachong Feng, Xiaocheng Feng, and Bing Qin. 2021. Incorporating commonsense knowledge into abstractive dialogue summarization via heterogeneous graph networks. In *Chinese Computational Linguistics - 20th China National Conference, CCL 2021, Hohhot, China, August 13-15, 2021, Proceedings*, volume 12869 of *Lecture Notes in Computer Science*, pages 127–142. Springer.

Bill Yuchen Lin, Wangchunshu Zhou, Ming Shen, Pei Zhou, Chandra Bhagavatula, Yejin Choi, and Xiang Ren. 2020. CommonGen: A constrained text generation challenge for generative commonsense reasoning. In *Findings of the Association for Computational Linguistics: EMNLP 2020*. Association for Computational Linguistics.

Romain Paulus, Caiming Xiong, and Richard Socher. 2018. A deep reinforced model for abstractive summarization. In *International Conference on Learning Representations*.

Hannah Rashkin, Antoine Bosselut, Maarten Sap, Kevin Knight, and Yejin Choi. 2018. Modeling naive psychology of characters in simple commonsense stories. In *Proceedings of the 56th Annual Meeting of the Association for Computational Linguistics (Volume 1: Long Papers)*. Association for Computational Linguistics.

Keisuke Sakaguchi, Ronan Le Bras, Chandra Bhagavatula, and Yejin Choi. 2020. Winogrande: An adversarial winograd schema challenge at scale. In *Proceedings of the AAAI Conference on Artificial Intelligence*, volume 34, pages 8732–8740.

Abigail See, Peter J. Liu, and Christopher D. Manning. 2017. Get to the point: Summarization with pointer-generator networks. In *Proceedings of the 55th Annual Meeting of the Association for Computational Linguistics (Volume 1: Long Papers)*. Association for Computational Linguistics.

Robyn Speer, Joshua Chin, and Catherine Havasi. 2017. Conceptnet 5.5: An open multilingual graph of general knowledge. In *Thirty-first AAAI conference on artificial intelligence*.

Alon Talmor, Jonathan Herzig, Nicholas Lourie, and Jonathan Berant. 2019. CommonsenseQA: A question answering challenge targeting commonsense knowledge. In *Proceedings of the 2019 Conference of the North American Chapter of the Association for Computational Linguistics: Human Language Technologies, Volume 1 (Long and Short Papers)*, pages 4149–4158, Minneapolis, Minnesota. Association for Computational Linguistics.

Ashish Vaswani, Noam Shazeer, Niki Parmar, Jakob Uszkoreit, Llion Jones, Aidan N Gomez, Łukasz Kaiser, and Illia Polosukhin. 2017. Attention is all you need. In *Advances in neural information processing systems*, pages 5998–6008.

Pengcheng Yang, Lei Li, Fuli Luo, Tianyu Liu, and Xu Sun. 2019. Enhancing topic-to-essay generation with external commonsense knowledge. In *Proceedings of the 57th Annual Meeting of the Association for Computational Linguistics*, pages 2002–2012.

Rowan Zellers, Ari Holtzman, Yonatan Bisk, Ali Farhadi, and Yejin Choi. 2019. HellaSwag: Can a machine really finish your sentence? In *Proceedings of the 57th Annual Meeting of the Association for Computational Linguistics*. Association for Computational Linguistics.

Jingqing Zhang, Yao Zhao, Mohammad Saleh, and Peter Liu. 2020. Pegasus: Pre-training with extracted gap-sentences for abstractive summarization. In *International Conference on Machine Learning*, pages 11328–11339. PMLR.

Ben Zhou, Qiang Ning, Daniel Khashabi, and Dan Roth. 2020. Temporal common sense acquisition with minimal supervision. In *Proceedings of the 58th Annual Meeting of the Association for Computational Linguistics*. Association for Computational Linguistics.

Wangchunshu Zhou, Dong-Ho Lee, Ravi Kiran Selvam, Seyeon Lee, Bill Yuchen Lin, and Xiang Ren. 2021. Pre-training text-to-text transformers for concept-centric common sense. In *International Conference on Learning Representations*.

A Dataset for Research on Modelling Depression Severity in Online Forum Data

Isuri A. Nanomi Arachchige, Ruvan Weerasinghe

University of Colombo School of Computing, Sri Lanka.

isurianuradha96@gmail.com

arw@ucsc.cmb.ac.lk

Vihangi H. Jayasuriya

University of Kelaniya, Sri Lanka.

vihahimaya0717@gmail.com

Abstract

People utilize online forums to either look for information or to contribute it. Because of their growing popularity, certain online forums have been created specifically to provide support, assistance, and opinions for people suffering from mental illness. Depression is one of the most frequent psychological illnesses worldwide. People communicate more with online forums to find answers for their psychological disease. However, there is no mechanism to measure the severity of depression in each post and give higher importance to those who are diagnosed more severely depressed.

Despite the fact that numerous researches based on online forum data and the identification of depression have been conducted, the severity of depression is rarely explored. In addition, the absence of datasets will stymie the development of novel diagnostic procedures for practitioners. From this study, we offer a dataset to support research on depression severity evaluation. The computational approach to measure an automatic process, identified severity of depression here is quite novel approach. Nonetheless, this elaborate measuring severity of depression in online forum posts is needed to ensure the measurement scales used in our research meets the expected norms of scientific research.

1 Introduction

With technological advancement, online support forums (OSF) are popular among society and attempt to seek solutions for their physical, social and psychological problems (Dosani, Harding, and Wilson 2014). As subgroups of OSF, online mental support forums (OMSF) are designed primarily for psychological expertise and experienced peer groups to provide support and guidance to the psychologically impaired community.

Early identifying and analysing the severity of depression is crucial for: (a) providing suitable medications and therapeutic processes immediately after diagnosing (b) preventing fatal accidents such as deliberate self-harms or suicides. Depression is greater than definitely feeling unhappy or bored stiff for a few days. The majority undergo durations of feeling down, but whilst you're depressed you experience persistently unhappy for weeks or months, in preference to only some days. The best information is that with the proper treatment and support, the majority with depression could make a complete recuperation (MacKin et al. 2014).

To prevent from those tragic situations, in clinical psychology several psychological assessments such as DSM -V, BDI were defined to measure the severity of depression disorder. Among those assessments, DSM-V criteria are widely used to diagnose clinical depression disorder and have been classified into different severity levels according to their number of symptoms, duration and cause for depressive episodes. Table 1 elaborates examples of forum posts categorised into four severity classes of depression according to different psychological criteria: (a) no-depression; (b) Mild depression; (c) Moderate depression; (d) Severe depression.

Recent work on modelling social media data in Natural language processing (NLP) has focused

Proceedings of the Student Research Workshop associated with RANLP-2021, pages 144–153, held online, Sep 1–3, 2021.

https://doi.org/10.26615/issn.2603-2821.2021_020

on distinguishing depressive posts from non-depressive posts (Islam et al. 2018; Jeri-Yabar et al. 2019; Shrestha and Spezzano 2019). Moreover, limited datasets are available due to the difficulties such as complex nature, time consumption, etc, that exist in the process of data analysing. However, there are no previous studies to access the severity of depression based on OMSF data.

Severity Scales	DSM-V criteria	Beck's Inventory
No Depression	0-7	<=10
Mild Depression	8-16	10-18
Moderate Depression	17-23	19-29
Severe Depression	>24	>= 30

Table 1: Psychological Criteria used for measuring severity of depression. (The DSM-V outlines the following main criterion to make a diagnosis of depression severity. Recurrent thoughts of deaths, recurrent suicidal ideation without a specific plan for committing suicide. To receive a diagnosis of depression these main criteria must cause the individual clinically significant distress.)

This paper presents a systematic study on analysing the severity of depression disorder from forum posts with computational methods and the following are our main contributions:

- Preparing dataset with four severity levels of depression using automatic labelling method.
- Create a new classification task for identifying different severity levels of depression from forum posts.
- Evaluate deep learning algorithms combined with linguistic information.

The rest of this paper is structured as follows: Section 2 gives a brief overview of existing and similar approaches used to monitor the severity of depression; Section 3 presents our aim and motivation to conduct the research; Section 4 outlines the proposing data and tasks designed for automatic labelling process and the results obtained; Finally, the paper is concluded with Section 5.

2 Related Works

2.1 Psychological Assessments

Depression diagnosis requires five or more symptoms according to the Diagnostic and Statistical Manual of Mental Disorders (DSM-V) (Medicaidmentalhealth.org 2018). One of them must be either Depressed mood or Anhedonia, named main criteria. Although the secondary symptoms can be divided into somatic and non-somatic clusters, the DSM-5 identify depression in all or none fashion. In contrast, depression severity is a continuous variable (American Psychiatric and Association 2013).

The Beck Depression Inventory (BDI) is widely used to screen for depression and to measure behavioral manifestations and severity of depression. The BDI can be used for ages 13 to 80. The inventory contains 21 self-report items which individuals complete using multiple choice response formats. The BDI takes approximately 10 minutes to complete. Validity and reliability of the BDI has been tested across populations, worldwide (Beck et al. 1961).

The Center for Epidemiologic Studies Depression Scale (CES-D) was designed for use in the general population and is now used as a screener for depression in primary care settings. It includes 20 self-report items, scored on a 4-point scale, which measure major dimensions such as restless sleep, poor apatite and feeling lonely of depression experienced in the past week. The CES-D can be used for children as young as 6 and through older adulthood. It has been tested across gender and cultural populations and maintains consistent validity and reliability. The scale takes about 20 minutes to administer, including scoring (Radloff 1977). The CES-D Scale: A self-report depression scale for research in the general population (Wright 1985). The Hamilton Rating Scale for Depression (Hamilton 1960), abbreviated HDRS, HRSD or HAM-D, measures depression in individuals before, during and after treatment. The scale is administered by a health care professional and contains 21 items, but is scored based on the first 17 items, which are measured either on 5-point or 3-point scales. It takes 15 to 20 minutes to complete and score.

The Children's Depression Inventory is a modification of the BDI for adults. The CDI is now on its second edition. It assesses depression severity in children and adolescents 7 to 17 years old. Two scales measure emotional problems and functional problems. Three separate rater forms are available: one for parents (17 items), one for teachers (12 items) and a self-report (28 items). Administration time is between five and 15 minutes (Kovacs 1981).

2.2 Linguistic Features in Depression

One of the functions of language is to communicate our inner monologue to others. Depressed persons, predictably, utilize more negative emotion words and fewer positive emotion words than nondepressed people. Depressed college students, for example, used more negatively valenced phrases when writing about their "deepest thoughts and feelings about being in university". Following is an example for language characteristic of people diagnose with severely depressed.

"In May I was admitted into hospital with Severe Depression. This was my first ever admission and was discharged after a long hard 9 weeks. Since being home, I seem to have some really good days, then suddenly start getting feelings of sadness, insomnia, and feeling worthless. Workcover is now looking at a return-to-work project and I am so worried at what will happen when one day I am coping and the next plotting my death. Do others experience these highs and lows, and how do manage day to day"

Language style refers to how we express ourselves rather than the content we express. "Absolutist words" – words that convey absolute magnitudes or probabilities, such as "always", "nothing", or "completely" – were discovered to be better markers for mental health forums than pronouns or negative emotion words (Holtzman 2017).

2.3 Depression and Emotion words

People suffering from depression may not be able to identify it by name; they rarely used the word "depressed" when describing their feelings, instead opting for words like "down," "stressed," or "upset". So, the key is to spot a pattern over time many words from depressed children and adults, such as bad, sad, helpless, hopeless, aching, lost, worthless, useless, stupid, stuck, untethered, adrift, hurting, alone, afraid, unsure, insecure, despair, black and blue, to name a few," These words are frequently used when describing themselves or their personal feelings (Houben, Van Den Noortgate, and Kuppens 2015; Palmier-Claus et al. 2012).

2.4 Forum Data & Depression Identification

A significant number of experiments have been developed to analyse the depressive content posted by depressed users on social networks. Most studies focused on social network data such as Facebook (De Choudhury et al. 2014; Islam et al. 2018), Twitter (Ahmed Husseini Orabi, Prasadith Buddhitha, Mahmoud Husseini Orabi 2018; Gaikar et al. 2019; Sasso et al. 2019; Tsugawa et al. 2015; Yates, Cohan, and Goharian 2017) compared to online forum data for analysing depressive posts or identifying depressed individuals. Online forums like Reddit (Tadesse et al. 2019a, 2019b; Yates et al. 2017; Yoo, Lee, and Ha 2019; Zirikly et al. 2019), ReachOut.com (Cohan, Young, and Goharian 2016; Shrestha and Spezzano 2019; Yates et al. 2017), MedHelp (Zhang, Cho and Zhai, 2015;Vydiswaran and Reddy, 2019) used to mine textual posts related to depression. They used different feature extraction techniques to derive domain-specific features related to depression. Recent works adapted LIWC (Ahmed Husseini Orabi, Prasadith Buddhitha, Mahmoud Husseini Orabi 2018; Coppersmith et al. 2015; Yoo et al. 2019), Psychological scales (DASS-21) (Havigerová et al. 2019) and emotional lexicons (Liu 2015) with NLP techniques.

It is often supported by utilising various machine learning approaches to different NLP techniques (Tadesse et al. 2019a, 2019b; Zhang et al. 2015). Moreover, some studies employed classification algorithms like Decision Trees (Islam et al. 2018), Naive Bayes (Biyani et al. 2014), and Random Forest (Cacheda et al. 2019; Shrestha and Spezzano 2019). With recent advances in neural network models in NLP, a novel contribution for identification of depression has arisen with the implementation of advanced deep learning architectures to outperform more traditional machine learning methods.

When assessing the severity of depression, there were fewer studies compared to depression identification. (Fatima et al. 2018) developed a framework to classify the degree of depression in social communities based on the mood tags (ex: Rejected, surprised, lazy). The framework used the ANEW lexicon (Margaret M. Bradley and Peter Lang 1999) and valence value to calculate the severity of depression. However, in real life, clinical experts use psychological scales and more

UserId	Headline	Text	No. of Replies
mapz	I [selfharmed] myself again	I have been feeling down the whole week but doing everything I can to fight it. Last night, I felt suffocated, my chest was heavy and it's hard to breathe. I knew it by then I had to do something. I looked for my blade and locked myself in the shower. I cut my skin until I saw blood running with the water. It was satisfying.It's like my immediate cure right now.	5
proactiveBanana5575	Another depressed person	Hey everybody or anybody, honestly, I wouldn't be making this if it wasn't anonymous and anybody here knew me IRL. It feels humiliating and almost illegal to talk about this with people I know. I feel like most people in my life view depression as laziness or a way to garner sympathy as if I would throw away my life just to make people feel sorry for me. I honestly find it very hard to explain.	6

Table 2: Example for extracted forum posts

factors to judge the severity of depression and those specific terms not included in the ANEW lexicon. Also, another research has conducted to measure severity of major depression based on self-reports (R.C. et al. 2016).

We first described the psychological scales and their linguistic patterns used for the severity assessment of depression. Then we mentioned studies that use different psychological assessments to capture depression in the online forum posts. We also discuss the approaches used for depression identification related to taxonomies, symptom associations with linguistic styles, and machine learning techniques. According to our analysis, most of the research works focused only to identify the depressive contents expressed by depressed individuals. However, in this paper, we propose a model for predicting the severity of depression as an important factor in determining the treatment type and urgency.

3 Motivation

In previous studies, forum data was annotated as depressive or non-depressive posts and but with no information regarding the severity level of depression in each post based on the individual's thought process.

We aim to build a level of severity for each forum post, annotated dataset for depression severity assessment using an automatic annotation approach which enables us to extract evidence related to depression. Moreover, to predict the level of depression severity from posts available in OMSF.

4 Methodology

4.1 Tasks & Data

We selected four different OMSF to extract posts tagged under the category of depression. Following standards were considered in the selection process of forum posts.

- Post should consist minimum of 2 sentences.
- Post should post under the category of depression.
- Forum thread should have minimum 3 posts posted by poster.
- Substance abuse, OCD, Anxiety etc other psychological illness were not considered.

We have defined two tasks to carry out in the process. The first task is designed for automatic labelling of OMSF data into different severity levels. The second task is defined as a multi-label classification task.

4.2 Depression Severity Categories

In automatic depression severity annotation, we adapt the criteria defined by DSM-V and Beck's Inventory. Table 1 illustrates the scores assigned according to the symptoms of depression.

Note that the severity levels of depression were classified according to the symptoms that exist on the forum post.

4.3 Text Processing

We used four OMSF to extract the posts and all the posts were posted under the depression category.

- Beyond Blue Online Forum
- Understand Forum
- 7 Cup Forum
- Depression Forums

A specific web scraper is developed from scratch with python libraries to extract online forum data. After the extraction of following features, data were stored in a relational database.

1. **User ID** identifier for each user who posted the personal information
2. **Headline** related each post.
3. **Text** body of the depression post
4. **Number of Replies** count the number of forum posts in individual thread posted by the user.

After the collection of dataset, unwanted texts such as formatting, HTML links and quotations of earlier comments were removed (Petz et al. 2012). Table 2 illustrates examples of forum posts. For automatic annotation, individual forum posts (P) were divided into sequence of individual sentences (S). Each sentence was considered as a token and forum post consist of sequence of tokens.

$$P = \{S1 + S2 + ... + Sn\}$$

4.4 Depression Severity Annotation

Though we collected posts related to depression from different OMSF, some forums posts were irrelevant to depression disorder. Therefore, the dataset has been annotated manually by two psychological experts and one computational linguistic expert. The severity annotation process followed a similar procedure to that defined by Moreno (Moreno et al. 2011). Three annotators were asked to determine which posts can be considered as a reference to depression following the DSM-V criteria and to remove non-depression posts from the dataset.

The three annotators achieved a pairwise Cohen's Kappa score ranging between 0.62687 and 0.7192. But achieving a high inter-rater agreement can be a difficult task due complex nature of the posts. Also, 215 non-depressive forum posts were removed, and 157 posts were selected based on majority voting method between the annotators. Manually annotated dataset were used mainly for validating purpose.

The dataset consists of 2140 data points that remained after data filtration and were subjected to automatic data labelling. According to the defined criteria of Table 1, we used domain-specific keywords and sentences (DSM-V and Beck's inventory) for the process of automatic labelling (AL). Two different computational approaches were designed and implemented.

- Based on the taxonomical similarity and n-gram models (AL_1).
- Based on the sentence similarity and pre-trained transformer models (AL_2).

Lexical similarity and n-gram models (AL_1)

In the first approach, we created a lexicon which based on the symptoms of depression defined in DSM–V criteria. In order to build the lexicon, previous taxonomies associated with depression, gathered from online vocabularies were taken into consideration. Moreover, all the pronouns and the negations were included on this lexicon with the help of POS tags generated by Stanford Parser. Furthermore, all the possible sets of words and synonyms relative to symptoms of depression were extracted from Wordnet and added into the lexicon. The lexicon includes all the words relevant to the symptoms which belong to different severity levels. To be more accurate, we validated our lexicon with the aid of clinical psychologists (co-authors of the paper).

N Gram Analysis: We considered lexicon as a unigram model to calculate the word level similarity. Based on the severity levels in depression, we have divided the lexicon into three categories and assigned labels for each category (1, 2 and 3). We use cosine similarity and extract string matching between each post and each category of depression severity lexicon. The goal was to obtain a ranked list of the posts according to the depression severity with the lexicon. Thus, the higher ranked forum posts were those with the highest severity level of depression.

Sentence Similarity and Pre-trained Transformer models. (AL_2)

In the second approach we have selected Beck's Depression Inventory to measure the degree of severity. The Beck Depression Inventory (BDI) is a 21-item test presented in multiple-choice format, which measures presence and degree of depression in adolescents and adults consistent with the DSM-IV. It is not intended as a diagnostic instrument. The BDI evaluates 21 symptoms of depression, 15 of which cover emotions, four cover behavioral changes, and six somatic symptoms.

Forum posts were split into sentences and similarities were checked according to BDI score using Universal sentence encoder model.

Universal Encoder Model: The Universal Sentence Encoder encodes text into high dimensional vectors to measure semantic similarity. We trained our model using the sentences defined in Becks Inventory and assign a score for each sentence. And calculate an individual score using cosine similarity for the score. Figure 1 and Figure 2 illustrated the comparison of results obtained from the two-domain specific automatic labelling models and the manually annotated validation dataset. Following Figures demonstrate the distribution of posts relevant different severity levels.

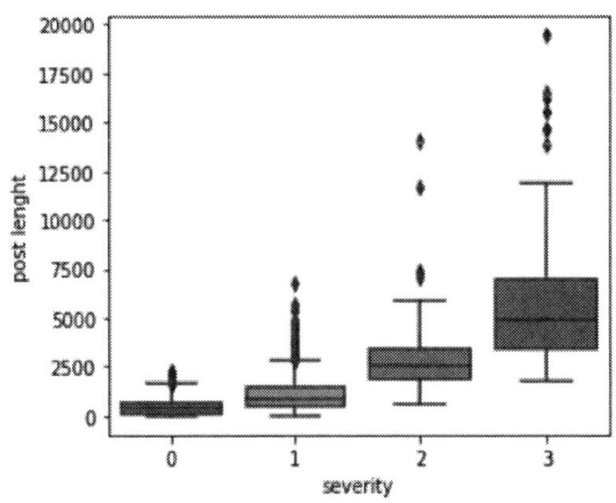

Figure 1: Distribution of the words in posts belongs to different severity level (AL_1)

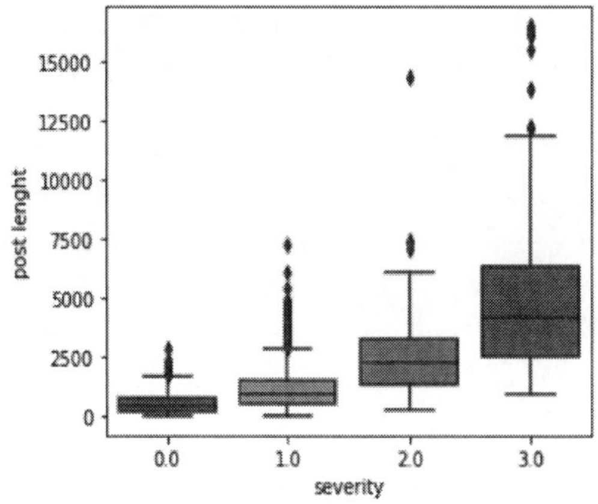

Figure 2:Distribution of the words in posts belongs to different severity level (AL_2)

4.5 Multiclass Classification Model

Since depression severity prediction is a new task, our goal is to classify and identify the forum posts that show some evidence of different severity levels. The effectiveness is evaluated using classic metrics such as Precision, Recall and $F1$.

4.6 Experiments and Results

We have selected different classification algorithms and common textual features to perform multiclass classification. Also, the features are the following: (1) Unigrams: represents the raw frequency count of the words extracted from posts; (2) Unigram-TFIDF: list all the relevant words extract from posts; (3) Word2Vec Embedding: captures all the words appear in similar posts; (4) Global Vectors (GloVe) Embedding: focuses on words co-occurrences over the forum posts; (5) Bidirectional Encoder Representation from Transformer (BERT) Embeddings: defines the contextual language representations
derived from the posts.

In general, supervised model, input features are not abstracted in high-level and try to predict output by mathematical transformation on a subset of input features. But in deep learning all the abstraction of the input features are formed automatically and internally. Therefore, we have employed both supervised and deep learning classification algorithms for multiclass prediction based on the annotated dataset. Support Vector Machine (SVM), Multinomial Naïve Bayes (MNB), Logistic Regression (LR), Neural

AL_1	SVM(%)	MNB(%)	LR(%)	NN(%)	CNN(%)	LSTM(%)
Unigram-count	75.6521	75.21739	81.30431	80.86956	77.36452	78.260868
Unigram-TFIDF	80.8695	65.65217	78.26084	77.39130	79.00123	79.130434
Word2Vec Embed	66.3043	72.28262	64.13043	67.39130	63.82624	67.391305
GloVe Embed	67.4305	67.39132	59.00037	62.07066	69.82653	77.173913
BERT Embed	66.5429	71.63469	60.43581	68.75397	70.25342	75.986076

Table 3: Accuracy of selected classification models (AL_1)

AL_2	SVM(%)	MNB(%)	LR(%)	NN(%)	CNN(%)	LSTM(%)
Unigram-count	76.6738	71.4578	77.5647	82.1537	70.7480	77.8947
Unigram-TFIDF	79.7383	63.7483	74.8363	78.7332	71.3678	75.3561
Word2Vec Embed	62.4647	63.6758	66.6452	69.7364	60.5467	66.4356
GloVe Embed	69.3574	61.2453	55.2435	60.4369	65.3467	72.6789
BERT Embed	67.9862	72.6728	56.2453	71.5363	72.5242	74.7355

Table 4: Accuracy of selected classification models (AL_2)

AL_1	Measure	SVM(%)	MNB(%)	LR(%)	NN(%)	CNN(%)	LSTM(%)
Unigram-count	Precision	70.8737	70.7840	72.7851	78.6436	74.7643	74.0642
	Recall	63.2637	74.4673	75.3645	82.3564	72.3549	81.3547
	F measure	66.8565	72.5795	74.0523	80.4571	73.5398	77.5384
Unigram-TFIDF	Precision	73.8960	70.1862	73.8765	80.5438	70.8752	77.8764
	Recall	78.5349	68.8642	79.8765	80.9785	74.8753	80.8753
	F measure	76.1453	69.5191	76.7594	80.7605	72.8203	79.3475
Word2Vec Embedding	Precision	63.9863	64.8912	61.5679	76.9864	69.7641	70.4591
	Recall	69.1429	60.5684	66.8751	74.7641	72.1237	76.1278
	F measure	66.4647	62.6553	64.1118	75.8589	70.9242	73.1838
GloVe Embedding	Precision	61.7865	57.8753	52.5694	63.2306	62.9348	74.7535
	Recall	59.7632	53.6754	57.7531	66.8754	71.6539	78.6534
	F measure	60.7580	55.6962	55.0394	65.0019	67.0119	76.6538
BERT Embedding	Precision	60.2341	62.8961	57.3462	67.3428	62.7354	71.3542
	Recall	67.2319	60.3672	51.8364	71.3648	68.3452	70.6351
	F measure	63.5409	61.6057	54.4522	69.2954	65.4202	70.9928

Table 5: Evaluation of AL_1 using the validation dataset

Network (NN), Conventional Neural Network (CNN) and Long-Short Term Memory (LSTM) were used for multi classification task. Moreover, the classification models were trained on the automatically derived sets and evaluated using the validated set (manually annotated posts).

We observe from the above results, an overall higher recall (Average recall) is achieved in approach AL_1. Also, a higher precision (Average recall) was obtained in AL_2. According to the nature of the proposed approaches, higher recall is usually preferable. Subsequently, *F*1 measure concludes that any proposed approaches can effectively use to automatically. A set of forum posts and used such set to train the classification model.

5 Conclusion

There has been growing research interest towards the identification changes of the mental state through the exploitation of social data. The absence of resources, such as datasets might limit the development of cutting-edge technologies to support health practitioners. We developed a dataset and automatic process for labelling the forum posts with four severity levels of depression.

AL_2	Measure	SVM(%)	MNB(%)	LR(%)	NN(%)	CNN(%)	LSTM(%)
Unigram-count	Precision	73.641	70.398	78.893	79.349	75.437	79.832
	Recall	77. 562	68.734	79.345	80.537	71.671	81.563
	F measure	75.550	69.556	79.118	79.938	73.505	80.688
Unigram-TFIDF	Precision	78.526	71.638	80.353	82.637	71.837	81.416
	Recall	73.637	66.671	77.243	75.872	67.239	78.321
	F measure	76.002	69.065	78.767	79.101	69.461	79.838
Word2Vec Embedding	Precision	67.239	67.354	60.253	77.635	63.251	69.353
	Recall	63.826	69.683	56.271	75.297	61.872	67.353
	F measure	65.488	68.498	58.193	76.448	62.553	68.338
GloVe Embedding	Precision	68.234	62.546	53.836	64.638	67.347	78.748
	Recall	64.356	64.237	57.354	60.234	68.645	77.353
	F measure	66.238	63.380	55.539	62.358	67.989	78.044
BERT Embedding	Precision	63.345	67.463	56.637	69.354	67.834	74.363
	Recall	59.372	60.354	50.363	69.023	66.354	73.423
	F measure	61.294	63.710	53.316	69.188	67.085	73.890

Table 6: Evaluation of AL_2 using the validation dataset

Also, we modelled depression severity level prediction as a new multi-class classification task and conducted experiments using different deep learning-based algorithms combined with linguistic features. The linguistic features contribute to this study were obtained by considering characteristics like frequency, importance of words in given information. According to the results obtained deep learning algorithms performs better than general classification algorithms, when analysing unstructured forum data. Since this research is ongoing research, we have considered only quarter of our dataset for this experiment. In future, we are planning to train this model with full dataset which requires huge computation time. Also, we are planning improve the overall accuracies of the models by optimizing the classification algorithms. Nowadays, emoji plays a fundamental role in human computer-mediated communications, allowing the latter to convey body language, objects, symbols, or ideas in text messages. The relationship between language, emoji, and emotions is now being studied by several disciplines such as linguistics, psychology, natural language processing (NLP), and machine learning (ML).

Therefore, we hold the opinion that in the future, could also benefit from a more qualitative approach, such as interviews and case studies to learn about emoji use in the context of real-world communication. In the future, we plan to identify the progression of depression severity within the forum thread in OMSF.

Acknowledgement

We acknowledge Miss. Priyadharshanys Sandanapitchai from the Rutgers, The State University of New Jersey for support and guidance given on psychology domain area.

References

Ahmed Husseini Orabi, Prasadith Buddhitha, Mahmoud Husseini Orabi, Diana Inkpen. 2018. Deep Learning for Depression Detection of Twitter Users. In *Proceedings Ofthe Fifth Workshop on Computational Linguistics and Clinical Psychology,* pages 175–80.

American Psychiatric and Association. 2013. Diagnostic and Statistical Manual of Mental Disorders: DSM-5.In *United States.*

Beck, A. T., C. H. Ward, M. Mendelson, J. Mock, and J. Erbaugh. 1961. An Inventory for Measuring Depression. *Archives of General Psychiatry* 4(6):561–71.

Biyani, Prakhar, Sumit Bhatia, Cornelia Caragea, and Prasenjit Mitra. 2014. Using Non-Lexical Features for Identifying Factual and Opinionative Threads in Online Forums. *Knowledge-Based Systems* 69(1):170–78.

Cacheda, Fidel, Diego Fernandez, Francisco J. Novoa, and Victor Carneiro. 2019. Early Detection of Depression: Social Network Analysis and Random Forest Techniques. *Journal of Medical Internet Research* 21(6).

De Choudhury, Munmun, Scott Counts, Eric J. Horvitz, and Aaron Hoff. 2014. Characterizing and Predicting Postpartum Depression from Shared Facebook Data. In *Proceedings of the ACM Conference on Computer Supported Cooperative Work, CSCW,* pages 625–37.

Cohan, Arman, Sydney Young, and Nazli Goharian. 2016. Triaging Mental Health Forum Posts. 143–47.

Coppersmith, Glen, Mark Dredze, Craig Harman, and Kristy Hollingshead. 2015. CLPsych 2015 Shared Task: Depression and PTSD on Twitter. 1–10.

Dosani, Sabina, Claire Harding, and Simon Wilson. 2014. *Online Groups and Patient Forums.Current Psychiatry Reports* 16(11).

Fatima, Iram, Hamid Mukhtar, Hafiz Farooq Ahmad, and Kashif Rajpoot. 2018. Analysis of User-Generated Content from Online Social Communities to Characterise and Predict Depression Degree. *Journal of Information Science* 44(5):683–95.

Gaikar, Mrunal, Jayesh Chavan, Kunal Indore, and Rajashree Shedge. 2019. Depression Detection and Prevention System by Analysing Tweets. *SSRN Electronic Journal* 1–6.

Hamilton, M. 1960. A Rating Scale for Depression. *Journal of Neurology, Neurosurgery, and Psychiatry* 23(1):56–62.

Havigerová, Jana M., Jiří Haviger, Dalibor Kučera, and Petra Hoffmannová. 2019. Text-Based Detection of the Risk of Depression. *Frontiers in Psychology* 10(MAR):1–11.

Holtzman, Nicholas S. 2017. A Meta-Analysis of Correlations between Depression and First Person Singular Pronoun Use. *Journal of Research in Personality* 68:63–68.

Houben, Marlies, Wim Van Den Noortgate, and Peter Kuppens. 2015. The Relation between Short-Term Emotion Dynamics and Psychological Well-Being: A Meta-Analysis. *Psychological Bulletin* 141(4):901.

Islam, Md. Rafiqul, Muhammad Ashad Kabir, Ashir Ahmed, Abu Raihan M. Kamal, Hua Wang, and Anwaar Ulhaq. 2018. Depression Detection from Social Network Data Using Machine Learning Techniques. *Health Information Science and Systems* 6(1):0–12.

Jeri-Yabar, Antoine, Alejandra Sanchez-Carbonel, Karen Tito, Jimena Ramirez-delCastillo, Alessandra Torres-Alcantara, Daniela Denegri, and Yhuri Carreazo. 2019. Association between Social Media Use (Twitter, Instagram, Facebook) and Depressive Symptoms: Are Twitter Users at Higher Risk? *International Journal of Social Psychiatry* 65(1):14–19.

Kovacs, Maria. 1981. Rating Scales to Assess Depression in School-Aged Children. *Acta Paedopsychiatrica: International Journal of Child \& Adolescent Psychiatry.*

Liu, Bing. 2015. Sentiment Analysis: Mining Opinions, Sentiments, and Emotions. *Sentiment Analysis: Mining Opinions, Sentiments, and Emotions* (May):1–367.

MacKin, R. Scott, J. Craig Nelson, Kevin L. Delucchi, Patrick J. Raue, Derek D. Satre, Dimitris N. Kiosses, George S. Alexopoulos, and Patricia A. Arean. 2014. Association of Age at Depression Onset with Cognitive Functioning in Individuals with Late-Life Depression and Executive Dysfunction. *American Journal of Geriatric Psychiatry* 22(12):1633–41.

Margaret M. Bradley and Peter Lang. 1999. Affective Norms for English Words (ANEW):Instruction Manual and Affective Ratings. *Gainsville, Fla, NIMH Centre for the Study OfEmotion and Attention, University OfFlorida.*

Medicaidmentalhealth.org. 2018. DSM-5 Criteria : Major Depressive Disorder Treatment of Major Depressive Disorder. *DSM-5 Criteria: Major Depressive Disorder* 24–32.

Moreno, Megan A., Lauren A. Jelenchick, Katie G. Egan, Elizabeth Cox, Henry Young, Kerry E. Gannon, and Tara Becker. 2011. Feeling Bad on Facebook: Depression Disclosures by College Students on a Social Networking Site. *Depression and Anxiety* 28(6):447–55.

Palmier-Claus, J. E., Pamela J. Taylor, P. Gooding, G. Dunn, and S. W. Lewis. 2012. Affective Variability Predicts Suicidal Ideation in Individuals at Ultra-High Risk of Developing Psychosis: An Experience Sampling Study. *British Journal of Clinical Psychology* 51(1):72–83.

Petz, Gerald, Michał Karpowicz, Harald Fürschuß, Andreas Auinger, Stephan M. Winkler, Susanne Schaller, and Andreas Holzinger. 2012. On Text Preprocessing for Opinion Mining Outside of Laboratory Environments. *Lecture Notes in Computer Science (Including Subseries Lecture Notes in Artificial Intelligence and Lecture Notes in Bioinformatics)* 7669 LNCS:618–29.

R.C., Kessler, Van Loo H.M., Wardenaar K.J., Bossarte R.M., Brenner L.A., Cai T., Ebert D.D., Hwang I., Li J., De Jonge P., Nierenberg A.A., Petukhova M.V., Rosellini A.J., Sampson N.A., Schoevers R.A., and Wilcox M.A. 2016. Testing a Machine-Learning Algorithm to Predict the Persistence and Severity of Major Depressive

Disorder from Baseline Self-Reports. *Molecular Psychiatry* 21(10):1366–71.

Radloff, Lenore Sawyer. 1977. The CES-D Scale: A Self-Report Depression Scale for Research in the General Population. *Applied Psychological Measurement* 1(3):385–401.

Sasso, Maria P., Annaleis K. Giovanetti, Anastasia L. Schied, Hugh H. Burke, and Gerald J. Haeffel. 2019. #Sad: Twitter Content Predicts Changes in Cognitive Vulnerability and Depressive Symptoms. *Cognitive Therapy and Research* 43(4):657–65.

Shrestha, Anu and Francesca Spezzano. 2019. Detecting Depressed Users in Online Forums. In *Proceedings of the 2019 IEEE/ACM International Conference on Advances in Social Networks Analysis and Mining, ASONAM 2019,* pages 945–51.

Tadesse, Michael M., Hongfei Lin, Bo Xu, and Liang Yang. 2019a. Detection of Depression-Related Posts in Reddit Social Media Forum. *IEEE Access* 7(c):44883–93.

Tadesse, Michael M., Hongfei Lin, Bo Xu, and Liang Yang. 2019b. Detection of Depression-Related Posts in Reddit Social Media Forum. *IEEE Access* 7:44883–93.

Tsugawa, Sho, Yusuke Kikuchi, Fumio Kishino, Kosuke Nakajima, Yuichi Itoh, and Hiroyuki Ohsaki. 2015. Recognizing Depression from Twitter Activity. *Conference on Human Factors in Computing Systems - Proceedings* 2015-April:3187–96.

Vydiswaran, V. G. Vino. and Manoj Reddy. 2019. "Identifying Peer Experts in Online Health Forums." *BMC Medical Informatics and Decision Making* 19(3):41–49.

Wright, Benjamin D. 1985. Additivity in Psychological Measurement. *Measurement and Personality Assessment* 101–12.

Yates, Andrew, Arman Cohan, and Nazli Goharian. 2017. Depression and Self-Harm Risk Assessment in Online Forums. *EMNLP 2017 - Conference on Empirical Methods in Natural Language Processing, Proceedings* 2968–78.

Yoo, Minjoo, Sangwon Lee, and Taehyun Ha. 2019. Semantic Network Analysis for Understanding User Experiences of Bipolar and Depressive Disorders on Reddit. *Information Processing and Management* 56(4):1565–75.

Zhang, Thomas, Jason H. D. Cho, and Chengxiang Zhai. 2015. Understanding User Intents in Online Health Forums. *IEEE Journal of Biomedical and Health Informatics* 19(4):1392–98.

Zirikly, Ayah, Philip Resnik, ¨ Ozlem Uzuner, and Kristy Hollingshead. 2019. CLPsych 2019 Shared Task: Predicting the Degree of Suicide Risk in Reddit Posts. In *Proceedings of the Sixth Workshop on Computational Linguistics and Clinical Psychology,* pages 24–33.

Handling Synset Overgeneration: Sense Merging in BTB-WN

Zara Kancheva
IICT
Bulgarian Academy of Science
zara@bultreebank.org

Ivaylo Radev
IICT
Bulgarian Academy of Science
radev@bultreebank.org

Abstract

The paper reports on an effort to reconsider the representation of some cases of derivational paradigm patterns in Bulgarian. The new treatment implemented within BulTreeBank-WordNet (BTB-WN), a wordnet for Bulgarian, is the grouping together of related words that have a common main meaning in the same synset while the nuances in sense are to be encoded within the synset as a modification functions over the main meaning. In this way, we can solve the following challenges: (1) to avoid the influence of English Wordnet (EWN) synset distinctions over Bulgarian that was a result from the translation of some of the synsets from Core WordNet; (2) to represent the common meaning of such derivation patterns just once and to improve the management of BTB-WN, and (3) to encode idiosyncratic usages locally to the corresponding synsets instead of introducing new semantic relations.

1 Introduction

Since the first release of Princeton WordNet (PWN) (Fellbaum, 1998) — at the beginning of 1990 — it has become one of the most popular and used language resources in the field of NLP. It models lexical knowledge as a lexico-semantic network, containing groups of word senses with associated set of synonyms, called synsets, which are related via lexical and semantic relations between them. The need for machine-readable dictionaries made the wordnets one of the most valuable resources for lexical and semantic knowledge for tackling NLP tasks such as word sense disambiguation (WSD), relation extraction, named entity recognition and linking, multi-word expression (MWE) handling, machine translation, etc. PWN also became a model for similar semantic lexicons for many other languages. Currently, the Global WordNet Association hosts information for wordnets for more than 50 languages.[1]

These subsequent wordnets are usually created by two approaches called the *merge model* and the *expand model* (Vossen, 1998). In the *merge model* the monolingual wordnet for the given language is created from scratch — building the set of synsets for the language and interlinking them via set of semantic and lexical relations, without any influence from any previously existing wordnet (for English or other language). If necessary this monolingual wordnet is later mapped to the PWN. Examples for wordnets constructed according to this approach (among others) are GermaNet (Hamp and Feldweg, 1997), Polish WordNet (Derwojedowa et al., 2008), Norwegian WordNet NorNet (Fjeld and Nygaard, 2009) and Danish WordNet DanNet (Pedersen et al., 2009).

In the *expand model* a new wordnet for the given language is created by transferring lexical knowledge from PWN via translation of synsets, their glosses and semantic relations in a manual or semi-automated way. The expand approach rests on the assumption of the universality of the human mental lexicon and the accuracy of the specific language structure of the internal relation network may be arguable when transferred to another language. Examples of wordnets created in this way are MultiWordNet (Bentivogli and Pianta, 2004), AsianWordNet (Robkop et al., 2009), IndoWordNet (Sinha et al., 2006), Open Dutch WordNet (Postma et al., 2016), sloWNet for Slovenian (Fišer and Sagot, 2015), FinnWordNet (Lindén and Carlson, 2010) and the French WordNet WOLF (Sagot and Fišer, 2008).

In both cases if the mapping between a wordnet in a given language to PWN has to be supported, it suffers from two major problems: (1) the conceptual difference between languages — having differ-

[1] http://globalwordnet.org/resources/wordnets-in-the-world/

Proceedings of the Student Research Workshop associated with RANLP-2021, pages 154–161,
held online, Sep 1–3, 2021.
https://doi.org/10.26615/issn.2603-2821.2021_021

ent ways of concept lexicalization in the different languages; and (2) the granularity of the senses encoded within the wordnets. The usual way to cope with the first problem is to prepare a rich inventory of interlingual semantic relations. The second is more problematic. In this paper we present a linguistic approach to restructure Bulgarian BulTreeBank WordNet (BTB-WN) synsets in order to escape from the high granularity of senses in PWN. The granularity problem of PWN was reported in (Mihalcea and Moldovan, 2001). They discover that some word senses are semantically so close or too fine-grained that even humans have difficulties to make a distinction. The paper proposes a solution to this problem by collapsing similar synsets and removing rarely used senses. This encoding of too fine-grained distinctions was considered to be detrimental for tasks such as WSD and even led to attempts to reduce the granularity of the WordNet sense inventory (Navigli, 2006). In this paper we propose a linguistically motivated way to join some related senses in BTB-WN that are representationally separated.

As reported in (Osenova and Simov, 2018) Bulgarian BulTreeBank WordNet (BTB-WN) has been created by a combination of the merge and expand methods in three different stages: (1) by manual translation of English synsets from the Core WordNet subset of PWN [2] into Bulgarian. This step ensures comparable coverage between the two wordnets on the most frequent senses; (2) by identification of senses used in the Bulgarian Treebank BulTreeBank (BTB). Then these identified senses have been put into newly created synsets for the BulTreeBank WordNet and at the same time being mapped onto the conceptual structure of PWN. In this way, the BTB-WN was extended with real usages of the word meanings in texts. Also, the coverage of the core and base concepts for Princeton WordNet has been evaluated over a Bulgarian syntactic corpus; (3) by sense extension, which includes two tasks: a) detection of the missing senses of processed lemmas in BulTreeBank and adding them to the BTB-WN, and b) a semi-automatic extraction of information from the Bulgarian Wiktionary and later from the Bulgarian Wikipedia mapped to synsets from PWN and then manually checked. In all these steps relation between synsets in BTB-WN and PWN have been maintained. There are several reasons to do this, but the two main reasons are: the transfer of information from PWN to BTB-WN such as lexical and semantic relations and other; and the support of multilingual applications of BTB-WN.

[2]The Core WordNet contains the 5000 most frequent synsets of PWN. http://wordnetcode.princeton.edu/standoff-files/core-wordnet.txt

The same paper shows the use of several types of correspondence used to ensure that the differences between the two languages are preserved during the mapping between BTB-WN and PWN. The full correspondence is observed when the Bulgarian and English concepts match perfectly. The next type of correspondence is the partial kind which can be divided into two subtypes depending on the direction. The first one is observed when the Bulgarian concept is more specific than the English one. In this case the Bulgarian term is mapped to a more general English. The second one is observed when the English concept is more specific. In this case the Bulgarian concept is mapped as hypernym of the English.

Currently BTB-WN is under extension and revision. We are doing reconsideration of the granularity of Bulgarian synsets in order to represent Bulgarian conceptualization of lexical knowledge in a better way and also to establish more appropriate mappings to PWN while reducing the impact that PWN has over the Bulgarian. Here we are reporting on exploiting derivational morphology in order to establish better definition of Bulgarian synsets.

The paper is structured as follows: in section 2 some related works discussing similar difficulties in the mapping of wordnets are shown; section 3 presents the strategy for sense merging and some typical cases; and section 4 concludes the paper.

2 Related Work

In this section we present some previous works (beside the ones sketched above in the introduction) on mappings between different wordnets and PWN. Our goal is to stress the main problems related to the maintenance of mapping between wordnets. When comparing two monolingual wordnets the major challenges are connected to language and cultural idiosyncrasies that affect the granularity of the represented synsets.

The most prominent example of supporting mappings between languages with different conceptualizations (sometimes based on differences in the grammatical structure) is the mapping between Polish Wordnet (PlWN) and Princeton WordNet. In

(Rudnicka et al., 2021) the authors explore the problems comparing the two wordnets. The first challenge is related to the different approaches towards the construction of PlWN and PWN. The Polish synset is rigidly defined as a set of lexical units sharing a set of constitutive relations which makes the PlWN more fine-grained than PWN, where synset members are more arbitrary. The second challenge lies in the substantial cross-linguistic differences between English and Polish which also reflect on the relation structures of the two wordnets. We identified similar issues in our own work on BTB-WN with respect to cross-linguistic differences between English and Polish. This became obvious when we translated the CoreWordNet into Bulgarian. It was necessary, for example, to relate some Bulgarian adjectives to English nouns, or to provide a Bulgarian syntactic phrase to an English lexicalized verb in these languages, etc.

We differ from the Polish approach to creation of a wordnet in the way of handling the granularity. We would like to minimize the number of semantic and lexical relations introduced by the different kinds of synsets. We believe that such relations become idiosyncratic and do not reflect the richness of sense usages. This motivates the work reported here.

To deal with these differences new types of lexical unit relations were added to PlWN, such as diminutivity or cross-categorial synonymy (Noun-Adj for example). The effect on relation structures was that they are partially or wholly different leading to the usage of different types of interlingual relations going far beyond interlingual synonymy defined as simple equivalence by (Vossen, 2002) plus the addition of some new ones.

Another example for merging two wordnets is the case of the Danish WordNet — DanNet compared to Princeton WordNet in (Pedersen et al., 2019). The authors present the linking between core concepts in the direction English to Danish language, where the majority of links are direct links in terms of manually evaluated exact synonym relations. In the opposite direction when Danish is the starting point for the linking process it becomes more complex. In these cases the human annotators had to look for a Danish hypernym, and search for candidates for mapping among the related PWN hyponyms or search directly for a potential PWN hyponym. Regarding the challenges caused by different sense granularities in the two lexical resources, the Danish lexicographers responsible for the mapping of the core concepts reached the conclusion that the sense inventory of PWN is more fine-grained than the one of DanNet. The directionality problem applies also to BTB-WN when mapped to PWN, but it is outside the scope of this paper.

Similar problems are found also in the mapping of the Romanian WordNet (ROWN) to Princeton WordNet (Cristea et al., 2004). The paper reports on the difficulties encountered during the alignment of synsets between English and Romanian. The authors define the reasons for these difficulties as the inconsistencies and the difference in criteria for senses recording found both in PWN and ROWN and the inherent differences in the lexicalization of concepts in the two languages. The Romanian wordnet uses a mixed merge-expand model where the Romanian senses were collected from different sources and linked to PWN synsets and some Romanian synsets were modified to match the linguistic concepts of PWN. The two major challenges reported in this work are: (1) the difference in the granularity between the second language (Romanian in this case) and the English language, and (2) the conceptual gaps in one or the other language.

The paper also puts forward a rarely discussed problem — that mapping a non-English wordnet to PWN is often done by non-native English speakers, who encounter difficulties in correctly perceiving the English senses especially in the fine-grained structure of the PWN. Similar observations were made also by us. Thus, further development in mapping might require involving native English speakers.

The granularity problem appears in the case of the Turkish WordNet — KeNet (Bakay et al., 2021). It is built as a monolingual resource on the base of the latest contemporary dictionary of Turkish with its semantic relations suggested by PWN, but manually checked and only the correct relations added to the KeNet. Before the addition of sense relations the Turkish synsets underwent a merge and a split processes. In the merge process "different synsets that should be grouped together were identified and grouped as a single synset". During that process three important rules were established: (1) each synset has to have one single and unique definition, (2) only true synonyms are valid synset members, and (3) a representative lemma for the whole synset must be a first member in each synset. In the split process wrongly grouped senses were identified and separated into new synsets. This allowed the creators of KeNet to control the synset members and identify which synsets had missing members or had extra members.

We use a similar approach to reconsider the structure of BTB-WN and its mapping to PWN. The main difference is that we try to be consistent with respect to whole sets of synsets in Bulgarian motivated by linguistic knowledge about related senses as it will be clear in the next section.

3 Linguistically Motivated Sense Merging

Currently BTB-WN is being developed in two directions: (1) refinement of the legacy synsets from the previous versions by editing synset definitions, synset members (lemmas) and sense relations, and (2) extending the word coverage of the BTB-WN with lemmas from a Bulgarian explanatory dictionary — (Popov, 1994) containing about 56,000 lemmas grouped in 46,000 entries. We consider this number of lemmas and entries as a medium-size lexicon of Bulgarian. In its current state the BTB-WN consists of nearly 23,400 synsets and 50,000 lemmas. For comparison at the start of this process of refinement and extension the BTB-WN had nearly 19,000 synsets and 38,300 lemmas. The current result shows that our strategy for reducing the granularity of senses is working well and the number of lemmas is growing faster than the number of synsets.

During the manual work on refinement the experts met the above reported problem with the granularity of the English WordNet (EWN), where every nuance in meaning is reflected, resulting in many similar synsets. For example the synset for "over and over again" with definition *repeatedly* and no relations and the synset for "repeatedly" with definition *several times* and one pertainym relation or the case with the lemma "marquess" where the EWN makes a distinction between a *nobleman (in various countries) ranking above a count* and *a British peer ranking below a duke and above an earl*, but the Bulgarian concept consider it just as *a nobleman in various countries with this title*. A decision had to be made to completely follow the structure of EWN thus making the BTB-WN an English language-dependent wordnet which would make it very difficult to map it with wordnets in other languages or to go in the direction of monolingual wordnets and take the approach of consolidation of the hierarchy, and therefore — unification of very similar meanings, supported by detailed definitions and diversified examples. Making the BTB-WN English-dependant does not correspond with the usage and the goals BTB-WN needs to achieve. This led to the only possible solution — diverging from the expand model of creation and going closer to the merge model.

The following subsections will outline several cases in which sense merging is the preferred choice instead of creating several very similar in meaning synsets. As we stressed earlier we use derivational patterns in Bulgarian for this purpose.

3.1 Diminutives

Diminutives are a specific linguistic category considered by scholars either as distinct lexical units or as forms of other, 'general' form (Krastev, 1976), because a diminutive form could be derived from almost all parts of speech and additionally it denotes the same object as the non-diminutive forms, but with some difference in the appearance or with a particular attitude towards this object. (Dimitrova, 1959) considers diminutives as an intermediate category between separate words and forms of general words, (Zidarova, 2004) outlines their unclear status. Anyway, there is an aspect of the diminutives that is not controversial — that their meaning is not limited only to the traditional smallness, but they can also express positive or negative attitude. Similar contradictions of the nature of diminutives in English are observed for example in (Jurafsky, 1996), (Bagasheva, 2018), (Schneider, 2013). Depending on the notion of diminutives, there can be observed several approaches of their presentation in dictionaries.

(Avramova, 2016) compiles three approaches for dictionary articles of diminutives: structural definition, semantic definition and structural-semantic definition. The structural definition says that the given term is a diminutive for the general term. It could be considered the poorest in terms of information given. The semantic definition is used mostly for diminutives for people and animals and it describes the diminutive as a young person/animal. The third type — structural-semantic — provides information that the term is diminutive, but also presents all of its possible meanings — it could express youngness, smallness, weakness, positive or negative attitude.

In the current work on BTB-WN we will take into consideration only the diminutives for nouns; such forms for adjectives could be part of future work. The approach towards the diminutives' definition will follow the idea of the structural-semantic definitions in the dictionaries with one difference — the diminutive forms of the nouns will be in one synset with the general form, but will have a special lemma marker. If we presume that a diminutive noun usually has around three meanings (for something small, for expressing affection or for expressing ridicule towards somebody or something), we can imagine how many synsets a wordnet could generate only from this category of words. The lemma markers that we will use would contain information about the different meanings of the given diminutive, but will prevent the wordnet to have great number of very similar synsets. Analogous markers will be used to present dialectical, archaic, slang and vulgar meanings on the level of lemmas. The same approach could be applied for the augmentative meanings.

A good example for the variety of meanings that a diminutive can bear is the noun даскалче "daskalche" (teacher-diminutive) — it could be interpreted as a young teacher, a rather short or thin teacher, it could express negative attitude towards the teacher, but it can also be a expression of affection.

3.2 Nouns vs. Human Gender

One of the productive derivational patterns in language are the masculine and feminine lemmas of nouns for professions, nationalities, etc. Similar is the case for some animals. Usually wordnets encode this difference in the lemmas as separate synsets. At the beginning in BTB-WN we have started to encode it in the same way. Later we discovered that in many cases this distinction is quite insignificant and not really important for the differences in the meaning.

With respect to the mapping to PWN the differences between Bulgarian and English became obvious. Only a few English nouns have a separate lemma for feminine. As a result many Bulgarian synsets did not have corresponding English synset to be mapped to. A decision was made to always unite the forms in one synset. Occupations like "actor" and "actress", "waiter" and "waitress" are divided in separate synsets, but many similar are combined, for example the synsets for "physician" or "teacher".

Another problem with this type of synsets is that when the synsets for male and female terms are separated, the female form is hyponym of the male, which is not the most precise relation, and when they are both put in one synset in BTB-WN it is very difficult to find the appropriate position in the hierarchy.

Other examples of that problem are the terms for nationality — in English often there are no distinct nouns denoting men, women and children (only one genderless form), but in Bulgarian such derivative nouns are productive, thus an effort was made to include them in one synset — българин, българка, българче "balgarin, balgarka, balgarche" (Bulgarian man, Bulgarian woman, Bulgarian child).

In order to solve the problem in Bulgarian and to encode the information we decided to add such lemmas to the same synset sharing the main meaning in the synset and the gender differences to be encoded with respect to the different lemmas in the synset.

There is a similar case with the English synsets for animals. Often the domestic animals are divided into two synsets (or sometimes more — including the young of this animal) — one for the meaning of female animal, and one for the male (like "hen" and "cock", "male horse" and "mare", "billy" and "nanny", "cow" and "bull"), but for wild animals there is usually one synset (wolf) in comparison to the Bulgarian where we have вълк and вълчица "valk and valchica" (male wolf and female wolf). In this cases we encode all the lemmas for the same animal in the same synset.

3.3 Variation in Verb Prefixation

Bulgarian verbal paradigm contains a great amount of verbs with prefixes that bear the semantics of start, end, duration, repetition, etc. of the action. (Todor Boyadzhiev and Penchev, 1998) state that "this type of prefix verbs do not denote new action, but the same action of their derivative verb — they only specify, fix this action in space, time and in quantitative terms". Synsets with such verbs do not have equal English synsets, so the decision is to map them to the synset for the general meaning of the verb and to use lemma markers which contain the specific semantic features of the distinct meanings. There is a variety of prefixes that compose such verbs, their semantics are thoroughly analysed in (Ivanova, 1974) (Velkova, 2019), but for the purposes of this research only the most common senses of the prefixes are outlined:

- въз- "vaz-" (renewing the action; bringing the action to result; producing effect; bringing the action to a higher or upper level)
- до- "do-" (bringing the action to result, to completion)
- за- "za-" (start of action; bringing to action; bringing to a new state; performing the action continuously and to a high degree)
- из- "iz-" (bringing to result, to completion; bringing something to a new state; moving the action outward)
- на- "na-" (bringing to result; bringing to new state; performing the action to a larger extent and with accumulation)
- над- "nad-" (bringing to result; performing the action beyond, over the area of the object; bringing the action to a higher level or better state (than someone/something else))
- по- "po-" (performing the action to a lesser degree; bringing to a new state; start of action; performing the action shortly and intermittently)
- под- "pod-" (develop the indicated action under the object or in its lower part; bringing the action to result; performing the action secretly, covertly; performing the action in a rather weak, slight, soft manner)
- пре- "pre-" (renewal or repetition of the action, sometimes in new way or with the inclusion with one more action; performing the action to a greater extent;)
- пред- "pred-" (performing the action before other action, preceding something)
- при- "pri-" (bringing something closer to some place or object; start of action; bringing something to result; renewal of the action; lower intensity of the action; parallel performance of two actions)
- про- "pro-" (bringing to a new state; performing the action shortly and intermittently; start of action)
- о- "o-" (bringing to result; spreading the action on the entire surface of the object)
- об- "ob-" (bringing to result; spreading the action on the entire surface of the object)
- раз- "raz-" (performing the action to a significant extent; bringing to result; setting the action in multiple directions; dividing something in parts by the action)
- с- "s-" (bringing to result; bringing to new state; performing the action suddenly and with great force)
- съ- "sa-" (performing the action by reducing (destroying) the distance between two or more objects within its range; parallel performance of two actions)
- у- "u-" (directing the action in depth or to the center of the object; directing to result)
- в- "v-" (bringing to a new state; bringing to result)
- въ- "va-" (bringing to a new state; bringing to result)
- от- "ot-" (taking out subject or the object from the definition area of the action by performing the action; end of the action)

Needless to say that not every verb has derivatives with all these prefixes, but still they are very productive.

For example the verbs пиша "pisha" (with meaning 'to write'), написвам "napisvam", напиша "napisha" ('to write (something) completely, till the end'), изписвам "izpisvam", изпиша "izpisha" ('to completely fill something with writing, text), записвам "zapisvam", запиша "zapisha" ('start to write'), дописвам "dopisvam", допиша "dopisha" ('write (something) to the end, write everything that is necessary') and прописвам "propisvam", пропиша "propisha" ('learn how and start to write') will be united in one synset; the verbs with prefixes will have lemma markers that further describe their meaning.

There is also a rather big group of poliprefixed verbs (with two or more prefixes — for example изпонапрепиша, изпонапреписвам "izponaprepisha", "izponaprepisvam" ('to completely write something down from a source')) in Bulgarian, but poliprefixation will be part further research.

The three cases of derivational relations presented above show the approach we took in BTB-WN — joining in the same synsets many of the derivatives that do not alternate on a large scale the main meaning of the lemma from which all the rest are derived. The borderline between modified sense and separate sense is a challenge on its own and we implement manual checks in several Bulgarian dictionaries to make this distinction. Then the differences are encoded as small modifications of the main meaning — modifying some characteristics of this meaning like the gender of the referent, the size, other features, etc. With this approach we have succeeded to reduce the number of synsets. Another benefit of this approach is that given meaning is represented just in one synset and any modification and the addition of new knowledge are in one place. In this way it becomes manageable in a better way.

4 Conclusion and Future Work

The paper presents an attempt at dealing with sense merging in the process of mapping two wordnets with a focus on the treatment of synsets for diminutives, verb forms with different ways of action and female and male forms of nouns for professions, roles, nationalities and animals. The work reported here is based on the notion that making the coverage of BTB-WN based on number of lemmas (synset members) instead on number of synsets will be beneficial when applying wordnet data to the tasks like WSD. As a secondary result of this work several suggestions for edits in the English WordNet were made.

In the future we hope to achieve even larger coverage of lemmas by including dialectal, archaic, slang, diminutive and vulgar words as new synsets or new synset members. One task still remaining is the ordering of the synset members relying on the notion that the first member has to be the exemplar.

We have reported some works on the mapping mainly of wordnets for languages from Indo-European language families to English PWN. It would be interesting to extend the study for mapping between different languages within the family (for example Bulgarian to Polish or Bulgarian to German) and also between wordnets for languages from different language families. We are aware of the even greater problems with the mapping between Asian wordnets and the English one.

Acknowledgments

This work was partially supported by the *Bulgarian Ministry of Education and Science under the National Research Programme "Young scientists and postdoctoral students" approved by DCM # 577 / 17.08.2018* and by *the Bulgarian National Interdisciplinary Research e-Infrastructure for Resources and Technologies in favor of the Bulgarian Language and Cultural Heritage, part of the EU infrastructures CLARIN and DARIAH – CLaDA-BG*, Grant number DO01-377/18.12.2020.

In addition the work of Zara Kancheva has been accomplished with the partial support by the Grant No. BG05M2OP001-1.001-0003, financed by the Science and Education for Smart Growth Operational Program (2014-2020) and co-financed by the European Union through the European structural and Investment funds.

References

Tsvetanka Avramova. 2016. Deminutivite kato rechnikovi edinitsi (Diminutives as dictionary units). pages 89–97, Sofia, Bulgaria. Prof. Marin Drinov Academic Publishing House.

Mariya Bagasheva. 2018. Ways of expressing the category of diminutiveness in english. volume 56, pages 460–469. Plovdivski universitet "Paisii Hilendarski (University of Plovdiv "Paisii Hilendarski").

Özge Bakay, Özlem Ergelen, Elif Sarmış, Selin Yıldırım, Bilge Nas Arıcan, Atilla Kocabalcıoğlu, Merve Özçelik, Ezgi Sanıyar, Oğuzhan Kuyrukçu, Begüm Avar, and Olcay Taner Yıldız. 2021. Turkish WordNet KeNet. In *Proceedings of the 11th Global Wordnet Conference*.

Luisa Bentivogli and Emanuele Pianta. 2004. Extending wordnet with syntagmatic information. In *Proceedings of second global WordNet conference*, pages 47–53.

D. Cristea, Cătălin Mihăilă, C. Forascu, Diana Trandabat, Maria Husarciuc, Gabriela Haja, and Oana Postolache. 2004. Mapping Princeton WordNet synsets onto Romanian wordnet synsets.

Magdalena Derwojedowa, Maciej Piasecki, Stan Szpakowicz, Magdalena Zawisławska, and Bartosz Broda. 2008. Words, concepts and relations in the construction of Polish WordNet. pages 162–177.

Milka Dimitrova. 1959. Umalitelnite imena v knizhovniya ezik (The Diminutives in the Literary Bulgarian Language). volume 6, page 263–319, Sofia, Bulgaria. Akademichno izdatelstvo "Prof. Marin Drinov" ("Prof. Marin Drinov" Academic Publishing House).

Christiane Fellbaum. 1998. *WordNet: An Electronic Lexical Database*. MIT Press.

Darja Fišer and Benoît Sagot. 2015. Constructing a poor man's wordnet in a resource-rich world. *Language Resources and Evaluation*, 49(3):601–635.

R. Fjeld and Lars Nygaard. 2009. Nornet — a monolingual wordnet of modern Norwegian. In *In NODALIDA 2009 workshop: WordNets and other Lexical Semantic Resources - between Lexical Semantics, Lexicography, Terminology and Formal Ontologies*, pages 13–16.

Birgit Hamp and Helmut Feldweg. 1997. GermaNet - a lexical-semantic net for German. In *Automatic Information Extraction and Building of Lexical Semantic Resources for NLP Applications*.

Kalina Ivanova. 1974. *Nachini na glagolnoto deystvie v savremenniya balgarski ezik (Ways of verb action in contemporary Bulgarian language)*. Akademichno izdatelstvo "Prof. Marin Drinov" (Prof. Marin Drinov Academic Publishing House), Sofia, Bulgaria.

Daniel Jurafsky. 1996. Universal tendencies in the semantics of the diminutive. *Language*, 72(3):533–578.

Borimir Krastev. 1976. Umalitelnostta v balgarskiya ezik (The diminutiveness in Bulgarian language). Sofia, Bulgaria. Narodna prosveta.

Krister Lindén and Lauri Carlson. 2010. FinnWordNet–Finnish WordNet by translation. *LexicoNordica–Nordic Journal of Lexicography*, 17:119–140.

Rada Mihalcea and Dan I Moldovan. 2001. Automatic generation of a coarse grained wordnet.

Roberto Navigli. 2006. Reducing the granularity of a computational lexicon via an automatic mapping to a coarse-grained sense inventory. In *Proceedings of the Fifth International Conference on Language Resources and Evaluation (LREC'06)*, Genoa, Italy. European Language Resources Association (ELRA).

Petya Osenova and Kiril Simov. 2018. The Data-driven Bulgarian WordNet: BTBWN. *Cognitive Studies — Études cognitives*, 18(1713).

Bolette S. Pedersen, Sanni Nimb, Ida Rørmann Olsen, and Sussi Olsen. 2019. Merging DanNet with Princeton Word Net. In *GWC*.

Bolette Sandford Pedersen, Sanni Nimb, Jørg Asmussen, Nicolai Hartvig Sørensen, Lars Trap-Jensen, and Henrik Lorentzen. 2009. DanNet: the challenge of compiling a wordnet for Danish by reusing a monolingual dictionary. *Language resources and evaluation*, 43(3):269–299.

Dimitar Popov. 1994. *Balgarski talkoven rechnik. Chetvarto izdanie, preraboteno i dopalneno (Bulgarian Explanatory Dictionary. Forth revised and extended edition)*. Nauka i izkustvo (Science and art), Sofia, Bulgaria.

Marten Postma, Emiel van Miltenburg, Roxane Segers, Anneleen Schoen, and Piek Vossen. 2016. Open Dutch WordNet. In *Proceedings of the 8th Global WordNet Conference (GWC)*, pages 302–310.

Kergrit Robkop, Sareewan Thoongsup, T. Charoenporn, V. Sornlertlamvanich, and H. Isahara. 2009. Wnms : Connecting the distributed wordnet in the case of Asian WordNet.

Ewa Rudnicka, Wojciech Witkowski, and Maciej Piasecki. 2021. A (non)-perfect match: Mapping plWordNet onto PrincetonWordNet. In *Proceedings of the 11th Global Wordnet Conference*, pages 137–146, University of South Africa (UNISA). Global Wordnet Association.

Benoît Sagot and Darja Fišer. 2008. Building a free French wordnet from multilingual resources. In *OntoLex*, Marrakech, Morocco.

Klaus P. Schneider. 2013. The truth about diminutives, and how we can find it: Some theoretical and methodological considerations.

Manish Sinha, Mahesh Reddy, and Pushpak Bhattacharyya. 2006. An approach towards construction and application of multilingual indo-wordnet. In *3rd Global Wordnet Conference (GWC 06), Jeju Island, Korea*. Citeseer.

Ivan Kutsarov Todor Boyadzhiev and Yordan Penchev. 1998. Savremenen balgarski ezik (Contemporary Bulgarian language).

Yordanka Velkova. 2019. Predtsavkite kato markeri na determinatsiya (Prefixes as markers of determination). *Materiali ot Mezhdunarodnata konfenetsiya "Balgaristichni ezikovedski cheteniya (Proceedings of The International Conference "Bulgarian Linguistic Readings"), 19–20.11.2018*, pages 209–217.

Piek Vossen. 1998. EuroWordNet: A multilingual database with lexical semantic networks.

Piek Vossen. 2002. WordNet, EuroWordNet and Global WordNet. *Revue Française de Linguistique Appliquée*, 7.

Vanya Zidarova. 2004. Deminutivi i leksikalna nominatsiya (Diminutives and lexical nomination). pages 114–122, Sofia, Bulgaria. Universitetsko izdatelstvo "St. Kliment Ohridski" (University press "St. Kliment Ohridski").

On the Evolution of Word Order

Idan Rejwan
Tel Aviv University and AI21 Labs
Tel Aviv, Israel
idanrejwan91@gmail.com

Avi Caciularu
Bar-Ilan University
Ramat-Gan, Israel
avi.c33@gmail.com

Abstract

Most natural languages have a predominant or fixed word order. For example in English the word order is usually Subject-Verb-Object. This work attempts to explain this phenomenon as well as other typological findings regarding word order from a functional perspective. In particular, we examine whether fixed word order provides a functional advantage, explaining why these languages are prevalent. To this end, we consider an evolutionary model of language and demonstrate, both theoretically and using genetic algorithms, that a language with a fixed word order is optimal. We also show that adding information to the sentence, such as case markers and noun-verb distinction, reduces the need for fixed word order, in accordance with the typological findings.

1 Introduction

Word order is a linguistic concept that refers to how syntactic elements are arranged in a sentence in different languages. Specifically, it deals with the relative position of the three prominent syntactic roles in a sentence: subject (*S*), verb (V), and object (O). The three syntactic roles can be ordered in six different arrangements: *SVO, SOV, VSO, VOS, OVS, OSV*. Apriori, there is no reason to assume that one order is superior to others. However, typological findings show that most natural languages have one preferred or fixed word order, with the vast majority of them belonging to the first two families: SVO or SOV (Comrie, 1989). Interestingly, languages that have developed spontaneously and did not contact other languages also have a distinct preference for particular word order, such as the Al-Sayyid Bedouin Sign Language (Sandler et al., 2005).

Another typological finding is related to case markers, which are morphological indicators (usually prefixes or suffixes) that indicate the syntactic role of a word in a sentence. For example, the word for *the boy* in Arabic is *al-walad-u* if it is the subject and *al-walad-a* if it is the object. Apparently, in languages with a rich system of case markers, such as Arabic, Latin and Sanskrit, the word order is more flexible (Sapir, 1921; McFadden, 2004).

These findings raise several research questions. First, why is there a preferred or fixed order in the majority of natural languages? Second, why do most languages have *SVO* or *SOV* as their preferred order? Third, how can we explain the relationship between case markers and flexible word order?

This work addresses the aforementioned questions within an evolutionary perspective (Pinker and Bloom, 1990; Nowak et al., 2000). As in the evolution theory of the animal world, if a particular feature appears in many different species, it is assumed to give a functional advantage to the organisms carrying it, thus helping them survive natural selection. Similarly, linguistic phenomena that are common to all or most languages are assumed to provide a functional advantage and facilitate better communication.

Within this perspective, a plethora of works suggested to use Genetic Algorithms (GA), an optimization method inspired by evolutionary principles, in order to investigate typological findings (Batali, 1998; Kirby, 1999; Levin, 1995; Kirby, 2001). In this work, we follow this framework and use GA to study the phenomenon of word order, yet not investigated to the best of our knowledge. In particular, we attempt to answer whether a fixed word order gives a functional advantage, which may explain its emergence in most natural languages. We also provide a theoretical analysis to prove that the optimal grammar, with respect to our functional assumptions, is a grammar with fixed word order. Although it would be interesting to explore why a specific word order is preferred, for example SVO or SOV, this work addresses the

Proceedings of the Student Research Workshop associated with RANLP-2021, pages 162–166,
held online, Sep 1–3, 2021.
https://doi.org/10.26615/issn.2603-2821.2021_022

fundamental question about why languages have fixed word orders at all, rather than specific ones.

2 Method

Following Pinker and Bloom (1990), we view language as a form of communication designed to transmit a message between a speaker and a hearer. Thus, if we are to speak of an "optimal" language, it is the one that facilitates precise delivery of a message between the speaker and the listener.

In this view, the hearer observes only the sentence received from the speaker, which does not contain information regarding the relationship between the words and their syntactic roles.

Intuitively, word order might impact the way the hearer understands the sentence. For example, compare the English sentence "*we ship a man*" with "*we man a ship*". In this case, as the words "*ship*" and "*man*" may function as both a noun and a verb, and due to the absence of case markers, the meaning is determined solely by the order of words in the sentence.

Under these assumptions, we use GA to simulate a language's evolution, starting with no preferred word order, and test whether communication constraints enforce a fixation of particular word order.

2.1 Algorithm

The algorithm is initialized with a *lexicon*, a fixed list of 1000 words, where each word is a string of three letters. The words are randomly initialized and are given to all agents. We test both options of one lexicon for all words or two lexicons for nouns and verbs (see elaboration in section 4).

We initialize a population of 100 *grammars*, where each one is a probability distribution over the six possible word orders and is initialized to the uniform probability. Each grammar is represented by a *speaker* and a *hearer* trying to communicate a message over a noisy channel, and their success in communication measures the fitness of the grammar. In other words, for every grammar, the *speaker* produces a sentence based on the grammar, and the *hearer* determines the syntactic role of each word in the sentence.

The GA runs for 1000 successive generations. In each one, the speaker samples three random words from the lexicon with their syntactic roles. Then, he samples an order according to the probability distribution in the grammar, concatenates the sampled words according to it, and sends it to the hearer. Then, a random noise flips every letter in the sentence with a probability of $p = 0.01$. Note that the noisy sentence might contain words that are out of the lexicon.

Next, the hearer receives the noisy sentence and matches the syntactic roles in two steps. First, for every word in the sentence, he removes the noise by looking for the nearest word in the lexicon, in terms of Levenshtein distance. Then, he outputs the most probable word order given the grammar and the words.

Finally, we measure the Hamming distance between the input and the output by counting the correct syntactic roles. For example, the distance between SVO and SOV is $2/3$ since O, and V are at different locations.

In each generation, 30% of the grammars with the smallest distances are replicated to the next generation, with some random mutations to the probability distributions - a Gaussian noise with variance 0.01 is added to each probability in the grammar, and then re-normalized, to sum up to 1. After many generations, the surviving grammars are expected to be the ones that allow optimal communication between the speaker and the hearer.

We use this method to examine whether adding information to the sentence, such as the distinction between nouns and verbs or explicit case markers, changes the optimal grammar.

We tested different values for the population size, selection rate, and mutation rate, but all the examined values yielded similar trends.

3 Theoretical Analysis

As mentioned, optimal communication occurs when the distance between the input and output is minimal. In this section, we prove that under this definition of optimality, and assuming the hearer always identifies the words in the lexicon correctly despite the noise (as indeed happens with a high probability), the following holds

Theorem 1. *Any optimal grammar has exactly one fixed word order.*

Proof. Let $X_1 \ldots X_n$ and $Y_1 \ldots Y_n$ be random variables of the occurrence of possible word orders, associated with the speaker and the hearer, respectively. We define

$$P(X_i = 1) = P(Y_i = 1) = p_i, \qquad i = 1, ..., n.$$

Let d_{ij} be the distance between X_i and Y_j, defined as the number of syntactic roles with different positions between X_i and Y_j. Then, the expected distance is given by

$$\mathbb{E}[d] = \sum_{(i,j)} d_{ij} P(X_i, Y_j),$$

where $P(X_i, Y_j)$ is the probability that the speaker chose order X_i (with probability of p_i) and the hearer chose order Y_j (with probability of p_j). Since the hearer has no additional information other than the observed sentence, he picks the most probable order from his grammar, independently of the speaker. Accordingly, $P(X_i, Y_j) = p_i p_j$, and therefore the expected value of the distance is given by

$$\mathbb{E}[d] = \sum_{(i,j)} p_i d_{ij} p_j.$$

Note that $p_i d_{ij} p_j \geq 0, \forall i, j$, since p_i, p_j are probabilities, and d_{ij} is a distance. Since $d_{ij} = 0$ only for $i = j$, to get the minimal expected distance 0 it should hold $\forall i \neq j$ either $p_i = 0$ or $p_j = 0$. Therefore, p_i can be greater than zero in exactly one entry. For other words, the only probability distributions that give an expected distance of zero have probability 1 for a particular word order X_i and zero for the rest. Accordingly, the optimal grammar must have fixed word order. □

4 Experiments

We tested the model in four different scenarios.

1. **Base** - all words are taken from a single lexicon, without distinction between nouns and verbs and without case markers.

2. **N-V** - separate lexicons for nouns and verbs, which enables the hearer to distinguish between nouns and verbs, thus identifying the verb in the sentence.

3. **Case** - each word in the sentence carries a suffix indicating its syntactic role (S, V or O).

4. **N-V & Case** - both 2 and 3, i.e., there is a distinction between nouns and verbs, and every word in the sentence carries a case marker.

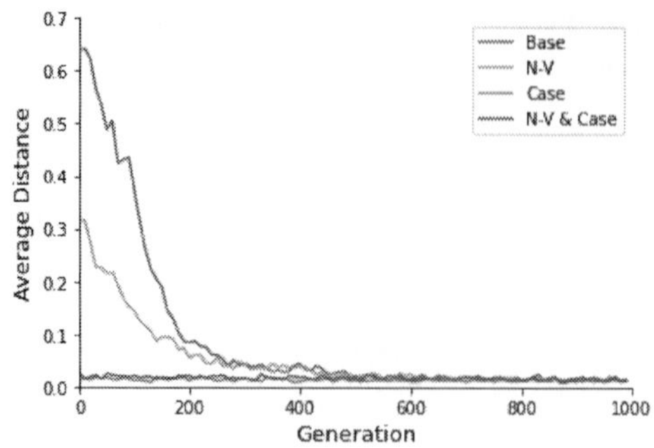

Figure 1: Average distance of sentences over generations.

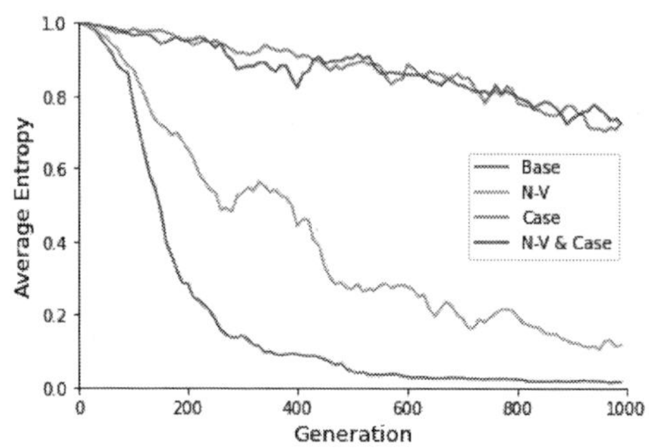

Figure 2: Average entropy of grammars over generations.

5 Results

For every scenario, we present the average distance between the input and the output among all grammars in each generation (Figure 1). It can be observed that the base scenario starts with the highest distance among the scenarios, as the sentences carry no information regarding the syntactic roles. A similar discussion could be held for the N-V scenario, in which the hearer can identify the verb in the sentence but cannot distinguish between the subject and object. In both scenarios, we observe a drop in the average distance, meaning that at some point, the hearers successfully parsed the sentences with only a small error. In the two scenarios with the case markers, we see that the distance is very close to zero even in the first generation, meaning that the hearers parsed the sentences correctly from the first generation.

To examine if the grammars converged to fixed word order, we present the grammars' average entropy in every generation (Figure 2). The entropy is defined by $H = -\sum_i p_i \log p_i$ and satisfies $0 \leq H \leq 1$ where $H = 1$ represents a uniform

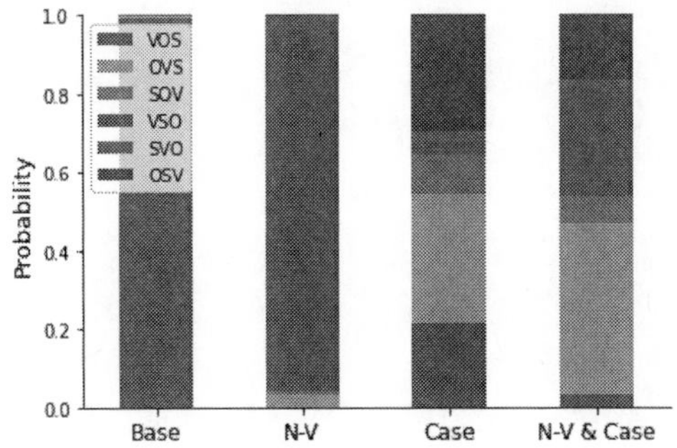

Figure 3: Word order probability after 1000 generations.

distribution (absolute randomness) and $H = 0$ represents probability 1 for one word order and zero for the rest (absolute determinism). It can be observed that the average entropy of grammars begins at 1 (absolute randomness) in all scenarios, as the probability for every word order is equal. In the base scenario, we observe a fast decline in entropy until it converges to zero, i.e., a fixed word order. A decline is also observed in the N-V scenario. However, it is slower and does not converge to zero even after 1000 generations. As for the scenarios with the case markers, in both cases, we observe that the entropy remains high even after 1000 generations, meaning that no particular word order was fixed.

We also present the grammar that had the smallest distance after 1000 generations (Figure 3). In the base and N-V scenarios, we observe that the grammar converged to an (almost) fixed word order, VOS in the base scenario, and VSO in the N-V scenario. In contrast, in both scenarios with case markers, the word order remained flexible even after 1000 generations.

6 Discussion

In the base scenario, we observed a fast fixation of single word order. Therefore, in line with the theoretical result, we conclude that given no additional information regarding the sentence's syntactic relations, fixed word order is necessary to allow successful communication. We also observed a fixation in the N-V scenario, meaning that a distinction between nouns and verbs does not provide sufficient information for communication, and thus fixed word order is also necessary in this case.

In contrast, both scenarios with case markers did not converge to preferred word order, meaning that the case markers by themselves are enough to allow communication. This finding is consistent with the result of artificial language learning experiments conducted on human learners (Fedzechkina et al., 2011). Note that since the case markers we used were just one letter, they could have been flipped by the random noise, leading to a wrong parsing by the hearer. However, the chances that two case markers in the same sentence will be flipped are small, and thus the hearer can parse the sentence correctly with high probability.

We note that additional experiments performed with a more significant number of syntactic roles yielded similar trends. Hence we conclude that these findings do not depend on the number of syntactic roles.

The reason why the base scenario converged to VOS and the N-V scenario converged to VSO is arbitrary, due to random drift, since there is no functional advantage to a particular word order over the others.

7 Conclusions

This work presents a simplistic functional model of language that demonstrates how a fixed word order in languages may result from a lack of information about syntactic relations.

Empirically, we used Genetic Algorithms (GA) in order to investigate whether additional information would render the fixed word order unnecessary. We showed that a distinction between nouns and verbs provides additional information to the hearer, but it is not sufficient. In contrast, case markers provide enough information to enable a flexible word order. These results are consistent with the typological findings.

Regarding the reason why most natural languages tend exhibit SVO or SOV orderings, the model used in this work does not seem to provide an explanation. It has been demonstrated that even where a single word order has been fixed, we have received various possible orders that are not necessarily one of these two. This is because we did not consider the functional advantages of certain orders over others, so the final order is entirely determined by random chance. Additional psycho-linguistic considerations are needed to explain the typological finding, as done in other studies (Gibson et al., 2013; Hengeveld et al., 2004).

References

John Batali. 1998. Computational simulations of the emergence of grammar. *Approach to the Evolution of Language*, pages 405–426.

Bernard Comrie. 1989. *Language universals and linguistic typology: Syntax and morphology*. University of Chicago press.

Maryia Fedzechkina, T Florian Jaeger, and Elissa L Newport. 2011. Functional biases in language learning: Evidence from word order and case-marking interaction. In *Proceedings of the Annual Meeting of the Cognitive Science Society*, volume 33.

Edward Gibson, Steven T Piantadosi, Kimberly Brink, Leon Bergen, Eunice Lim, and Rebecca Saxe. 2013. A noisy-channel account of crosslinguistic word-order variation. *Psychological science*, 24(7):1079–1088.

Kees Hengeveld, Jan Rijkhoff, and Anna Siewierska. 2004. Parts-of-speech systems and word order. *Journal of linguistics*, pages 527–570.

Simon Kirby. 1999. Syntax out of learning: The cultural evolution of structured communication in a population of induction algorithms. In *European Conference on Artificial Life*, pages 694–703. Springer.

Simon Kirby. 2001. Spontaneous evolution of linguistic structure-an iterated learning model of the emergence of regularity and irregularity. *IEEE Transactions on Evolutionary Computation*, 5(2):102–110.

Michael Levin. 1995. The evolution of understanding: A genetic algorithm model of the evolution of communication. *BioSystems*, 36(3):167–178.

Thomas McFadden. 2004. The position of morphological case in the derivation. *PhD diss., University of Pennsylvania*.

Martin A Nowak, Joshua B Plotkin, and Vincent AA Jansen. 2000. The evolution of syntactic communication. *Nature*, 404(6777):495–498.

Steven Pinker and Paul Bloom. 1990. Natural language and natural selection. *Behavioral and brain sciences*, 13(4):707–727.

Wendy Sandler, Irit Meir, Carol Padden, and Mark Aronoff. 2005. The emergence of grammar: Systematic structure in a new language. *Proceedings of the National Academy of Sciences*, 102(7):2661–2665.

Edward Sapir. 1921. *Language: An introduction to the study of speech*. Harcourt, Brace.

EmoPars: A Collection of 30K Emotion-Annotated Persian Social Media Texts

Nazanin Sabri, Reyhane Akhavan, Behnam Bahrak
School of Electrical and Computer Engineering, College of Engineering
University of Tehran, Tehran, Iran
{nazanin.sabri,reyhane.akhavan,bahrak}@ut.ac.ir

Abstract

The wide reach of social media platforms, such as Twitter, have enabled many users to share their thoughts, opinions and emotions on various topics online. The ability to detect these emotions automatically would allow social scientists, as well as, businesses to better understand responses from nations and costumers. In this study we introduce a dataset of 30,000 Persian Tweets labeled with Ekman's six basic emotions (Anger, Fear, Happiness, Sadness, Hatred, and Wonder). This is the first publicly available emotion dataset in the Persian language. In this paper, we explain the data collection and labeling scheme used for the creation of this dataset. We also analyze the created dataset, showing the different features and characteristics of the data. Among other things, we investigate co-occurrence of different emotions in the dataset, and the relationship between sentiment and emotion of textual instances. The dataset is publicly available at https://github.com/nazaninsbr/Persian-Emotion-Detection.

1 Introduction

As humans communicate emotions through text (Alm et al., 2005), the creation of text-based emotion detection models are a necessity for the analysis and understanding of the content posted online, more-natural speech generation, and better human-computer interaction tasks which are categorized as affective computing [1]. The lack of any other signals for emotions within text (i.e., facial expressions or body language) and the subjective nature of emotions, makes this task a challenging one.
Despite the availability of a number of studies on the topic of emotion recognition in NLP, they have been predominantly conducted in the English language. The unavailability of annotated data in the Persian language hinders the study of emotions in this language. As a result, in this study, we introduce a dataset of 30K Persian Tweets labeled with Ekman's six basic emotions (Ekman, 1999). To the best of our knowledge this is the first publicly available emotion-labeled dataset in the Persian language, which we believe will allow Persian NLP to progress and start the study of emotions.
The rest of this paper is structured as follows: in Section 2 we provide a brief review of studies on emotions and the automatic detection of emotions. We additionally point to other datasets available on the topic in other languages. Next, we discuss our data collection and labeling methods in Section 3. The statistics and properties of our datasets are presented in Section 4. Finally, we conclude the study in Section 5.

2 Related Work

Even though a significant body of work is available on the topic of emotions, a commonly agreed-upon definition is still lacking (Mulligan and Scherer, 2012). The American Psychology Association (APA) defines emotion as "a complex reaction pattern, involving experiential, behavioral, and physiological elements, by which an individual attempts to deal with a personally significant matter or event" (apa, (accessed December 1, 2020). The three key components of emotions, stated in the aforementioned definition, are subjective experience, physiological response, and behavioral response (Hockenbury and Hockenbury, 2010). Subjective experience has been explored in studies looking at the effects of culture, age, and gender on the emotions people feel (Barrett et al., 2007; Shaver et al., 1992; Fischer et al., 2004; Ekman et al., 1987; Kunzmann and Grühn, 2005). The physiological response to emotions could range from sweaty palms to a churning stomach. For instance, (Fernández

[1] "computing that relates to, arises from, or deliberately influences emotion" (Picard, 1999)

Proceedings of the Student Research Workshop associated with RANLP-2021, pages 167–173,
held online, Sep 1–3, 2021.
https://doi.org/10.26615/issn.2603-2821.2021_023

et al., 2012) shows that heart rate is significantly increased when people watch movies conveying fear or anger, (Waldstein et al., 2000) also explores frontal EEG activation in response to anger and happiness, and (LeDoux, 1995) reviews studies on the neurological aspects of emotion, focusing mostly on fear. In part one of (Philippot et al., 2004), the physiological processes during emotion regulation are discussed. Additionally, (Dalgleish, 2004) offers a comprehensive historical overview of studies on the neural bases of emotions. Lastly, behavioral responses could include smiling, sighing, and crying. These responses are found to often depend on societal norms and individual differences (Krys et al., 2016; Gross and Levenson, 1997; Van Hemert et al., 2011).

There is some debate on what basic emotions are and what we really mean by "basic". (Ortony and Turner, 1990) discusses this issue at length. The paper refutes the claim that there exist basic emotions out of which all other emotions are built. (Ekman and Cordaro, 2011) disagrees and offers a concrete list of characteristics that basic emotions have. Nevertheless, multiple classifications of emotions have been introduced in the literature. One categorization, offered by Paul Ekman, suggests basic emotions to be: anger, disgust, fear, happiness, sadness and surprise (Ekman, 1999, 1992). Later on, however, Ekman does name other emotions that could potentially be proven to be basic (Ekman and Cordaro, 2011). Another well-known classification, offered by Plutchik, introduces 8 basic emotions composed of anger, fear, disgust, sadness, surprise, anticipation, trust, and joy (Plutchik, 1980).

With the growth of social media platforms, the automatic detection of emotions through text has come into focus in recent years. Several surveys of studies on emotion detection from text have been conducted, one in 2014 (Canales and Martínez-Barco, 2014), and two others in 2018 (Seyeditabari et al., 2018; Sailunaz et al., 2018). As a result, in our review, we will mainly focus on newer studies. In 2019, a shared task on the detection of emotions in textual dialogue was organized (emo, (accessed December 1, 2020; Chatterjee et al., 2019), which resulted in a wave of studies on the topic. The best model on the task achieves an F1-score of 0.79, however the best two models on the task did not submit system description papers (Chatterjee et al., 2019). The third ranking model on the task (Agrawal and Suri, 2019), uses lexical features such as emotional intensity, valence-arousal-dominance scores (Warriner et al., 2013), and sentiment classifiers' scores to train a Light-GBM tree (Ke et al., 2017) model which achieves a micro-averaged F1 score of 0.77. (Basile et al., 2019) which was ranked fourth, uses a neural ensemble system made up of 4 neural models. The most used embedding-model among the top systems, was reported to be GloVe (Pennington et al., 2014). It is important to keep in mind that achieving the same level of accuracy on our dataset will be harder for two reasons: (1) our dataset does not include context for each Tweet which was available in the aforementioned task, and (2) Persian language is a low-resource language, thus some of the features that the participants used are not in our disposal.

Another shared-task in WASSA-2021 Workshop (Tafreshi et al., 2021) required participants to predict emotional tags (Ekman's six basic emotions) and empathy of news stories. The highest accuracy on the task was reported to be 0.62 with a corresponding F1 of 0.55 (Mundra et al., 2021). This result was obtained through data augmentation and fine-tuning of the ELECTRA (Clark et al., 2020) model. (Butala et al., 2021), another participant of the task, compares different conditional generation models (T5 (Raffel et al., 2019) and pegasus (Jingqing et al., 2019)) and pre-trained contextual embeddings (BERT (Devlin et al., 2019) and AlBERT (Lan et al., 2019)) and reports AlBERT to outperform BERT (Macro-F1 of 0.47 vs. 0.37). However, T5 is reported to have the best performance with a Macro-F1 of 0.57.

There are a number of studies unrelated to the shared-tasks as well. (Hasan et al., 2019) explores using a soft-classification model that assigns probabilities to each emotion. (Shoeb and de Melo, 2020) creates a dataset and introduces a method to find the correspondence between emojis and particular emotions. (Ishiwatari et al., 2020) tries to detect emotions in conversation. The authors incorporate speaker dependency into the model using graph attention networks (Veličković et al., 2017) as well as introducing a novel relational position encoding which is shown to improve the accuracy of the model. (Polignano et al., 2019) introduces a model made up of CNN, BiLSTM, and self-attention components, and compare different word-embeddings, finding that FastText vector spaces (Bojanowski et al., 2016) better capture the information they want. (Gollapalli et al., 2020) introduces an unsupervised emotion detection method which is built upon word co-occurrences and word associations. Some emotion datasets include: (Sosea and Caragea, 2020) from an English online health community with a focus on cancer, (Demszky et al., 2020) from English Reddit comments, (Liu et al., 2019) from long-form narratives in English, (Kumar et al., 2019) from Hindi stories, and (Almahdawi and Teahan, 2019) an Arabic dataset from Facebook posts written in the Iraqi dialect. While (Khosravi et al., 2019) uses machine learning models to detect emotions of Persian news texts, the dataset has not been published. Additionally, to the best of our knowledge, the dataset presented as part of this study is the first emotion dataset on the Persian social media texts. As social media content and formally-written news articles are structured differently, we believe that this dataset is of great value for the study of user-created content in social networks.

3 Data Collection and Labeling

In this section, we begin by going over the data collection method (3.1), continuing on to explaining the labeling and validation process (3.2). The statistics of our dataset are explained in Section 4. The data is publicly available on GitHub[2].

3.1 Collection

The data presented as part of this study was collected using Twitter's official developer API (twi, (accessed December 2, 2020). To make sure our data is not biased by any topic or the discussions of a particular time we take two measures:

(1) we collect tweets using different keywords including articles and prepositions which are not specific to any particular topic and thus make sure no bias is introduced.

(2) the data is sampled from Tweets posted since the mid-2019 up until mid-2020, making sure to include at least some Tweets from each time period. As a result no time-specific issue dominates our dataset.

After the data has been collected we randomly sample 30,000 instances of the Tweets with a minimum character length of 20 (the minimum length is placed to ensure the Tweet is long enough to potentially reflect emotions). To preserve the anonymity of the Tweets, we replace any user mentions with *@USERNAME* and any link with *www.LINK.com* before the data has been inputted for labeling. In this manner we make sure to indicate there was a link or mention but that it was removed for anonymity purposes.

3.2 Labeling

We use iToll (ito, (accessed January 2, 2021), a Persian crowd-sourcing website to label the texts in our dataset. The labeling is done through Yes/No questions, where the user is shown the text and asked if emotion X is present in the text. This question is then repeated for all 6 basic emotions. Each question is shown to 5 different individuals and the final result is calculated through max voting[3].

To make certain the labels are valid, after the first round of labeling has been completed, any user whom more than 50% of their votes contradict the majority vote are considered to be unreliable user and his/her votes are removed from the dataset. These votes are then replaced with new votes by asking the questions from other individuals. A similar method of labeling was used by (Sosea and Caragea, 2020) and was shown to obtain satisfactory results. However, it is important to keep in mind that the perception of emotions can be quite subjective. Additionally since no context is available for each text, each user might read and perceive a text with a different attitude/tone. These differences could all lead to difficulties when it comes to labeling emotions.

4 Dataset Statistics

4.1 Instances of Each Emotion

As previously mentioned, our dataset is made up of 30,000 Tweets, labeled with six different emotion labels. Figure 1 shows the number of tweets in our dataset that are simultaneously labeled with N different emotions. We can see that 80% of the data does not have any emotion label at all, and less than 5% have 3 or more emotion labels. The large proportion of Tweets that do not have any emotion, make the task of automatic emotion detection,

[2] https://github.com/nazaninsbr/Persian-Emotion-Detection

[3] In the published dataset the vote counts have been provided. These numbers are in the range of $[0, 5]$. As a result, to ascertain whether or not an emotion is present (a binary classification), the user must check if the number is more than 2 (in other words if more than 2 people out of 5 have voted YES for that emotion). Should you want more certain labels (with less room for annotation errors), you could select a higher threshold for each emotion.

difficult. Figure 2 displays the number of Tweets with each emotion. We can see sadness is the most observed emotion, followed by anger and hatred. Fear is the least observed emotion, with only 690 instances among our data (closely followed by Happiness with only 692 positive instances).

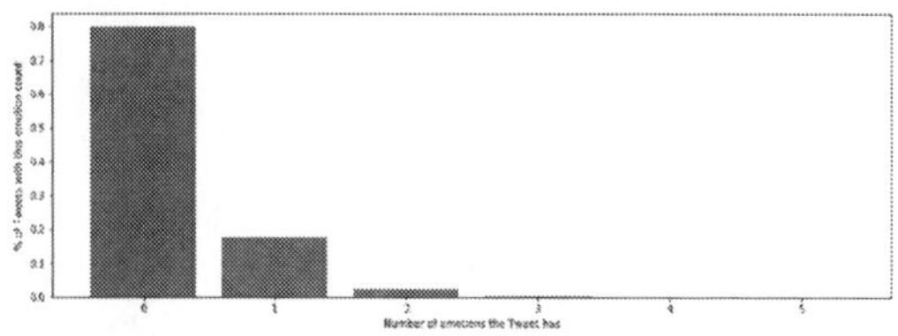

Figure 1: Number of Tweets in our dataset with zero to at most five labeled emotions

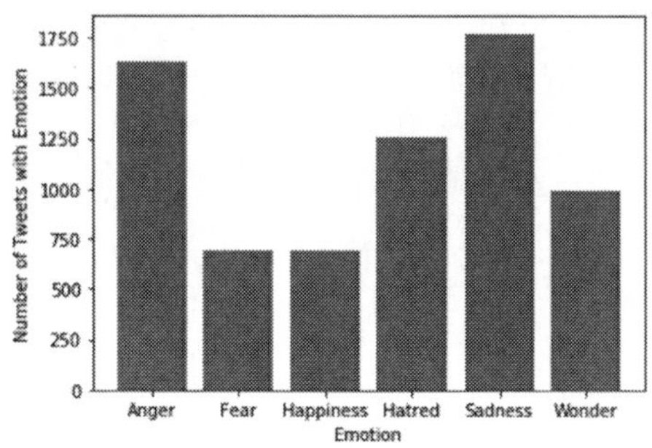

Figure 2: Number of Tweets with each emotion

4.2 Co-occurrence of Emotions

Co-occurrence of emotions is another issue we investigate in Figure 3. The value in each cell represents the proportion $\frac{e_1 \cap e_2}{e_1 \cup e_2}$ (where e_i represent the emotions on the row or column). We can see that positive and negative emotions are very unlikely to be labeled in the same text, further proving the validity of our labeling scheme.

4.3 Agreement on the Existence of Emotions

Next we explored whether there is more agreement on the availability of some emotions compared to others. To answer this question, we begin by defining the following metric for each emotion:

$$\text{Average Agreement} = \frac{1}{M} * \sum_{i=1}^{M} \frac{|n_{yes}^{(i)} - n_{no}^{(i)}|}{5} \quad (1)$$

In Equation 1, M represents the number of texts in our dataset ($M = 30,000$) and $n_{yes}^{(i)}$ is the number of positive votes for Tweet i. The closer the metric is to 1, there is more agreement on existence of the emotion. The results are presented in Table 1. We observe that the most agreement is on happiness and the least agreement is on the presence of sadness.

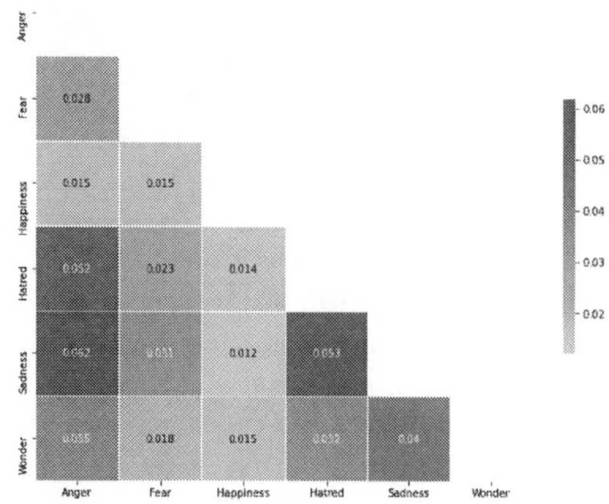

Figure 3: Emotion Co-occurrences, normalized by the total number of instances in the dataset

Emotion	Value of Equation 1
Anger	0.67
Sadness	0.65
Hatred	0.69
Happiness	0.75
Wonder	0.71
Fear	0.73

Table 1: Average agreement for different emotions on the sentences available in our dataset

4.4 Tweet Length

Next, we look into the average character length of instances of each emotion. The results are shown in Table 2. As Twitter allows 280 characters for each Tweet (twi), the average lengths are small. However this is not a phenomena limited to our dataset as (twi) also reports that only 1% of Tweets reach the limit.

4.5 Emojis, and Hashtags

Looking at the emojis used in the dataset, we see that 90% of sentences in the dataset do not have any emojis. Hashtags are also only observed in 19.3% of the data.

Emotion	Avg. Char. Len.	# Instances
Anger	133.3	1,632
Sadness	129.6	1,770
Hatred	132.6	1,256
Happiness	110.1	692
Wonder	124.1	986
Fear	140.5	690

Table 2: Average character length of sentences in our dataset

4.6 Sentiment vs. Emotion

To understand how the sentiment of each sentence relates to its emotion, we use Quecst (Jung et al., 2020), an online tool which labels texts with their sentiment score. We were able to detect the sentiment of 21,485 texts (71%) in our dataset. Figure 4 depicts these sentiment values. *0* means a negative sentiment and *1* refers to a positive one. We can see there are high number of tweets for both negative and positive extremes. Additionally, the majority of the data (45%) is shown to have a positive (> 0.5) sentiment. While neutral sentiment ($= 0.5$) makes up 17% and negative sentiment (< 0.5) makes up 37% of the data.

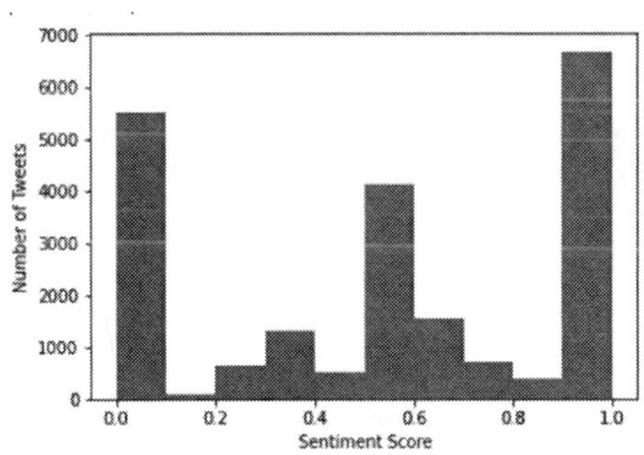

Figure 4: Histogram of sentiment scores of the tweets in our dataset

We further explore the distribution of sentiment scores for each emotion as shown in Figure 5. While some plausible relationships can be seen (for instance the availability of more positive tweets with the "happiness" label), no clear relationship can be observed between most other emotions (such as "anger") and the sentiment values.

5 Conclusion

In this study we presented a dataset of Emotion-labeled Persian Tweets and discussed the properties

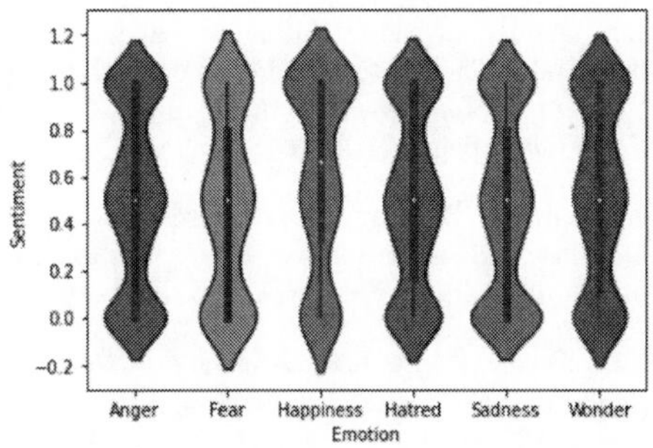

Figure 5: Distribution of sentiment scores for each emotion

of the dataset. We believe this dataset is a valuable resource for future studies in Persian NLP. Future work could investigate models for the task of emotion detection and investigate emotions surrounding various topics on social media platforms.

References

Twitters doubling of character count from 140 to 280 had little impact on length of tweets. https://techcrunch.com/2018/10/30/twitters-doubling-of-character-count-from-140-to-280-had-little-impact-on-length-of-tweets/?guccounter=1&guce_referrer=aHR0cHM6Ly93d3cuZ29vZ2xlLmNvbS8&guce_referrer_sig=AQAAAGtt9NmxoAHZ5quCVKsd9mzI7Qso9sy1WW3QjFWfLyoLuTuA0kETvOI3PnlMpVirGuqogD7pRxNSQEovhs-nyPmOYxQrDSzJd3vkhvQ-X3LvBk77KDYPhILYaski5hJ3BUr7inLE-r9laS7A-7XQRMetXJM1DXVVpUzNMvStbR7H.

(accessed December 1, 2020). *APA Dictionary of Psychology*. https://dictionary.apa.org/emotion.

(accessed December 1, 2020). *EMOCONTEXT : A SHARED TASK AT SEMEVAL 2019*. https://www.humanizing-ai.com/emocontext.html.

(accessed December 2, 2020). *Twitter Developer API*. https://developer.twitter.com/en/docs/api-reference-index.

(accessed January 2, 2021). *Itoll*. https://check.itoll.ir.

Parag Agrawal and Anshuman Suri. 2019. Nelec at semeval-2019 task 3: think twice before going deep. *arXiv preprint arXiv:1904.03223*.

Cecilia Ovesdotter Alm, Dan Roth, and Richard Sproat. 2005. Emotions from text: machine learning for text-based emotion prediction. In *Proceedings of human language technology conference and conference on empirical methods in natural language processing*, pages 579–586.

Amer J Almahdawi and William J Teahan. 2019. A new arabic dataset for emotion recognition. In *Intelligent Computing-Proceedings of the Computing Conference*, pages 200–216. Springer.

Lisa Feldman Barrett, Batja Mesquita, Kevin N Ochsner, and James J Gross. 2007. The experience of emotion. *Annu. Rev. Psychol.*, 58:373–403.

Angelo Basile, Marc Franco-Salvador, Neha Pawar, Sanja Štajner, Mara Chinea Rios, and Yassine Benajiba. 2019. Symantoresearch at semeval-2019 task 3: combined neural models for emotion classification in human-chatbot conversations. In *Proceedings of the 13th International Workshop on Semantic Evaluation*, pages 330–334.

Piotr Bojanowski, Edouard Grave, Armand Joulin, and Tomas Mikolov. 2016. Enriching word vectors with subword information. *arXiv preprint arXiv:1607.04606*.

Yash Butala, Kanishk Singh, Adarsh Kumar, and Shrey Shrivastava. 2021. Team phoenix at wassa 2021: Emotion analysis on news stories with pre-trained language models. *arXiv preprint arXiv:2103.06057*.

Lea Canales and Patricio Martínez-Barco. 2014. Emotion detection from text: A survey. In *Proceedings of the Workshop on Natural Language Processing in the 5th Information Systems Research Working Days (JISIC)*, pages 37–43.

Ankush Chatterjee, Kedhar Nath Narahari, Meghana Joshi, and Puneet Agrawal. 2019. Semeval-2019 task 3: Emocontext contextual emotion detection in text. In *Proceedings of the 13th International Workshop on Semantic Evaluation*, pages 39–48.

Kevin Clark, Minh-Thang Luong, Quoc V Le, and Christopher D Manning. 2020. Electra: Pre-training text encoders as discriminators rather than generators. *arXiv preprint arXiv:2003.10555*.

Tim Dalgleish. 2004. The emotional brain. *Nature Reviews Neuroscience*, 5(7):583–589.

Dorottya Demszky, Dana Movshovitz-Attias, Jeongwoo Ko, Alan Cowen, Gaurav Nemade, and Sujith Ravi. 2020. Goemotions: A dataset of fine-grained emotions. *arXiv preprint arXiv:2005.00547*.

Jacob Devlin, Ming-Wei Chang, Kenton Lee, and Kristina Toutanova. 2019. BERT: Pre-training of deep bidirectional transformers for language understanding.

Paul Ekman. 1992. An argument for basic emotions. *Cognition & emotion*, 6(3-4):169–200.

Paul Ekman. 1999. Basic emotions. *Handbook of cognition and emotion*, 98(45-60):16.

Paul Ekman and Daniel Cordaro. 2011. What is meant by calling emotions basic. *Emotion review*, 3(4):364–370.

Paul Ekman, Wallace V Friesen, Maureen O'sullivan, Anthony Chan, Irene Diacoyanni-Tarlatzis, Karl Heider, Rainer Krause, William Ayhan LeCompte, Tom Pitcairn, Pio E Ricci-Bitti, et al. 1987. Universals and cultural differences in the judgments of facial expressions of emotion. *Journal of personality and social psychology*, 53(4):712.

Cristina Fernández, Juan C Pascual, Joaquim Soler, Matilde Elices, Maria J Portella, and Enrique Fernández-Abascal. 2012. Physiological responses induced by emotion-eliciting films. *Applied psychophysiology and biofeedback*, 37(2):73–79.

Agneta H Fischer, Patricia M Rodriguez Mosquera, Annelies EM Van Vianen, and Antony SR Manstead. 2004. Gender and culture differences in emotion. *Emotion*, 4(1):87.

Sujatha Das Gollapalli, Polina Rozenshtein, and See Kiong Ng. 2020. Ester: Combining word cooccurrences and word associations for unsupervised emotion detection. In *Proceedings of the 2020 Conference on Empirical Methods in Natural Language Processing: Findings*, pages 1043–1056.

James J Gross and Robert W Levenson. 1997. Hiding feelings: the acute effects of inhibiting negative and positive emotion. *Journal of abnormal psychology*, 106(1):95.

Maryam Hasan, Elke Rundensteiner, and Emmanuel Agu. 2019. Automatic emotion detection in text streams by analyzing twitter data. *International Journal of Data Science and Analytics*, 7(1):35–51.

Don H Hockenbury and Sandra E Hockenbury. 2010. *Discovering psychology*. Macmillan.

Taichi Ishiwatari, Yuki Yasuda, Taro Miyazaki, and Jun Goto. 2020. Relation-aware graph attention networks with relational position encodings for emotion recognition in conversations. In *Proceedings of the 2020 Conference on Empirical Methods in Natural Language Processing (EMNLP)*, pages 7360–7370.

Zhang Jingqing, Zhao Yao, Saleh Mohammad, et al. 2019. Pegasus: Pre-training with extracted gap-sentences for abstractive summarization. *arXiv preprint arXiv: 1912.08777*.

S. Jung, J. Salminen, and B. J. Jansen. 2020. *Text2Sentiment (Version 1.0) [Computer software]*. Qatar Computing Research Institute. `https://quecst.qcri.org/tool/Text2Sentiment`.

Guolin Ke, Qi Meng, Thomas Finley, Taifeng Wang, Wei Chen, Weidong Ma, Qiwei Ye, and Tie-Yan Liu. 2017. Lightgbm: A highly efficient gradient boosting decision tree. In *Advances in neural information processing systems*, pages 3146–3154.

Ali Khosravi, Manoochehr Kelarestaghi, and Mehdi Purmohammad. 2019. Emotion detection in persian text; a machine learning model. *Contemporary Psychology, Biannual Journal of the Iranian Psychological Association*, 14(1):42–48.

Kuba Krys, C-Melanie Vauclair, Colin A Capaldi, Vivian Miu-Chi Lun, Michael Harris Bond, Alejandra Domínguez-Espinosa, Claudio Torres, Ottmar V Lipp, L Sam S Manickam, Cai Xing, et al. 2016. Be careful where you smile: Culture shapes judgments of intelligence and honesty of smiling individuals. *Journal of nonverbal behavior*, 40(2):101–116.

Yaman Kumar, Debanjan Mahata, Sagar Aggarwal, Anmol Chugh, Rajat Maheshwari, and Rajiv Ratn Shah. 2019. Bhaav-a text corpus for emotion analysis from hindi stories. *arXiv preprint arXiv:1910.04073*.

Ute Kunzmann and Daniel Grühn. 2005. Age differences in emotional reactivity: the sample case of sadness. *Psychology and aging*, 20(1):47.

Zhenzhong Lan, Mingda Chen, Sebastian Goodman, Kevin Gimpel, Piyush Sharma, and Radu Soricut. 2019. Albert: A lite bert for self-supervised learning of language representations. *arXiv preprint arXiv:1909.11942*.

Joseph E LeDoux. 1995. Emotion: Clues from the brain. *Annual review of psychology*, 46(1):209–235.

Chen Liu, Muhammad Osama, and Anderson De Andrade. 2019. Dens: a dataset for multi-class emotion analysis. *arXiv preprint arXiv:1910.11769*.

Kevin Mulligan and Klaus R Scherer. 2012. Toward a working definition of emotion. *Emotion Review*, 4(4):345–357.

Jay Mundra, Rohan Gupta, and Sagnik Mukherjee. 2021. Wassa@ iitk at wassa 2021: Multi-task learning and transformer finetuning for emotion classification and empathy prediction. *arXiv preprint arXiv:2104.09827*.

Andrew Ortony and Terence J Turner. 1990. What's basic about basic emotions? *Psychological review*, 97(3):315.

Jeffrey Pennington, Richard Socher, and Christopher D Manning. 2014. Glove: Global vectors for word representation. In *Proceedings of the 2014 conference on empirical methods in natural language processing (EMNLP)*, pages 1532–1543.

Pierre Philippot, Robert S Feldman, et al. 2004. *The regulation of emotion*. Psychology Press.

Rosalind W Picard. 1999. Affective computing for hci. In *HCI (1)*, pages 829–833. Citeseer.

Robert Plutchik. 1980. A general psychoevolutionary theory of emotion. In *Theories of emotion*, pages 3–33. Elsevier.

Marco Polignano, Pierpaolo Basile, Marco de Gemmis, and Giovanni Semeraro. 2019. A comparison of word-embeddings in emotion detection from text using bilstm, cnn and self-attention. In *Adjunct Publication of the 27th Conference on User Modeling, Adaptation and Personalization*, pages 63–68.

Colin Raffel, Noam Shazeer, Adam Roberts, Katherine Lee, Sharan Narang, Michael Matena, Yanqi Zhou, Wei Li, and Peter J Liu. 2019. Exploring the limits of transfer learning with a unified text-to-text transformer. *arXiv preprint arXiv:1910.10683*.

Kashfia Sailunaz, Manmeet Dhaliwal, Jon Rokne, and Reda Alhajj. 2018. Emotion detection from text and speech: a survey. *Social Network Analysis and Mining*, 8(1):28.

Armin Seyeditabari, Narges Tabari, and Wlodek Zadrozny. 2018. Emotion detection in text: a review. *arXiv preprint arXiv:1806.00674*.

Phillip R Shaver, Shelley Wu, and Judith C Schwartz. 1992. Cross-cultural similarities and differences in emotion and its representation.

Abu Awal Md Shoeb and Gerard de Melo. 2020. EmoTag1200: Understanding the association between emojis and emotions. In *Proceedings of the 2020 Conference on Empirical Methods in Natural Language Processing (EMNLP)*, pages 8957–8967, Online. Association for Computational Linguistics.

Tiberiu Sosea and Cornelia Caragea. 2020. Canceremo: A dataset for fine-grained emotion detection. In *Proceedings of the 2020 Conference on Empirical Methods in Natural Language Processing (EMNLP)*, pages 8892–8904.

Shabnam Tafreshi, Orphée De Clercq, Valentin Barriere, Sven Buechel, João Sedoc, and Alexandra Balahur. 2021. Wassa 2021 shared task: Predicting empathy and emotion in reaction to news stories. In *Proceedings of the Eleventh Workshop on Computational Approaches to Subjectivity, Sentiment and Social Media Analysis*, pages 92–104.

Dianne A Van Hemert, Fons JR van de Vijver, and Ad JJM Vingerhoets. 2011. Culture and crying: Prevalences and gender differences. *Cross-Cultural Research*, 45(4):399–431.

Petar Veličković, Guillem Cucurull, Arantxa Casanova, Adriana Romero, Pietro Lio, and Yoshua Bengio. 2017. Graph attention networks. *arXiv preprint arXiv:1710.10903*.

Shari R Waldstein, Willem J Kop, Louis A Schmidt, Amy J Haufler, David S Krantz, and Nathan A Fox. 2000. Frontal electrocortical and cardiovascular reactivity during happiness and anger. *Biological psychology*, 55(1):3–23.

Amy Beth Warriner, Victor Kuperman, and Marc Brysbaert. 2013. Norms of valence, arousal, and dominance for 13,915 english lemmas. *Behavior research methods*, 45(4):1191–1207.

A Review on Document Information Extraction Approaches

Kanishka Silva[1] Thushari Silva[2]
[1,2]Faculty of Information Technology, University of Moratuwa, Moratuwa, Sri Lanka

Abstract

Information extraction from documents has become great use of novel natural language processing areas. Most of the entity extraction methodologies are variant in a context such as medical area, financial area, also come even limited to the given language. It is better to have one generic approach applicable for any document type to extract entity information regardless of language, context, and structure. Also, another issue in such research is structural analysis while keeping the hierarchical, semantic, and heuristic features. Another problem identified is that usually, it requires a massive training corpus. Therefore, this research focus on mitigating such barriers. Several approaches have been identifying towards building document information extractors focusing on different disciplines. This research area involves natural language processing, semantic analysis, information extraction, and conceptual modelling. This paper presents a review of the information extraction mechanism to construct a generic framework for document extraction with aim of providing a solid base for upcoming research.

1 Introduction

Digitization of documents and moving forward for the paperless community has been in crucial discussion in the past few decades, contributed to many research opportunities advancing from image processing, Natural Language Processing, ontology, semantic analysis. Such research has the focus on one particular narrowed problem. But none or fewer are supporting to provide a generalized approach for information extraction from documents. Document processing is tremendous due to its diversity; even document generation could be in different ways, i.e., handwritten, scanned-handwritten, typewritten, machine-generated, machine-printed. In terms of content, again it is possible to divide among purpose (business, legal, technical, medical, academic, historical) (Ritter et al., 2011) (An and Park, 2018), language (English, Hindi, Arabic, Multi-lingual) (Tao et al., 2014).

It is better to have a more generalized solution than limited to the scope of each application area. However, this would not be an easy task due to diversities in document nature, but worth exercising since it provides a novel way of addressing document processing issues. This paper focuses on querying documents tasks, such as in question answering, due to the expandability for several other applications. But, notably, the information extraction area itself is a vast research area employing different methodologies not only for targeting documents. Such examples would be (Corro and Gemulla, 2013) and (Yates et al., 2007) discussing legacy open information extraction approaches. Later, the works of (Zhu et al., 2019), (Jia et al., 2019), (Zhang et al., 2019a) and (Zhang et al., 2019b) explains more advanced approaches in open information extraction, but this is not the scope in this paper as this emphasis on document information extraction aspects.

In (Weikan et al., 2018) explain a reading strategy of the humanized approach of document extraction, where first skim through the test to get a general idea, read the question or query carefully with the equipped general understanding from the document and then search for the answer with the prior knowledge.

This paper is structured to guide through a step-by-step approach of document information extraction while checking on crucial research at a legacy level and recent advancements. These

Proceedings of the Student Research Workshop associated with RANLP-2021, pages 174–179,
held online, Sep 1–3, 2021.
https://doi.org/10.26615/issn.2603-2821.2021_024

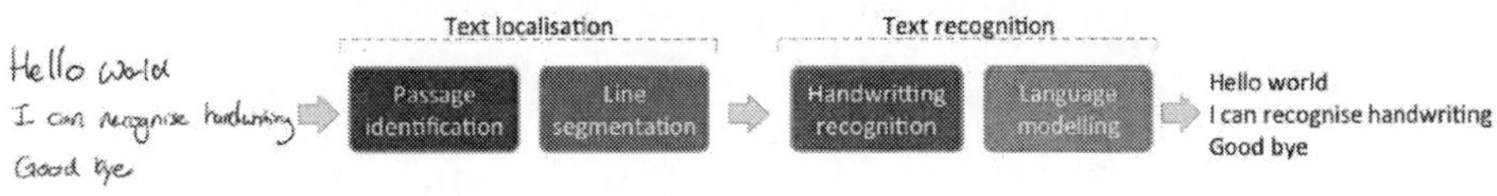

Figure 2: Overview of the Text Recognition System (Chung and Delteil, 2019)

groups could be used as segments in any proposed generic framework for document processing.

2 OCR Handwritten Documents

The paper (Saba et al., 2015) discusses language-independent rule-based classification for handwritten text and the printed text for data entry forms, mainly used in extracting information from form documents. It uses structural and statistical features derived into a rule-based system to determine the origin of the text. It considers baseline characteristics and stroke characteristics to differentiate.

(Chung and Delteil, 2019) propose a methodology for full-page offline text recognition using deep neural networks incorporating object detection neural networks, multi-scale CNN and bidirectional LSTM to perform text localization and then text recognition. In-text localization performs passage identification and line segmentation using IAM datasets and ResNet34 on ImageNet. Then during the text recognition phase, CNN-biLSTM will output NXM in terms of probabilities, and with the language modelling, it has converted to a string of text using the beam search approach. Figure 2 illustrates the overview of the system they proposed.

3 Derive Concept Relations

A Segmenting stream of documents using structural and factual descriptions discuss in (Karpinski and Bela¨ıd, 2016). It explains 4 document levels: records, technical documents, cases, and fundamental documents. This research proposes a novel method for stream segmentation in stream data. In the paper, a logbook for the previous pages they have used to compare descriptors. The system diagram illustrates as follows in Figure 1.

Logical labelling has been discussed in the study (Tao et al., 2014), using 2D Conditional Random Fields to derive the page structure in machine-printed documents. It constructs neighbourhood graphs and pairwise cliques templated while combining local and contextual features obtained from the PDF document. Using an SVM classifier, it derives the baseline without any contextual information considered. Early knowledge-based context analysis considers primary context, the relation between text and text, non-text, and text.

One of the OCR applications is digitizing historical books in libraries where the searchable text is derived. Although the existing OCR applications extract simple structures such as

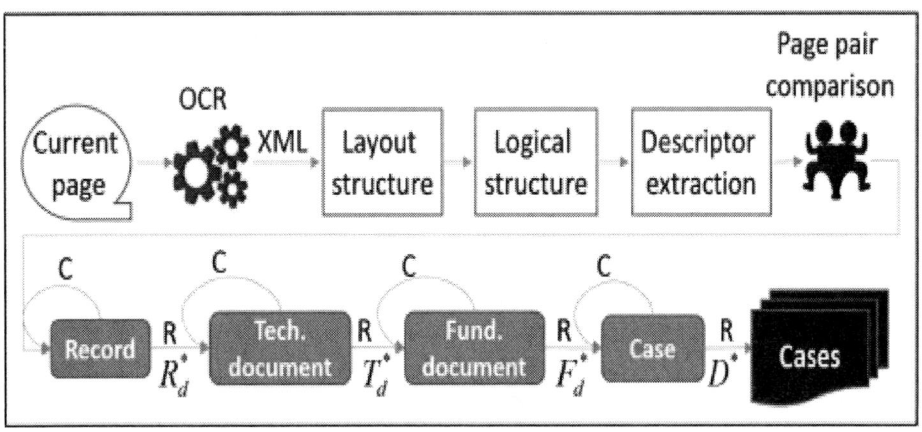

Figure 1: System Diagram of Descriptors (Karpinski and Bela¨ıd, 2016)

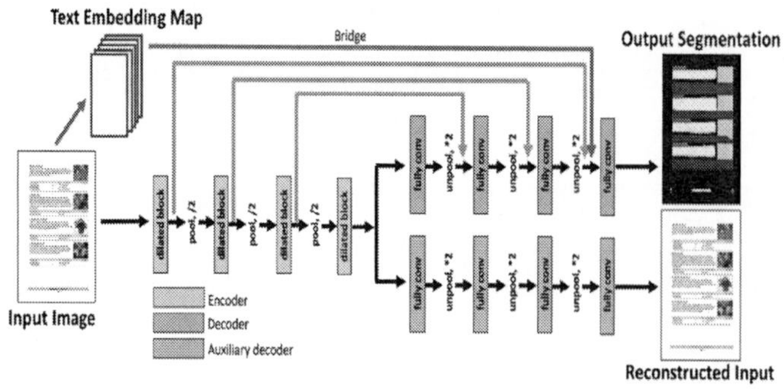

Figure 3: Multimodal Fully Convolutional Neural Network (Yang, et al., 2017)

paragraphs and pages, it is harder to identify complex formatting such as chapters, sections. Mapping such information to a table of content to provide more structural information is proposed by (Nguyen et al., 2017). It introduced an aggregation-based method on two set operators and properties of the table of content entries.

4 Derive Semantic Structure

Document Semantic Structure Extraction is a separate research discipline where document image is segmented into the region of interest and provide a semantic explanation for each (Yang et al., 2017). This paper involves two phases, page segmentation and Concept-Relation analysis. (Yang et al., 2017) present a multimodal fully convolutional network to extract semantic structure in terms of pixel-wise segmentation task.

The paper (Elhadad et al., 2017) proposes an approach to dimensionality reduction of feature vector size for web text document classification using WordNet ontology. This paper has proposed a Vector Space Model for the mining task and used Term Frequency Inverse Document Frequency for the task weighting. The suggested approach is ontology base, and for the evaluation, it uses Principal Component Analysis.

5 Document Entity Recognition

Differential tools use for document entity recognition evaluate in (Marrero et al., 2009). In the entity recognition process, it analyses the features of lexical, semantic, and heuristic. English corpus included around 579 words. Based on entity types of results are evaluated. Finally, this paper proposes a model that eliminates the limitations identified. Also, the corresponding model. is based on the small corpus. The best tools are Supersense - WNSS and the lowest performance from Afner. In (Ritter et al., 2011) uses an NLP pipeline that begins with part of speech tagging and then use chunking to obtain NER. It uses shallow syntax in tweets using annotated tweets and build-tools trained on data. Also, have used features generated from T-POS & T-Chunk in segmenting named entity. The paper (Marrero et al., 2013) discusses the meaning behind Named Entity Recognition and analyses the field from theoretical and practical views considering drawbacks, challenges, and opportunities in the area. It brought the argument to show that this task mainly depends on the development and evaluation of the tools.

NER can apply in many practical scenarios, such as in Twitter post analysis as explained in (Locke and Martin, 2009). It identifies several Named Entities and classifies them among People, Locations and Organizations. Also, it discusses identifying the language-specific features and methods effectively. Further, this paper elaborates on how it can improve to the areas of NER performing on other text sources such as news articles and less structured microblogging texts. Throughout the process of research, it identifies the difference between the microblogging text and the formal process.

The paper (Toral and Munoz, 2006) proposes a framework for named entity detection from Web content associated with semi-structured text data records by exploiting the inherent structure via a transformation process facilitating collective detection. This framework does not require training labels on the data records to learn the sequential classification model. Instead, it makes use of existing named entity repositories such as

DBpedia. It incorporates this external clue via distant supervision by making use of the Generalized Expectation constraint. Finally, a collective detection model supporting the logical inference proposed to consider the consistency among potential named entities and header text.

6 State-of-the-Art Language Models

Several language models have been emerged in more recent research, word embeddings, transformer-based models being key highlights. These model architectures and pre-trained models are used for document-based language modelling successfully.

The paper (Vasvani et al.,2017) presents an attention-based novel architecture named. Transformers. It mainly uses in natural language processing for tasks such as text summarization and translations. The main advantage in transformers is it does not require sequential data to insert in an orderly manner. Because of that, it allows parallelization compared to Recurrent Neural Networks and reduces the overall training time due to that. Pretrained models such as BERT (Bidirectional Encoder Representations from Transformers) (Devlin et al., 2019) are using this model. Transformers follows encoder-decoder architecture where the encoder contains several encoding layers, and the decoder consists of several decoder layers. It was designed based on how long sentences memorize in neural machine translation. The input sentence is first embedded and then passed into a stack of encoders. Then the output from the last encoder pass to each decoder layer. In terms of the internal architecture, there are two main parts in the encoder, namely, self-attention and feed-forward neural network. And the decoder follows similar architecture to the encoder. There is an Encoder-Decoder Attention in between these two, which follows the same pattern as multiheaded self-attention. It takes sequential input for the decoder. The output will pass to another linear layer with SoftMax activations following the same concepts as forwarding propagation and loss functions such as cross-entropy to update trainable parameters.

ELMo (Peters et al., 2018) provides deep contextualized word representation using a bi-directional LSTM model to get word representations. It analyses the words by considering the context used. As it uses character-based representation, it creates dynamic vectors from the given input text. In ELMo, it learns both word and linguistic context. The pre-trained model can utilize for any downstream required NLP task, such as question answering, coreference resolution, textual entailment, named entity extraction, semantic role labelling and sentiment analysis. Multiple word embeddings produce for every single word considering different scenarios. Higher-level layers use to capture context-dependent aspects. And the model aspects such as syntax are captured by lower-level layers. ELMo (Peters et al., 2018) performs Language Modelling by training to predict the next word for the given word sequence. This contextual embedding is by grouping hidden states by concatenation.

The encoder part in BERT (Devlin et al., 2019) is similar to the architecture in transformers as it consists of a feed-forward neural network and self-attention heads. These two segments act as the training parameters to differentiate within different BERT (Devlin et al., 2018) models. The various applications of BERT are question-answer modelling, classification tasks such as spam detection, answer generation from a given passage, sentence tagging such as entity recognition.

7 Question Answering from Documents

Since any generic document information extraction framework should be able to provide answers for the given queries, we must consider the design aspects of question answering systems, where it requires the composing of several components, Named Entity Recognition, Semantic Analysis of the question, Named Entity Disambiguation, query expansion and execution. The study (Jayalakshmi and Sheshasaayee, 2017) has proposed, Web And semantic knowledge Driven (WAD) approach to increase the accuracy of the document selection. This approach first evaluates the user query, entity linking method and the query expansion technique. Finally, ontological information uses to rank the answers.

The paper (Veena et al., 2017) suggests a graph-based Question Answering system for reading comprehension tests, where it picks the sentence in the given passage which gives the best answer. It uses combined techniques of morphological analysis, coreference resolution and synonym checks to achieve higher accuracy.

8 Conclusion

Most of the research is firmly dependent upon the dataset/corpus and limited to the addressed language. The suggested model is usually trained and implemented within the given environment, whereas less performance for complex unstructured documents. For some research, a precompiled training dataset requires building the model so that when applying within a different environment, an additional effort need for preparing such datasets. Also, the current state of art referring to this study is usually subjective for the problem area such as academic, business, biomedical.

As per future trends regarding this research area, most recent studies are moving towards extracting information by considering the conceptual factors rather than digitizing the text and then grabbing the semantics. Current approaches are limited to given scope, document type, structure, language. Applying this research in real-time applications will not provide aid for day-to-day applications. In the existing approaches, a large corpus of documents uses for training and fitting the model. A requirement for a generalized framework capable of extracting information from any document exists due to that. The key idea is to mimic how a human understands an unknown text document through the content and the relation between the sections. Such a generalized framework will employ the benefits from existing approaches, but not solely dependent, as the main framework components could be replaceable by any other future approaches by providing a baseline. This review will provide a solid background analysis before approaching this generic framework.

References

Alan Ritter, Sam Clark, Mausam and Oren Etzioni. (2011). Named Entity Recognition in Tweets: An Experimental Study. EMNLP. (pp. 1524–1534) https://aclanthology.org/D11-1141.

Alexander Yates, Michael Cafarella, Michele Banko, Oren Etzioni, Matthew Broadhead, and Stephen Soderland. 2007. TextRunner: open information extraction on the web. In Proceedings of *Human Language Technologies: The Annual Conference of the North American Chapter of the Association for Computational Linguistics: Demonstrations (NAACL-Demonstrations '07).* Association for Computational Linguistics, USA, 25–26. https://doi.org/10.3115/1614164.1614177.

Antonio Toral and Rafael Munoz (2006). A proposal to automatically build and maintain gazetteers for Named Entity Recognition by using Wikipedia. *Workshop On New Text Wikis And Blogs And Other Dynamic Text Sources.* https://aclanthology.org/W06-2809

Ashish Vaswani, Noam Shazeer, Niki Parmar, Jakob Uszkoreit, Llion Jones, Aidan N. Gomez, Łukasz Kaiser, and Illia Polosukhin. 2017. Attention is all you need. In Proceedings of the *31st International Conference on Neural Information Processing Systems (NIPS'17).* Curran Associates Inc., Red Hook, NY, USA, 6000–6010.

Brian Locke, and James Martin (2009). Named entity recognition: adapting to microblogging. *In Computer Science Undergraduate Contributions* (p. 29).

Dongxu Zhang, Subhabrata Mukherjee, Colin Lockard, Xin Dong and A. McCallum (2019). Integrating Web-Scale OpenIE Extractions and Knowledge Bases with Entity Neighborhood Encoder.

Dongxu Zhang, Subhabrata Mukherjee, Colin Lockard, Xin Dong and A. McCallum (2019). OpenKI: Integrating Open Information Extraction and Knowledge Bases with Relation Inference. NAACL. https://doi.org/10.18653/V1/N19-1083

G. Veena, S. Athulya, S. Shaji and D. Gupta, "A graph-based relation extraction method for question answering system," 2017 *International Conference on Advances in Computing, Communications and Informatics (ICACCI),* 2017, pp. 944-949, https://doi.org/ 10.1109/ICACCI.2017.8125963.

Jacob Devlin, Ming-Wei Chang, Kenton Lee and Kristina Toutanova, "BERT: Pre-training of Deep Bidirectional Transformers for Language Understanding" In Proceedings of the *2019 Conference of the North American Chapter of the Association for Computational Linguistics: Human Language Technologies*, Volume 1 (Long and Short Papers), https://doi.org/10.18653/v1%2FN19-1423

Jonathan Chung and Thomas Delteil, "A Computationally Efficient Pipeline Approach to Full Page Offline Handwritten Text Recognition," *International Conference on Document Analysis and Recognition Workshops (ICDARW)*, 2019, pp. 35-40, https://doi.org/10.1109/ICDARW.2019.40078.

JungHyen An and Y. B. Park (2018). Methodology for Automatic Ontology Generation Using Database Schema Information. *Mobile Information Systems*. 2018. 1-13. https:/doi.org/10.1155/2018/1359174.

Luciano Del Corro and Rainer Gemulla. 2013. ClausIE: clause-based open information extraction. In Proceedings of the *22nd international conference on World Wide Web (WWW '13)*. Association for Computing Machinery, New York, NY, USA, 355–366. https://doi.org/10.1145/2488388.2488420

Matthew E. Peters, Mark Neumann, Mohit Iyyer, Matt Gardner, Christopher Clark, Kenton Lee and Luke Zettlemoyer, (2018). Deep Contextualized Word Representations,*NAAC*,.https://doi.org/10.18653/v1/N18-1202

Mohamed K. Elhadad, Khaled M. Badran and Gouda I. Salama, "A novel approach for ontology-based dimensionality reduction for web text document classification," *IEEE/ACIS 16th International Conference on Computer and Information Science (ICIS),* 2017, pp. 373-378, https://doi.org/10.1109/ICIS.2017.7960021.

Mónica Marrero, Julián Urbano, Sonia Sánchez-Cuadrado, Jorge Morato, Juan Miguel Gómez-Berbís, Named Entity Recognition: Fallacies, challenges and opportunities, *Computer Standards & Interfaces*,Volume 35, Issue 5, 2013, Pages 482-489, ISSN 0920-5489, https://doi.org/10.1016/j.csi.2012.09.004.

Mónica Marrero, Sonia Sanchez-Cuadrado, Jorge Morato and George Andreadakis (2009). Evaluation of named entity extraction systems. In *Advances in Computational Linguistics Research in Computing Science* (pp. 47-58).

Romain Karpinski and Abdel Belaïd, "Combination of Structural and Factual Descriptors for Document Stream Segmentation," 2016 *12th IAPR Workshop on Document Analysis Systems (DAS),* 2016, pp. 221-226, https://doi.org/10.1109/DAS.2016.21.

S. Jayalakshmi and Ananthi Sheshasaayee, "Automated question answering system using ontology and semantic role," 2017 *International Conference on Innovative Mechanisms for Industry Applications (ICIMIA)*, 2017, pp. 528-532, https://doi.org/10.1109/ICIMIA.2017.7975515.

Shengbin Jia, E. Shijia and Yang Xiang (2019). Neural Open Relation Extraction via an Overlap-aware Sequence Tagging Scheme.

Tanzila Saba, Abdulaziz S. Almazyad and Amjad Rehman "Language independent rule based classification of printed & handwritten text," 2015 *IEEE International Conference on Evolving and Adaptive Intelligent Systems (EAIS)*, 2015, pp. 1-4, https://doi.org/10.1109/EAIS.2015.7368806.

Thi-Tuyet-Hai Nguyen, Antoine Doucet and Mickael Coustaty, "Enhancing Table of Contents Extraction by System Aggregation," 2017 *14th IAPR International Conference on Document Analysis and Recognition (ICDAR)*, 2017, pp. 242-247, https://doi.org/10.1109/ICDAR.2017.48.

Weikang Li, Wei Li, Yunfang Wu. A Unified Model for Document-Based Question Answering Based on Human-Like Reading Strategy. *Proceedings of the Thirty-Second AAAI Conference on Artificial Intelligence*, New Orleans, Louisiana, USA, February 2-7, 2018. pages 604-611, AAAI Press, 2018.

Xiao Yang, Ersin Yumer, Paul Asente, Mike Kraley and Daniel Kifer "Learning to Extract Semantic Structure from Documents Using Multimodal Fully Convolutional Neural Networks," 2017 *IEEE Conference on Computer Vision and Pattern Recognition (CVPR),* 2017, pp. 4342-4351, https://doi.org/10.1109/CVPR.2017.462.

Xin Tao, Zhi Tang, Canhui Xu and Yongtao Wang, "Logical Labeling of Fixed Layout PDF Documents Using Multiple Contexts," 2014 *11th IAPR International Workshop on Document Analysis Systems, 2014*, pp. 360-364, https://doi.org/10.1109/DAS.2014.54.

Zhu, Q., Ren, X., Shang, J., Zhang, Y., El-Kishky, A., Xu, F.F., & Han, J. (2019). Integrating Local Context and Global Cohesiveness for Open Information Extraction. Proceedings of the *Twelfth ACM International Conference on Web Search and Data Mining.*

Towards New Generation Translation Memory Systems

Nikola Spasovski, Ruslan Mitkov

Research group in Computational Linguistics
University of Wolverhampton
{n.spasovski,r.mitkov}@wlv.ac.uk

Abstract

Despite the enormous popularity of Translation Memory systems and the active research in the field, their language processing features still suffer from certain limitations. While many recent papers focus on semantic matching capabilities of TMs, this planned study will address how these tools perform when dealing with longer segments and whether this could be a cause of lower match scores. An experiment will be carried out on corpora from two different (repetitive) domains. Following the results, recommendations for future developments of new TMs will be made.

1 Introduction

Translation Memory systems are one of the many translation technology tools available in the translation market. Their main purpose is to accelerate translators' productivity and improve the overall translation process. As many authors recognise, Translation Memories have achieved remarkable success among both translation companies and individual translators, and have positively impacted translators' work. (Lagoudaki (2008); Bowker (2008)). Their popularity is evidenced by the results of the 2018 Language Industry Survey[1] – Expectations and Concerns of the European Language Industry, which show that the use of computer assisted translation (CAT) tools is widespread in both language service companies and in individual professionals/freelancers, with only less than 1% of companies reporting that they do not use CAT tools, and only around 13% of individual language professionals.

By virtue of the lively interest CAT tools have received from the industry and academia over the last three decades, the software and technical features of these tools have also been evolving at rapid pace, thus successfully 'surpassing' rival tools and technologies in the extremely competitive translation market. Furthermore, as a consequence of an increasing demand for this type of technology, we have witnessed a diversification and multiplication of the range of TM systems on the market today.

The concept of Translation Memory is a simple one. It can be defined as a database used to store previously translated segments. This database consists of parallel texts and their translations, which are segmented and then aligned according to a sentence-based method. Whenever there is an equal or similar phrase to be translated, these segments are offered as exact or fuzzy matches. The chances of a retrieval increase as the translator stores more translations in the database. Nonetheless, if there are no exact/fuzzy matches to be suggested, nowadays the TM can offer 'similar matches', or a match from the Machine Translation extension of most CAT tools. It is left to the translator to decide whether the 'similar' or MT matches are useful, and these can be used in the translation by editing the differences.

The sentence matching in TMs is based on 'string-edit' distance, or more precisely, the 'Levenshtein distance' (Levenshtein, 1966). Levenshtein distance, in the words of Somer (2003), is the 'minimum number of changes (e.g. insertions, deletions and substitutions) needed to replace one segment with another'. In TM terms, this means that the database segments/chunks are compared to the sentence to be translated based on the number of changed characters, or distance, between words.

Using 'string-edit' distance makes TMs practical for repetitive texts, such as technical ones, that abound in similar terminology as these systems simplify the task of reusing previously translated content. In line with the aforementioned, Zaretskaya (2016) notes that translators of

[1] The European Language Industry Survey can be accessed on the following link.

technical content are the most likely candidates to benefit from TM tools, followed by legal translators and those translating financial and/or marketing documents.

Nevertheless, many researchers (Macklovitch and Russell (2000); Pekar and Mitkov (2007); Reinke (2013); Baquero and Mitkov (2017)), Mitkov et al. (2021) point out the main limitation of the Levenshtein distance - the lack of language processing functionalities - which stands in the way of TMs recognising matches between syntactically different but semantically equal segments.

Consequently, research including TM systems has been constantly sparked by a single question: *How to improve these systems so that translators can benefit from them even more?*

2 Related work

In academia, TMs have been approached from both the technical (NLP) aspect, which includes work on their capabilities of semantic matching, and the user aspect, which addresses users' necessities regarding the tools.

From the user aspect, Lagoudaki (2008) performed extensive research on users' needs regarding translation memories. The results of her work showed that translators would not accept any changes in TM tools if the existing processing speed were affected and if those changes resulted in additional time–consuming tasks in the translation process. Furthermore, translators consider that changes are not necessary unless they make the software perform tasks faster and better than a human. However, most experienced respondents answered that 'the system's computational efforts must stop at the point where the imagination of the translator risks being compromised'. Nevertheless, young translators believe that the matching capabilities of a TM system could be improved with the implementation of machine translation techniques.

Zarteskaya et al. (2016) conducted a user survey on CAT tools, which included a section dedicated to the 'functionality' features of the tools. According to the results obtained by the survey, speed is a fundamental part of translators' work. Hence, the most important characteristics that a TM system should have are a high working speed, followed by a user-friendly interface, and ease of use.

On the NLP side, Pekar and Mitkov (2007) proposed a new generation of translation memory capable of performing semantic matching of sentences. Several studies that consisted of paraphrase recognition experiments on TMs were conducted as an answer to this semantic matching approach. Among them are: Marsye (2011), Timonera and Mitkov (2015), Chatzitheodorou (2015).

In Marsye (2011), authors assessed how TM systems would perform in terms of suggesting possible match segments that were paraphrases of the source segment. In order to identify synonym words and recognise paraphrases, the author suggests using WordNet as an extension of the TMs as a possible solution.

Later work included Chatzitheodorou (2015), who used the NooJ module to create equivalent paraphrases from the source texts of a TM. He proved that this method could increase fuzzy matches; however, the implemented module failed to paraphrase certain chunks.

Furthermore, in order to improve match retrieval, Timonera and Mitkov (2015) carried out experiments with clause splitting as well as paraphrasing. Following the experiments, the authors came to the conclusion that paraphrasing and the use of a Paraphrase database (PPDB) does result in an improved match retrieval.

More recent attempts to improve translation memory systems involve experiments with neural networks and deep learning methods (Mitkov 2021). Among them, Ranasinghe, et al. (2020) are worth mentioning, who employed NLP and DL techniques such as word and sentence embeddings to match segments from the TM database instead of the previously used Levenshtein (edit) distance.

Although the aforementioned studies performed reasonably well and enhanced the capabilities of semantic matching, all of them present limitations. Most have not been tested in real-life scenarios, and some even lack information on the time required by the system to suggest a segment from the TM database. Considering all user-conducted surveys pointed out speed as the most valued component of the tools, it remains to be seen whether the - updated - system outperforms Translation Memories in terms of speed and is able to offer matches faster.

Moreover, two of the experiments see storage space-related issues. In one of the studies, as the database grows, the TM processing/retrieval time becomes slower, while the second study found that the larger the database, the more RAM space is needed. Thus, applied to a real-life scenario, translators' speed would be affected and additional storage space would be required.

3 Methodology

Across the different literature reviewed, at the time of writing this research proposal, it was found that there exists little to no work that explores in depth the topic of translation memories and their performance on longer segments. This fact stands out when we consider that some of the available tools, such as MateCat and MemoQ, fail to return a high-percent fuzzy match if the segment is significantly longer. Hence, a methodology for carrying out the study is designed:

A known deficiency, an analysis of performance in a defined setting (long repetitive segments in financial and scientific texts), and possible suggestions for what to come afterwards.

The overall goal of this project is to evaluate to what degree TMs fail in retrieving matches for longer (repetitive) segments by using their in-built text processing algorithms, hence; the main research question in this study will be *how can matching (of longer segments) in existing translation memories be improved, making the tools more useful for translators?*

3.1 Language data (Parallel Corpora as Translation Memories)

The working languages of the study are English and Spanish – each one will be treated as a source language. To this end, available parallel corpora from two different domains will be used. The corpora will be imported and aligned. They will then be processed into the database as a TM, so that they can be properly exploited. The first corpus is the European Central Bank corpus, which contains financial vocabulary extracted from the Bank's website, and the second corpus is going to be selected in a later stage of the study. It is expected that the focus will be on a medical domain (anatomy, more specifically). The main assumption is that certain domains are more repetitive, and this characteristic influences the final TM output in terms of retrieving higher fuzzy matches. Therefore, as part of the corpora preprocessing, we will iterate over them and measure the degree of segment repetition. The repetition measurement will be performed using n-grams (trigrams, fourgrams) in the Natural Language Toolkit (NLTK) library in Python. After performing the repetition measurement, shorter and longer segments will be divided and experimented with. For the purposes of this research, the reference size will be 1700/1800 characters, so that a "short segment" will be shorter than 1700 and a "longer one" will be equal or longer than 1700. Given that existing corpora often present some issues, another procedure as part of the text-preprocessing will be to perform data cleaning. This will include three steps:

1. check whether both corpora in Spanish and English use the same XML tags;
2. check for mismatches in date format, numbers (whether they are written with digits or letters);
3. check for empty segments in one of the languages and/or segments in different languages than the required.

These details are considered important since they could influence the fuzzy match percentage of the TMs to be used. For the data cleaning, one of the publicly available sources suggested by Barbu (2017) will be used.

3.2 Experiments

In order to answer the research question, this study will assess the TMs' output and try to find ways to improve them. One of the most important components of the investigation to focus on will be the fuzzy matches. We will seek to investigate and compare the attributes and translation output of several TM systems: commercial (e.g. MemoQ, Wordfast), open (e.g. SmartCAT, MateCat), as well as TM tools with web interface (e.g. Memsource, Matecat). Both word-based and character-based Levenshtein distance typically employed in commercial TM systems will be put to the test. Ideally, in order to assess performance, the matching threshold will be set between 70 and 80 percent. We will observe how the fuzzy match algorithm works with longer segments and whether a greater length could be a reason for a lower score match. If this is the case, we will measure to what degree TMs fail in retrieving matches for longer segments. Additionally, a comparison regarding speed and matching accuracy between both types of segments will be carried out.

Finally, the influence of formatting and tags on the match retrieval and how they could impact the semantic recognition when they are not well placed within long (or short) segments will be analyzed.

3.3 Future work

Following these experiments, the typical errors will be categorised and recommendations for the development of a new generation of TM systems (that integrate linguistic knowledge) will be made. We will be aiming for this work to be a base for NLP engineers seeking to improve TMs, as well as for other researchers in translation technologies working with longer or repetitive segments (from finance and science) in general and to (eventually) prepare a basis for future interpreting memory tools or other language tools that rely on TMs.

References

2018 Language Industry Survey – Expectations and Concerns of the European Language Industry

Baquero Silvestre A., Mitkov R. (2017). Translation Memory Systems have a long way to go. In proceedings of the Workshop Human-Informed Translation and Interpreting Technology https://doi.org/10.26615/978-954-452-042-7_006

Barbu E. (2017). Ensembles of Classifiers for Cleaning Web Parallel Corpora and Translation Memories. In proceedings of the International Conference Recent Advances in Natural Language Processing (RANLP) https://doi.org/10.26615/978-954-452-049-6_011

Bowker L. (2008) Computer - Aided Translation Technology: A Practical Introduction. Ottawa: University of Ottawa Press

Chatzitheodorou K. (2015). Improving translation memory fuzzy matching by paraphrasing. In proceedings of the Workshop on Natural Language Processing for Translation Memories (NLP4TM), pages 24–30.

European Central Bank corpus J. Tiedemann, (2012), Parallel Data, Tools and Interfaces in OPUS. In Proceedings of the 8th International Conference on Language Resources and Evaluation (LREC 2012)

Lagoudaki E. (2008). Expanding the Possibilities of Translation Memory Systems From the Translator's Wishlist to the Developer's Design. PhD thesis, Imperial College London

Levenshtein, Vladimir I. (1966). "Binary codes capable of correcting deletions, insertions, and reversals". In Soviet physics doklady , volume 10, 707–710.

Macklovitch E, Russell G. (2000). What's been Forgotten in Translation Memory. In: Proceedings of the 4th Conference of the Association for Machine Translation in the Americas on Envisioning Machine Translation in the Information Future, London, UK, pages 137–146

Marsye A. (2011). Towards a New Generation Translation Memory: A Paraphrase Recognition Study for Translation Memory System Development. Master thesis, University of Wolverhampton

Mitkov, R. (2021). Translation Memory. In S. Deane-Cox and A. Spiessens (Eds), The Routledge Handbook of Translation and Memory. Basingstoke: Routledge.

Pekar V, Mitkov R. (2007). New Generation Translation Memory: Content - Sensitive Matching. In proceedings of the 40th anniversary congress of the Swiss association of translators, terminologists and interpreters.

Ranasinghe T, Mitkov R, Orăsan C and Caro Quintana R. (2020). Semantic Textual Similarity based on Deep Learning: Can it improve matching and retrieval for Translation Memory tools?

Reinke U. (2013). State of the Art in Translation Memory Technology. In proceedings of the Workshop on Natural Language Processing for Translation Memories (NLP4TM), pages 17–23

Somers H. (2003). Computers and Translation: A Translator's Guide. Amsterdam and Philadelphia: John Benjamins.

Timonera K, Mitkov R. (2015). Improving Translation Memory Matching through Clause Splitting. In proceedings of the Workshop on Natural Language Processing for Translation Memories (NLP4TM), pages 17–23

Zaretskaya A, Corpas G, Seghiri M. (2016). User Perspective on Translation Tools: Findings of a User Survey

Zaretskaya A. (2016). Translators' requirements for translation technologies: user study on translation tools. PhD thesis, Universidad de Málaga

Question Answering in Natural Language: the Special Case of Temporal Expressions

Armand Stricker
LISN-CNRS, Université Paris-Saclay
armand.stricker@universite-paris-saclay.fr

Abstract

Although general question answering has been well explored in recent years, temporal question answering is a task which has not received as much focus. Our work aims to leverage a popular approach used for general question answering, answer extraction, in order to find answers to temporal questions within a paragraph. To train our model, we propose a new dataset, inspired by SQuAD, specifically tailored to provide rich temporal information. We chose to adapt the corpus WikiWars, which contains several documents on history's greatest conflicts. Our evaluation shows that a deep learning model trained to perform pattern matching, often used in general question answering, can be adapted to temporal question answering, if we accept to ask questions whose answers must be directly present within a text.

1 Introduction

Question answering is an automatic language processing task that aims to search for information in a text or database to answer a question in natural language. It is a task that differs from the query of a search engine, because it aims to exempt the user from querying the data using a formal language query. This type of method is particularly useful when the database is very large or poorly documented, or when the textual data to be queried is difficult to structure.

General question answering is a subject that has already been widely explored, and we have therefore decided to focus on a particular part of this research domain. The purpose of this paper will be to explore question answering as it relates to temporal information in English texts.

This is a task that can vary in difficulty: the temporal structure and the amount of temporal data can fluctuate quite a lot depending on the text, which can therefore be relatively simple to analyze or relatively complex, depending also on the questions asked. A set of clear definitions is therefore imperative.

1.1 Definitions

First, we need to define and limit what constitutes a *temporal expression*. Temporal information is most often expressed through a phrase or expression that describes a point in time or duration.

For this work, we define a temporal expression (timex) as any expression that denotes a moment or interval, or any other temporal reference that is not based on an event. Indeed, although an event can be located in time, it does not allow it to be measured (Derczynski, 2013). Thus, *after the rain fell* is not valid, unlike an expression such as *the day after the rain fell* which is centered around *day*, a measure of time. From this definition, we can establish a typology of temporal expressions. A temporal expression can most often be (see Derczynski et al., 2012 for a more thorough and complete typology):

Absolute, when a moment is totally explicit and unambiguous such as *Monday, October 6th, 2019.*

Deictic, when the moment of enunciation must be used to determine the moment to which the expression refers: *two weeks ago.* We can assume, for example, that the moment of

Proceedings of the Student Research Workshop associated with RANLP-2021, pages 184–192,
held online, Sep 1–3, 2021.
https://doi.org/10.26615/issn.2603-2821.2021_026

enunciation is the moment when the text was written.

Anaphoric, when the moment of enunciation is distinct from the moment when the reference is made, when a person is telling a story in the past tense for example (*that evening*). The moment of enunciation (the moment when she tells the story) is not enough, it is necessary to determine the moment of reference within her story.

Given this typology, we can more easily identify in a text what we will call temporal expressions and what our questions will focus on. Here is an overview of what our system will have to process (text extracted from the WikiWars corpus (Mazur, Pawel, and Robert Dale (2010))):

Royal flight to Varennes

> *(...)On the night of 20 June 1791 the royal family fled the Tuileries wearing the clothes of servants, while their servants dressed as nobles. However, the next day the King was recognised and arrested at Varennes (in the Meuse departement). He and his family were paraded back to Paris under guard, still dressed as servants. From this time, Barnave became a counselor and supporter of the royal family.*

A temporal question answering system will have to be able to answer questions on the temporal expressions highlighted in yellow. We can distinguish different types of temporal questions.

Questions which have a ***literal*** *answer.* The answer is found literally in the text and the system will need to be able to select the appropriate passage, corresponding to the answer sought. Questions that would fit into this category would be: *When did the royal family flee from Paris? When was the king arrested? When did Barnave become counselor of the royal family?*

Questions that require ***inference***. The answer is not directly present in the text and the system will need to be able to identify the temporal information it will need before reaching a conclusion: *How long was the king away from Paris?* (He left on June 20 and was arrested the next day, so he was gone 2 days). *What was the date when the king was arrested?* (*the next day* corresponds in fact to June 21st since the previous day was the 20th)

In this paper, we limit ourselves to literal questions, but these examples already give us a glimpse of how complex temporal question answering can be. We will begin by presenting the methods generally used in question answering, explaining which method we preferred and why. We will then review state of the art corpora by presenting the SQuAD (Rajpurkar & al., 2016) and especially the WikiWars (Mazur & Dale, 2010) corpora, explaining how we combined WikiWars with the SQuAD approach to create our own temporal corpus. We will then detail our model and explain how the data is represented and which features were used, before finally presenting and discussing the results obtained.

2 State of the Art and Methods

Traditional information retrieval involves finding a short passage of text within a set of documents. A selection of relevant documents is first made, then these documents are subdivided into sections, paragraphs, or sentences. We focus only the second part of this task, which we adapt to the case of temporal question answering.

We decided to mainly use the **information extraction** method (vs the Knowledge-Base approach) which means using literal questions as we stated above, mainly because annotating the data is faster: when building the dataset, we can write the questions as they are without worrying about translating them into logical form. It is also possible to ask a third party to help build the dataset since all that is needed is to write a question and identify the answer within the text. These advantages make it possible to build a larger dataset more quickly. However, we are not opposed to the Knowledge-Base approach and we even think that combining the two approaches could be something to explore in the future.

Answer type	Percentage	Example
Date	8.9%	19 October 1512
Other Numeric	10.9%	12
Person	12.9%	Thomas Coke
Location	4.4%	Germany
Other Entity	15.3%	ABC Sports
Common Noun Phrase	31.8%	property damage
Adjective Phrase	3.9%	second-largest
Verb Phrase	5.5%	returned to Earth
Clause	3.7%	to avoid trivialization
Other	2.7%	quietly

Table 1: Classification of answer types for SQuAD

2.1 The SQuAD corpus

SQuAD (Rajpurkar & al, SQuAD: 100,000+ Questions for Machine Comprehension of Text, 2016) is certainly one of the most well-known corpora when it comes to question answering. It is a corpus developed for question answering by extraction (the answer is literally present in the text and must be extracted) and it is for this reason that we have chosen to analyze it more closely, and eventually to draw inspiration from the methodology used.

The corpus is composed of articles from the English Wikipedia divided into paragraphs. There are 536 articles, chosen among the 10,000 most popular articles. The popularity of an article was determined using Wikipedia's Internal PageRanks from Project Nayuki, a site that offers a variety of practical computer applications (https://www.nayuki.io/page/computing-wikipedias-internal-pageranks). The PageRank of a document is the probability that a visitor will arrive at that document after performing a uniform random web search (uniform random browsing). From this selection, individual paragraphs are then extracted from each article, with those under 500 characters being eliminated.

As stated above, a response is equivalent to a passage extracted from a paragraph, which greatly simplifies the annotation of the data, and explains how the corpus can be so large (23,215 paragraphs in all). Indeed, the questions were produced through intensive crowdsourcing. It is important to note that any type of question is valid, as long as a passage of text can be selected to answer it. SQuAD is therefore not a corpus that is particularly adapted to questions on temporal expressions, and this is one of the limitations of this corpus, as far as we are concerned.

Indeed, when looking at the types of responses contained in the corpus in Table 1 and the percentages they represent, few dates (proportionally) are highlighted as responses. Only 9% of the answers are dates, which shows that they are not the primary concern of the corpus. Moreover, these statistics, given by the authors, make it difficult to determine to what extent other types of temporal expressions (defined in the introduction) are present (durations, deictic expressions, anaphors, etc.)

2.2 The WikiWars corpus

On the other hand, WikiWars: A New Corpus for Research on Temporal Expressions, (2010) is better suited to our task in terms of content. The corpus was developed from 22 English Wikipedia documents that describe the historical courses of wars. The authors of the corpus searched Google for these two phrases: "most famous wars in history" and "biggest wars". They found a page describing the 10 most famous wars in history and a page describing the 20 most important wars of the 20th century. They then combined these two lists, eliminated duplicates and searched Wikipedia for articles about these wars. Here is an example of a paragraph from the WikiWars corpus:

> *On* ***<TIMEX2 val="1791-06-20TNI">****the night of 20 June 1791****</TIMEX2>*** *the royal family fled the Tuileries wearing the clothes of servants, while their servants dressed as nobles. However,* ***<TIMEX2 val="1791-06-21">****the next day****</TIMEX2>*** *the King was recognised and arrested at Varennes (in the Meuse departement)*

We have highlighted the temporal expressions as well as the TIMEX2 tags that surround them. The TIMEX2 annotation scheme (Ferro et al., 2005) allows us to associate a temporal value with the expression in question, which could be leveraged in further work involving inference questions (expressions such as "the next day" have dates associated with them (1791-06-21), which would allow for questions such as "What day was it when the King was arrested ?" to have a more precise answer than simply "the next day"). However, given our focus on purely extracting responses from the text, the ***val*** attribute was not used.

WikiWars holds a greater number of references to the distant past and the temporal structures of the texts are more elaborate than those found in SQuAD. Furthermore, the number of temporal expressions per document is higher than other popular temporal corpora (121.41 timex/doc vs. 7.73 for the ACE corpus (Doddington, 2005)). This therefore makes it a better fit for our task. However, unlike SQuAD, it is not annotated for question answering. We believe that the combination of these two types of corpora has not yet been sufficiently explored and we therefore created a dataset that addresses this shortcoming.

3 Data and Model

3.1 Using the SQuAD approach on the WikiWars corpus

We combined the SQuAD approach with the WikiWars corpus, in order to test the extraction method on a corpus suitable for the study of temporal expressions. WikiWars is not annotated with question-answer pairs, so we augmented this dataset to suit our task, by breaking the text into paragraphs, like the SQuAD documents, and adding a list of questions and answers under each of them, using XML tags.

In order to enrich our dataset considerably, we decided that three questions would be associated with each temporal expression. As well as providing a larger training set, this meant that copying elements from the text to formulate the questions (and therefore simplifying the task of finding and extracting the answer for the model) was necessarily limited since the questions could not resemble each other exactly, as illustrated in the following example:

On September 1, 1939 Germany and Slovakia (...) attacked Poland and World War II broke out.

This extract could have as associated questions: *When did World War II break out? What day was it when WWII started? When was Poland attacked?*

Rephrasing makes it more difficult for the model to determine which part of the paragraph the question is about. In the example above, the first question uses information at the end of the sentence while the answer is at the beginning; the second question uses *started* instead of *broke out* and synthesizes *World War II* into *WWII*; the last question is in the passive voice, thus reversing the order of the words found in the text. The efficiency of the model is therefore tested by using such examples, especially since some paragraphs can be quite long (the longest ones contain approximately 300 words).

Given the amount of question-answer pairs to annotate (approximately 6000) and the straightforwardness of the annotation task, the annotations were performed manually by 2 bilingual annotators (French and English). In the annotation protocol, the annotators were provided with a presentation of the WikiWars corpus and with an explanation of our aim in creating this corpus. They were also provided with several examples of annotated paragraphs and guidelines which insisted on reformulating the text when writing the questions and on finding various formulations.

Not all temporal expressions were taken into account. Indeed, it was sometimes difficult to ask coherent questions which took these expressions as answers. Given that the priority of our task was to have logical and coherent questions that a user could ask, we felt that if questions became too artificial (to accommodate a particular temporal expression as an answer), then they should not appear in our dataset.

For example, the adjective *former* sometimes caused problems. Although we can see how this adjective can provide useful temporal information, formulating a question which has this specific word as an answer does not sound natural, as can be seen in the following example:

(...)Republican former vice president Richard Nixon.

What vice president was Nixon? => (?)Former

We therefore asked our annotators to leave the field blank if they felt that a question might be difficult to phrase and proof-read their annotations.

In total, our corpus contains 702 paragraphs (paragraphs without temporal expressions were not counted) and 6120 question-answer pairs, which were annotated in approximately a month and a half. By comparison, SQuAD has around 23,000 paragraphs and 107,000 question-answer pairs. Although the amount of data is not as large, it is much more specific and only targets temporal information.

The dataset can be acquired and used for other experiments by contacting armand.stricker@universite-paris-saclay.fr or benoit.crabbe@linguist.univ-paris-diderot.fr.

3.2 Model

Neural networks are particularly well suited for extracting answers from a text and it is this approach that we have chosen. Indeed, to try to answer the question, the model will try to find similarities between the words in the question and the words of the paragraph by comparing their respective distributional representations. We chose to use recurrent neural networks, since they are ideal to encode the information contained in a sequence.

We implemented a model inspired by the Document Reader component of the DrQA system designed by Chen & al. (2017), a system that allows a user to search for a document and then select a passage within it. Thus, a question is composed of l tokens :

$$Q = \{q_1, q_2, \dots, q_l\} \qquad (1)$$

and a paragraph is composed of m tokens :

$$P = \{p_1, p_2, \dots, p_m\} \qquad (2)$$

Paragraph encoding For each word in the paragraph, we first create a vector representation which is the concatenation of 4 components, all of which are intended to try to draw the model's attention to certain words in the paragraph, rather than others. Here are the functions that translate these different features:

Word embeddings - We first use 300-dimensional GloVE pre-trained embeddings (Pennington & al., 2014) to obtain the embedding of a word p_i:

$$f_{embedding}(p_i) = \boldsymbol{E}(p_i) \qquad (3)$$

Exact match - This function creates two features: the fact that a word p_i is identical in the question and in the paragraph, and the fact that the lemmatized forms of the token are also identical:

$$f_{exact\_match}(p_i) = \mathbb{I}(p_i \in Q) \qquad (4)$$

Token Features - We encoded the various characteristics of a token p_i , namely its grammatical category (POS, part of speech), whether it is part of a named entity (NER, named entity recognition), and the TF-IDF (term frequency - inverse document frequency):

$$f_{token}(p_i) = concat(POS(p_i), \dots) \qquad (5)$$

To obtain the POS of a word, we used the automatic nltk POS-tagger (https://www.nltk.org/book/ch05.html). To obtain named entities, we used spaCy (https://spacy.io/usage/linguistic-features#named-entities), who trained its algorithm on OntoNotes (Weischedel & al., 2011). The algorithm is capable of identifying a range of entities, and most importantly dates. As for the TF-IDF, this measure allows us to weigh the frequency of the token p_i by seeing if it is present in other examples. The more the token is present in the corpus, the lower its weighted frequency will be.

Aligned embedding of the question (attention mechanism) - Finally we added an attention vector: often, in addition to encoding the exact match, question answering systems use an attention mechanism to represent in a more sophisticated way the similarity between a passage and a question, for similar but non-identical words like *flight* and *plane* for example. The vector is supposed to reflect the proximity between the token and the words in the question. We use a weighted similarity function where p_i represents the queries and q_j the keys:

$$f_{aligned}(p_i) = \sum_j a_{i,j} \boldsymbol{E}(q_j) \qquad (6)$$

The attention weight $a_{i,j}$ encodes the similarity between the token p_i and each word q_j in the question. This attention weight can be calculated as the dot product between the functions α of the question words' embeddings and the paragraph's, where α can be a simple feed forward neural network:

$$a_{i,j} = \frac{\exp\left(\alpha(E(p_i))^T . \alpha\left(E(q_j)\right)\right)}{\sum_{j'} \exp\left(\alpha(\boldsymbol{E}(p_i))^T . \alpha\left(\boldsymbol{E}(q_{j'})\right)\right)} \qquad (7)$$

We concatenate all these feature vectors to obtain a vector representation for each token in the paragraph:

$$\widetilde{\boldsymbol{p}}_i = concat(f_{embedding}(p_i), \dots) \quad (8)$$

Finally, each $\widetilde{\boldsymbol{p}}_i$ is passed through an RNN so as to obtain a final $\boldsymbol{p}'_i$ for each token:

$$\{\boldsymbol{p}'_1, \boldsymbol{p}'_2, \dots, \boldsymbol{p}'_m\} = RNN(\{\widetilde{\boldsymbol{p}}_1, \widetilde{\boldsymbol{p}}_2, \dots, \widetilde{\boldsymbol{p}}_m\}) \quad (9)$$

Question encoding The question encoding is similar to the paragraph encoding but is simpler because not as many features are used to represent each token in the question. Pre-trained embeddings such as GloVE (Pennington & al., 2014) are used to obtain the vector representation $\widetilde{\boldsymbol{q}}_i$ which will be transmitted to the RNN (an LSTM (Hochreiter & al., 1997) in our case). We do not create any other features for the tokens in the question:

$$\widetilde{\boldsymbol{q}}_i = f_{embedding}(q_i) \quad (10)$$

The sequence is encoded and we output the hidden representations of the network:

$$\{\boldsymbol{q}'_1, \boldsymbol{q}'_2, \dots, \boldsymbol{q}'_l\} = RNN(\{\widetilde{\boldsymbol{q}}_1, \widetilde{\boldsymbol{q}}_2, \dots, \widetilde{\boldsymbol{q}}_l\}) \quad (11)$$

These vector representations are then combined through a weighted sum to produce a single vector **q** which represents the question:

$$\boldsymbol{q} = \sum_j b_j \boldsymbol{q}'_j \quad (12)$$

The weight b_j is a measure that reflects the relevance of each word in the question and can be learned from a weight vector **w**:

$$b_j = \frac{\exp(w.q'_j)}{\sum_{j'} \exp(w.q'_{j'})} \quad (13)$$

Prediction of a span - Once the two previous steps are completed, we obtain an embedding of the question **q** and a vector representation for each token of the paragraph $\{\boldsymbol{p}'_1, \boldsymbol{p}'_2, \dots, \boldsymbol{p}'_m\}$. We then train two different classifiers: one to calculate the probability $P_{start}(i)$ that a word p_i marks the beginning of the answer and one to calculate $P_{end}(i)$. We use a bilinear attention layer as a similarity function, where W_{start} and W_{end} are matrices of learned weights:

$$P_{start} \exp(\boldsymbol{p}'_i W_{start} \boldsymbol{q}) \quad (14)$$

$$P_{end} \propto \exp(\boldsymbol{p}'_i W_{end} \boldsymbol{q}) \quad (15)$$

One way to determine which passage is the answer is to take the word with the highest start probability and the one with the highest end probability, in order to deduce that the words in between are part of the answer. This is obviously not the only way to proceed, and it would also have been possible to build a model that goes through the text predicting whether or not a word is part of the answer.

We use cross-entropy loss as our loss function, where the argmax position of the vectors containing the start and end probabilities is compared to the indices of the gold labels in the example in order to update the model's parameters.

3.3 Training

We split our documents into three csv files: train, dev and test. The paragraphs of each document were split into three temporary datasets with the following proportions: 80%, 10%, 10%. Since each paragraph contains several questions, distributing the data in this way and not per question, avoids that a paragraph be present in both the dev and the train dataset, which would distort the results.

4 Results and discussion

4.1 Metrics

We used several metrics to evaluate the performance of our model. The model systematically predicts a start and end token, so we evaluated: *the percentage* of tokens at the beginning of an answer correctly predicted, *the percentage* of correctly predicted tokens at the end of a response, *the mean* of the two previous measures, *the percentage* of whole passages correctly predicted (the start token and the end token are correct, it is an exact match).

The table below shows our results, on the development and test sets:

Our Model	Dev		Test	
	Mean	Exact match	Mean	Exact Match
	61.5	52.6	54.7	41.4

Table 2: Results on dev and test

We see that our model manages to predict correctly about 50% of the passages on the dev set. We also notice that the performances are lower on the test corpus. It is difficult to evaluate why, except to consider the fact that the corpus may present examples that are too different from those encountered during training. We will take a closer look at the errors made by our model in the next section.

4.2 Ablation Analysis

We also conducted an analysis of the features used to encode the paragraphs on the development set by ablation, as shown in the table below:

Features	F-measure
Full	52.6
No NER	48.3
No POS	50.1
No TF-IDF	51.5
No f_{token}	43.5
No $f_{aligned}$	46.3
No f_{exact_match}	49.4
No $f_{aligned}$ et f_{exact_match}	35.11
No $f_{aligned}$ et NER	46.2
No f_{exact_match} et NER	43.3

Table 3: Ablation analysis for the features used

We notice that the f-measure (which boils down to the percentage of exact matches in this case) does not drop much (3%) when we remove the exact match, traditionally a very important feature for general question answering. We also notice that the removal of the NER (named entity recognition) does not lead to a drastic drop either (4.3%) even if the algorithm used (https://spacy.io/usage/linguistic-features#named-entities) allows us to identify temporal expressions quite reliably. This means that even when the possible answers are indicated in the paragraph, our model does not rely only on this feature to find the answer, and that it is not enough to simply extract the temporal expressions of a paragraph to find the right answer. The features that account for the link between the question and the text are therefore of great importance.

What is interesting to note is the interaction of the different features with each other. Indeed, the individual ablations of attention ($f_{aligned}$) and of f_{exact_match} generate relatively small decreases (6.3% and 3.2%). But when we remove both features simultaneously, the performance of the model drops drastically: by 17.4%. We can conclude that these two features play a similar but complementary role and that they are quite essential in the search for the passage in the paragraph, allowing to identify the context within which to look for the answer.

Nevertheless, not all features interact with each other. In another case, the decrease is additive: the simultaneous removal of the information on the grammatical category (POS), on the named entities (NER) and of the TF-IDF generates a score of 43.5% ("No f_{token}" in table 3, where f_{token} is a concatenation of the features mentioned). This score corresponds approximately to the sum of the individual losses caused by each feature (respectively - 2.5%, - 4.3% and - 1.1%, which would result in a score of 44.7%). However, 43.5% is indeed slightly lower than 44.7%, so there must be some interaction. We also tested the interaction between named entity recognition and contextualization features f_{exact_match} and $f_{aligned}$, but the drop in performance was not significant.

4.3 Qualitative Analysis of Model Inference

In the following examples, "(START)" and "(END)" indicate the boundaries of the expected response, while "****_" and "_****" indicate the start and end tokens predicted by our model. They appear only when the prediction is wrong. The examples were taken directly from the output of the model.

Overall, our model predicts almost only temporal expressions. When there is an error, the answer is often not the temporal expression expected or turns out to be incomplete, as we will see through the following series of examples.

Correctly handled cases - The most favorable case for predicting a correct answer is when the paragraph is relatively short and the question is formulated in such a way that the context of the answer is easy to identify and relatively close to the answer. The model also performs better when the choice of temporal expressions within the paragraph is limited, as in the following example:

> *when did emperor charles i attempt secret negotiations with <unk> ?*
>
> *in (START)1917(END) , emperor charles i of austria secretly attempted separate peace negotiations with <unk> , with his <unk> ' s brother <unk> in belgium as an intermediary , without the knowledge of germany . (...)*

This example is quite short and *1917* is the only temporal expression. We have highlighted the shared passages in the question and the paragraph. The words are exact matches here, except for "attempt" and "attempted" although they still have the same lemma.

Partially correct answers - The fact that our model is trying to predict a start and end token means that several temporal expressions are sometimes combined by our model, as in the example below:

> *when was south africa invaded by german troops ?*
> *some of the first clashes of the war involved british , french and german colonial forces in africa . on ****_7 august , french and british troops invaded the german <unk> of <unk> . on (START)10 august(END) german forces in south - west africa attacked south Africa; sporadic and fierce fighting continued for the remainder of the war .*

Our model predicted the wrong start token but the correct end token. The predicted start token is indeed a date but is not part of the correct temporal expression. It is as if the model had tried to combine *7* and *august*, surely because the context around these two terms fits the question well (we have highlighted the exact matches around the two temporal expressions). Modeling the proximity between temporal expressions within a paragraph could therefore be considered during future experiments. Nevertheless, we see the importance of the model's ability to contextualize correctly, and this type of error can even lead to completely inconsistent answers, where the end token is predicted to be before the start token.

Embeddings - We also observed a lack of expressiveness in the embeddings used. When a token in the question had a synonym in the paragraph, this did not always help guide the model. Indeed, the model seemed sometimes disoriented when a synonym for a word near the answer was used, resulting in an incorrect prediction.

Year, day, and season - Our model seemed to be able to recognize these key words in the questions and understood what format the answer was expected to have. This was especially apparent when we compared the answers for "when" questions (which were note as precise) with "what year", "what day", "which season" questions for the same paragraph.

5 Conclusion

In this work, we chose to simplify the temporal question answering problem and limit our work to literal questions. We were thus able to apply an extractive approach with some success.

Indeed, this method allowed us to create a rather large dataset, annotated by hand, over a rather short period of time (only about a month and a half). Thanks to this, we were also able to devote time to the state-of-the-art implementation of a deep machine learning model, the results of which demonstrated some of this model's strengths.

Nevertheless, it is not clear that the model is capable of understanding the underlying structure of the text it is dealing with. When the model has to choose between several temporal expressions, searching for the tokens closest to the answer does not always lead to the right prediction.

Moreover, our model is certainly not capable of making inferences and determining, for example, the date to which a deictic temporal expression, such as "this day", refers. In future work, we propose to broaden the definition of a temporal question in order to be able to deal with a larger variety of questions, especially inferential questions.

References

Allen, James F. (1983) "Maintaining Knowledge about Temporal Intervals." *Communications of the ACM* 26, no. 11 (November 1, 1983): 832–43.

Chen, Danqi, Adam Fisch, Jason Weston, and Antoine Bordes. (2017) "Reading Wikipedia to Answer Open-Domain Questions." *ArXiv:1704.00051 [Cs]*, April 27, 2017.

Derczynski, L., H. Llorens, and E. Saquete (2012), "Massively increasing TIMEX3 resources: a transduction approach." In Proceedings of the Language Resources and Evaluation Conference.

Derczynski, Leon R A. (2013) "Determining the Types of Temporal Relations in Discourse," n.d., 218.

Doddington, George. (2004) « The Automatic Content Extraction (ACE) Program », s. d., 4.

Lisa Ferro, L. Gerber, I. Mani, B. Sundheim, and G. Wil- son. 2005. TIDES 2005 Standard for the Annotation of Temporal Expressions. Technical report, MITRE, September.

Hochreiter, Sepp & Schmidhuber, Jürgen. (1997). Long Short-term Memory. Neural computation. 9. 1735-80. 10.1162/neco.1997.9.8.1735.

Jurafsky, Daniel and James H. Martin (2019), *Speech and Language Processing, An Introduction to Natural Language Processing, Computational Linguistics, and Speech Recognition*, Third Edition Draft

Diederik Kingma and Jimmy Ba. 2014. Adam: A method for stochastic optimization. *arXiv preprint arXiv:1412.6980* .

Pawel Mazur and Robert Dale. 2007. The DANTE Temporal Expression Tagger. In Zygmunt Vetulani, editor, *Proceedings of the 3rd Language And Technology Conference (LTC)*, Poznan, Poland, October.

Mazur, Pawel, et Robert Dale. (2010) « WikiWars: A New Corpus for Research on Temporal Expressions ». In *Proceedings of the 2010 Conference on Empirical Methods in Natural Language Processing*, 913–922. Cambridge, MA: Association for Computational Linguistics, 2010

Meng, Yuanliang, Anna Rumshisky, and Alexey Romanov. (2017) "Temporal Information Extraction for Question Answering Using Syntactic Dependencies in an LSTM-Based Architecture." In *Proceedings of the 2017 Conference on Empirical Methods in Natural Language Processing*, 887–896. Copenhagen, Denmark: Association for Computational Linguistics, 2017.

Neji, Zeineb, Marieme Ellouze, and Lamia Hadrich Belguith. (2016) "Question Answering Based on Temporal Inference." *Research in Computing Science* 117, no. 1 (December 31, 2016): 133–41.

Pennington, J., Socher, R., and Manning, C. D. (2014). Glove: Global vectors for word representation. In *EMNLP 2014*, pp. 1532–1543.

Pustejovsky P, Castaño, J, Ingria R, Saurí R, Gaizauskas R, Setzer A, and Katz G TimeML: Robust Specification of Event and Temporal Expressions in Text. In: Proceedings of the IWCS-5 Fifth International Workshop on Computational Semantics, 2003.

Pustejovsky, James & Hanks, Patrick & Saurí, Roser & See, Andrew & Gaizauskas, Rob & Setzer, Andrea & Radev, Dragomir & Sundheim, Beth & Day, David & Ferro, Lisa & Lazo, Marcia. (2003). The TimeBank corpus. Proceedings of Corpus Linguistics.

Rajpurkar, Pranav, Jian Zhang, Konstantin Lopyrev, and Percy Liang. (2016) "SQuAD: 100,000+ Questions for Machine Comprehension of Text." *ArXiv:1606.05250 [Cs]*, October 10, 2016.

Saquete, Estela, Jose Luis Vicedo, Patricio Martínez-Barco, Rafael Muñoz, and Hector Llorens. (2009) "Enhancing QA Systems with Complex Temporal Question Processing Capabilities." *Journal of Artificial Intelligence Research* 35 (August 28, 2009): 775–811.

Verhagen, Marc & Gaizauskas, Rob & Schilder, Frank & Hepple, M. & Moszkowicz, Jessica & Pustejovsky, James. (2009). The tempEval challenge: Identifying temporal relations in text. Language Resources and Evaluation. 43. 161-179.

Weischedel, Ralph & Hovy, Eduard & Marcus, Mitchell & Palmer, Martha & Belvin, Robert & Pradhan, Sameer & Ramshaw, Lance & Xue, Nianwen. (2011). OntoNotes: A Large Training Corpus for Enhanced Processing.

Building A Corporate Corpus For Threads Constitution

Lionel Tadonfouet Tadjou[1,2,3] **Fabrice Bourge[1]** **Tiphaine Marie[1]**
Laurent Romary[2] **Eric De La Clergerie[2]**
[1]Orange Caen, [2]Inria Paris, [3]Sorbonne University Paris, France
{lionel.tadjou,fabrice.bourge,tiphaine.marie}@orange.com
{laurent.romary,Eric.De_La_Clergerie}@inria.fr

Abstract

In this paper we describe the process of building a corporate corpus that will be used as a reference for modelling and computing threads from conversations generated using communication and collaboration tools. The overall goal of the reconstruction of threads is to be able to provide value to the collorator in various use cases, such as higlighting the important parts of a running discussion, reviewing the upcoming commitments or deadlines, etc.

Since, to our knowledge, there is no available corporate corpus for the French language which could allow us to address this problem of thread constitution, we present here a method for building such corpora including different aspects and steps which allowed the creation of a pipeline to pseudo-anonymise data. Such a pipeline is a response to the constraints induced by the General Data Protection Regulation GDPR [1] in Europe and the compliance to the secrecy of correspondence.

1 Introduction

Computer mediated communication (CMC) tools are used to produce and exchange an enormous amount of contents such as emails, chats and fora. But these contents are usually little or not structured, which makes the automatic extraction of knowledge difficult. In this paper, we tackle the issue of the constitution of threads in conversations within a specific company. This problem strongly relates to that of conversations disentanglement which have been addressed in several research works. Jiang et al. (2018) computed message similarity using language representation to address this problem. Such problems requires the existence of a corpus to analyse. It is why Kummerfeld et al. (2019) have built a large-scale corpus for conversations disentanglement, also the ENRON corpus was created by Klimt and Yang (2004) for email classification research. In the same way Chanier et al. (2014) built the CoMeRe corpus for French and Douglas et al. (2015) created the Avocado Research Email Collection. More recently Bevendorff et al. (2020) built the Webis Gmane Email Corpus from the archive of Gmane mailing list. Among these corpora, some are from ENRON and AVOCADO companies, but they are in English and their content have specific contexts different from those of the company of which we will create a corpus. Those that are in French have very few emails around 2030 (CoMeRe) or are mailing list conversations with themes and context that do not fit with corporate conversations. One approach could be transfer learning, (Bornea et al., 2020) use multilingual transfer learning for question answering problem. But the context of a company is very circumscribed and specific.

In this paper we describe a method for building a corporate corpus based on emails data. We specifically address the process of collecting, preprocessing and pseudo-anonymizing emails in order to meet legal, personal, acceptability and social constraints. This comprises the use of models for Named Entity Recognition (NER), rule-based systems and their evaluation. In the upcoming sections, we will present research works on corpus building and constraints related to it.

2 Related Work

Building a corpus is a prerequisite step to various research work in different fields such as discourse analysis, automatic translation and transcription, image recognition, emails segmentation, named entities recognition, etc. Chanier et al. (2014) built the CoMeRe corpus for discourse analysis and carried out linguistic studies of idiolects that appear

[1]https://ec.europa.eu/info/law/law-topic/data-protection/data-protection-eu_en

Proceedings of the Student Research Workshop associated with RANLP-2021, pages 193–202,
held online, Sep 1–3, 2021.
https://doi.org/10.26615/issn.2603-2821.2021_027

in different types of CMC. The CoMeRe corpus consists of heterogeneous CMC in French including 3 million chats, 44K SMS, 2,030 emails, 2,700 forum messages and 34k Tweets.

Automatically classifying emails in specific email directories and extracting information from them are issues that led to the creation of the ENRON Corpus by Klimt and Yang (2004), a corpus of emails in English from a private company. The ENRON corpus has been widely used: email formalities in work environments are studied by Peterson et al. (2011), also Chhaya et al. (2018) quantify the feelings and tone used in emails.

In order to disentangle conversations in the same message stream, Kummerfeld et al. (2019) developed a large corpus of 77,563 messages including 74,963 from Ubuntu's Internet Relay Chat (IRC) channel and 2,600 messages from Linux's that highly contribute to research in dialogue analysis.

Recently, Bevendorff et al. (2020) developed the largest corpus available named Webis Gmane Email Corpus 2019 consisting of 153 million emails extracted from 14,669 mailing lists. This corpus data exists in three major languages: English, German and French. These emails are segmented into 15 classes of emails by a neural model with a performance of 96%.

As a whole, the scarcity of reference data in general and in particular for the French language justifies our approach to build a corpus that covers the need of thread analysis in CMC context.

3 Constraints: Legal, personal and psychological

Certain conditions govern the exploitation of public data, including forum, mailing list or web site data. These types of conditions are generally displayed to and agreed upon by the user when registering for these forums and or mailing lists. Mentions contained in these terms and conditions often refer to the exploitation of user data for the purposes of training, service improvements and or advertising. Unlike this process of joining forums, mailing lists or websites, employees in corporate do not always have to explicitly validate such conditions, but are required to keep secret certain company information on the one hand and on the other hand the private information exchanged in corporate via CMC are governed by the secrecy of correspondence and the General Data Protection Regulation (GDPR) adopted in 2016 and became effective on 25 May 2018 in the European union.

Personal data protection concerns have been elicited since 1970 Hallinan and Zuiderveen Borgesius (2020), with Ann Cavoukain, the Privacy Commissioner of Ontario, Canada, co-author of the 1995 international report on Privacy Enhancing Technologies (PET) acting as a forerunner in the domain of data privacy in any technological design. Cavoukian (2010) further clarified that "the future of privacy cannot be assured solely by compliance with regulatory frameworks; rather, privacy assurance must ideally become an organization's default mode of operation".

With regard to the secrecy of correspondence, it would be a violation if a third party managed to access even a conversation of collaborators without their consent. Our goal of disentangling forum conversations, chats and corporate emails could only be carried out under the respect of the secrecy of correspondence. Thus obliging us to submit consent requests to the various collaborators involved in these conversations. This is a tedious task given the number of collaborators in the different teams or entities in a company.

In the same vein, the GDPR was established in the European Union territory to protect personal data. It applies to any organisation, public and private, that processes personal data on its behalf or not, provided that it is established in the territory of the European Union, or that its activity directly targets European residents. The GDPR strengthens the obligation of information and transparency towards the persons (collaborators in our case) whose data we process. Despite this obligation of transparency towards collaborators, they are able to exercise their rights of refusal, withdrawal (if committed beforehand) of exploitation of their data. Secure and substitute some information from this data are part of the conditions to be respected in order to be GDPR compliance. These conditions are binding for the data acquisition process because require to set up stable and streamlined processes that include administrative and material aspects.

The two previous forms of constraints put collaborators at the centre of any data acquisition process in a company. They need to know why and how their data will be used. And depending on the answers given to them, they are free to give their consent or not. Unwillingness to share their content which potentially includes personal or highly sensitive data, brings out another group of constraints that are personal, acceptability and even psychological.

All these constraints need to be addressed when dealing with business data acquisition and processing.

4 Methodology and Implementation

Our process is based upon three main stages: collecting conversations, preprocessing them and pseudo-anonymizing sensitive information in these conversations. For the global aim of conversation disentanglement, it is important to mention that the data will be further analysed by a limited number of people from two different teams, one within the company and another the associated public research team. Our goal is to process the data, with anonymization or pseudo-anonymization techniques in particular, so that it is not possible for any person outside that team to identify any participant in the conversations nor to be able to detect participants' personal data. In order to verify our compliance with GDPR and the secrecy of correspondences, our project has gone through an internal validation procedure supervised by a legal commission within the company on the basis of a data life-cycle and a completed risk analysis form. The data life-cycle describes in detail which operations would be performed by which person acting with what role. In particular it helped us identify the possible leaks in the process and their potential consequences. It also specifies that before the anonymization or pseudo-anonymization stage, only specific researcher, who bears the role of *technical data controller (TDC)* - can access the whole collected data on a secure storage device. The other collaborators in the team can only access the data collected from their own computer. This legal commission evaluated defined the process to follow.

This process consists first in obtaining a consent from the targeted collaborators. Then, once the data has been collected, any text string that directly or indirectly allows identification of a person or access to personal information must either be removed, modified or pseudo-anonymized. It is worth mentioning that the consent provided by the collaborators is valid for a maximum of one year at a time.

To obtain collaborators' consent, we produced media content (video and slides) explaining why and how the process of collecting and analysing data would take place. This is to provide transparency, as requested by GDPR. Obtaining a collaborator's consent means having him/her sign a document explaining why we want to collect emails he/she is involved in and under what conditions it is done. For COVID-19 reasons these documents were signed electronically and stored on a secure file system.

4.1 First stage: Collecting conversations

Since our objective was to collect a large corpus of French interactions occurring in the context of computer mediated exchanges in a business environment, we focused specifically on emails since a) these are still widely used in professional context and b) other sources appeared to be more fragmented and difficult to gather in a coherent way. Our main goal is to reconstruct threads from those conversations so that each thread only deals with a clear and well-circumscribed topic. After dealing with emails conversations, we will then explore other types of CMC in corporate such as forums, chats, IM, etc.

Still, the sole gathering of emails can appear to be a painful task. Beyond the difficulty of just gathering users' consents, the resulting issue is to be able to collect those messages or threads that only relate to the collaborators that have actually given their consent since obviously many threads involve several collaborators. Finally, the technical deployment of the mailing environment (in our case: Microsoft's Exchange server) can in itself be a hindrance to the precise querying and retrieval of the appropriate content.

As a consequence, we chose to collect emails directly from the collaborators' desktop computers. This choice was guided by two main reasons, namely:

- It is easier to obtain consents of some targeted collaborators. Aspects of security and confidence are in this way easily approached and collaborators have the full control of what is collected from their computer.
- It also allows us to limit the extraction to relevant emails, thus preventing that we come across, for instance, emails that the collaborator wants to keep confidential.

In order to build a corpus of significant size it is necessary to have the consent of a minimum number of collaborators. However targeting collaborators at random proved not to be sufficient. Indeed since we can only collect emails for which all the collaborators involved gave their consent, we would then take the risk of collecting conversations with many missing emails. This would probably result in having a negative impact when extracting meaningful threads from these amputated conversations. Our approach was to try to maximise the number of emails/conversations to extract while minimising the number of collaborators to contact. In doing so we distinguished collaborators who gave their consent into two groups, namely: - *anchor*, are collaborators within our project and with whom we can perform manipulations on their workstation to extract data; - *participant*, the rest of those collaborators who gave their consent. The above approach is divided into two steps. The first one consists in selecting *participant* who are"close" to an *anchor*.

The output of this first step is a list of interlocutors that will be used as a guide when selecting potential *participant* or anchors on other *anchor*' workstations. The second step is focusing on the actual extraction of emails and conversations on *anchor's* workstations. During this emails/conversations extraction, we also made sure that we extrated metadata such as senders, receivers, emails and conversations identifiers, dates and times from emails headers. These metadata helped us later for the pseudo-anonymization step and to keep the real links between the different messages of a conversation. To bootstrap this phase we first contacted collaborators from a single team, then from a project, from a larger entity and so on until a substantial amount of data would be collected.

In a more practical way and because Microsoft Outlook is the application used in the company for emails exchanges, we developed a C# Windows Presentation Foundation (WPF)[2] application based on *Microsoft Office Interface*[3] that allows us to interact with Outlook application and also with backup files from Outlook. With this tool we can select and unselect folders and contacts from a collbaborator's Outlook mailbox. Once the tool is installed on a *anchor's* workstation, the *anchor* uses it with the support of one of the people who designed the tool. Thus it is easy for an *anchor* to choose the emails folders from which the emails may be extracted and to choose the collaborators that could be contacted to become participants. This gives the possibility to avoid folders with private or personal contents and contacts with whom he/she has confidential exchanges. It also helps to provide data in JSON and CSV formats for future processing.

Until now we have obtained 78 consents from close collaborators involved in shared projects. Based on these 78 consents and as a first stage of data collection, we succeeded in extracting 11K unique emails for a total of 1 023 736 tokens, from the workstations of four *anchors* (the TDC and three other collaborators of the same team). These emails included conversations dating back to 2013 which shows the extent and richness of the information collected. The current size of this extracted data is 194 MB. These extracted data are only a first part of our final corpus, as we will contact collaborators from other teams and involved in other projects to increase the size of this corpus.

4.2 Second stage: Preprocessing collected data

Emails are not structured due to the explosion of different email formats and styles, coupled with the ad hoc ways in which people vary the structure and layout of their messages Carvalho and Cohen (2004). Emails contain different zones that can be easily identified by humans. Estival et al. (2007) identify five categories of zone within emails, namely: *Author Text, Signature, Advertisement*(automatically appended advertising), *Quoted Text* (extended quotations), and *Reply Lines* (including forwarded and reply text). Three years later Carvalho and Cohen (2004) refined and extended to nine categories. Two of them caught our attention: there are **Quoted Conversation Zones** (reply and forwoard message) and **Boilerplate Zones** (*signature, advertising, disclaimer* and *attachment*).

Preprocessing collected data initially consisted in deleting all duplicated emails, followed by identifying, dissociating or removing content from the quoted conversation and boiler-plates zones. To identify and extract quoted messages and signatures from an email, we used Talon[4], a python library. This library is inspired from the research work of Carvalho and Cohen (2004) and Joachims

[2]https://docs.microsoft.com/en-us/dotnet/desktop/wpf/overview/?view=netdesktop-5.0

[3]https://docs.microsoft.com/en-us/dotnet/api/microsoft.office.interop.outlook.application?view=outlook-pia

[4]https://github.com/mailgun/talon

(2001). As provided, this library works quite well for French e-mails both for the extraction of quoted messages and signatures with an average of predictions of 95% and 70%, respectively, despite the fact that the model within this library has been trained on ENRON corpus, a corpus in English.

Figure 1 shows the large gap between the number of tokens of an email with its quoted messages(in red on the figure) and without them (in blue). These quoted messages are actually the content of all or some previous emails in a conversation that are added to a new email.

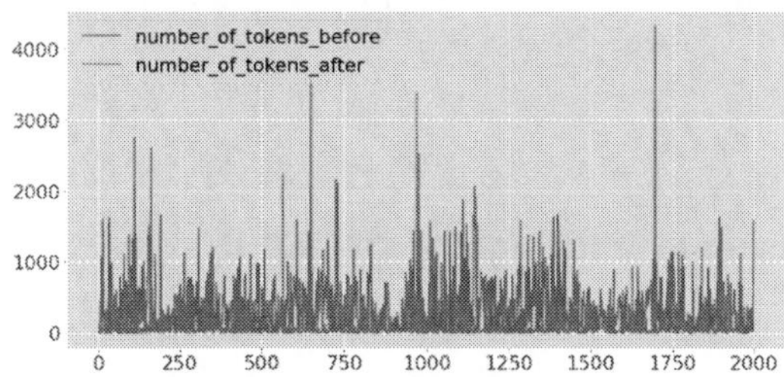

Figure 1. Number of tokens per email before and after quoted messages and signatures extraction for 2k emails sample

To comply with GDPR and the secrecy of correspondence, we started by replacing anything in the email body and subject that could indirectly lead to the identification of any person. Here, we were rather in an anonymisation process as we were trying to keep the semantic logic of sentences while substituting expressions. This meant replacing each email address, phone number, URL, path and any user's identifier respectively by *@EMAIL*, *@PHONE*, *@URL*, *@PATH* and *@ID* using python's internal *regular expression library*[5]. *@PATH* and *@ID* correspond respectively to any absolute or relative path of a folder or file and to sequences of text that uniquely identify the corporate collaborators. All these anonymized sequences do not have a great importance for the problem of thread reconstruction.

Within our collected data, emails are identified by two alphanumeric strings, namely:

- **ConversationID**: identifies a conversation, so it is the same for all emails within the same conversation
- **ConversationIndex**: is the unique identifier of an email, it contains its conversation identifier (*conversationID*). It helps to know what the position of an email is in the conversation tree.

We also replace those two strings for each email while keeping emails in their respective conversation and all relationships between emails.

This preprocessing step gives us an overview of the substitution method on strings easily identifiable. There are others whose identification is complex and we must find and substitute them. That is why we have conducted experiments of data annotation, Named Entity Recognition (NER) and disambiguation of collaborators names.

4.3 Third stage: Entities pseudo-anonymization

Besides indirect content which leads to the identification of a person in emails body, there are strings directly linked to collaborators such as their first names and last names. Emails body may also contain corporate sensitive data or intellectual property such as project names, tools, groups and/or entities names within it, conversation identifiers or any other kind of identifiers. Because of GDPR and secrecy of correspondence compliance, the identification and substitution of these data is necessary.

Identify direct strings listed above or sensitive data is become a general problem for a few decades called Named Entity Recognition (NER) in the field of NLP. A new state of art for French Named Entity Recognition has been recently established by Ortiz Suárez et al. (2020). However, some prior work has been carried out on NER in context of informal text such as emails. Minkov et al. (2005) propose a method based on Conditional Random Fields (CRF) and combined with rule-based system to extract personal names from emails. Zhang et al. (2018) use regular expressions to collect weak labels from web noisy data for the entity mentions and train a neural network to predict those RE-generated weak labels. These work show that regular expressions, rule-based system are still viable approach to Named Entity Recognition despite good results of recent transformers models which need some fine tuning. As our collected data could not be move on a cloud or GPU server for fine-tuning, we were constraint to approach the problem with a simple computer. We combine several approaches including annotation, CRF, fine-tuned **CamemBERT**[6] on NER task, regular

[5]https://docs.python.org/3/library/re.html

[6]https://camembert-model.fr/

expressions and rule-based system to achieve our goal of identifying and substitute information to be GDPR compliance.

4.3.1 Data annotation

Building up the ground truth for a downstream NLP task is a necessary step and usually corresponds to annotation which is time consuming especially when it is handcrafted. For NER case, tools have been built to accelerate annotations. **Prodigy**[7] and **INCEpTION**[8] are such tools. These are both accessible via web interfaces. In addition *Prodigy* offers command-line features. They are all based on *active learning (AL)* defined by Ren et al. (2020) as a method that aims to select the most useful samples from the unlabelled data set and hand it over to the "oracle" (e.g., human annotator) for labelling, so as to reduce the cost of labelling as much as possible while still maintaining performance. As *prodigy* is not free and *INCEpTION* needs some time to get hands on it, we used a tool built by a former intern of our team.

Tags of Named Entities	To annotate
PERSON (B-, I-)	first name, surname, full name and short forms for these
ORG (B-, I-)	known corporate
SUBGROUP(B-,I-)	company entities, departments, etc.
EMAIL	For email identification
PHONE(B-, I-)	phone number
PROJECT (B-, I-)	project names in the company
LOC (B-, I-)	any type of locations
ID	any identifier linked to a person
ROLE (B-, I-)	job names (Manager, Engineer, etc.)
UNCERTAIN	any identified entity that does not fall into the previous tags

Table 1. Tags used to annotate 1k emails

This tool is based on Conditional Random Fields (CRF) and active learning method and as well as being accessible via web interface. From the 11K extracted emails, we selected 1k emails containing at least 142 916 tokens. Three annotators did the annotation exercise on the 1k emails each with Named Entities(NE) tags we defined based on what we considered sensitive information to substitute. Those annotators come from the pool of *anchor* collaborators from whom we extracted the 11k emails and they annotated a total of 8689 tokens.. They are thus well aware of the general context of the task and therefore ended up being good raters for the task. Table 1 lists the various tags according to the BIO standard. Figure 2 shows the annotation statistics. We can see the very low rate of *ID*, *ROLE*, *LOC* and *ORG*, which is actually due to the pre-processing stage where we extracted signatures that usually contain identifiers (which have been annotated as *ID*), roles or functions, phone number, and addresses.

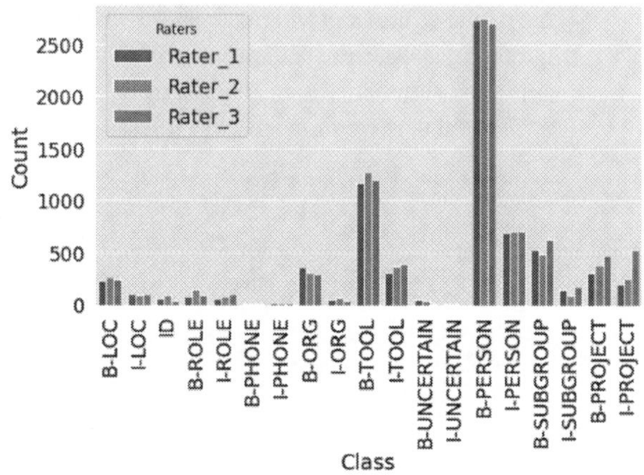

Figure 2. Statistics of annotations by three annotators

The very low rate of *phone number* is also related to the pre-processing stage described in section 4.2 with the use of regular expressions to identify and substitute *phone number*, *email address*, *url* and *path* (which sometimes contains the company ID of employees). Also *UNCERTAIN* is low because raters know well the context of emails that they annotated, otherwise we would have had a high number of *UNCERTAIN* tags. This shared knowledge of the context of annotated emails is also observed on several tags (*LOC*, *ID*, *TOOL*, *PERSON*) which are not very disproportionate for raters 1 and 2. Rater 3 annotated more *PROJECT* and *TOOL* than two others raters, this shows some ambiguity on strings related to those two tags. This effectively reflects the reality of distinction between project and tool because sometimes in a company, a tool developed in a project can bear the same name of the project. There is also such ambiguity between *SUBGROUP* (for departments or teams in the company) and *PROJECT*, due to the fact that sometimes a team name is identical to the product being developed. From the 8689 annotated tokens, we identified 236 different annotations among the three raters, in which the *SUBGROUP*, *PROJECT* and *TOOL* categories are predominant. These disparities show that certain concepts in corporate context are not accurate and may be subject to mis-

[7] https://prodi.gy/

[8] https://inception-project.github.io/

understanding.

For data annotation, we evaluated inter-annotator agreements (IAA) by means of the standard Cohen Kappa measure McHugh (2012) from the biomedical field. Cohen's Kappa measure is not the most relevant for NER as mentioned e.g. in Hripcsak and Rothschild (2005); Grouin et al. (2011), because it requires negative cases that do not exist for NER. Also Cohen's Kappa measure can not be used when there is more than two annotators. Since there are three raters for our data, we use Cohen's Kappa to evaluate pairs of raters (R_1, R_2), (R_1, R_3) and (R_2, R_3). To evaluate nominal inter-annotator agreements (IAA) with more than two annotators, Zapf et al. (2016) advise to use **Fleiss's Kappa** or **Krippendorff's alpha**. They study different cases and show that these measures are similar. Annotated data is very unbalanced because of the un-annotated tokens labelled with "O" which are highly represented compared to all existing tokens. As Brandsen et al. (2020) did, we computed all IAA scores in both cases with all tokens and only with annotated tokens. Table 2 shows different scores computed, and we observe that the scores with all tokens are quite high, but this is due to the bias of non-labelled tokens. Cohen's Kappa on annotated tokens only is **substantial** agreement with values in $[0.61 - 0.80]$ interval according to the interpretations in Viera and Garrett (2005) for three pairs of raters. Computed values for both Krippendorff's alpha and Fleiss's Kappa are identical 0.70 and belong to the same previous interval, interpret as substantial agreement. Based on these computed measures and their interpretation, we can find some correlations with diagram on the Figure 2. These annotations made it possible to build a repository of annotated tokens that we combined with CamemBERT-ner results and a rule-based system to pseudo-anonymize our entire data. This combination is what we call *data pseudo-anonymization chain* represented by Figure 3.

4.3.2 Data pseudo-anonymization chain

Pseudo-anonymising sensitive information starts with recognising them, and this is done by NER task. As we use a tool based on CRF coupled with active learning to annotate our data, we test the resulting model on unseen emails and the result was very bad compared to the test performed with **CamemBERT-ner**[9], a transformers based model.

[9] https://huggingface.co/Jean-Baptiste/camembert-ner

	(R_1,R_2)	(R_1,R_3)	(R_2,R_3)
Cohen's Kappa*	0.8879	0.8450	0.8344
Cohen's Kappa #	0.7832	0.6959	0.6690
Krippendorff's alpha*		0.8554	
Krippendorff's alpha #		0.7155	
Fleiss's Kappa*		0.8554	
Fleiss's Kappa #		0.7158	

Table 2. Inter-annotator agreement measures on 1k emails with Cohen's Kappa, Krippendorff's alpha and Fleiss's Kappa. R_i $stands\ for\ Rater_i$, $i \in \{1, 2, 3\}$; * For all tokens and # For annotated tokens only

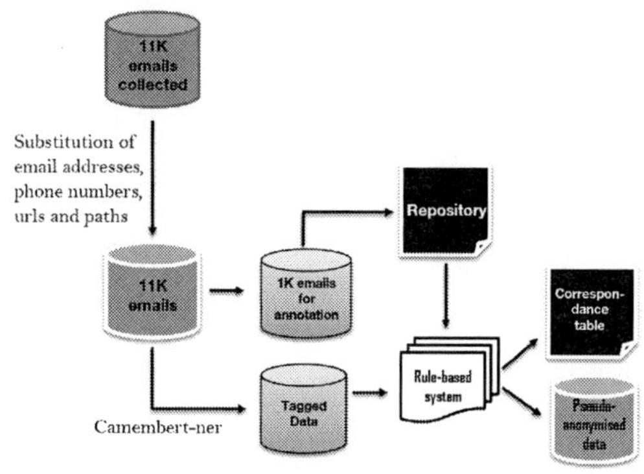

Figure 3. Data pseudo-anonymization chain

Figure 4 shows statistics of *CamemBERT-ner* model on the bunch of 1k emails data with a total number of 6952 identified strings of which 3915 are classified in the miscellaneous category (MISC).

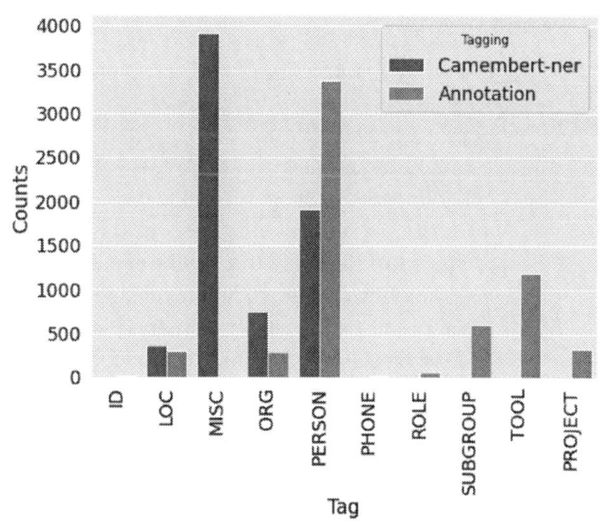

Figure 4. Number of elements identified and classified by CamemBERT-ner and tags identified by annotators on 1K emails

From the data annotation stage (carried out on the same 1k emails), there are 6219 identified strings that have been similarly annotated by the three annotators or by two of them. The difference of about 733 entities identified by CamemBERT-ner compared to manual annotations shows its performance in identifying elements that it cannot classify. This comes from the fact that CamemBERT-ner has been fine-tuned from CamemBERT on the wikiner-fr data set ($\sim$ 170 634 sentences). We anticipate that we will have to compare these results with those obtained with fine tuning *CamemBERT* on our own data in order to recognise additional entities (tool, project, ID, subgroup, etc.) used by raters during the annotation process.

As can be seen in figure 4, the main challenge is to be able to reclassify on these categories those from MISC. Also the organisations recognised by CamemBERT-ner are more than double of those from the annotation and need to be reclassified into other categories like subgroup or project. A rule-based system was used to refine category of entities from MISC. During the annotation process, a repository was built, containing a list of string with their respective tags (tags from table 1) without duplicates. The rule-based system consists of comparing strings identified as *miscellaneous* by *CamemBERT-ner* with same from the annotation repository and finally use his tag (defined by raters) to refine *miscellaneous* category. This Refining stage helps the rule-based system in creating semantic code for the substitution of those strings from emails content ans subjects. Created codes look like *user_xxxxxxxx*, *org_xxxxxxxx*, *tool_xxxxxxxx* respectively for identified collaborators, organisations, tools and this same coding pattern was used for all other entities classes. When substituting collaborators first names or last names or both in an email, the rule-based system checks sender or recipients of the email to keep the email and conversation thread context. While running, the rule-based system builds a new repository containing all pairs of substituted string and their respective code. This repository is call **correspondence table** and could be use later to rebuild emails and subjects without codes but strings which was substituted before. Below is an example of a paragraph before and after pseudo-anonymisation.

Les espaces de co-working sont plutôt traités dans le ***Research Paper*** *en cours de rédaction par* ***Pierre, Paul, Louise****. L'étude de* ***Louise*** *(seule) devait porter initialement sur la valeur pour* ***NomEntreprise*** *des tierslieux (fablabs, espaces de coworking) pour ce qui concerne l'apprentissage et la transmission de connaissances à distance. A part le recentrage sur une population interne* ***NomEntreprise****, l'idée générale est globalement conservée.*

The above paragraph contains bold text segments that are names of collaborators and companies that have been replaced by code as in the pseudo-anonymised text below.

Les espaces de coworking sont plutôt traités dans le ***misc_55e6a*** *en cours de rédaction par* ***user_8e47d, user_c6f1d, user_5ff59****. L'étude de* ***user_5ff59*** *(seule) devait porter initialement sur la valeur pour* ***org_252f2a*** *des tiers-lieux (fablabs, espaces de co-working) pour ce qui concerne l'apprentissage et la transmission de connaissances à distance. A part le recentrage sur une population interne* ***org_252f2a*** *, l'idée générale est globalement conservée.*

Everything that has been done so far has allowed to set up a data processing pipeline that takes data collected in CSV format as input and produces pseudo-anonymized data as output in the same format.

5 Future work

After obtaining pseudo-anonymised data, we will analyze this data in order to approach the problem of threads constitution with its inherent problems including conversation disentanglement, dialog acts identification and text segmentations. To reconstruct conversation threads, Domeniconi et al. (2016) propose an approach that combines similarity calculations of 8 *features* built from each email. These features actually bring out the context of an email. Taking into account the context of messages or emails allowed researchers of *Yahoo* and *Amazon* Avigdor-Elgrabli et al. (2018) to automatically evaluate the semantic relationship between messages within a mailbox.

Regarding conversation disentanglement, Elsner and Charniak (2010) and Elsner and Charniak (2011) approach chat disentanglement by first using binary classifier and local Coherence Models one year later. Jiang et al. (2018) take advantage of learning language representations to disentangle conversations. compute similarities between messages using a model they name ***Siamese Hierarchical Convolutional Neural Network (SHCNN)*** which is a Siamese hierarchical convolutional network.

SegBot was developed by Li et al. (2018) to propose a solution to the problem of text segmentation.

Koshorek et al. (2018) address text segmentation as a supervised learning problem and present a large dataset for this problem. Dialog acts identification could be seen as determining interlocutors intentions within a conversation. Wang et al. (2019) study the identification of intentions in emails in a workplace situation.

All these work give us some leads of experience to be carried out very soon with our data in order to approach our problem of threads constitution.

6 Conclusion

In this paper, we presented a method for building corporate corpora including different aspects and steps which allowed the creation of a pipeline to pseudo-anonymise data. Such a pipeline is a response to the constraints induced by the GDPR and the secrecy of correspondence compliance.

The process we described consists of several steps: first we prospected with our collaborators to obtain their consent agreement, this in order to be GDPR and secrecy of correspondence compliant; second we collected and pre-processed emails from Outlook mailboxes; the third step dealt with manual annotation and Named Entities Recognition; fourth, we performed data pseudo-anonymization. During the second step, we developed a tool called OutlookScraping that allowed us to collect a first batch of 11k emails on the workstations of 4 close collaborators out of 78 collaborators who gave their consent agreement.

All these steps contributed to the production of pseudo-anonymized data that we will use for our future work of thread constitution. For our constitution of threads problem, we will focus on conversations disentanglement, dialog acts identification and text segmentation.

References

Noa Avigdor-Elgrabli, Roei Gelbhart, Irena Grabovitch-Zuyev, and Ariel Raviv. 2018. More than threads: Identifying related email messages. CIKM '18, page 1711–1714, New York, NY, USA. Association for Computing Machinery.

Janek Bevendorff, Khalid Al Khatib, Martin Potthast, and Benno Stein. 2020. Crawling and preprocessing mailing lists at scale for dialog analysis. In *Proceedings of the 58th Annual Meeting of the Association for Computational Linguistics*, pages 1151–1158, Online. Association for Computational Linguistics.

Mihaela Bornea, Lin Pan, Sara Rosenthal, Radu Florian, and Avirup Sil. 2020. Multilingual transfer learning for qa using translation as data augmentation.

Alex Brandsen, Suzan Verberne, Milco Wansleeben, and Karsten Lambers. 2020. Creating a dataset for named entity recognition in the archaeology domain. In *Proceedings of the 12th Language Resources and Evaluation Conference*, pages 4573–4577, Marseille, France. European Language Resources Association.

Vitor R. Carvalho and William W. Cohen. 2004. Learning to extract signature and reply lines from email. In *IN PROCEEDINGS OF THE CONFERENCE ON EMAIL AND ANTI-SPAM*.

Ann Cavoukian. 2010. Privacy by design: The definitive workshop. a foreword by ann cavoukian, ph.d. *Identity in the Information Society*, 3(2):247–251.

Thierry Chanier, Céline Poudat, Benoît Sagot, Georges Antoniadis, Ciara R. Wigham, Linda Hriba, Julien Longhi, and Djamé Seddah. 2014. The CoMeRe corpus for French: structuring and annotating heterogeneous CMC genres. *Journal for language technology and computational linguistics*, 29(2):1–30. Final version to Special Issue of JLCL (Journal of Language Technology and Computational Linguistics (JLCL, http://jlcl.org/): BUILDING AND ANNOTATING CORPORA OF COMPUTER-MEDIATED DISCOURSE: Issues and Challenges at the Interface of Corpus and Computational Linguistics (ed. by Michael Beißwenger, Nelleke Oostdijk, Angelika Storrer & Henk van den Heuvel).

Niyati Chhaya, Kushal Chawla, Tanya Goyal, Projjal Chanda, and Jaya Singh. 2018. Frustrated, polite, or formal: Quantifying feelings and tone in email. In *Proceedings of the Second Workshop on Computational Modeling of People's Opinions, Personality, and Emotions in Social Media*, pages 76–86, New Orleans, Louisiana, USA. Association for Computational Linguistics.

Giacomo Domeniconi, Konstantinos Semertzidis, Vanessa Lopez, Elizabeth M. Daly, Spyros Kotoulas, and Gianluca Moro. 2016. A novel method for unsupervised and supervised conversational message thread detection. In *Proceedings of the 5th International Conference on Data Management Technologies and Applications*, DATA 2016, page 43–54, Setubal, PRT. SCITEPRESS - Science and Technology Publications, Lda.

Oard Douglas, Webber William, A. Kirsch David, and Golitsynskiy Sergey. 2015. Avocado research email collection. Linguistic Data Consortium (LDC).

Micha Elsner and Eugene Charniak. 2010. Disentangling chat. *Computational Linguistics*, 36(3):389–409.

Micha Elsner and Eugene Charniak. 2011. Disentangling chat with local coherence models. In *Proceedings of the 49th Annual Meeting of the Association for Computational Linguistics: Human Language Technologies*, pages 1179–1189, Portland, Oregon, USA. Association for Computational Linguistics.

Dominique Estival, Tanja Gaustad, Ben Hutchinson, Son Bao Pham, and Will Radford. 2007. Author profiling for english emails. In *In Proceedings of the 10th Conference of the Pacific Association for Computational Linguistics*, pages 263–272.

Cyril Grouin, Sophie Rosset, Pierre Zweigenbaum, Karën Fort, Olivier Galibert, and Ludovic Quintard. 2011. Proposal for an extension of traditional named entities: From guidelines to evaluation, an overview. In *Proceedings of the 5th Linguistic Annotation Workshop*, pages 92–100, Portland, Oregon, USA. Association for Computational Linguistics.

Dara Hallinan and Frederik Zuiderveen Borgesius. 2020. Opinions can be incorrect (in our opinion)! On data protection law's accuracy principle. *International Data Privacy Law*, 10(1):1–10.

G. Hripcsak and A. S. Rothschild. 2005. Agreement, the f-measure, and reliability in information retrieval. *J Am Med Inform Assoc*, 12(3):296–298.

Jyun-Yu Jiang, Francine Chen, Yan-Ying Chen, and Wei Wang. 2018. Learning to disentangle interleaved conversational threads with a Siamese hierarchical network and similarity ranking. In *Proceedings of the 2018 Conference of the North American Chapter of the Association for Computational Linguistics: Human Language Technologies, Volume 1 (Long Papers)*, pages 1812–1822, New Orleans, Louisiana. Association for Computational Linguistics.

Thorsten Joachims. 2001. A statistical learning learning model of text classification for support vector machines. In *Proceedings of the 24th Annual International ACM SIGIR Conference on Research and Development in Information Retrieval*, SIGIR '01, page 128–136, New York, NY, USA. Association for Computing Machinery.

Bryan Klimt and Yiming Yang. 2004. The enron corpus: A new dataset for email classification research. In *Machine Learning: ECML 2004*, pages 217–226, Berlin, Heidelberg. Springer Berlin Heidelberg.

Omri Koshorek, Adir Cohen, Noam Mor, Michael Rotman, and Jonathan Berant. 2018. Text segmentation as a supervised learning task.

Jonathan K. Kummerfeld, Sai R. Gouravajhala, Joseph J. Peper, Vignesh Athreya, Chulaka Gunasekara, Jatin Ganhotra, Siva Sankalp Patel, Lazaros C Polymenakos, and Walter Lasecki. 2019. A large-scale corpus for conversation disentanglement. In *Proceedings of the 57th Annual Meeting of the Association for Computational Linguistics*, pages 3846–3856, Florence, Italy. Association for Computational Linguistics.

Jing Li, Aixin Sun, and Shafiq Joty. 2018. Segbot: A generic neural text segmentation model with pointer network. In *Proceedings of the Twenty-Seventh International Joint Conference on Artificial Intelligence, IJCAI-18*, pages 4166–4172. International Joint Conferences on Artificial Intelligence Organization.

M. L. McHugh. 2012. Interrater reliability: the kappa statistic. *Biochem Med (Zagreb)*, 22(3):276–282.

Einat Minkov, Richard C. Wang, and William W. Cohen. 2005. Extracting personal names from email: Applying named entity recognition to informal text. In *Proceedings of Human Language Technology Conference and Conference on Empirical Methods in Natural Language Processing*, pages 443–450, Vancouver, British Columbia, Canada. Association for Computational Linguistics.

Pedro Javier Ortiz Suárez, Yoann Dupont, Benjamin Muller, Laurent Romary, and Benoît Sagot. 2020. Establishing a new state-of-the-art for French named entity recognition. In *Proceedings of the 12th Language Resources and Evaluation Conference*, pages 4631–4638, Marseille, France. European Language Resources Association.

Kelly Peterson, Matt Hohensee, and Fei Xia. 2011. Email formality in the workplace: A case study on the Enron corpus. In *Proceedings of the Workshop on Language in Social Media (LSM 2011)*, pages 86–95, Portland, Oregon. Association for Computational Linguistics.

Pengzhen Ren, Yun Xiao, Xiaojun Chang, Po-Yao Huang, Zhihui Li, Xiaojiang Chen, and Xin Wang. 2020. A survey of deep active learning.

A. Viera and J. Garrett. 2005. Understanding interobserver agreement: the kappa statistic. *Family medicine*, 37 5:360–3.

Wei Wang, Saghar Hosseini, Ahmed Hassan Awadallah, Paul N. Bennett, and Chris Quirk. 2019. Context-aware intent identification in email conversations. In *Proceedings of the 42nd International ACM SIGIR Conference on Research and Development in Information Retrieval*, SIGIR'19, page 585–594, New York, NY, USA. Association for Computing Machinery.

Antonia Zapf, Stefanie Castell, Lars Morawietz, and André Karch. 2016. Measuring inter-rater reliability for nominal data – which coefficients and confidence intervals are appropriate? *BMC Medical Research Methodology*, 16(1).

Shanshan Zhang, Lihong He, Slobodan Vucetic, and Eduard Dragut. 2018. Regular expression guided entity mention mining from noisy web data. In *Proceedings of the 2018 Conference on Empirical Methods in Natural Language Processing*, pages 1991–2000, Brussels, Belgium. Association for Computational Linguistics.

Generating Answer Candidates for Quizzes and Answer-Aware Question Generators

Kristiyan Vachev
FMI, Sofia University
"St. Kliment Ohridski"
Sofia, Bulgaria
vachevkd@gmail.com

Momchil Hardalov
FMI, Sofia University
"St. Kliment Ohridski"
Sofia, Bulgaria
hardalov@fmi.uni-sofia.bg

Georgi Karadzhov
Department of Computer Science and Technology
University of Cambridge, UK
gmk34@cam.ac.uk

Georgi Georgiev
Releva AI
Sofia, Bulgaria
georgi@releva.ai

Ivan Koychev
FMI and GATE
Sofia University
Sofia, Bulgaria
koychev@fmi.uni-sofia.bg

Preslav Nakov
Qatar Computing Research Institute
HBKU
Doha, Qatar
pnakov@hbku.edu.qa

Abstract

In education, quiz questions have become an important tool for assessing the knowledge of students. Yet, manually preparing such questions is a tedious task, and thus automatic question generation has been proposed as a possible alternative. So far, the vast majority of research has focused on generating the question text, relying on question answering datasets with readily picked answers, and the problem of how to come up with answer candidates in the first place has been largely ignored. Here, we aim to bridge this gap. In particular, we propose a model that can generate a specified number of answer candidates for a given passage of text, which can then be used by instructors to write questions manually or can be passed as an input to automatic answer-aware question generators. Our experiments show that our proposed answer candidate generation model outperforms several baselines.

1 Introduction

Testing with quiz questions can help both learning and retention, e.g., it could be used for self-study or as a way to detect knowledge gaps in a classroom setting, thus allowing instructors to adapt their teaching (Roediger III et al., 2011).

As creating such quiz questions is a tedious job, automatic methods have been proposed. The task is often formulated as an answer-aware question generation (Heilman and Smith, 2010; Zhang et al., 2014; Du et al., 2017; Du and Cardie, 2018; Sun et al., 2018; Dong et al., 2019; Bao et al., 2020; CH and Saha, 2020): given an input text and a target answer, generate a corresponding question.

Context: *One of the most famous people born in Warsaw was* ***Maria Skłodowska-Curie****, who achieved international recognition for her research on radioactivity and was the first female recipient of the* ***Nobel Prize****.* ***Famous musicians*** *include Władysław Szpilman and Frédéric Chopin. Though Chopin was born in the village of Żelazowa Wola, about 60 km (37 mi) from Warsaw, he moved to the city with his family when he was* ***seven months old****. Casimir Pulaski, a Polish general and hero of the American Revolutionary War, was born here in* ***1745****.*

Q1: *What was Maria Curie the first female recipient of?*
A1: *Nobel Prize*

Q2: *What year was Casimir Pulaski born in Warsaw?*
A2: *1745*

Q3: *How old was Chopin when he moved to Warsaw with his family?*
A3: *seven months old*

Figure 1: Example passage from the SQuAD1.1 dataset showing three of the questions created by humans and all answers to those and other questions in bold.

Many researchers have used the Stanford Question Answering Dataset (SQuAD1.1) dataset (Rajpurkar et al., 2016) as a source of training and testing data for answer-aware question generation. It contains human-generated questions and answers about articles in Wikipedia, as shown in Figure 1.

Proceedings of the Student Research Workshop associated with RANLP-2021, pages 203–209,
held online, Sep 1–3, 2021.
https://doi.org/10.26615/issn.2603-2821.2021_028

However, this formulation requires that answers be picked beforehand, which may not be practical for real-world situations. Here we aim to address this limitation by proposing a method for generating answers, which can in turn serve as an input to answer-aware question generation models. Our model combines orthographic, lexical, syntactic, and semantic information, and shows promising results. It further allows the user to specify the number of answer to propose. Our contributions can be summarized as follows:

- We propose a new task: generate answer candidates that can serve as an input to answer-aware question generation models.
- We create a dataset for this new task.
- We propose a suitable model for the task, which combines orthographic, lexical, syntactic, and semantic information, and can generate a pre-specified number of answers.
- We demonstrate improvements over simple approaches based on named entities, and competitiveness over complex neural models.

2 Related Work

The success of large-scale pre-trained Transformers such as BERT (Devlin et al., 2019), RoBERTa (Liu et al., 2019), ALBERT (Lan et al., 2020), and generative ones such as T5 (Raffel et al., 2020) or BART (Lewis et al., 2020), has led to the rise in popularity of the Question Generation task. Models such as BERT (Devlin et al., 2019), T5 (Raffel et al., 2020) and PEGASUS (Zhang et al., 2020) have been used to generate questions for the SQuAD1.1 dataset and have been commonly evaluated (Du et al., 2017) using BLEU (Papineni et al., 2002), ROUGE (Lin, 2004), and METEOR (Lavie and Agarwal, 2007). Strong models for this task include NQG++ (Zhou et al., 2017), ProphetNet (Qi et al., 2020), MPQG (Song et al., 2018), UniLM (Dong et al., 2019), UniLMv2 (Bao et al., 2020), and ERNIE-GEN (Xiao et al., 2020).

All these models were trained for answer-aware question generation, which takes the answer and the textual context as an input and outputs a question for that answer. In contrast, our task formulation takes a textual context as an input and generates possible answers; in turn, these answers can be used as an input to the above answer-aware question generation models.

The Quiz-Style Question Generation for News Stories task (Lelkes et al., 2021) uses a formulation that asks to generate a single question as well as the corresponding answer, which is to be extracted from the given context.

Follow-up research has tried to avoid the limitation of generating a single question or a single question–answer pair by generating a question for each sentence in the input context or by using all named entities in the context as answer keys (Montgomerie, 2020).

Finally, there has been a proliferation of educational datasets in recent years (Zeng et al., 2020; Dzendzik et al., 2021; Rogers et al., 2021), which includes Crowdsourcing (Welbl et al., 2017), ARC (Clark et al., 2018), OpenBookQA (Mihaylov et al., 2018), multiple-choice exams in Bulgarian (Hardalov et al., 2019), Vietnamese (Nguyen et al., 2020), and EXAMS, which covers 16 different languages (Hardalov et al., 2020). Yet, these datasets are not directly applicable for our task as their questions do not expect the answers to be exact matches from the textual context. While there are also span-based extraction datasets such as NewsQA (Trischler et al., 2017), SearchQA (Dunn et al., 2017) and Natural Questions: A Benchmark for Question Answering Research (Kwiatkowski et al., 2019) they contains a mix of long and short spans rather than factoid answers. Thus, we opted to use SQuAD1.1 in our experiments, but focusing on generating answers rather than on questions.

3 Method

Given an input textual context, we first extract phrases from it, then we calculate a representation for each phrase, and finally, we predict which phrases are appropriate of being an answer to a quiz question based on these representations.

3.1 Data

To train our classifier, we need a labeled dataset of key phrases. In particular, we use SQuAD1.1, which consists of more than 100,000 questions created by humans from Wikipedia articles, and was extensively used for question answering. An example is shown in Figure 1. We use version 1.1 of the dataset instead of 2.0 (Rajpurkar et al., 2018) because it contains the exact position of the answers in the text, which allows us to easily match them against the candidate phrases. Version 2.0 only adds examples whose answer is not present.

We created a dataset for our task using 87,600 questions from the SQuAD1.1 training set and their associated textual contexts. Because only 33% of the answers consisted of one word, it is important to also extract phrases longer than a single word. Thus, we also added all named entities; note that they have a variable word length. We further included all noun chunks, which we then extended by combining two or more noun chunks if the only words between them were connectors like *and*, *of*, and *or*. Here is an example of a complex chunk with three pieces: *a Marian place* ***of*** *prayer* ***and*** *reflection*. We considered as positive examples the phrases for which there was a question asked in the SQuAD1.1 dataset, and we considered as negative examples the additional phrases we created.

3.2 Features

We extracted the following features, adapted for the use of phrases containing multiple words:

TFIDFArticle, **TFIDFParagraph**: The average TF.IDF score for all words in the key phrase, where the Inverse Document Frequency (IDF) is computed from the words in all paragraphs of the article (*TFIDFArticle*) or only from the paragraph of the given key phrase (*TFIDFParagraph*).

TitleSimilarity: The average cosine similarity between the vectors of the words in the key phrase and the article title.

POS, **TAG**, **DEP**: The coarse-grained part-of-speech tag (*POS*), the fine-grained part-of-speech tag (*TAG*), and the syntactic dependency relation (*DEP*). If the phrase contains multiple words, we only consider the word with the highest TF.IDF.

EntityType: The named entity type of the phrase if any.

IsAlpha: True if all characters in the phrase are alphabetic.

IsAscii: True if the phrase consists only of characters contained in the standard ASCII table.

IsDigit: True if the phrase only contains digits.

IsLower: True if all words in the phrase are in lowercase.

IsCapital: True if the first word in the phrase is in uppercase.

IsCurrency: True if some word in the phrase contains a currency symbol, e.g., *$23*.

LikeNum: True if some word in the phrase represents a number, e.g., *13.4*, *42*, *twenty*, etc.

3.3 Model

We convert all the above features to binary, and then we use a Bernoulli Naïve Bayes classifier, which can account both for the presence and for the absence of a feature. To achieve this, we encode categorical features (e.g., *POS*, *TAG*) using one-hot encoding, and we put continuous features (e.g., *TFIDFArticle*, *TitleSimilarity*) into bins of five.

3.4 Evaluation Measures

As there is no established measure for evaluating key phrases for answer generation, we use and adapt the original evaluation script[1] created for the Question Answering task on the SQuAD1.1 dataset (Rajpurkar et al., 2016), which calculates an exact match (*EM*) and the harmonic mean of precision and recall (*F1*).

In the SQuAD1.1 dataset, there can be multiple correct versions of the answer for a question (e.g., *third*, *third-most*). Thus, the evaluation script calculates EM and F1 for each such version and then returns the highest value. As there can be also multiple question–answer pairs in a given passage, we further adapted the script to include all human-created answers, we calculated these scores against all answers in the passage, and finally, we took the highest values.

Finally, in order to allow for a more practical use of question generation algorithms, it is desirable to be able to generate multiple question–answer pairs for a given passage. To compute EM and F1 over multiple answer candidates, we adopted the following two approaches:

EM-Any and **F1-Any** show how likely it is to pick a ground-truth answer (also, how likely it is to be chosen by a human annotator of SQuAD1.1) out of N returned candidate answers. To calculate them, we took only the best EM and F1 scores after computing all scores for each candidate answer.

Using **EM-Avg** and **F1-Avg**, we can measure what percentage of all returned candidate answers have also been marked as an answer by a human. To calculate them, we took the average of all EM and F1 scores computed for the proposed candidate answers.

The results for the SQuAD1.1 development split, which consists of 2,067 unique passages, are shown in Table 1 and Table 2.

[1] `http://github.com/allenai/bi-att-flow/blob/master/squad/evaluate-v1.1.py`

4 Experiments and Evaluation

We used our model to generate ten candidate answers per passage (taking the ones with the highest classifier confidence), and we compared the results to other commonly used methods.

4.1 Baselines

Below, we list the baselines that we compared against:

- **NER:** Extracting all named entities from the passage and using them as candidate answers. On average, there are 13.64 named entities per SQuAD1.1 passage.
- **Noun Chunks:** Extracting all noun chunks from the passage and using them as candidate answers. On average, there are 33.15 noun chunks per SQuAD1.1 passage.
- **NE + NCh:** Combining all extracted named entities and noun chunks from the passage after using the SQuAD1.1 normalization script[2] to remove duplicate words (e.g., *the third* matches *third*).
- **T5-small:** We fine-tuned the small version of T5, which has 220M parameters. We trained the model to accept the passage as an input and to output the answer. We used a learning rate of 0.0001, a source token length of 300, and a target token length of 24. The best validation loss was achieved in the forth out of ten epochs.

4.2 Results

In this section, we describe our experimental results and we compare them to the baselines described in Section 4.1 above.

4.2.1 Best Over Multiple Candidates

Table 1 shows the results for EM-Any and F1-Any, i.e., how often, among the top-N candidates by the model, at least one was picked by a human.

We can see that, compared to using named entities, our model achieves a better EM-Any score with just eight answer candidates rather than using all named entities in the passage (which are 13.6 on average). It also achieves a higher F1-Any score with just six answer candidates.

Method	Answers	EM-Any	F1-Any
Our Model	1	29.63	38.80
	2	42.50	55.47
	3	52.92	66.83
	4	59.67	73.92
	5	65.50	79.11
	6	69.33	82.50
	7	72.90	85.58
	8	**75.43**	**87.70**
	9	77.66	89.20
	10	79.17	90.32
NER	**13.6**	**74.36**	**82.12**
NCh	33.2	86.79	95.90
NER + NCh	35.4	95.02	98.48
T5-small	1	37.56	49.16

Table 1: **Best over multiple candidates (EM-Any and F1-Any).** Measuring how often, among the top-N candidates proposed by the model, at least one was picked by a human.

Method	Answers	EM-Avg	F1-Avg
Our Model	1	**29.63**	**38.80**
	2	25.58	36.03
	3	24.18	35.15
	4	22.74	34.15
	5	22.07	33.65
	6	20.90	32.81
	7	20.02	32.05
	8	19.25	31.43
	9	18.45	30.57
	10	17.64	29.75
NER	13.6	16.33	25.24
NCh	33.2	7.86	17.75
NER + NCh	35.4	8.97	18.84
T5-small	1	**37.56**	**49.16**

Table 2: **Average over multiple candidates (EM-Avg, F1-Avg).** Measuring what percentage of the proposed answers were also selected as an answer by a human.

We further see that using the combination of all named entities and noun chunks yields the best score, but it produces 35 candidates on average, which is the majority of the words in the passage.

4.2.2 Average Over Multiple Candidates

Table 2 shows the results for EM-Avg and F1-Avg, i.e., measuring what percentage of the proposed answers were also selected as an answer by a human.

[2] `http://github.com/allenai/bi-att-flow/blob/master/squad/evaluate-v1.1.py#L11`

Due to the ability of the classifier to take a lower number of candidate questions, we can see that it outperforms taking all named entities or all noun chunks by a sizable margin.

We further see that the average scores consistently drop with the increase of the number of answer candidates. This also explains the lower scores of the named entity and noun chunks approaches as they produce much longer lists of candidate answers.

4.2.3 Single Answer Candidate

Finally, we see in both tables, that the T5 model achieves the highest average result. However, in our setup it cannot produce multiple candidates. We plan to extend it accordingly in future work.

5 Discussion

Figure 2 shows a passage from the development split of the SQuAD1.1 dataset and the top-10 answers that our model proposed for it. We can see that these answers represent a diverse set, including named entities, noun chunks, and individual words. Indeed, this is a typical example, as our analysis across the entire development dataset shows that on average, among the top-10 candidates, our model proposes 4.82 named entities and 6.40 noun chunks.

Note also that our evaluation setup could be unfair to the model in some cases, e.g., if the model proposes a good candidate answer but one that was not chosen by the human annotators, it would receive no credit for it.

Finally, note that our model can produce top-N results for user-defined values of N, which is an advantage over simple baselines based on entities or chunks, as well as over our setup for T5.

Context: *Oxygen is a chemical element with symbol O and atomic number 8. It is a member of the chalcogen group on the periodic table and is a highly reactive nonmetal and oxidizing agent that readily forms compounds (notably oxides) with most elements. By mass, oxygen is the third-most abundant element in the universe, after hydrogen and helium. At standard temperature and pressure, two atoms of the element bind to form dioxygen, a colorless and odorless diatomic gas with the formula O2. Diatomic oxygen gas constitutes 20.8% of the Earth's atmosphere. However, monitoring of atmospheric oxygen levels show a global downward trend, because of fossil-fuel burning. Oxygen is the most abundant element by mass in the Earth's crust as part of oxide compounds such as silicon dioxide, making up almost half of the crust's mass.*

Top 10 answers:

1. 8
2. 20.8 % of the Earth 's atmosphere
3. Oxygen
4. a member of the chalcogen group
5. Diatomic oxygen gas
6. almost half
7. O
8. two atoms of the element
9. the formula O2
10. fossil-fuel burning

Figure 2: The top-10 answer candidates generated by our model for a sample passage from SQuAD1.1. The human-selected ground truth answers are underlined, and the answer candidates are shown in brown.

6 Conclusion and Future Work

We proposed a new task: generate answer candidates that can serve as an input to answer-aware question generation models. We further created a dataset for this new task. Moreover, we proposed a suitable model for the task, which combines orthographic, lexical, syntactic, and semantic information, and can generate a pre-specified number of answers. Finally, we demonstrated improvements over simple approaches based on named entities, and competitiveness over complex, computationally expensive neural network models such as T5.

In future work, we plan to analyze and to improve the features. We also want to extend T5 to generate multiple candidates. We further plan to reduce the impact of false negatives, e.g., by means of manual evaluation by domain experts, and eventually by producing datasets with (potentially ranked) annotations of all suitable candidate answers.

Acknowledgments

This research is partially funded via Project UNITe by the OP "Science and Education for Smart Growth" and co-funded by the EU through the ESI Funds under GA No. BG05M2OP001-1.001-0004.

References

Hangbo Bao, Li Dong, Furu Wei, Wenhui Wang, Nan Yang, Xiaodong Liu, Yu Wang, Jianfeng Gao, Songhao Piao, Ming Zhou, and Hsiao-Wuen Hon. 2020. Unilmv2: Pseudo-masked language models for unified language model pre-training. In *Proceedings of the 37th International Conference on Machine Learning*, volume 119 of *Proceedings of Machine Learning Research*, pages 642–652.

Dhawaleswar Rao CH and Sujan Kumar Saha. 2020. Automatic multiple choice question generation from text: A survey. *IEEE Transactions on Learning Technologies*, 13(1):14–25.

Peter Clark, Isaac Cowhey, Oren Etzioni, Tushar Khot, Ashish Sabharwal, Carissa Schoenick, and Oyvind Tafjord. 2018. Think you have solved question answering? Try ARC, the AI2 reasoning challenge. *arXiv:1803.05457*.

Jacob Devlin, Ming-Wei Chang, Kenton Lee, and Kristina Toutanova. 2019. BERT: Pre-training of deep bidirectional transformers for language understanding. In *Proceedings of the 2019 Conference of the North American Chapter of the Association for Computational Linguistics: Human Language Technologies*, NAACL-HLT '19, pages 4171–4186, Minneapolis, Minnesota, USA.

Li Dong, Nan Yang, Wenhui Wang, Furu Wei, Xiaodong Liu, Yu Wang, Jianfeng Gao, Ming Zhou, and Hsiao-Wuen Hon. 2019. Unified language model pre-training for natural language understanding and generation. In *Advances in Neural Information Processing Systems 32: Annual Conference on Neural Information Processing Systems 2019*, NeurIPS '19, pages 13042–13054, Vancouver, BC, Canada.

Xinya Du and Claire Cardie. 2018. Harvesting paragraph-level question-answer pairs from Wikipedia. In *Proceedings of the 56th Annual Meeting of the Association for Computational Linguistics*, ACL '18, pages 1907–1917, Melbourne, Australia.

Xinya Du, Junru Shao, and Claire Cardie. 2017. Learning to ask: Neural question generation for reading comprehension. In *Proceedings of the 55th Annual Meeting of the Association for Computational Linguistics*, ACL '17, pages 1342–1352, Vancouver, Canada.

Matthew Dunn, Levent Sagun, Mike Higgins, V. Ugur Guney, Volkan Cirik, and Kyunghyun Cho. 2017. SearchQA: A new Q&A dataset augmented with context from a search engine. *arXiv:1704.05179*.

Daria Dzendzik, Carl Vogel, and Jennifer Foster. 2021. English machine reading comprehension datasets: A survey. *arXiv:2101.10421*.

Momchil Hardalov, Ivan Koychev, and Preslav Nakov. 2019. Beyond English-only reading comprehension: Experiments in zero-shot multilingual transfer for Bulgarian. In *Proceedings of the International Conference on Recent Advances in Natural Language Processing*, RANLP '19, pages 447–459, Varna, Bulgaria.

Momchil Hardalov, Todor Mihaylov, Dimitrina Zlatkova, Yoan Dinkov, Ivan Koychev, and Preslav Nakov. 2020. EXAMS: A multi-subject high school examinations dataset for cross-lingual and multilingual question answering. In *Proceedings of the 2020 Conference on Empirical Methods in Natural Language Processing*, EMNLP '20, pages 5427–5444, Online.

Michael Heilman and Noah A. Smith. 2010. Good question! statistical ranking for question generation. In *Human Language Technologies: The 2010 Annual Conference of the North American Chapter of the Association for Computational Linguistics*, NAACL-HLT '10, pages 609–617, Los Angeles, California, USA. Association for Computational Linguistics.

Tom Kwiatkowski, Jennimaria Palomaki, Olivia Redfield, Michael Collins, Ankur Parikh, Chris Alberti, Danielle Epstein, Illia Polosukhin, Jacob Devlin, Kenton Lee, Kristina Toutanova, Llion Jones, Matthew Kelcey, Ming-Wei Chang, Andrew M. Dai, Jakob Uszkoreit, Quoc Le, and Slav Petrov. 2019. Natural questions: A benchmark for question answering research. *Transactions of the Association for Computational Linguistics*, 7:452–466.

Zhenzhong Lan, Mingda Chen, Sebastian Goodman, Kevin Gimpel, Piyush Sharma, and Radu Soricut. 2020. ALBERT: A lite BERT for self-supervised learning of language representations. In *Proceedigs of the 8th International Conference on Learning Representations*, ICLR '20, Addis Ababa, Ethiopia.

Alon Lavie and Abhaya Agarwal. 2007. METEOR: An automatic metric for MT evaluation with high levels of correlation with human judgments. In *Proceedings of the Second Workshop on Statistical Machine Translation*, WMT '07, pages 228–231, Prague, Czech Republic.

Adam D. Lelkes, Vinh Q. Tran, and Cong Yu. 2021. Quiz-style question generation for news stories. In *Proceedings of the Web Conference 2021*, WWW '21, pages 2501–2511.

Mike Lewis, Yinhan Liu, Naman Goyal, Marjan Ghazvininejad, Abdelrahman Mohamed, Omer Levy, Veselin Stoyanov, and Luke Zettlemoyer. 2020. BART: Denoising sequence-to-sequence pretraining for natural language generation, translation, and comprehension. In *Proceedings of the 58th Annual Meeting of the Association for Computational Linguistics*, ACL '20, pages 7871–7880.

Chin-Yew Lin. 2004. ROUGE: A package for automatic evaluation of summaries. In *Proceedigs of the Workshop on Text Summarization Branches Out*, pages 74–81, Barcelona, Spain.

Yinhan Liu, Myle Ott, Naman Goyal, Jingfei Du, Mandar Joshi, Danqi Chen, Omer Levy, Mike Lewis, Luke Zettlemoyer, and Veselin Stoyanov. 2019. RoBERTa: A robustly optimized BERT pretraining approach. *arXiv:1907.11692*.

Todor Mihaylov, Peter Clark, Tushar Khot, and Ashish Sabharwal. 2018. Can a suit of armor conduct electricity? A new dataset for open book question answering. In *Proceedings of the 2018 Conference on Empirical Methods in Natural Language Processing*, EMNLP '18, pages 2381–2391, Brussels, Belgium.

Adam Montgomerie. 2020. Question generator. `https://github.com/AMontgomerie/question_generator`.

Kiet Van Nguyen, Khiem Vinh Tran, Son T. Luu, Anh Gia-Tuan Nguyen, and Ngan Luu-Thuy Nguyen. 2020. Enhancing lexical-based approach with external knowledge for Vietnamese multiple-choice machine reading comprehension. *IEEE Access*, 8:201404–201417.

Kishore Papineni, Salim Roukos, Todd Ward, and Wei-Jing Zhu. 2002. Bleu: a method for automatic evaluation of machine translation. In *Proceedings of the 40th Annual Meeting of the Association for Computational Linguistics*, ACL '02, pages 311–318, Philadelphia, Pennsylvania, USA.

Weizhen Qi, Yu Yan, Yeyun Gong, Dayiheng Liu, Nan Duan, Jiusheng Chen, Ruofei Zhang, and Ming Zhou. 2020. ProphetNet: Predicting future n-gram for sequence-to-SequencePre-training. In *Findings of the Association for Computational Linguistics: EMNLP 2020*, pages 2401–2410.

Colin Raffel, Noam Shazeer, Adam Roberts, Katherine Lee, Sharan Narang, Michael Matena, Yanqi Zhou, Wei Li, and Peter J. Liu. 2020. Exploring the limits of transfer learning with a unified text-to-text transformer. *arXiv:1910.10683*.

Pranav Rajpurkar, Robin Jia, and Percy Liang. 2018. Know what you don't know: Unanswerable questions for SQuAD. In *Proceedings of the 56th Annual Meeting of the Association for Computational Linguistics*, ACL '18, pages 784–789, Melbourne, Australia.

Pranav Rajpurkar, Jian Zhang, Konstantin Lopyrev, and Percy Liang. 2016. SQuAD: 100,000+ questions for machine comprehension of text. In *Proceedings of the 2016 Conference on Empirical Methods in Natural Language Processing*, EMNLP '16, pages 2383–2392, Austin, Texas.

Henry L. Roediger III, Adam L. Putnam, and Megan A. Smith. 2011. Chapter one - ten benefits of testing and their applications to educational practice. In Jose P. Mestre and Brian H. Ross, editors, *Psychology of Learning and Motivation*, volume 55, pages 1–36. Academic Press.

Anna Rogers, Matt Gardner, and Isabelle Augenstein. 2021. QA dataset explosion: A taxonomy of NLP resources for question answering and reading comprehension. *arXiv:2107.12708*.

Linfeng Song, Zhiguo Wang, Wael Hamza, Yue Zhang, and Daniel Gildea. 2018. Leveraging context information for natural question generation. In *Proceedings of the 2018 Conference of the North American Chapter of the Association for Computational Linguistics: Human Language Technologies*, NAACL-HLT '18, pages 569–574, New Orleans, Louisiana, USA.

Xingwu Sun, Jing Liu, Yajuan Lyu, Wei He, Yanjun Ma, and Shi Wang. 2018. Answer-focused and position-aware neural question generation. In *Proceedings of the 2018 Conference on Empirical Methods in Natural Language Processing*, EMNLP '18, pages 3930–3939, Brussels, Belgium.

Adam Trischler, Tong Wang, Xingdi Yuan, Justin Harris, Alessandro Sordoni, Philip Bachman, and Kaheer Suleman. 2017. NewsQA: A machine comprehension dataset. In *Proceedings of the 2nd Workshop on Representation Learning for NLP*, RepL4NLP '17, pages 191–200, Vancouver, Canada.

Johannes Welbl, Nelson F. Liu, and Matt Gardner. 2017. Crowdsourcing multiple choice science questions. In *Proceedings of the 3rd Workshop on Noisy User-generated Text*, W-NUT '17, pages 94–106, Copenhagen, Denmark.

Dongling Xiao, Han Zhang, Yu-Kun Li, Yu Sun, Hao Tian, Hua Wu, and Haifeng Wang. 2020. ERNIE-GEN: an enhanced multi-flow pre-training and fine-tuning framework for natural language generation. In *Proceedings of the Twenty-Ninth International Joint Conference on Artificial Intelligence*, IJCAI '20, pages 3997–4003.

Changchang Zeng, Shaobo Li, Qin Li, Jie Hu, and Jianjun Hu. 2020. A survey on machine reading comprehension—tasks, evaluation metrics and benchmark datasets. *Applied Sciences*, 10(21).

Jingqing Zhang, Yao Zhao, Mohammad Saleh, and Peter J. Liu. 2020. PEGASUS: Pre-training with extracted gap-sentences for abstractive summarization. In *Proceedings of the 37th International Conference on Machine Learning*, ICML '20, pages 11328–11339.

Kai Zhang, Wei Wu, Haocheng Wu, Zhoujun Li, and Ming Zhou. 2014. Question retrieval with high quality answers in community question answering. In *Proceedings of the 23rd ACM International Conference on Conference on Information and Knowledge Management*, CIKM '14, page 371–380, Shanghai, China.

Qingyu Zhou, Nan Yang, Furu Wei, Chuanqi Tan, Hangbo Bao, and Ming Zhou. 2017. Neural question generation from text: A preliminary study. *arXiv:1704.01792*.

Toward Discourse-Aware Models for Multilingual Fake News Detection

Francielle Vargas[1 2], Fabrício Benevenuto[2], Thiago A. S. Pardo[1]
[1]Interinstitutional Center for Computational Linguistics, University of São Paulo, Brazil
[2]Social Computing Laboratory, Federal University of Minas Gerais, Brazil
francielleavargas@usp.br
fabricio@dcc.ufmg.br taspardo@icmc.usp.br

Abstract

Statements that are intentionally misstated (or manipulated) are of considerable interest to researchers, government, security, and financial systems. According to deception literature, there are reliable cues for detecting deception and the belief that liars give off cues that may indicate their deception is near-universal. Therefore, given that deceiving actions require advanced cognitive development that honesty simply does not require, as well as people's cognitive mechanisms have promising guidance for deception detection, in this Ph.D. ongoing research, we propose to examine discourse structure patterns in multilingual deceptive news corpora using the Rhetorical Structure Theory framework. Considering that our work is the first to exploit multilingual discourse-aware strategies for fake news detection, the research community currently lacks multilingual deceptive annotated corpora. Accordingly, this paper describes the current progress in this thesis, including (i) the construction of the first multilingual deceptive corpus, which was annotated by specialists according to the Rhetorical Structure Theory framework, and (ii) the introduction of two new proposed rhetorical relations: INTERJECTION and IMPERATIVE, which we assume to be relevant for the fake news detection task.

1 Introduction

According to DePaulo et al. (2003), liars may be identified by their words, and a fairly straightforward element to mitigate risks of deceptive activities consists of the ability to correctly interpret and codify the underlying intent of the speakers (Ho and Hancock, 2019).

Several models have proposed to automatically identify statements that are intentionally misstated (or manipulated). The vast majority of deception detection methods rely on linguistic features such as n-grams, language complexity, part-of-speech tags, and syntactic and semantic features.

More recently, discourse frameworks of the computational linguistics area, such as Rhetorical Structure Theory (RST) (Mann and Thompson, 1987), have been adopted as the basis to automatically detect deceptive stories (e.g., fake news or fake reviews) on the web and social media. Figure 1 shows an example of a fake news annotated using the Rhetorical Structure Theory framework.

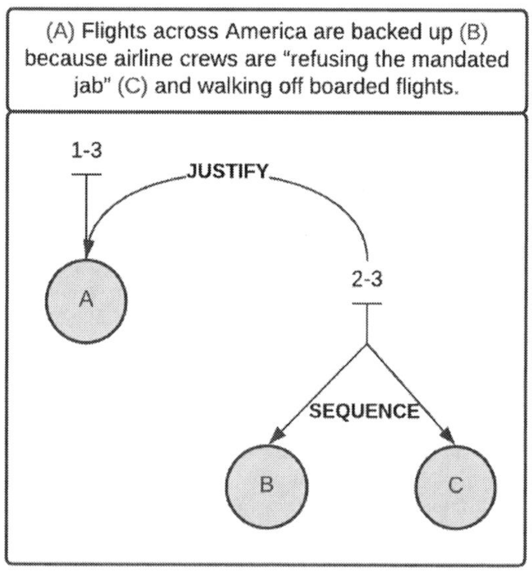

Figure 1: Example of a fake news extracted from Politifact stated on August 8, 2021 in a Facebook post, which was annotated using Rhetorical Structure Theory framework.

As shown in Figure 1, a deceptive story (also called fake news or deceptive news) was segmented into three elementary discourse units (EDU's), as well as hierarchically organized according to the following coherence relations: JUSTIFY and SEQUENCE. Moreover, there are spans of texts that

Proceedings of the Student Research Workshop associated with RANLP-2021, pages 210–218,
held online, Sep 1-3, 2021.
https://doi.org/10.26615/issn.2603-2821.2021_029

are more central (nucleus) to the text's purpose than others (satellite), and the nucleus is signaled by an arrow.

Kumar and Geethakumari (2014) argue that research on people's cognitive mechanisms has promising guidance for the detection and refutation of fake content. Nevertheless, most approaches for fake news detection are focused on the content-based classification, as well as "shallow" linguistic features, even without considering the potential of cognitive mechanisms or contextual information. Therefore, taking into account the considerable impact of discourse and contextual information for deception detection, we allow ourselves to argue that would be a carelessness rely not on rich and more sophisticated approaches for the fake news detection task.

Although there is an acknowledged potential for a discourse-aware analysis as a cognitive-based approach, there is a considerable lack of research on discourse in deceptive stories. To Meibauer (2018), we do not have significant knowledge of the embedded lies in text or discourse, with the notable exception of the studies proposed in Galasińki (2000) and Meibauer and Dynel (2016), although these studies deal with fictional discourse. Indeed, a very plausible assumption to explain the lack of research on deception in real discourses would be that this is rather a difficult requirement to satisfy.

More recent proposals have explored discourse-aware models for deception detection, more specifically, fake news and fake reviews detection, nevertheless, to the best of our knowledge, no previous multilingual discourse-aware studies exist. The first discourse approach for fake news detection was proposed by Rubin et al. (2015), in which a discourse-aware model that embodies rhetorical structure features using classical learning methods was used for the English language. In the same settings, for the Russian language, Kuzmin et al. (2020), and Pisarevskaya (2017) also developed a classical Bag-of-RST representation using Support Vector Machine (SVM) (Scholkopf and Smola, 2001) and Random Forest (Breiman, 2001), as well as pre-trained contextual embeddings (e.g., BERT) were used for fake news detection. In Atanasova et al. (2019), a robust framework was proposed, which embodies discourse features extracted from a RST-discourse parser, using Long Short-Term Memory (LSTM) (Hochreiter and Schmidhuber, 1997) and Convolutional Neural Networks (CNN) sophisticated learning methods for fake news detection in English. The authors claim that discourse and contextual features improve the fake news detection system performance. For fake reviews detection, Popoola (2017) analyzes rhetorical structure coherence relations from a forensic collection of authentic and fake Amazon book reviews and concludes that paid review writers deploy deceptive pragmatics (i.e., a coherent set of linguistic strategies) are deployed to support the intent to deceive.

In this thesis, we embrace the challenges and opportunities of the study on the rhetorical structure patterns in fake news from different languages. The main goal of this thesis is to assess whether, from the study on the discourse structure patterns in a multilingual fake news corpora, it is possible to propose efficient computational discourse-aware models for multilingual fake news detection. Accordingly, this investigation is an inquiry into the nature of the high-level, discourse structure of deceptive natural language texts, whereby the long-term main goal is to uncover systematic language differences and inform them for deception or falsification verification systems.

In what follows, we will give a summary of our research effort so far. In Section 2, we briefly discuss decetive language, as well the state-of-the-art on discourse structure applied to deception detection. Moving forward, in Section 3, we present this ongoing research and describe the progress toward this thesis's goals by (1) the construction of the first multilingual deceptive corpus annotated according to the Rhetorical Structure Theory framework, and (2) introducing two new proposed rhetorical relations: INTERJECTION and IMPERATIVE, which we suggest to be relevant for fake news detection. Section 4 describes the future research paths for further exploration. In Section 5, some conclusions are presented.

2 Deceptive Language and Discourse

Information is mainly passed on in the form of language. Consequently, research on how people use language to inform and misinform, as well as how meaning may be automatically extracted from large amounts of text, is unquestionably relevant. Moreover, the main literature on deception suggests that liars may be identified by their stories (Newman, 2003; DePaulo et al., 2003; Hancock and Guillory, 2015; Ho and Hancock, 2019).

According to DePaulo et al. (2003), deceptive linguistic style in general presents negative polarity, weak employment of singular and third-person pronouns, and high employment of movement verbs. In the same settings, Nahari et al. (2019) claim that the basic assumption on deceptive language is that liars differ from truth-tellers in their verbal behavior, accordingly, lying stories may be identified by inspecting the verbal behavior patterns. In the same setting, Newman (2003) proposes a set of linguistic behaviors, which, according to the authors, predict deception, such as tones of words, kind of preposition, conjunctions, and pronouns.

A very plausible assumption would be that there are different discourse structure patterns in deceptive and truthful stories. Indeed, this has been claimed by various authors (Rubin et al., 2015; Popoola, 2017; Kuzmin et al., 2020; Pisarevskaya, 2017; Atanasova et al., 2019). Discourse-aware approaches for deception detection are usually framed as a supervised learning problem, which embodies in a model coherence relations followed by hierarchical nuclearity information to build automatic classifies. Moreover, the discourse features may be also used as a complement for other stylistic-based linguistic features. Therefore, discourse analysis applied to automated deception detection intends to assess the potential for the application of discourse coherence analysis, developing linguistic heuristics to automatically classify statements that are intentionally misstated (or manipulated).

3 Ongoing Research

In this Ph.D. ongoing research, we are especially interested in discourse-aware approaches for deception detection, more specifically, using the Rhetorical Structure Theory framework for fake news detection. Our aim is to develop computational models for deception detection where discourse structure is a first-class citizen. We have already made progress toward this goal by: (1) developing the first multilingual deceptive corpus, which we called Deceiver [1], annotated by specialists according to the RST framework. Deceiver multilingual corpus consists of 600 pieces of news classified in deceptive versus truthful documents, as well split in 300 documents in Brazilian Portuguese, and 300 documents in English; and (2) introducing two new rhetorical relations: INTERJECTION and IMPERATIVE, which we consider to be relevant for the fake news detection task.

[1] https://github.com/francielleavargas/Deceiver

Moving forward, we propose to examine the discourse structure. Our aim is to develop patterns that show deception. Secondly, we will assess whether a computational model that embodies the multilingual discourse structure patterns is an efficient approach for multilingual fake news detection on the web and social media. Therefore, the proposed research is divided among three main fronts described in what follows and shown in Figure 2:

- Multilingual Corpus Construction;
- Rhetorical Structure Theory Modeling;
- Deception Detection.

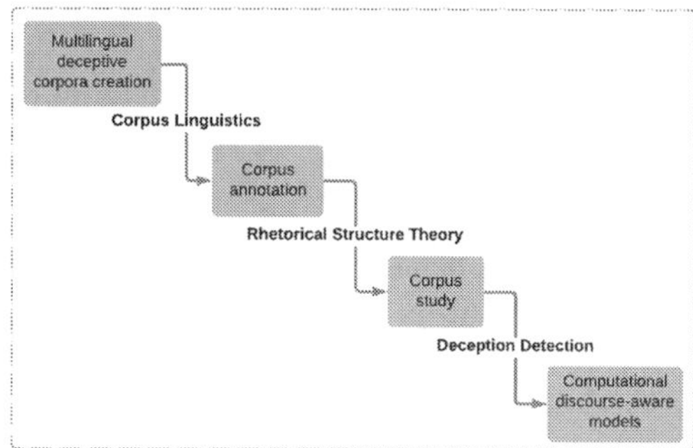

Figure 2: Methodology

3.1 Multilingual Corpus Construction

As our work is the first to explore multilingual discourse-aware strategies for deception detection, the research community currently lacks multilingual deceptive annotated corpora. Therefore, we provide a new corpus composed of fake news and truthful stories in Portuguese and English, which was annotated by two skilled linguistics using the Rhetorical Structure Theory framework.

3.1.1 Corpus Development

According to Bachenko et al. (2008), obtaining reliable positive and negative data samples is one of the challenges in automated deception detection research, especially concerning deception detection tasks that require careful selection of data. The difficulty is in-ground truth verification: finding suitable data "in the wild" and conducting fact checking to obtain ground truth is costly, time-consuming, and labor-intensive. Furthermore, as a matter of ongoing debate, exactly what counts as a representative corpus is an open question and difficult to satisfy.

In this thesis, we created and annotated the first multilingual deceptive corpus, which we named "Deceiver" [2], which consists of deceptive and truthful news shared on the web and social media. The Deceiver multilingual corpus consists of 600 pieces of truthful and deceptive news divided into 300 pieces of news in Brazilian Portuguese, and 300 pieces of news in English classified equally into deceptive and truthful classes. Table 1 exhibits the corpus overview.

Table 1: Deceiver multilingual corpus overview

Deceiver Corpus	Data	Total	Language
Fake News	New stories	150	Portuguese
Truthful News	CSTnews	150	Portuguese
Fake News	MisInfoText	150	English
Truthful News	MisInfoText	150	English

New stories consists of unpublished deceptive stories manually collected from 3 (tree) Brazilian fact-checking agencies: G1 Fato ou Fake[3], Lupa[4] and E-farsas[5]. The collected stories were checked by the mentioned agencies during the period of July-2018 to June-2021. We also used a couple of pieces from another fake news corpus in Brazilian Portuguese proposed by our research laboratories.

CSTnews (Cardoso et al., 2011) consists of a corpus composed of 140 news texts written in Brazilian Portuguese and counts with several annotation layers, including annotation in the morphosyntax/syntax, semantics, and discourse levels. The annotation has been performed by computer scientists and linguists. We revisited the discourse annotation level of the CSTnews corpus and included the annotation of new coherence relations proposed by this research (see Sections 3.2.1 and 3.2.2). Note that CSTnews provides only 140 news texts. Therefore, we additionally collected 10 pieces of truthful news written in the Brazilian Portuguese language from Folha de São Paulo [6], which consists of a referential Brazilian newspaper. The new documents were randomly collected during July 2021 on issues related to coronavirus pandemic topics.

MisInfoText (Torabi Asr and Taboada, 2018) consists of a large dataset containing instances of fact-checked news articles, which were automatically collected from fact-checking websites for false/true claims and headlines, links to the original news articles spreading them, and the veracity labels given by the fact-checkers. We randomly selected 150 fake and 150 real stories and annotated them using rhetorical structure theory.

3.1.2 Corpus Annotation

Consistency and quality of the data are directly related to the performance of the machine learning classifiers. In particular, subjective tasks, such as fake news and fake reviews detection present high complexity and a wide range of challenges, and an annotation schema provides a suitable characterization of domain specificity, as well as improves the labeled data.

In this thesis, we annotated 600 deceptive and truthful stories using the Rhetorical Structure Theory framework. The annotation process was performed by two specialists and conducted by an experienced linguist, in order to warrant the quality of the labeled data, as well as to minimize the subjectivity of this task, including the natural ambiguity related to RST coherence relations classification. Accordingly, we propose an annotation approach, which encompasses three main steps: (i) selection of annotators, (ii) annotation schema definition, and (iii) evaluation, which we describe in what follows:

1. **Selection of annotators**: firstly, we selected annotators with suitable background. Given that the RST is a linguistic theory, we selected two skilled linguists with backgrounds in the RST framework. Table 2, exhibit the specialists profile.

Table 2: Specialist's profile.

Degree	Occupation	Knowledge in Portuguese	Knowledge in English
Linguistics	Professor of Syntax	Mother language	Proficient
Linguistics	NLP Specialist	Mother language	Proficient

2. **Annotation schema definition**: we propose a well-defined annotation schema to minimize mistakes arising from human subjectivity, as well as leverage the annotation precision. We use the Rhetorical Structure Theory framework, and supply a well-written and clear guideline in the specialist's mother language,

[2] https://github.com/francielleavargas/Deceiver

[3] https://g1.globo.com/fato-ou-fake/

[4] https://piaui.folha.uol.com.br/lupa/

[5] https://www.e-farsas.com/

[6] https://www.folha.uol.com.br/

which guided the annotators during the entire annotation process. Our guideline was build using the RST-annotation guideline proposed by Stede et al. (Stede et al.) and Carlson and Marcu (2001), as well as the original RST proposal Mann and Thompson (1987); Thompson and Mann (1988). In total, 38 (thirty-eight) rhetorical relations were annotated, being 32 (thirty-two) rhetorical relations proposed in Mann and Thompson (1987), 4 (four) rhetorical relations proposed in Carlson and Marcu (2001), and 2 (two) new rhetorical relations identified during this ongoing thesis research. Table 3 describes the set of rhetorical relations used to annotate the proposed Deceiver multilingual corpus.

Table 3: Rhetorical relations used to annotate the Deceiver multilingual corpus

Author	Total	Description
(Mann and Thompson, 1987)	32	ANTITHESIS, BACKGROUND, CIRCUMSTANCE, CONCESSION, CONDITION, ELABORATION, ENABLEMENT, EVALUATION, EVIDENCE, INTERPRETATION, JUSTIFY, MOTIVATION, NON-VOLITIONAL CAUSE, NON-VOLITIONAL RESULT, OTHERWISE, PURPOSE, RESTATEMENT, SOLUTIONHOOD, SUMMARY, VOLITIONAL CAUSE, VOLITIONAL RESULT, CONTRAST, SEQUENCE, JOINT, ATTRIBUTION, COMPARISON, PRESENTATION, DISJUNCTION, MEANS, PREPARATION, UNCONDITIONAL, UNLESS.
(Carlson and Marcu, 2001)	4	LIST, CONCLUSION, PARENTHETICAL, SAME-UNIT
Proposed Relations	2	INTERJECTION, IMPERATIVE

Moreover, we selected easy-accessible platforms for discussion among annotators (e.g., WhatsApp and e-mail), where the annotators could discuss aspects related to the chosen theory, as well as on the ambiguities inherent in natural languages.

3. **Evaluation**: Our evaluation approach is divided into two steps. In the first step, 45% of the corpus was annotated by specialist 1, and other 45% of the corpus was annotated by specialist 2. In the second step, 10% of the corpus was annotated by both annotators. We evaluated the annotation process using this sample of the full corpus, composed of 10% of documents, which were annotated by both linguists. Figure 3 shows our evaluation approach.

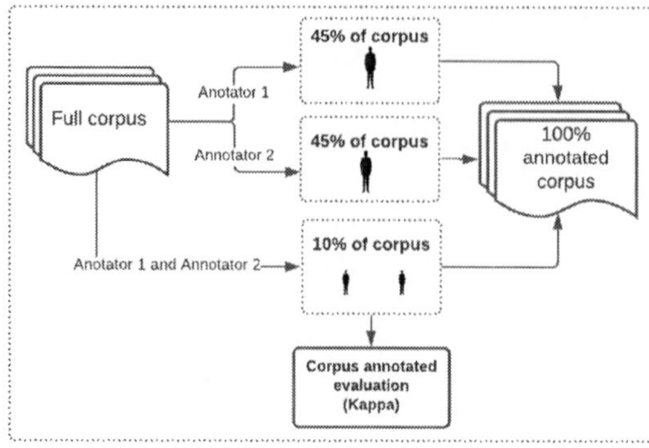

Figure 3: Evaluation

Currently, the annotation evaluation is ongoing. We further intend to apply the Kappa (McHugh, 2012) to measure inter-human annotation agreement.

3.2 Rhetorical Structure Theory

Mann and Thompson (1987) claim that Rhetorical Structure Theory is "a linguistic theory of how text hangs together, and extended discourses are made out of sequences of sentences that are related to one another". RST presents three mechanisms that are central above all for understanding the proposed framework. Mann and Thompson (1987) define these mechanisms by nuclearity, schema, and rhetorical (or coherence) relations.

Rhetorical relations contain nuclei and satellites. The nucleus consists of text elements that are more central and relevant to the relation. On the other hand, the supporting units are called satellites. Coherence relations are also classified in mononuclear and multinuclear relations, and described in terms of the used schema (i.e., how one or more satellites or nuclei relate to each other).

In this paper, we present two unpublished rhetorical relations, which were identified during the annotation process of the first multilingual deceptive corpus. In Sections 3.2.1 and 3.2.2, we describe the 1INTERJECTION and IMPERATIVE rhetorical relations, that we suggest to be relevant to signal deceptive intentions.

3.2.1 INTERJECTION

We agree that natural languages are ultimately socially transmitted. Accordingly, Dingemanse (2017) claims that the structure of language forms the evolutionary landscape for linguistic items, and there are unrefined linguistic structures that signal characteristics of the margins of language. Wilkins

(1992) defines this type of linguistic structure as conventional lexical forms that are monomorphemic and typically constitute an utterance of their own. Therefore, in natural languages, an interjection also may be defined as an expression that transmits sudden emotions.

As already mentioned, deceptive news may be analogous to satires, as well as emotions are noted. Moreover, despite that RST provides some coherence relations that supply pragmatic information, no previous coherence relations exist to signal intentions that manifest emotions, sensations, and states of mind using unrefined linguistic structures. Therefore, in this thesis, we assume that a new rhetorical relation provides relevant information for deception detection tasks, and propose a new mononuclear relation named INTERJECTION, described in Table 4 in terms of constraints on the nucleus, satellite, and effects on the reader.

Table 4: INTERJECTION rhetorical relation: brief description of the constraints on the nucleus and satellites, nuclearity classification, and type of relation (information or intentional). We should point out that *N/A* means that there are not any constraints.

Type	Description
Brief description	INTERJECTION is a type of rhetorical relation that signals the intent to act on the reader, leading him to adopt a type of behavior, making use of the unrefined linguistic structures that express information analogous to sudden emotions, sensations, and states of mind.
Type of nucleus	Mononuclear.
Type of relation	Intentional.
Constraints on the nucleus (N)	N/A
Constraints on the satellite (S)	The satellite presents any context that provides a piece of information with sudden emotions, sensations, states of mind.
Constraints on the combination between nucleus and satellite (N+S)	N/A
Effect on the reader	Writer's intention consists of leading the reader to adopt a certain behavior without the need to make use of more elaborate linguistic structures.

As shown in Table 4, the proposed INTERJECTION relation is mononuclear and presents pragmatic information. The satellite presents necessarily uncomplicated linguistic structures that express information analogous to sudden emotions, sensations, and states of mind information. Moreover, there are not any constraints on the nucleus, and the writer leads the reader to adopt a type of behavior using an unrefined linguistic structure analogous to sudden emotion, sensations, and states of mind. An example of INTERJECTION is shown in Figure 4.

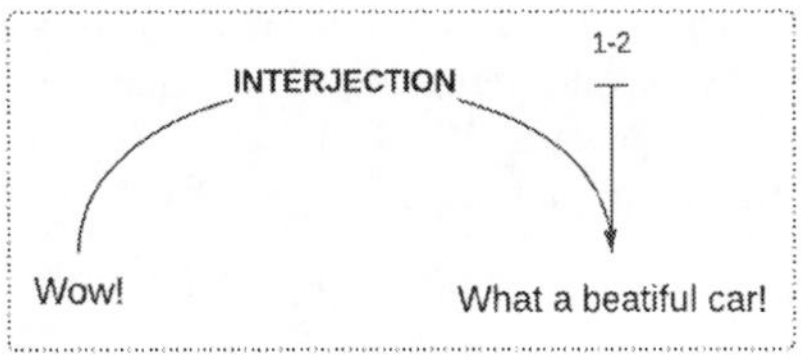

Figure 4: INTERJECTION rhetorical relation.

3.2.2 IMPERATIVE

Levels of analysis followed by different linguistic structures encompass the information passed in natural languages. Linguists around the world have been spending thousands of centuries understanding and proposing theories that explain the complex human language phenomena. An elementary fundamental of language structure is that the vocabulary of most languages is classified according to word-class or grammatical categories. The languages usually present the following distinctive word classes: noun, adjective, pronoun, verb, article, numeral, adverb, conjunction, and interjection. Each one of these categories is responsible for signaling events into natural language. For instance, note that nouns are responsible for naming the objects and beings in the world. Differently, the actions performed by the objects and beings in the world are usually signaled by verbs. Therefore, verbs are an important word class that expresses an action, state, or process. Furthermore, a wide variety of verbs may supply discourse and pragmatics information. For instance, observe the following sentence:

1. *I insist that he leaves the house right now.*
2. *Get out of the house right now!*

Note that, in the second example, we observe that the writer intends explicitly to give an order in an authoritative way. On the other hand, in the first example, even though there is a typical order intentionally signaled by the verb "insist", it is not expressed explicitly in an authoritative way. Taking into account the RST framework, the first sentence would be classified as a MOTIVATION rhetorical relation. Moving forward, since this type of coherence relation was identified in the deceptive stories, we propose a new rhetorical relation named IMPERATIVE. Table 5 presents the definition that we propose to this relation.

Table 5: IMPERATIVE rhetorical relation: brief description of the constraints on the nucleus and satellites, nuclearity classification, and type of relation (information or intentional). We should point out that "N/A" means that there are not any constraints.

Type	Description
Brief description	IMPERATIVE rhetorical relation expresses order, request or advice, whose writer imposingly intends that the reader accomplish an action. Moreover, this type of rhetorical relation may be found in an affirmative or negative way.
Type of nucleus	Mononuclear.
Type of relation	Intentional.
Constraints on the nucleus (N)	N/A.
Constraints on the satellite (S)	The satellite expresses an explicit order, advice, or request.
Constraints on the combination between nucleus and satellite (N+S)	The nucleus precedes the satellite in the text.
Effect on the reader	The writer intends explicitly to give an order in an authoritative way. The reader recognizes the presence of an order, advice, or request.

As shown in Table 5, the proposed IMPERATIVE relation is mononuclear and presents pragmatic information. The satellite expresses an explicit order, advice, or request, and there are not any constraints on the nucleus. On the effects on the reader, the reader understands that there is the presence of order, advice, or request. Figure 5 exhibits an example of IMPERATIVE rhetorical relation.

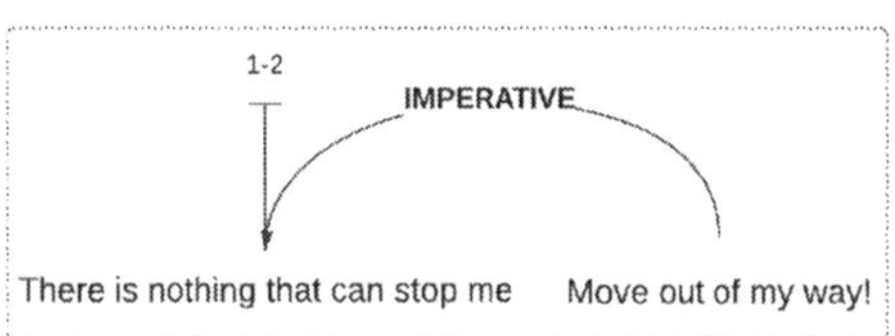

Figure 5: IMPERATIVE rhetorical relation.

4 Further Research Exploration

4.1 Deception Detection

In the last few years, there was a growth in the number of web and social media users. Consequently, the potential of deceptive activities also increased, resulting in the production of fake news, fake reviews (also known as opinion spam), deceptive discussion, simple lies, etc. Fake news detection is defined as the prediction of the chances of a particular news article being intentionally deceptive (Rubin et al., 2015). Fake reviews or opinion spams are inappropriate or fraudulent reviews (Ott et al., 2011). Deceptive discussions consist of narratives or statements intentionally misstated (or manipulated) (Larcker and Zakolyukina, 2012).

As it is known from previous discussions, Rhetorical Structure Theory has been adopted for fake news detection. Accordingly, in this Ph.D. ongoing research, we propose to examine rhetorical structure patterns from the proposed multilingual deceptive corpus and to build and evaluate computational discourse-aware models for multilingual fake news detection on the web and social media. Moving forward, the next steps of this thesis include (a) performing a corpus study with the proposed RST-annotated multilingual deceptive corpus, and (b) building computational models, which embody discourse structure information, and evaluating whether our approach is efficient to automatically detect fake news in different languages. In Sections 4.1.1 and 4.1.2, we discuss the future research paths for further exploration in this thesis.

4.1.1 Corpus Study

The next step of this ongoing research consists of performing a skilled corpus study, in which a specialist will theoretically and empirically analyze linguistic patterns in deceptive and truthful news, in order to identify linguistic structures that show deception. Firstly, we will analyze lexical, syntactic, and semantic phenomena in deceptive and truthful stories, and assess the relationship between these phenomena in both analyzed languages: Portuguese and English.

Secondly, we propose to examine the discourse structure in deceptive and truthful stories in order to assess whether deceptive and truthful discourse structure presents similar multilingual patterns. In order to achieve that, we intend to investigate different types of coherence relations, as well as the nuclearity properties.

4.1.2 Building Discourse-Aware Computational Models

Recently proposed approaches in the literature assess discourse structure from deceptive and truthful stories, and build models, which embody discourse structure information for monolingual deception detection. Differently from previous discourse-based approaches for fake news detection, we intend to examine discourse structures from deceptive and truthful stories for multilingual fake news detection. In order to archive that, the next step of this ongoing research consists of building computational discourse-aware models, which embody discourse structure patterns learned from a multilingual deceptive corpus study, as well as evaluating whether the proposed approach may efficiently distinguish fake news from real news in different languages.

In general, previous work on fake news detection uses neural networks or traditional machine learning techniques for specific languages (Rubin et al., 2015; Kuzmin et al., 2020; Pisarevskaya, 2017; Atanasova et al., 2019). In particular, due to the high performance presented by the deep artificial neural networks, which differs from traditional machine learning techniques due to the learning of abstract feature representations through its multiple layers, we intend to evaluate classical machine learning classifiers and employ deep neural network learning methods and pre-trained models of word embeddings, such as BERT (Devlin et al., 2019).

5 Conclusions

Statements that are intentionally misstated (or manipulated) present linguistic features that are different in relation to the statements that are not intentionally misstated. According to Fallis (2009), lying is saying something that you believe to be false with the intent to deceive, as well as deceptive language consists of a type of language deliberately used to attempt to mislead others (DePaulo et al., 2003). In recent years, there is a considerable increase in deceptive activities on the web and social media, including, for example, fake news, which consist in a global and relevant social, political, and economic problem.

Prior researches on fake news detection use a variety of linguistic styles and psychologist-based features for monolingual and multilingual fact-checking systems. Rather than using the classical linguistic style approach, recent research works propose successfully discourse-aware computational models for predicting online deception, more specifically, fake news and fake reviews. Nevertheless, to the best of our knowledge, there are not any multilingual discourse-aware studies on deceptive texts. Therefore, in this Ph.D. ongoing research, we embrace the challenges and opportunities on the study of multilingual discourse structure in deceptive natural language texts for prediction of online deception, more specifically, fake news.

We aim further to investigate discourse structure patterns from the first proposed multilingual deceptive corpus, annotated according to the Rhetorical Structure Theory framework. Then, we intend to build computational models that embody the discourse structure patterns that show deception, as well as to evaluate whether our approach is efficient for the multilingual fake news detection task.

In this paper, we presented the ongoing Ph.D. research and described the already in progress work toward this thesis's goals. Ours research method includes (a) the construction of the first multilingual corpus of deceptive versus truthful stories (news) in Portuguese and English languages, and (b) the introduction of two new rhetorical relations, which consist of the second contribution of this research. The proposed rhetorical relations, named INTERJECTION and IMPERATIVE, present pragmatic information and are mononuclear. Moreover, we suggest that these proposed relations are relevant for discourse-aware approaches for fake news detection. Finally, we discuss the future research paths for further exploration related to this thesis's goals.

References

Pepa Atanasova, Preslav Nakov, Lluís Màrquez, Alberto Barrón-Cedeño, Georgi Karadzhov, Tsvetomila Mihaylova, Mitra Mohtarami, and James Glass. 2019. Automatic fact-checking using context and discourse information. *J. Data and Information Quality*, 11(3).

Joan Bachenko, Eileen Fitzpatrick, and Michael Schonwetter. 2008. Verification and implementation of language-based deception indicators in civil and criminal narratives. In *Proceedings of the 22th International Conference on Computational Linguistics*, pages 41–48, Manchester, UK.

Leo Breiman. 2001. Random forests. *Machine Learning*, 45:5–32.

P.C.F. Cardoso, E.G. Maziero, M.L.R. Castro Jorge, E.M.R. Seno, A. Di Felippo, L.H.M. Rino, M.G.V. Nunes, and T.A.S. Pardo. 2011. Cstnews - a discourse-annotated corpus for single and multi-document summarization of news texts in brazilian portuguese. In *Proceedings of the 3rd RST Brazilian Meeting*, pages 88–105, Cuiabá, Brazil.

Lynn Carlson and Daniel Marcu. 2001. Discourse tagging manual. *Tech. rep. ISI-TR-545*, pages 01–87.

Bella DePaulo, James J Lindsay, Brian Malone, Laura Muhlenbruck, Kelly Charlton, and Harris Cooper. 2003. Cues to deception. *Psychological Bulletin*, 129:74–118.

Jacob Devlin, Ming-Wei Chang, Kenton Lee, and Kristina Toutanova. 2019. BERT: Pre-training of deep bidirectional transformers for language understanding. In *Proceedings of the 2019 Conference of the North American Chapter of the Association for Computational Linguistics: Human Language Technologies.*, pages 4171–4186, Minnesota, USA.

Mark Dingemanse. 2017. On the margins of language: Ideophones, interjections and dependencies in linguistic theory. In N. J. Enfield, editor, *Dependencies in language*, volume 15, page 195–203. Language Science Press.

D. Fallis. 2009. What is lying? *Journal of Philosophy*, 106(1):29–56.

Dariusz Galasińki. 2000. *The language of deception: a discourse analytical study*. SAGE Publications.

Jeffrey T. Hancock and Jamie Guillory. 2015. Deception with technology. In *The Handbook of the Psychology of Communication Technology*, volume 16, pages 270–289.

Shuyuan Mary Ho and Jeffrey T. Hancock. 2019. Context in a bottle: Language-action cues in spontaneous computer-mediated deception. *Computers in Human Behavior*, 91:33–41.

Sepp Hochreiter and Jürgen Schmidhuber. 1997. Long short-term memory. *Neural computation*, 9(8):1735–1780.

KP Krishna Kumar and G Geethakumari. 2014. Detecting misinformation in online social networks using cognitive psychology. *Human-centric Computing and Information Sciences*, 4(14).

Gleb Kuzmin, Daniil Larionov, Dina Pisarevskaya, and Ivan Smirnov. 2020. Fake news detection for the Russian language. In *Proceedings of the 3rd International Workshop on Rumours and Deception in Social Media*, pages 45–57, Barcelona, Spain.

David F. Larcker and Anastasia A. Zakolyukina. 2012. Detecting deceptive discussions in conference calls. *Journal of Accounting Research*, 50(2):495–540.

William C. Mann and Sandra A. Thompson. 1987. *Rhetorical structure theory: a theory of text organization*. University of Southern California, Information Sciences Institute Los Angeles.

Mary L McHugh. 2012. Interrater reliability: the kappa statistic. *Biochemia medica*, 22(3):276–282.

Jörg Meibauer. 2018. The linguistics of lying. *Annual Review of Linguistics*, 4(1):357–375.

Jörg Meibauer and Marta Dynel. 2016. Empirical approaches to lying and deception. *International Review of Pragmatics*, 8(3).

Galit Nahari, Tzachi Ashkenazi, Ronald Fisher, Pär Granhag, Irit Hershkowitz, Jaume Masip, Ewout Meijer, Zvi Nisin, Nadav Sarid, Paul Taylor, Bruno Verschuere, and Aldert Vrij. 2019. Language of lies: Urgent issues and prospects in verbal lie detection research. *Legal and Criminological Psychology*, 24:1–23.

Pennebaker J. W. Berry D. S. Richards J. M. Newman, M. L. 2003. Lying words: Predicting deception from linguistic styles. *Personality and Social Psychology Bulletin*, 5(29):665–675.

Myle Ott, Yejin Choi, Claire Cardie, and Jeffrey T. Hancock. 2011. Finding deceptive opinion spam by any stretch of the imagination. In *Proceedings of the 49th Annual Meeting of the Association for Computational Linguistics: Human Language Technologies*, pages 309–319, Oregon, USA.

D Pisarevskaya. 2017. Rhetorical structure theory as a feature for deception detection in news reports in the russian language. In *Computational Linguistics and Intellectual Technologies: Proceedings of the International Conference Dialogue 2017*. ACM.

Olu Popoola. 2017. Using rhetorical structure theory for detection of fake online reviews. In *Proceedings of the 6th Workshop Recent Advances in RST and Related Formalisms*, pages 58–63, Santiago de Compostela, Spain.

Victoria L Rubin, Niall J Conroy, and Yimin Chen. 2015. Towards news verification: Deception detection methods for news discourse. In *Proceedings of the The Rapid Screening Technologies, Deception Detection and Credibility Assessment Symposium co-located with HICSS48*, page 01–11, Hawaii, USA.

Bernhard Scholkopf and Alexander J Smola. 2001. *Learning with kernels: support vector machines, regularization, optimization, and beyond*. MIT press, Cambridge.

Manfred Stede, Maite Taboada, and Debopam Das. 2017. Annotation guidelines for rhetorical structure. *Linguistics Department at The University of Potsdam*, 1:1–31.

Sandra A. Thompson and William C. Mann. 1988. Rhetorical structure theory: A fremework for the analysis of texts. *IPRA Papers in Pragmatics*, 1:79–105.

Fatemeh Torabi Asr and Maite Taboada. 2018. The data challenge in misinformation detection: Source reputation vs. content veracity. In *Proceedings of the First Workshop on Fact Extraction and VERification (FEVER)*, pages 10–15, Brussels, Belgium.

David P. Wilkins. 1992. Interjections as deictics. *Journal of Pragmatics*, 18(2-3):119–158.

Automatic Transformation of Clinical Narratives into Structured Format

Sylvia Vassileva[1], **Gergana Todorova**[1], **Kristina Ivanova**[1], **Boris Velichkov**[1,2], **Ivan Koychev**[1,2], **Galia Angelova**[3] and **Svetla Boytcheva**[3]

[1] Faculty of Mathematics and Informatics, Sofia University "St. Kliment Ohridski", Sofia, Bulgaria
sylvia.vassileva@gmail.com, gergana.d.todorova@gmail.com, kiivanova735@gmail.com, koychev@fmi.uni-sofia.bg

[2] GATE Institute, Sofia University "St. Kliment Ohridski", Sofia, Bulgaria
boris.velichkov@gate-ai.eu

[3] Institute of Information and Communication Technologies, Bulgarian Academy of Sciences, Sofia, Bulgaria
galia@lml.bas.bg, svetla.boytcheva@iict.bas.bg

Abstract

Vast amounts of data in healthcare are available in unstructured text format, usually in the local language of the countries. These documents contain valuable information. Secondary use of clinical narratives and information extraction of key facts and relations from them about the patient disease history can foster preventive medicine and improve healthcare. In this paper, we propose a hybrid method for the automatic transformation of clinical text into a structured format. The documents are automatically sectioned into the following parts: diagnosis, patient history, patient status, lab results. For the "Diagnosis" section a deep learning text-based encoding into ICD-10 codes is applied using MBG-ClinicalBERT - a fine-tuned ClinicalBERT model for Bulgarian medical text. From the "Patient History" section, we identify patient symptoms using a rule-based approach enhanced with similarity search based on MBG-ClinicalBERT word embeddings. We also identify symptom relations like negation. For the "Patient Status" description, binary classification is used to determine the status of each anatomic organ. In this paper, we demonstrate different methods for adapting NLP tools for English and other languages to a low resource language like Bulgarian.

1 Introduction

The analysis of medical data can lead to the discovery of knowledge that has a significant effect on healthcare and the effectiveness of treatment. Unfortunately, large amounts of health data are available in an unstructured text format, usually in the local language of the countries. These documents contain valuable information, but it cannot be extracted directly from them. Transformation of the clinical record from unstructured text format into a structured presentation that includes key facts and relations will enable further analysis, which can help to obtain valuable information about the patient's medical history and in this way to support preventive medicine and improve healthcare.

Vaci et al. (2020) use huge manually annotated corpora for patients with depression with expert-selected terms of interest. They apply statistical models and active learning for structured information extraction with an average F1-score of 74% for temporal characteristics, diagnosis, disease history, symptoms, cognitive scores, medications, response, and adverse effects. Taira et al. (2001) also apply statistical methods for structuring information from radiology reports. Denecke (2008) presents a method SeReMeD, based on semantic transformation rules that achieves precision 93% and recall 88% for chest X-ray reports. Kreimeyer et al. (2017) investigate in their systematic review the clinical NLP methods. Still, the rule-based approaches predominate.

Zhan et al. (2021) apply different word embedding techniques for automatic prediction of ICD-10 codes for free-text clinical notes for 8 cardio-vascular diseases. The reported AU-ROC rating is in the range from 94% up to 99%. Chen et al. (2021) apply hybrid methods combining keyword-based method and deep learning methods (word2vec and sentence2vec), achieving F1-score 83% and 88% correspondingly for both methods.

There is limited research for languages other

Proceedings of the Student Research Workshop associated with RANLP-2021, pages 219–227,
held online, Sep 1–3, 2021.
https://doi.org/10.26615/issn.2603-2821.2021_030

than English about NER from clinical text Névéol et al. (2018). Lei et al. (2014) present NLP techniques for Name Entity Recognition (NER) for clinical text in Chinese. The authors explore the application of different classical machine learning techniques like conditional random fields (CRF), support vector machines (SVM), maximum entropy (ME), and structural SVM (SSVM) over about 400 manually annotated admission notes and discharge letters. The best score is 93% for the former and 90% for the latter datatype. Zhang et al. (2018) propose an entropy-based model for temporal information extraction for medical facts and medical events from Chinese clinical text.

Some preliminary work was reported for structuring clinical information in Bulgarian - for extraction of various numerical values related to lab test by Boytcheva et al. (2015), medication extraction by Boytcheva (2011), and annotation with ICD-10 codes by Velichkov et al. (2020a). The automatic generation of diabetes register from unstructured clinical texts using rule-based NLP techniques is presented in Tcharaktchiev et al. (2018).

Therefore, we aim to develop a Natural Language Processing (NLP) pipeline for automatically extracting information from clinical texts and presenting it in a structured format. This task is even more challenging for low-resource languages like Bulgarian. The developed approach employs both classical methods such as those based on dictionaries and rules and modern language models based on Deep Neural Networks Transformers such as BERT (Bidirectional Encoder Representations from Transformers by Devlin et al. (2018)) and can be easily adapted to other languages.

2 Data

2.1 Diagnosis Dataset

The ICD-10 classification [1] is a hierarchical classification of diseases that consists of multiple levels. Each diagnosis is a description of a disease and is associated with one or more ICD-10 codes. Categories using 3 and 4 signs are used in the Bulgarian healthcare system to encode the diseases. For example, the 3-sign code "C00" is used to encode "Malignant neoplasm of lip", and its 4-sign child "C00.0" encodes "Malignant neoplasm of external upper lip". The ICD-10 classification has 2,035 3-sign classes and almost 11,000 4-sign classes. In this paper, we classify each diagnosis by choosing the most relevant 4-sign classes.

For the purposes of ICD-10 diagnosis classification task, a dataset created by Velichkov et al. (2020a) was used with additional cleaning and preprocessing to reduce the noise. It contains 345,591 sample diagnoses with their corresponding ICD-10 codes.

2.2 Bulgarian Medical Articles Dataset

We compile a dataset of Bulgarian medical articles starting with a dataset from Velichkov et al. (2020a) and enhancing it by scraping Bulgarian medical websites, containing general medical articles. The final dataset consists of about 10,000 articles. The Bulgarian Medical Articles Dataset is used in the Diagnosis encoding task.

2.3 Patient History Dataset

The Patient History Dataset is used for evaluation purposes and consists of 30 samples of manually annotated patient history records from outpatient records. The records are anonymized and contain 170 sentences, 582 entity token instances across 9 categories. It contains 446 tokens linked to WikiData entities for 111 unique entities. The Patient History Dataset is used in the Patient History information extraction task.

2.4 Patient History Entity Knowledge Base

As part of the Patient History extraction task, we perform entity linking of recognized entities against a knowledge base. We compile a knowledge base from WikiData symptoms, clinical signs, organs, including parts of the body, and anatomical systems which represent UMLS[2] or MeSH[3] ontology concepts. In total, we collected 40,417 entities with 169,359 aliases and translated automatically all aliases in Bulgarian using Google translate. Some data cleaning was performed on the result translation. Unfortunately, there is no official reliable translation of UMLS or MeSH in Bulgarian.

2.5 Patient Status Dataset

For the task of patient status classification, we use a dataset of anonymized patient records. The records include patient status from General Practitioners (GPs) outpatient records. Each sentence in the

[1] https://icd.who.int/browse10/2010/en

[2] https://www.nlm.nih.gov/research/umls/index.html

[3] https://www.nlm.nih.gov/mesh/meshhome.html

dataset is manually annotated with the organ it refers to and whether or not the organ is healthy or abnormal. The dataset consists of 7,554 sample sentences.

The patient status record contains information about basic patient exams like blood pressure, pulse, Succusio renalis, BMI (Body Mass Index), Height, Waist, Weight, VOD/VOS (Visio oculus dexter/Visio oculus sinistra - visual acuity of the right and left eyes), as well as a description of the patient's symptoms based on a doctor's visual examination. For example, the status may contain "УНГ - зачервено гърло" *("ENT - sore throat")* or *"RR:120/80" (Blood pressure measured using Riva-Rocci method: 120/80).*

3 Methods for Clinical Text Structuring

3.1 Information Extraction from Medical Texts in Bulgarian

This work aims to develop a prototype system for recognizing and extracting medical concepts from clinical texts in Bulgarian. The developed NLP approach consists of the following modules:

- Document sectioning - The discharge letters in Bulgaria follow a standard structure of sections. The documents are automatically divided into the following parts: diagnosis, patient history, patient status, lab test results.
- Diagnosis encoding into ICD-10 - For the "Diagnosis" section, we use MBG-ClinicalBERT model - based on ClinicalBERT, fine-tuned for Bulgarian medical text, to automatically generate ICD-10 codes of diagnoses from the row text.
- Patient History information extraction - From the patient history section, we identify the patient's symptoms using a rule-based approach, improved by similarity search, based on MBG-ClinicalBERT word embeddings. We also identify relationships between symptoms including negation.
- Patient status classification - For the patient status description, binary classification is used to determine the condition of each anatomic organ.
- Lab test results extraction - The laboratory results section is also processed to extract the test and result values for the patient. In this section, we use a rule-based approach.

As smaller contributions, we also consider the presented below various methods for adapting the NLP tools for English and other widely spread languages to a low-resource language such as Bulgarian.

3.2 Automatic Encoding of Diagnosis into ICD-10 codes

Most of the medical diagnoses are presented in discharge letters as unstructured text and concept normalization using a standard classification or ontology needs to be applied for disease identification. The task for automatic encoding of diagnosis into ICD-10 codes can be considered as an extreme multi-class classification task with about 2,000 classes of 3-sign codes and nearly 11,000 classes of 4-sign codes, as well as multi-label, as there can be more than one valid code for a diagnosis.

3.2.1 Fine-Tuning MBG-ClinicalBERT Language Model

For this task we develop MBG-ClinicalBERT - a model based on ClinicalBERT (Alsentzer et al., 2019). ClinicalBERT is a deep learning language model, a variant of BERT (Bidirectional Encoder Representations from Transformers proposed by Devlin et al. (2018)), originally trained on approximately 2 million clinical notes in English. ClinicalBERT is trained on clinical texts only in English and therefore requires additional training to be applied to Bulgarian texts.

The MBG-ClinicalBERT model we develop is based on ClinicalBERT and additionally trained on about 10,000 medical articles from the Bulgarian Medical Articles Dataset (Section 2.2) containing descriptions of diseases in Bulgarian to improve the model's understanding of Bulgarian medical vocabulary and its context use. We split the dataset and use 80% for training, 10% for hyper-parameter tuning, and 10% for testing. The training is performed using the masked language model task by masking 15% of the tokens in the text and training the model to predict them. We use WordPiece tokenization and the original vocabulary of the model and report the resulting perplexity of the model.

3.2.2 Fine-Tuning ICD-10 Diagnosis Classifier

The MBG-ClinicalBERT model is then fine-tuned for the ICD-10 diagnosis classification task by using the standard classification architecture proposed by Devlin et al. (2018). We use the output [CLS] token from MBG-ClinicalBERT, add a softmax linear layer on top, and train it to predict the ICD-10 code using the Diagnosis Dataset from Section 2.1. As a result, we show the top 5 classes with the highest probability. The accuracy, macro-F1 and Mean Reciprocal Rank (MRR) of the model are reported.
The MRR is the mean reciprocal rank and its formula is shown below, where Q is the number of test samples and rank is the rank position of the first relevant document[4]:

$$MRR = \frac{1}{Q}\sum_{i=1}^{Q}\frac{1}{rank_i} \tag{1}$$

3.3 Hybrid Method for Information Extraction from Patient History

There are different approaches to recognizing objects in text. The main types are dictionary-based, rule-based, using machine learning - supervised or unsupervised methods.

The task of information extraction from the patient history section is performed using a hybrid approach combining a rule-based named entity recognizer and an entity linker working with a knowledge base of symptoms, complaints, organs, and anatomical systems. This module of the system should be able to recognize patient disease history, as well as risk factors, and family history. The system must also recognize connections between symptoms, complaints, and anatomical organs and systems, as well as detect negations of complaints and symptoms.

The overall architecture (Fig. 1) is using a spaCy stanza pipeline [5] [6] which provides sentence splitting, tokenization, POS tagging, lemmatization, and dependency parsing for Bulgarian out of the box. The stanza pipeline is trained using BulTreeBank universal dependencies treebank [7] and is available for direct usage.

3.3.1 Patient History Named Entity Recognition

A custom named entity recognition (NER) component is created using a rule-based approach. The component recognizes entities in 11 categories (Table 1). The idea of the developed method is to find simpler objects through dictionaries and then, with the help of rules, find the connections between the individual objects and identify the concepts sought. Using spaCy's Entity Ruler, the NER matches phrases generated using entity lexicons and rules of several types: matching the lexicon phrases, matching the lexicon phrases combined with adjectives or other parts of speech, matching negation of risk factors, complaints, or symptoms. The rules have been crafted manually by analyzing the Patient History Dataset from Section 2.3. spaCy's matcher automatically matches entities using the predefined rules. The entity category lexicons are compiled manually from the Patient History Dataset (Section 2.3) and WikiData[8] results for the respective categories.

Some of the entity categories can contain nested categories. For example, the family history usually contains symptoms of the family members, and negations can be applied to symptoms, complaints, or risk factors. Therefore, the rules for these categories are generated using previously detected sub-entities. Identifying part of the nested entities is also valuable so it is counted as a correctly recognized token.

For the NER task we report the token-based accuracy of the approach.

3.3.2 Patient History Entity Linking

We use the fine-tuned MBG-ClinicalBERT language model as an encoder to generate word embeddings for each alias in the knowledge base from Section 2.4. The fine-tuning process was described in Section 3.2. The word embeddings are generated using the mean pooling strategy of the last four layers of the BERT model with the help of HuggingFace transformers library[9]. Since BERT provides contextualized word embeddings, the pipeline should be able to use the sentence context information carried in the embeddings to disambiguate entities. To link each recognized entity

[4] https://en.wikipedia.org/wiki/Mean_reciprocal_rank

[5] spaCy https://spacy.io/

[6] spaCy Stanza https://github.com/explosion/spacy-stanza

[7] BulTreeBank https://universaldependencies.org/treebanks/bg_btb/index.html

[8] https://www.wikidata.org/

[9] https://huggingface.co/

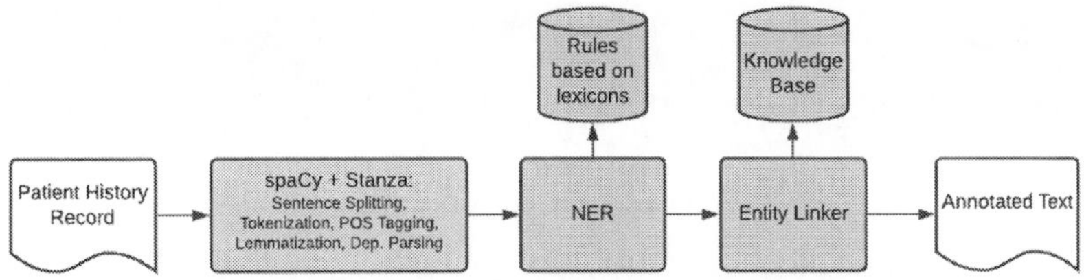

Figure 1: Architecture of the patient history pipeline.

Table 1: Entity categories recognized by the NER component

Category	**Description**	**Lexicon Phrase Count**
ORGAN	Human Organs	1200
COMPLAINT	A patient's subjective report of their problems	1110
SYMPTOM	A doctor's assessment of the patient's problems (supported by clinical signs)	1646
ANATOMICAL SYSTEM	Anatomical systems in the human body	35
FAMILY	Family relation types	52
FAMILY HISTORY	Family history phrases	27
RISK FACTOR	Risk factors to health	50
NEGATION	Negative phrases	25
NO RISK FACTOR	Lack of risk factors	3
NO SYMPTOM	Lack of symptoms	2
NO COMPLAINT	Lack of complaints	1

to the corresponding entity in the knowledge base, we search for the entity with the highest cosine similarity score.

The threshold for accepting an entity is 0.8 and the entity linker uses the entity candidate with the highest score. The entity linker performs entity disambiguation. For each entity recognized by the NER component, it tries to find the associated entity in the knowledge base with the highest similarity score. As a baseline for entity linking, we perform an exact string match search in the knowledge base. We report the accuracy of the entity linker component.

3.4 Classification of the Patient Status Data

For the patient status task, the pipeline extracts several pieces of information - the basic exam results, the organ being described, and whether or not the organ is healthy/abnormal. The pipeline consists of pre-processing, extraction of exam results, organ classification, followed by abnormality classification, as shown in Fig. 2.

The pre-processing consists of sentence splitting and tokenization using NLTK library[10], abbreviation expansion using a list of predefined medical abbreviations, removing stop words using the BTB stop word list[11], transliteration of terms from Latin to Cyrillic using Python Transliterate library [12], and converting to lower case and stemming using BulStem [13].

3.4.1 Patient Status Information Extraction and Classification

The extraction of exam results is performed using regular expressions created by analyzing the Patient Status Dataset (Section 2.5).

To recognize the organ which is being described in each sentence, we use a multi-class classifier developed previously by Velichkov et al. (2020b) since it has shown almost 99% accuracy in their

[10] https://www.nltk.org/

[11] http://bultreebank.org/wp-content/uploads/2017/04/BTB-StopWordList.zip

[12] https://pypi.org/project/transliterate/

[13] https://github.com/mhardalov/bulstem-py

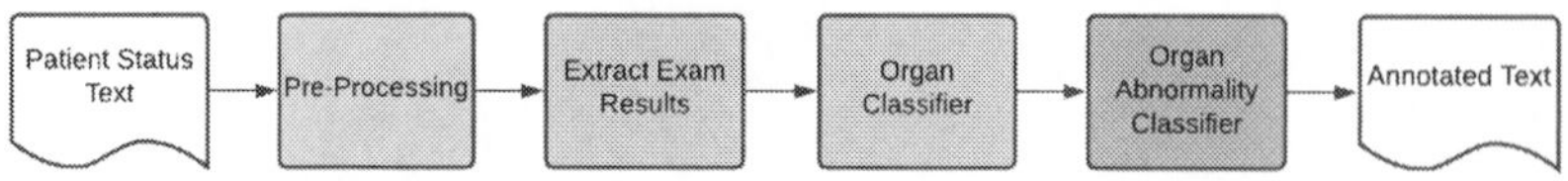

Figure 2: Architecture of the patient status pipeline.

experiments.

For the organ abnormality classification, we train a binary classifier using the Patient Status Dataset from Section 2.5. Support Vector Machine (SVM) is used to classify each record against the hypothesis "is diseased or abnormal". Based on the results, we can determine whether a particular organ is healthy or not.

The pre-processed text is transformed to feature vectors using tf-idf (TfIdfVectorizer from scikit-learn library [14]). The dataset is split into two parts - 80% for training and 20% for testing. Hyper-parameter tuning is performed using grid search. In addition, 10 fold cross-validation is used and the classification accuracy, precision, recall, and F1 scores are reported.

4 Experiments and Results

4.1 Automatic Encoding of Diagnosis into ICD-10 codes

4.1.1 Fine-Tuning MBG-ClinicalBERT Language Model

As we described above, the MBG-ClinicalBERT model is additionally trained with 10,000 articles in Bulgarian using the Bulgarian Medical Articles Dataset from Section 2.2. The dataset is split into three parts: 80% for training, 10% for hyper-parameter fine-tuning, and 10% for testing, 15% masking of the words in the text was used. In NLP the Perplexity is a measurement of how well the language model predicts a test sample. In other words, lower perplexity is better. The best result on the tuning set was achieved using the following configuration: learning rate - 4e-15, max epochs - 20. The MBG-ClinicalBERT achieved perplexity of 1.7606.

4.1.2 Fine-Tuning ICD-10 Diagnosis Classifier

For the classification task of diagnoses to ICD-10 codes, the dataset from Section 2.1 is used and was split using stratification and assigned 80% for training, 10% for hyper-parameter tuning, and 10% for testing. The best results were observed with the following configuration: learning rate - 5e-5, max epochs - 10.

The fine-tuned MBG-ClinicalBERT classifier achieved an accuracy of 92%, macro F1 of 87%, and MRR of 94%.

In order to better illustrate the task, we are solving, an example of a text and its ICD-10 classification is shown in Table 2.

The classifier is doing relatively well achieving 92% accuracy in the top 5 predictions, even though it did not predict the exact code for the sample diagnoses. The trained model can be used to suggest the top 5 codes to the doctor and have the doctor pick the most appropriate one.

For the first diagnosis, the model was able to correctly predict the 3-sign code of the disease, and the predicted 4-sign codes are quite close to the actual correct code. In the second diagnosis example, the results were slightly worse, but again all predictions are quite close to the true class. Given the presence of almost 11,000 classes, MBG-ClinicalBERT shows encouraging results for complex diagnoses.

4.2 Hybrid Method for Information Extraction from Patient History

4.2.1 Patient History Named Entity Recognition

To evaluate the NER and entity linking components, we use the Patient History Dataset from Section 2.3. A sample patient history excerpt from the test set can be seen in Table 3. A sample annotated text by the NER is displayed in Fig. 3. The symptom *"astheno-adynamia"*[15] is a complex condition of general weakness, fatigue, and helplessness that is not present in any of the dictionaries and thus cannot be recognized by the NER.

The accuracy of the NER on the test set is 87%. The majority of the errors (80%) are entities that are not recognized at all as the terms are outside of the NER dictionary. The analysis of the results of the experiments shows that the system is highly dependent on the completeness of the dictionaries it

[14] `https://scikit-learn.org/stable/`

[15] `http://www.medik.bg/?page=test&id=367`

Table 2: Example of diagnosis text and the correct and predicted ICD-10 codes.

Diagnosis Text	**Correct Code**	**Top 5 Predicted Codes**
"Неходжкинов лимфом – фоликуларен 1 ст. по СЗО, IV A кл.ст.(левкемизация, костен мозък) , FLIPI score 2 (intermediate risk), GELF score 2 (intermediate risk)." *("Non-Hodgkin's lymphoma - follicular 1 st according to WHO, IV A class (leukemia, bone marrow), FLIPI score 2 (intermediate risk), GELF score 2 (intermediate risk).")*	C82.2	C81.7 C82.1 C83 C82.9 C82
"Медикаментозно предизвикана апластична анемия." *("Drug-induced aplastic anemia.")*	D61.1	D61.9 D62 D64.0 D63 D63.8

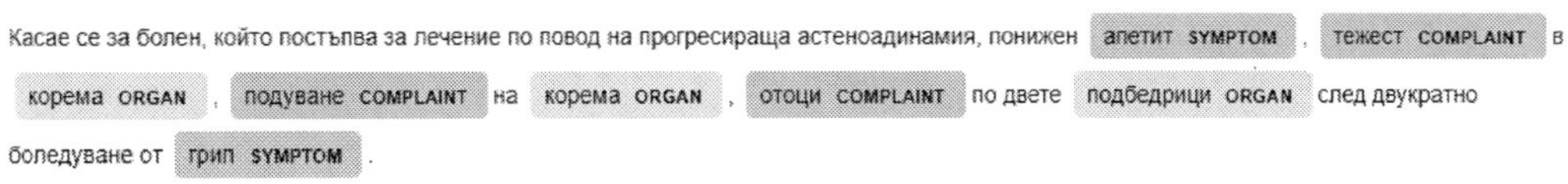

Figure 3: Sample patient history annotated by the NER.

Table 3: Sample text from the test set.

Bulgarian Text	**Translation**
Касае се за болен, който постъпва за лечение по повод на прогресираща астеноадинамия, понижен апетит, тежест в корема, подуване на корема, отоци по двете подбедрици след двукратно боледуване от грип.	*The patient was admitted for treatment with progressive astheno-adynamia, decreased appetite, heaviness in the abdomen, bloating, swelling in both lower legs after two illnesses from the flu.*

Table 4: Entities and categories predicted by the pipeline on the sample text.

Bulgarian Phrase	**Translation**	**Category**	**Correct**	**WikiData Entity ID**	**Correct**
астеноадинамия	astheno-adynamia	SYMPTOM	False	-	False
апетит	appetite	SYMPTOM	True	Q5731733	False
тежест	heaviness	COMPLAINT	True	Q104851419	False
корема	abdomen	ORGAN	True	Q9597	True
подуване	bloating	COMPLAINT	True	Q4927059	True
отоци	swelling	COMPLAINT	True	Q152234	True
подбедрици	lower leg	ORGAN	True	Q8265768	True
грип	influenza	SYMPTOM	True	Q2840	True

uses. The system can be improved by adding more entities to the dictionaries by the user. Difficulties for the system are spelling mistakes, abbreviations, and sentences, built outside the generally accepted grammatical norms.

4.2.2 Patient History Entity Linking

The entity linker produces a list of recognized entities and their respective entity IDs from WikiData as displayed in Table 4.

The overall accuracy of the Entity Linking using similarity search with MBG-ClinicalBERT embed-

Table 5: Examples of correct and incorrect organ and abnormality classification.

Sentence	Organ	Abnormal
Глава - правилна конфигурация. *(Head - normal configuration.)*	Глава *(Head)*	No
Сук реналис пол двустранно *(Sucussio renalis positive bilateral)*	Бъбрек *(Kidney)*	Yes
В добро общо състояние. *(Good overall condition.)*	None	No
Контактна, адекватна, афебрилна. *(Responsive, adequate, afebrile.)*	None	Yes

dings is 49% while the naive exact match baseline is 41%. MBG-ClinicalBERT embeddings show a statistically significant improvement over the baseline but are not high enough to be used in a real-world system. Improvements can be made using annotated data for disambiguation and fine-tuning clinical entity embeddings. Due to the huge variance in medical vocabulary as well as context-dependent abbreviations, the task of identifying the exact entity is very hard. In addition, the automatically generated translations create noise and sometimes confuse the search.

4.3 Classification of Patient Status Data

The organ abnormality classifier using an SVM model is evaluated on the Patient Status Dataset from Section 2.5. The SVM classifier shows very good results - accuracy of 93%, precision - 92%, recall - 93%, and F1 score - 92%.

Examples of the organ and abnormality classification can be viewed in Table 5. The model correctly classifies abnormality in different organs, including numerical data from basic exams, for example, sucussio renalis positive or negative. The organ abnormality classification is having issues when the sentence is describing the overall patient status using words like *"responsive"*, *"afebrile"*, which are commonly used by GPs. In these cases, the classifier incorrectly predicts the status as abnormal, even though the training dataset does not contain any abnormal samples with these words. This could be due to the short concise sentences and insufficient examples containing these words in the training dataset.

5 Conclusion and Further Work

In this paper, we presented a method for automatic extraction of data from clinical text and displaying it in a structured format for the Bulgarian language. The developed approach employs both classical methods such as those based on dictionaries and rules and modern language models based on Deep Neural Networks Transformers such as BERT. As the targeted language is a low resource one we also presented various methods for adapting the NLP tools for English and other widely spread languages. We also present results from conducted experiments to evaluate the trained ML models, which show competitive performance, making them applicable for the considered tasks.

Table 6: Results for discharge letter transformation in structure form

	Diagnosis	Patient History	Patient Status
Accuracy	92%	87%	93%
F1	87%	-	92%

Despite the presented methods are developed for a particular language they are general and can be easily adapted to other languages.

Further improvements of the presented approach can include extending the dictionaries and investigating other deep learning language models and using a semi-supervised approach to train them on the named entity recognition and text classification tasks.

Acknowledgments

This research is funded by the Bulgarian Ministry of Education and Science, grant DO1-200/2018 'Electronic health care in Bulgaria' (e-Zdrave).

Also is partially funded via GATE project by the EU Horizon 2020 WIDESPREAD-2018-2020 TEAMING Phase 2 under GA No. 857155 and OP SE4SG under GA No. BG05M2OP001-1.003-0002-C01.

References

Emily Alsentzer, John R. Murphy, Willie Boag, Wei-Hung Weng, Di Jin, Tristan Naumann, and Matthew B. A. McDermott. 2019. Publicly available clinical bert embeddings.

Svetla Boytcheva. 2011. Shallow medication extraction from hospital patient records. In *Patient Safety Informatics*, pages 119–128. IOS Press.

Svetla Boytcheva, Galia Angelova, Zhivko Angelov, and Dimitar Tcharaktchiev. 2015. Text mining and big data analytics for retrospective analysis of clinical texts from outpatient care. *Cybernetics and Information Technologies*, 15(4):58–77.

Qingxiao Chen, Xuesi Zhou, Ji Wu, and Yongsheng Zhou. 2021. Structuring electronic dental records through deep learning for a clinical decision support system. *Health Informatics Journal*, 27(1):1460458220980036.

Karl Denecke. 2008. Semantic structuring of and information extraction from medical documents using the umls. *Methods of Information in Medicine*, 47(05):425–434.

Jacob Devlin, Ming-Wei Chang, Kenton Lee, and Kristina Toutanova. 2018. Bert: Pre-training of deep bidirectional transformers for language understanding. *arXiv preprint arXiv:1810.04805*.

Kory Kreimeyer, Matthew Foster, Abhishek Pandey, Nina Arya, Gwendolyn Halford, Sandra F Jones, Richard Forshee, Mark Walderhaug, and Taxiarchis Botsis. 2017. Natural language processing systems for capturing and standardizing unstructured clinical information: a systematic review. *Journal of biomedical informatics*, 73:14–29.

Jianbo Lei, Buzhou Tang, Xueqin Lu, Kaihua Gao, Min Jiang, and Hua Xu. 2014. A comprehensive study of named entity recognition in chinese clinical text. *Journal of the American Medical Informatics Association*, 21(5):808–814.

Aurélie Névéol, Hercules Dalianis, Sumithra Velupillai, Guergana Savova, and Pierre Zweigenbaum. 2018. Clinical natural language processing in languages other than english: opportunities and challenges. *Journal of biomedical semantics*, 9(1):1–13.

Ricky K Taira, Stephen G Soderland, and Rex M Jakobovits. 2001. Automatic structuring of radiology free-text reports. *Radiographics*, 21(1):237–245.

Dimitar Tcharaktchiev, Zhivko Angelov, Svetla Boytcheva, and Galia Angelova. 2018. Automatic generation of a national diabetes register from outpatient records. *Mathematical Modeling*, 2(4):163–166.

Nemanja Vaci, Qiang Liu, Andrey Kormilitzin, Franco De Crescenzo, Ayse Kurtulmus, Jade Harvey, Bessie O'Dell, Simeon Innocent, Anneka Tomlinson, Andrea Cipriani, et al. 2020. Natural language processing for structuring clinical text data on depression using uk-cris. *Evidence-based mental health*, 23(1):21–26.

Boris Velichkov, Simeon Gerginov, Panayot Panayotov, Sylvia Vassileva, Gerasim Velchev, Ivan Koychev, and Svetla Boytcheva. 2020a. Automatic icd-10 codes association to diagnosis: Bulgarian case. In *CSBio'20: Proceedings of the Eleventh International Conference on Computational Systems-Biology and Bioinformatics*, pages 46–53.

Boris Velichkov, Kristina Ivanova, Valeri Hristov, Ivan Borisov, Alexander Peychev, Ivan Koychev, and Svetla Boytcheva. 2020b. Ai-driven approach for automatic synthetic patient status corpus generation. In *2020 4th International Conference on Artificial Intelligence and Virtual Reality*, AIVR2020, page 29–35, New York, NY, USA. Association for Computing Machinery.

Xianghao Zhan, Marie Humbert-Droz, Pritam Mukherjee, and Olivier Gevaert. 2021. Structuring clinical text with ai: old vs. new natural language processing techniques evaluated on eight common cardiovascular diseases. *medRxiv*.

Runtong Zhang, Fuzhi Chu, Donghua Chen, and Xiaopu Shang. 2018. A text structuring method for chinese medical text based on temporal information. *International journal of environmental research and public health*, 15(3):402.

Association for Computational Linguistics
209 N. Eighth Street
Stroudsburg, Pennsylvania 18360

ISBN 978-1-7138-4096-1

CURRAN ASSOCIATES INC.
proceedings.com